ENTREPRENEURIAL LAW

■ ■ ■

George W. Kuney
*Lindsay Young Distinguished Professor of Law and
Director, James L. Clayton Center for Entrepreneurial Law
Director of the L.L.M. in United States Business Law
The University of Tennessee College of Law*

Brian K. Krumm
*Associate Professor of Law
The University of Tennessee College of Law
Anderson Center for Entrepreneurship and Innovation
Research Council, Haslam College of Business*

WEST
ACADEMIC
PUBLISHING

© 2019 LEG, Inc. d/b/a West Academic
    444 Cedar Street, Suite 700
    St. Paul, MN 55101
    1-877-888-1330

West, West Academic Publishing, and West Academic are trademarks of West Publishing Corporation, used under license.

Printed in the United States of America

ISBN: 978-1-64242-251-1

ACKNOWLEDGMENTS

Brian K. Krumm joined the faculty of the University of Tennessee in 2012 as an Associate Professor in the College of Law's Business Clinic and a Member of the Anderson Center for Entrepreneurship and Innovation Research Council, Haslam College of Business. He previously has held positions a management consultant in an international consulting firm, as Policy Advisor to the Governor of Tennessee, and in private practice where he primarily focused on business and commercial transactions.

George W. Kuney is the Lindsay Young Distinguished Professor of Law and the Director of the Clayton Center for Entrepreneurial Law at the University of Tennessee College of Law. Prior to joining the faculty in 2000, he was in private practice with California-based firms where he specialized in business law and reorganizations under chapter 11 of the bankruptcy code nationwide.

The authors appreciate the contributions from our colleagues Professor Don Leatherman, Associate Professor Michelle Kwon, and Associate Professor Gary Pulsinelli of The University of Tennessee College of Law, for their review and insightful contributions to the book. Thanks also to JIANG Dong, Associate Professor at Renmin University of China Law School who has collaborated with us on a Chinese edition of this book. http://www.law.ruc.edu.cn/eng/show.asp?No=141. We would also like to acknowledge the support and encouragement that we received from Director Lynn Youngs and the faculty of the Anderson Center for Entrepreneurship and Innovation, Haslam College of Business and for the invaluable business perspectives that have become a part of this book. https://haslam.utk.edu/anderson-center.

The authors would like to acknowledge the significant contributions of time and effort of University of Tennessee College of Law Research Assistants Tyler S. Williams, Charlotte A. Houser, Sallie W. Papajohn, Sloane R. Davis, and Derrick M. Davis. Additional appreciation is extended to Clayton Center for Entrepreneurial Law Research Associate Wendy G. Patrick and the University of Tennessee Research Grant Associate Jeffrey Scott Carter, who assisted with the first edition of this work.

The early collaboration on this book began while Professor Krumm was serving as the Clayton Center for Entrepreneurial Law Visiting Professor of Law with Professor Kuney. Through conference participation with both the transactional and business clinic academic communities, it became apparent that a book that was able to help students in a business clinic catering to start-ups and entrepreneurs bridge the gap between theory and practice would be a valuable resource. As such, the book contains many points absorbed from individuals at other institutions and other resources. Additionally, the bibliography at the close of the text lists books and other sources of authority that the authors have worked with or think highly of, and which have unquestionably influenced the content of this book to one extent or another. Where specific attribution to a source was possible, it has been made in the text. Any omissions are unintentional.

More information on The University of Tennessee's Clayton Center for Entrepreneurial Law and its Business Law Clinic may be found at https://law.utk.edu/programs/clayton/ and https://law.utk.edu/clinics/.

INTRODUCTION

The idea for this book, Entrepreneurial Law, has grown from a number of sources. Discussions at the First Biennial Transactional Law Conference at Emory Law School highlighted awareness of the need for ways in which business and law schools can better prepare students for careers in business and transactional law. Subsequent conversations with representatives from West Publishing indicated that they were interested in creating a training course for entrepreneurs and new associates in law firms that would focus on helping individuals to develop the necessary transactional skills to pursue their endeavors. The focus of the Clayton Center for Entrepreneurial Law and the growth of the Business Law Clinic at the University of Tennessee and its interactions with technology transfer and other entrepreneurial pursuits have led the authors to create a resource which can be used by both business and law students in creating business entities, interacting with counsel, drafting transactional documents, protecting intellectual property, and dealing with securities issues.

The book does not purport to be a comprehensive treatment in any of the areas of business or law covered here. Its objective is to serve as single source of reference with extensive links to other resources and exemplars, for those attempting to resolve and address business related transactional challenges.

The book first introduces the reader to the importance of case management and professionally handling the client assignment. It emphasizes the need and techniques for business people and lawyers to effectively connect through the initial interview and the steps necessary to effectively establish the attorney-client relationship and successfully navigate the waters of an entrepreneurial voyage. In addition, it stresses the need and benefits of continuously documenting and updating the client file and creating a transactional record to keep all the business "ducks in a row."

The second chapter discusses the development and creation of a business plan. This section is crucial in understanding and preparing for entrepreneurial development. This chapter illustrates each section of a business plan and provides examples of some generally included material. It is designed to keep the entrepreneur on track and to guide the business on a certain and efficient route. The chapter sets forth a helpful tool that can turn an entrepreneurial idea into a well thought out approach to develop the idea into a prosperous business entity.

The third chapter discusses the various factors that the attorney and client must consider when choosing the appropriate business entity to support a particular venture's business objective. Once the optimal entity choice is made, the mechanics of filing the state required documents and the creation, adoption, and maintenance of the internal organic documents are discussed. Also included are suggestions for the proper management and governance of the enterprise and compliance with regulatory requirements.

The fourth chapter provides insight on how business deals are structured and imparts the skills and knowledge to the reader that are essential in drafting effective contracts on behalf of their client. The chapter instructs the student on how to analyze the transaction, assess the risks involved, and effectively spread those risks between the parties to the contract based on the deal negotiations.

The fifth chapter provides a thorough discussion of the various forms of intellectual property rights as they are protected by state trade secret law, federal patent and copyright law, and state and federal trademark law. This provides the reader with a basic understanding of the various concepts and an ability to effectively deal with them in transactional documents.

The final chapter provides an overview and discussion of the state and federal securities registration process. It emphasizes the complexity of this process, discusses various exemptions for particular securities offerings from full registration, and stresses the need to obtain competent co-counsel when the attorney's lack of experience so dictates.

Entrepreneurial Law will not make the reader an expert on the topic; it will, however, introduce the reader to the multitude of components of both business and law that support entrepreneurial and business transactions. In other words, it collects, explains, and gives the reader a good start and a resource of first impression.

SUMMARY OF CONTENTS

TABLE OF CONTENTS

TABLE OF CASES

ENTREPRENEURIAL LAW

CHAPTER 1

GETTING STARTED

■ ■ ■

A. CASE MANAGEMENT

Although it may seem mundane, one of the most important skills for an attorney to develop is how to best manage the client assignment and case file. Not only are these skills essential in cultivating the attorney-client relationship, but also in successfully planning, organizing, and documenting the business transaction. Because the focus of this book is aimed at the student attorney and client within an academic clinical setting, matters such as setting up a law practice, quoting fees, or establishing an IOLTA account[1] will not be addressed. Rather, the focus of this chapter will be to provide insight into the process of interviewing, counseling, and documenting the needs of the business client.

Unlike clients that seek lawyers for litigation matters, many business clients do not fully appreciate the value of the transactional attorney. When the client has been served with a complaint, arrested, or suffered some sort of damage, she knows that she needs an attorney immediately to either prosecute their case or defend her interests. However, with a business transaction, many clients perceive the role of the attorney as someone who is merely filling out forms which are necessary for a particular business deal. Some clients will even enter into agreements without the benefit of an attorney and draft documents of their own based on exemplars that they find on the Internet or in office supply stores. When the deal turns sour, they are surprised that they have placed themselves in a precarious position. The true art and value of a competent and successful transactional attorney is the ability not only to create business entities and document transactions, but also to counsel and educate the client along the way.

Business ventures can be risky. The attorney should explain to the client that their role is to assist in identifying the potential risks of the

---

[1] A lawyer who receives funds that belong to a client must place those funds in a trust account separate from the lawyer's own money. Client funds are deposited in an IOLTA (Interest on Lawyer Trust Accounts) account when the funds cannot otherwise earn enough income for the client to be more than the cost of securing that income. The client—not the IOLTA program—receives the interest if the funds are large enough or will be held for a long enough period of time to generate net interest that is sufficient to allocate directly to the client. Every state operates an IOLTA program. Interest from these trust accounts are collected and pooled to provide civil legal aid to the un- or under-represented and support improvements to the justice system.

venture and to draft documents that will protect the client or the business entity which the client represents, as best as possible, in the event that things do not turn out as planned.

When drafting organizational documents to form a business entity, the attorney should make it clear that he or she represents the entity and not the individuals that are forming the entity (assuming this is, in fact, the case). While it is not always possible to get all of the parties involved in a new venture together for the initial interview, it is strongly encouraged. It is critical that all of the founders of a new venture clearly understand the liabilities, responsibilities, and fiduciary duties that they will undertake in forming a business entity. Equally important is that they gain an appreciation for their continued responsibilities of entity oversight and compliance with the organizational documents' provisions on director and officer responsibilities, voting procedures, and documentation of the entity's decision-making process. Too often clients are so focused on their new business prospects that they fail to follow the required formalities that go along with state-sponsored entity recognition. The consequences of not following corporate formalities can range from inability to obtain necessary financing to the loss of liability protection through piercing of the corporate veil. This is where the attorney plays the valuable role of counselor, discussing and advising on the processes and documentation that are necessary to protect and promote the business entity.

B. THE INITIAL INTERVIEW

Although clients occasionally just walk into the office to obtain legal advice, most often the initial contact will be made by telephone or by e-mail. One should never give off-the-cuff legal advice over the phone or in an e-mail; this is an invitation for a future malpractice claim. Legal advice should only be given after carefully interviewing the client concerning all the relevant facts and reviewing the essential documents. The interview should be scheduled in advance and the client should be instructed to supply any important documents for review beforehand so that the attorney has time to read them carefully.

The initial interview is much like a first date. The client and attorney do not know each other but hope to become better acquainted and perhaps form a mutually beneficial relationship. In a profession where credibility is essential, professional dress is imperative. The attorney should not be informal or casual, and clients should be addressed by their title unless and until they specify otherwise. The initial interview is your first opportunity to show the client how you can assist in addressing their particular legal issues and problems.

Once an interview time has been established, the attorney should be prompt. Nothing will start the attorney-client relationship or interview off more poorly than keeping a new client waiting. To ensure that this does not happen, initial interviews should be scheduled for a time when the attorney knows they will be in the office and have the time (approximately an hour and a half) available to dedicate to the interview. First impressions are very important. When greeting the client, shake hands while looking the client in the eye. However, keep in mind that all touching should be appropriate for the client's age, gender, and culture (for example, in some cultures male-female touching in public is not appropriate).

Remember, the client is depending on you to solve or resolve their problem, so take command of the situation. Give directions on where to go and where to sit. Ensure that your conference or interview room provides privacy. Notify the receptionist that there should be no interruptions unless there is an emergency. The client deserves all of your attention and it is inappropriate to discuss another client's legal matters in front of another client.

There are many types of barriers to effective communication and having a laptop computer between you and the client can be one of them. If a computer is to be used to take notes in an interview it should be accomplished with the screen down flat or on a tablet computer, by two attorneys, or with the assistance of a paralegal or secretary; the lead attorney should focus directly on the client, explaining that the other is present to take notes of the important details. The interview should be conducted in a room where there are no preventable visual, audible, or temperature detractions. Remember, at this stage not only are you interviewing the client, but the client is also interviewing you.

There is no right or wrong way to begin an interview. However, asking the client an open-ended question like "what are we here to talk about today?" allows the potential client to provide information and describe the circumstances in their own words. While it is often difficult for an analytical attorney not to interrupt the client and ask questions, it is best to allow them to do all of the talking, at least initially. This will provide a broad understanding of the framework and context of the entire transaction. If you need to clarify a point or have a question, make a quick note and discuss it when the client is finished speaking.

One of the best qualities an attorney can have while interviewing a potential client is being a good listener. Act like you are paying attention (and do so as well). Maintaining eye contact while the client is talking assures them that they are the focus of your attention. Be an active listener rather than a passive one, encouraging the interviewee with nods and other non-verbal feedback. Be alert for non-verbal cues given by the client, observing their posture, tone, and expression. An effective way of verifying your understanding of the communication is to rephrase what the client has said and repeat it back to them. This can serve to reassure the client that you clearly understand what they are saying and provide an opportunity for them to correct any misunderstandings.

After the client has paused from telling their story, the attorney then has the opportunity to ask for clarification and details. This is a good opportunity to complete the in-house forms that your office should use to obtain information during the initial interviews. Such forms collect client contact and other information necessary to determine if the client and the legal matter is one that the clinic has an interest in representing. Each office typically has established case acceptance criteria. After determining that the office will accept the matter, you must assess whether the firm's capabilities are an appropriate fit to meet the client's needs before formally entering into an attorney-client relationship.

There are some clients that you should just not represent. It may be that they have unrealistic expectations and do not want to hear an opposing view. In some instances, your intuition may tell you that you should not represent them. If a client is unwilling to listen and accept your advice in the initial meeting, then you should consider whether you want to spend time convincing the client to accept your advice throughout the representation. This is a difficult lesson for many lawyers to learn, but you do not have to represent everyone, and if there are indications in the initial interview that the client is vague about the transaction, or seems to complain excessively, it may be best to decline to represent this client.

Remember that the client will also be evaluating the attorney, that their main concern will be the ultimate outcome of the matter, and that how much attention you will give to their case will be very important to them. While the attorney must talk about timeframes and potential outcomes, she should refrain from guaranteeing results. In law, things are seldom free from doubt. One of the authors makes it a practice to never tell a client that there is a better than a fifty percent chance of success in any business deal or litigation. It is better to make representations concerning things that are under the lawyer's control, such as how they have handled similar assignments like this in the past and how they will keep the client informed as the matter progresses.

This may also be a good time to discuss the confidentiality of the matter, the attorney-client privilege, and any limitations the attorney and client may have in that regard. Attorney-client privilege is a legal privilege designed to keep confidential communications between an attorney and her client secret. This privilege helps to encourage a client to make a full disclosure about the facts without fear of confidences being exposed to others. The privilege allows attorneys to provide direct and candid advice, resulting in more effective representation.

Once you have listened to the client's story, followed up for more details on any unclear areas, and explained the concepts of confidentiality and attorney-client privilege, you should begin to wrap-up the interview. After the interview is finished you should show the client to the door and inform them that you will be back in touch with them by a certain date. You should also inform them of any actions that they should take or materials that you would like them to provide to you, again with a deadline for each. It is good practice to follow this verbal request with a written confirmation to ensure a clear record and to assist the client in remembering what needs to be done, when.

C. THE INTAKE MEMO AND CONFLICTS CHECK

After the initial interview, the attorney should immediately prepare a thorough intake memo detailing the information obtained during the interview and your thoughts on the matter. This written analysis should be used to determine if the attorney, after consulting with his or her supervisor, should accept or reject the matter. The lawyer will then need to run a conflicts check to determine whether there is anything that might impair effective representation of the client because of preexisting relationships with other clients. For example, when dealing with corporations, remember that directors, officers, employees, stockholders, and corporations are separate entities and may have conflicting interests, and you are not permitted under the rules of professional responsibility to represent actual, present conflicting interests. Most offices today maintain a computer database of clients, former clients, adverse parties, and contacts for just this purpose. However, there are still some card file conflict systems in existence, and these can and do work effectively. As you obtain additional information in the case, you should stay attuned to conflicts that may develop and update the office's files accordingly.

There is a multitude of potential conflict-of-interest situations and the lawyer as a fiduciary has an absolute duty of loyalty. Anything that even appears to compromise that loyalty is a conflict. The Model Rules of Professional Conduct do not prevent representation of a client where there might be a future conflict, as long as the clients understand the potential conflict and knowingly waives it after enjoying an opportunity to seek outside counsel. The waiver should always be reduced to writing so there is a record. Like the intake memo, the waiver letter should be printed for inclusion in the paper case file, as well as saved in a computer file cross-referenced with the case file name and number. Decisions on case acceptance or rejection are generally made after the conflicts check and a thorough discussion with the supervising attorney.

D. ENGAGEMENT AND NON-ENGAGEMENT AGREEMENTS

Once the decision of whether or not to represent the client has been made, an engagement or non-engagement letter should be sent informing the client of your decision. The purpose of the engagement letter is to establish the scope of representation and the duties of attorney and client necessary to avoid any future misunderstandings. Such a letter establishes the responsibilities that the attorney will undertake, outlines limitations on the services to be performed, and provides protection from claims that the attorney failed to provide the services.

Everything in the engagement letter should have been discussed in the initial interview. The letter should include an introduction that clearly identifies the client. If the client is a corporate client, make it clear that it is the corporation being represented and not the individual directors, officers, or employees. If there are other individuals involved in the transaction whose interests will not be handled by the attorney, this should also be expressly stated. The letter should outline the work to be performed, with the qualification that delays can arise due to circumstances outside the attorney's control and these should be expected. The primary attorney working on the matter should be identified along with another person that the client can speak with in the event that the primary attorney is unavailable. Finally, the new client should be instructed to sign and return the engagement agreement, and the attorney should include it in the case file, providing the client with a copy upon receipt.

A non-engagement letter serves to protect the interests of both the attorney and the non-client. The non-client is protected by receiving notice that they are not represented and should seek the services of another attorney. The attorney is protected from a potential malpractice action, even where they have not provided any legal advice or received any fees. This is because the standard for whether an attorney-client relationship has been established is whether the non-client reasonably believed that they were represented or received legal advice.[2] Without evidence to the contrary, courts may also rule that the non-client detrimentally relied on the attorney's advice, even if there was a reasonable misunderstanding. Claims for detrimental reliance can also arise where an attorney offers opinions on a transaction that another party to the transaction relies upon, even if represented by their own attorney. While including a disclaimer

---

[2]   *See* Broyhill v. Aycock & Spence, 102 N.C. App. 382, 402 S.E. 167 (1991) (an express verbal agreement, fees, or a formal contract is not necessary to establish an attorney-client agreement because such can be implied in conduct) citing North Carolina State Bar v. Sheffield, 73 N.C. App. 349, 326 S.E. 2nd 320 (1985).

stating that the opinion was intended only for their client may suffice, a formal non-engagement letter can provide further protection.

When drafting the non-engagement letter, specify the matter for which the attorney was consulted and unequivocally state that the matter is not being accepted. It is not necessary to give a reason for declining representation; however, you should indicate that no research has been conducted nor investigation made on the matter and that no opinion is being offered. You should advise the non-client to consult with another attorney but do not give either advice or recommend another attorney. Return all documents that the client has provided you with the letter by registered mail. Non-engagement letters and the signed registered mail receipt should be maintained in files for a period of at least six years to protect the attorney against claims of representation and malpractice.

E. THE PLANNING MEMO

Once the engagement letter with the client's signature has been received, the attorney should create a case planning memo. This memo should refer to the facts contained in the intake memo, any issues that have been raised by the supervising attorney, and any additional facts or issues relevant to the matter. It should outline the parties to the transaction, the central legal issues, areas that need additional fact finding and research, and the proposed plan of action with time frames for completion. When a case is completed or when it needs to be transferred to another attorney, a transfer/closing memo should be completed and added to the case file. Again, once reviewed and approved by the case supervisor, the case planning memo, like the intake memo and engagement letter, should be printed and included in the case file, as well as saved in a computer file cross-referenced with the case file name and number.

F. MANAGING AND MAINTAINING
CASE RECORDS

Although it may seem duplicative to maintain both a computer and hard copy case file, they both have value and, to some extent, different purposes. The hard copy case file is the working file in which all original memos, correspondence, client e-mails, interview and meeting notes, drafts and finals of transactional documents, and any other written material or legal documents related to the mater are contained. Although attorneys in practice differ on the topic, in the authors' view, it is a good practice to keep not only the final documents but also the drafts. In the event that there is later confusion over who made what changes to the final document, you will have the ability to review the changes made by the parties to clarify the issue. (The counter argument that supports destroying drafts is based on the theory that one is thereby reducing the issues and evidence should litigation later arise.) Proper and thorough documentation of the matter as it progresses is not only essential for the attorney initially handling the matter, but crucial to any subsequent attorney who may have to take over the matter due to extenuating circumstances. The computer-based files on the other hand allow you to easily revise drafts of transactional documents. However, computers can crash and files can be deleted inadvertently. In addition, it can be difficult to remember to transcribe and input handwritten notes. Thus, it is always wise to maintain both sets of files.

Much like the case files, attorneys should also maintain a double entry calendaring system. Missed deadlines are very common errors that cause numerous malpractice and grievance claims every year. To avoid a lawsuit resulting from a missed deadline, every attorney should have their own well-organized calendaring system designed for multiple independent inputs, whether kept in time management software, Outlook, or an organized paper system. If at all possible, each system should have a backup. In law offices where there is more than one practicing attorney, it is typical for the calendaring system to be office-wide, with dates entered through a single data entry point, with all critical dates provided to the same contact person. The office system generates an automatic reminder to the responsible attorney, to their secretary or assistant, and to their supervising attorney. The individual attorney should also keep an independent calendar as a double check. However, this process does not necessarily eliminate all errors, especially deadlines that are missed when the wrong date is entered into the calendaring system. Thus, it's always a good practice for the office to assign a detail-oriented person to input the calendar entries, and to have a process to double check entries after they are entered. A properly implemented system can eliminate or reduce errors caused by missed statutes of limitations and other deadlines. Such a system also has the added benefits of improving office management and client relations.

When an attorney tells a client how long it will take to accomplish a certain matter, it creates an expectation in that client. When that expectation is not realized, the result is a disgruntled client. By the same token, if you are able to contact the client and tell them that you were able to complete their work a bit early, you have exceeded their expectations, and they are more likely to retain you in the future and refer you to other potential clients. A calendaring system that provides periodic notices of important delivery dates (a tickler system) can help the attorney keep on top of their workload and ensure timely delivery of the work product. However, transactional work involving a number of different parties can impose scheduling constraints over which the attorney has no control. For example, a closing date on a transaction may be scheduled and the work completed on your part; however, one of the other parties is having difficulties completing their financing arrangements. Since most attorneys handle more than one matter at a time, rescheduling the closing may take days or weeks to arrange. On both small and large or complex matters, multiple reschedulings should be anticipated. In these situations, immediate and effective communication with the client, followed by a formal letter explaining that the circumstances are not under your control, will give the client some assurance that you are on top of things and looking out for their best interests.

Routine communications are critical to maintaining a good attorney-client relationship. Telephone communications are an effective and low-cost way to keeping your client informed and it is important to return clients phone calls as promptly as possible when they call you. Since it is not always possible for the attorney to return a client's call within a reasonable time frame (two hours), it is wise to designate someone to return the call and reassure the client that the attorney is unavailable and will return the call as soon as they are available. Ineffective telephone communication is one of the most common grievances about lawyers and often leads to both malpractice claims and disciplinary complaints. By the same token, lawyers who punctually return calls will find that this is often a factor in their clients' decisions to retain them as counsel in other matters and in referring outside business to them. It is important to keep a record of client calls. This record should document the client's name, the date and time, and what was said in all incoming client calls. The same record should be used to document all attempts to return calls, including answered calls, as well as voicemail and answering machine calls. Such records can be maintained in your hard copy file as evidence of the attorney's due diligence in effectively responding to client telephone queries.

Written client communication is also an effective means of keeping the client involved and informed in their legal matters, in addition to being a good way to avoid problems. Whether it is a formal letter on letterhead or an e-mail, anything sent to the client reminds them that their matter is not being neglected. As a practical matter, the client should get a copy of any incoming and outgoing correspondence, as well as a copy of formal filings and documents relating to the matter. It is also the responsibility of the attorney to decide what information should not be sent to the client and if withholding the particular information is in the client's best interest. Whether the written communication is a formal letter or an e-mail, all correspondence should be checked for spelling and marked either with an indication that additional materials are enclosed or with the notation "without enclosures." Always make sure that the client's name is spelled correctly; name mistakes send the client a message that they are unimportant and suggest that the attorney may be neglecting their matter in other respects as well. The communication status of every file should be checked every sixty days. If the client has not been communicated with during this time period, a letter updating them on the matter should be sent, even if little or no activity has occurred.

Maintaining accurate attorney time records is also an important part of properly managing a client assignment. While these records may or may not be used for billing purposes, the structure of recording your time in an organized fashion serves a number of purposes. It can inform you of how long it takes to handle a particular matter, and also provide a measure of how you are progressing as an attorney over time. Whether you will enter private practice, government work, or serve as in-house counsel, keeping a time record of how your day is spent is an important way of establishing your worth to the client and the organization. Whether you use a manual or computerized time tracking system, it is important to record all of your time as soon as you move from one matter to another. All services rendered should be recorded—later writeoffs in an exercise of billing judgment can always be made, if appropriate. Remember that you are focusing on keeping time records and not billing records; if you attempt to be selective you will not record enough. A running list should be maintained and reviewed at the end of the day. Ideally, time records for each client will be maintained in both the hard copy case file and the computerized file. Such records have served as evidence in disciplinary hearings when a client has accused an attorney of neglecting their case.

G. DISENGAGEMENT LETTERS AND CLOSING FILES

The primary purpose of the closing (disengagement) letter is to let the client know that you consider the legal matter that you were handling on their behalf to be over and that the attorney-client relationship is terminated. The letter should be sent to the latest address on file and identify the completed matter as thoroughly as possible. This letter is important in establishing a date for purposes of malpractice and grievance statutes of limitations. The letter also describes the file and document retention policies of your office and offers the client the opportunity to request its file. All reasonable attempts should be made to return documents such as leases, share certificates, mortgages, deeds, wills, and other documents that bear seals and original signatures to the client. Give the client the opportunity to make an affirmative act if they want their records returned. For example, you can offer to allow the client to pick the records up and have them sign a receipt, or to direct your office in writing where they want the records sent. In both situations, your office will have a record that the documents were given back to the client.

Where appropriate, the letter should sincerely express how much the attorney enjoyed working with the client and that they would welcome the opportunity to assist them with future matters. In some situations, a postage paid form survey can also be enclosed as a further attempt to express that the attorney values the client's opinion and that you want to ensure customer satisfaction. A returned survey also serves as proof that the client received the closing letter and may provide awareness of client dissatisfaction, which can then be handled proactively.

The question of how long an attorney must retain client files that are closed prior to destruction is difficult to answer, as laws differ from state to state. Every office should have a document retention policy to control the volume of files and to make files more useful and accessible. The policy should provide guidelines as to what the office should and should not retain and establish procedures for the destruction or return of files that are no longer needed. Some states require records to be retained for as long as seven years.

CHAPTER 2

BUSINESS PLANS

■ ■ ■

A. INTRODUCTION

The development and creation of a business plan is a crucial element in the formation of a business. A business plan is like a roadmap. This roadmap is meant to keep the entrepreneur on track and guide the business on a certain and efficient route. Although some successful companies did not have a business plan at their inception, investors, bankers, and entrepreneurial professors strongly believe that a business plan is a relevant and essential part of business formation. The business plan is a helpful tool that can turn an entrepreneurial idea into a well thought out approach to develop the idea into a prosperous business entity. While a business plan does not guarantee success, it can help avoid frequent mistakes that lead to business failure.

The business plan is more like a Global Positioning System ("GPS") map than a paper roadmap one might find in the glove compartment of an automobile. Like a GPS map, the business plan provides specific step by step directions for the business. A business plan accomplishes the following:

- Communicates business goals.

- Sets forth strategies to meet business goals.

- Identifies potential problems the business might face.

- Provides solutions to solve problems the business might face.

- Outlines the organizational structure of the business.

- Creates financial statements for the business.

- Discusses the capital needed to get the business started.

- Identifies potential customers, the industry, and the competition.

Having a thorough business plan in place can confer many benefits upon the entrepreneur and the new business. For example, the development of a business plan helps the entrepreneur think through the business and determine how everything will work together. This can include examining why and how the operations of the business affect sales and vice versa. During this process the entrepreneur and the business plan become one.

Developing a business plan is not only for the process of borrowing money for the business. While a plan is key to reassure investors and bankers, having a plan can also help the entrepreneur think about strategic partnerships he or she might pursue or how to attract a lucrative customer.

Overall, a business plan is a guide to define and meet goals. The plan details the "bigger picture" for the business and helps keep operations on track when smaller issues may arise. It is important to keep in mind that as the business grows and changes, the business plan should be adapted to reflect those changes.

The business plan consists of somewhere between eight (8) and ten (10) sections. Depending on the type of business and the style of the entrepreneur, the sections of the plan may vary, as some sections may be combined. However, the most common sections of a business plan include:

- Executive Summary
- Business Description
- Marketing Section
- Operations
- Management Team
- Financial Information
- Risk Analysis
- Harvest Strategy and Milestones
- Appendix

The remainder of this chapter will discuss each section of the business plan and detail the process of creating the plan. Keep in mind that this chapter is a suggestion of how to create your business plan, and that you should create a unique plan that will conform to your business.

B. EXECUTIVE SUMMARY

The executive summary is designed to serve as a snapshot of the proposed business. This document provides an overview of the business, what will be sold in the business, target customers, key features of the market, the business' capital needs, and basic financial projections. An executive summary must communicate a vast amount of information in as few pages and paragraphs as possible. The document should be concise, business-like, and should avoid flowery language. The ideal executive summary should consist of 1–3 pages of the most vital information. It should also grab the reader's attention immediately and get the reader excited about the business venture.

A well written executive summary effectively communicates the problem the business will solve and why the problem is worth solving. This provides the entrepreneur his or her first chance to tell the story of the business. Many investors and bankers base their initial interest entirely on this portion of the business plan. Therefore, it is essential that the executive summary sets forth the business goals while also telling a compelling story.

Almost everyone in the business world suggests writing the executive summary of the business plan last. Even though it is placed at the beginning of the business plan, it is comprised entirely of information from the other sections. Therefore, some entrepreneurs find it easier to write the executive summary after the completion of the other sections of the business plan. On the other hand, drafting the executive summary first can serve as a good way to collect and organize your thoughts as you begin writing your plan. Once the plan is otherwise complete, you can return to the executive summary to complete it.

When writing your summary, think of it as an "elevator pitch," including key points that you want to get across to the reader quickly. The executive summary should boil down to the basic concepts of business: customer $\longrightarrow$ problem $\longrightarrow$ solution. For help in explaining your business ideas effectively, think about the following questions:

- How many people/customers have this problem?
- Is there a growing trend related to this problem?
- How is the problem currently being addressed?
- Why are current solutions to the problem lacking?
- Why is your solution to the problem better than the others?

The goal for any executive summary is to catch the reader's attention within the first paragraph. You may also find success by including valuable information about yourself and the proposed business that will set you apart from everyone else. This can range from having proprietary information or intellectual property that others do not. It can also include having a talented team that can get the job done or having access to valuable resources that give you an advantage over the competition.

It is a good idea to include key financial numbers in your executive summary as well. Including these numbers and projections will give the reader a sense of how much you think you will sell and how much money you think the business will generate.

Finally, use the executive summary as a chance to sell your idea and turn your opportunity into the reader's opportunity. Put forth a compelling story about your business that will leave the reader ready to immediately join in on your venture.

When the reader has finished reading your executive summary they should have a clear sense of who you are, what the business is, what you need to succeed, and why you will succeed. If you are successful, the reader will see your idea as an opportunity that consumers are going to enthusiastically support.

As a last step, test your work by having a friend, relative, or colleague read the summary. Additionally, if you have access to a small business development center, or the like, utilize their services to critique, tweak, and test your executive summary, as well as your entire business plan.

C. BUSINESS DESCRIPTION

The business description section of the business plan is designed to identify the name of the business, the industry in which the business will complete, the type of business, and any intellectual property associated with the business. This description expands on, and provides important details that were left out of, the executive summary.

When you are describing the industry in which the business will compete, think about these questions as you complete your research and compile your findings:

- What is the size of the industry?

- What are the overall trends of the industry?

- Is the industry growing rapidly, growing slowly, experiencing a resurgence, or in decline?

Much of this information can be gained by researching the Standard Industrial Classification (SIC) and North American Industry Classification System (NAICS) codes associated with the industry. You may also wish to consult the United States Census Bureau (https://www.census.gov) and the United States Bureau of Labor Statistics (https://bls.gov.) websites to learn more about your specific industry.

The next step in writing your business description is to narrow your focus on the market in which you wish to compete. Determine where your customer is within the industry. Furthermore, establish whether your customer is the end user of the product or if you will be selling to a distributor or supplier to another company.

Any successful business description must also include a section dedicated to describing the business' product. A product description may include the following information:

- What is the product?

- What makes your product or service unique?

- What are the features that your product has that sets it apart from the competition?

- Who will use the product?

- How will the product be distributed?

When the business description is boiled down, think about what you want your business to be known for in the future. Make your business memorable and explain why people will use your product or service rather than any other. Point out advantages that your business will provided versus the competition.

The goal of your business description should be to describe what your business is and what industry you are competing in. When you make this concept clear, investors and bankers will see exactly what they are looking for and will see signs that you are the person in whom they wish to invest.

Take your enthusiasm for your business and let it shape how you write your business description, as well as the rest of your business plan. If you are successful in doing so, investors, bankers, and consumers will begin to share the same enthusiasm, which will lead to a successful business venture.

D. MARKETING SECTION

The marketing section of the business plan is one that many people fear, due to the amount of work and research required to comprise it thoroughly. However, by this point in the process of creating your business plan, you should have a well-rounded idea about your business and have most of the research already completed and compiled. This section is one of the most important sections of the business plan because it covers how many customers you plan to reach, how much you plan to charge them, and how you intend to make them aware of your company.

Most marketing sections of a business plan contain two parts. The first part is based on research and analysis, and the second section presents a marketing plan for the business. The main goal of the entire marketing section is to explore the customer, pricing, and the competition in much greater detail.

The first step in compiling the marketing section is to tie together primary market research, secondary market research, qualitative market research, and quantitative market research to create and tell a story about who your target customer is going to be. Primary research consists of information such as surveys, while secondary research may be gained from assessing government databases. Qualitative research is gained through focus groups and interviews, while quantitative research can be ascertained by asking people and potential customers direct questions.

When discussing the customer portion of your marketing section, the following actions may help to point you in the right direction. The information relating to these tasks can be gathered from industry research.

- Determine who your target customer will be.

- Identify the critical needs of the customer that are not currently being met.

- Assess demographic information of potential customers.

- Identify any seasonal, cyclical, or predictable purchasing trends within your industry.

- Discuss fluctuation in your revenue stream and how you plan to deal with fluctuation issues that may arise.

- Numerically identify and demonstrate the size of the market and then show how you plan to capture your customers.

The second step in putting together your marketing section is to determine pricing for your product. Keep in mind that there is a distinct difference between pricing and selling. While these two terms are often used interchangeably, pricing focuses on maintaining a balance between profitability and competitiveness, while selling focuses on advertising and other marketing techniques.

If you are pricing a service (music lessons, tax preparation, lawn care and landscaping, pet grooming, etc.) there is a standard formula that most entrepreneurs use to determine pricing. If you are familiar with the industry you may have some idea of what pricing needs to be based on experience. However, if you are just starting out, the standard formula set forth below can help to guide you through this process.

This formula considers four factors: desired annual salary (S), overhead costs (OH), desired annual profit margin (PM), and desired annual billable hours (BH).

A desired annual salary is a simple statement of how much you would like to make in take home pay for the entire year. Overhead costs include any costs you will incur to do business (equipment, rent, utilities, supplies, travel expenses, etc.). The annual profit margin is a percentage amount that you wish for your business to make, over and above salary and overhead expenses. A common goal for a profit margin is 10%–20%.

Billable hours refer to the number of hours you will work to provide revenue to the business. Many business owners assume that they will be able to bill 2,080 hours for the year (52 weeks × 40 hours per week). However, you must be careful to factor in vacation time, administrative duties, accounting, marketing time, and holidays. The number of billable hours will differ from company to company, but most businesses expect around 65%–75% of time to be billable.

To determine pricing using these factors, add your desired annual salary (S) with your overhead costs (OH). Then, multiply this number by your desired profit margin (PM). Next, take that number and add it to your salary and overhead costs. Divide the sum of those three numbers by your billable hours (BH), and you will come up with the rate you must charge per hour.

$$\frac{S+OH(PM\%)+S+OH}{BH} = \text{Hourly rate}$$

Example:

Salary:	$100,000.00
Overhead:	$25,000.00
Profit Margin:	20%
Billable Hours:	1,560 (75% of 40 hours per week × 52 weeks)

Price Per Hour = $96.15

After completing a calculation of this formula to determine your pricing, evaluate your rate with other competitors in the industry. If this rate is higher than what your competitors charge, seek ways to cut overhead costs, or adjust your salary. On the other hand, if your rate is higher, simply offer a better service that warrants the higher price. Evaluating your rate in comparison to the industry will help you achieve your goal of being both profitable and competitive.

If you are pricing a product, the main sources of influence are location and financial demographics of the area in which you wish to sell. For example, a high-end story in an affluent section of town will warrant and provide for higher pricing. On the other hand, a low-end store in an extremely rural area will warrant and provide for lower, more affordable pricing. Location and financial demographics have a major impact on how much a product must be marked up or marked down.

It is also essential to explain how your pricing system works. Include information, such as costs for materials, distribution methods and costs, advertising costs, and overhead costs. Also, be sure to include the annual profit margin percentage you wish to retain.

Additionally, include any information pertaining to discounts or special offers you wish to employ (introductory offers, coupons, refer a friend discounts, free trials, special financing options, buy one get one offers, etc.).

Once you have obtained this information and tied it all together, you will have successfully completed the first part of the Marketing Section of your Business Plan.

The second part of the Marketing Section is known as the Marketing Plan. This section should include a marketing penetration strategy, growth strategy, strategy on how to reach customers, and a sales strategy.

The second section should also include a short competitive analysis. This analysis should mention your direct and indirect competition, highlight the competition's strength and weaknesses, and discuss how you plan to compete within the industry. This analysis should be brief, as you will have another opportunity to fully discuss your analysis in a separate portion of the Business Plan.

When writing the Marketing Plan, you may find it helpful to rely on a sales strategy, marketing strategy, or a combination of both. If you choose to rely on a sales strategy, make a list of prospects you wish to reach with your business. Then, map out how you're going to reach those prospects by answering the following questions:

- What kind of sales force do you plan to have?

- Do you plan to rely on outside distributors and resellers, and, if so, how?

- How many salespeople do you plan to employ?

- How will you pay your salespeople?

This list is not all inclusive, so thoroughly think through these questions, as well as other questions that might be pertinent to your specific business, should you decided to rely on a sales strategy approach.

Should you choose to use a marketing approach, you should analyze the usefulness and effectiveness of print ads, radio and television ads, and direct mail.

Some may say that print ads (newspapers, magazines, and billboards) are going out of style. However, with the use of QR codes and the like, print ads are beginning to make a resurgence, and may prove to be an effective marketing tool for your new business. If using print ads, consider that newspaper ads are generally good for one day only and that magazine ads tend to generally have a longer shelf life. Furthermore, if you decide to utilize print ads, run multiple ads over time to test effectiveness, and don't give up after only trying once.

While national radio and television ads are expensive and not ideal for a local customer base, local radio and television ads are generally more affordable and can provide a positive return on investment. In analyzing this form of marketing, look at your target customer base and choose a local medium most suitable to that group.

Direct mail is an option available that pinpoints who received your ad and when they receive it. Direct mail campaigns include sending catalogs, brochures, letters, postcards, and coupons directly to the customers you wish to pursue. It is common practice for businesses to buy a specific mailing list of people within a demographic area and send a direct mailing to them. A helpful resource to consider with direct mailing is the Direct Marketing Association (https://thedma.org).

There are also newer and less traditional marketing tools available, such as online marketing tools, purchasing paid search items, social media advertising, and display advertising. These are cheap and effective options that can reach the online demographic, as well as younger generations of customers.

You may also wish to consider partnership marketing. This takes place when you join forces with an established company to get your name out within the community. You can also accomplish this by sponsoring local events, such as marathons, concerts, and sporting events. Your local news station or newspaper might also be willing to do a feature on your local business, as this is a common portion of local news.

As you prepare the Marketing Plan of your Marketing Section, carefully consider as many strategies as possible before committing to a single approach. In sum, find a strategy that makes the most sense for your product, your service, and most importantly, your customer.

E. OPERATIONS

The operations section of your business plan should be centered on the concept of logistics. Logistics is the management of the resource flow between the point of origin and the point of consumption of the product you are selling. The process of logistics is described by your operations, which boils down to what you do and how you do it. The companies that thrive in the market place are those that compete better on the ground through logistics. This level of execution in the marketplace can be the difference between a successful or unsuccessful business.

Logistics is more than finding a warehouse to store your product or finding trucks or a shipping service to deliver your goods. If you, as an entrepreneur, treat logistics as an essential component of your market strategy, you will have a much higher chance of successfully growing your business.

It is important to dedicate an entire section of your business plan to operations because the reader of your plan may not fully understand the market or industry in which you operate. This section showcases your competitive advantage and shows how your operations are more efficient and different than the competition. Depending on your type of business, this section may be very involved and labor intensive, or it may be simple.

When writing this section of your business plan, you should attempt to answer the following questions:

- Where are you going to get your supplies?

- How is your product made?

- How do you plan to deliver the product to your customers?

This section should also explain your processes, systems, and operational controls. Be sure to discuss the location of your business also, as well as any regulations you must abide by. For some businesses, regulations and location play a major part in operations, while being a small consideration in others.

The processes portion of your operations section processes should define all the processes and operations that your business will be involved in to do business. It should look to capacity (will you be able to satisfy the market demand, as well as delivery (where and how you plan to ship your product).

In describing your operations, seek to provide answers to these questions:

- What does your business do?

- How long does it take you to make your product or provide your service?

- How many units can you produce during a specified time?

- What percentage of total capacity do you plan to maintain?

- How many people are needed to maintain your operation?

- How do you plan to get your product to the customer in a satisfactory way?

Additionally, break down the process of your business by demonstrating how long it takes to make one unit, how much one unit costs, and when you plan to begin selling your product or service.

The next step in the operations section of the business plan is to create an operations flow chart. This is a picture-based flow chart that shows how your product goes from supplier to customer. This step by step diagram is helpful to ensure that your business has the most efficient practices in place. It is important to demonstrate, through this section, that you fully understand the manufacturing and delivery process for your product or service.

It is key to include specific details about your business in this section, such as hours of operation, days open each week, and any seasonal schedule changes. Describe the systems you will use to get the job done, as well. For example, you may wish to describe what computer systems you will use to receive orders, place orders, complete accounting, and administer payroll. List any details of your equipment by providing any information about assets, buildings, land, furniture, inventory, or vehicles the business owns.

As you write the operations section of your business plan, assess your operational controls (How are you going to maintain inventory levels?) and control systems (What are you going to do if something goes wrong? Do you have a backup plan?).

To finalize this section, there are three main considerations that you should evaluate regarding your business. These are supply, location, and distribution.

Supply boils down to making sustainable relationships with those who meet your supply, manufacturing, and delivery needs. When thinking about supply chain management, it is necessary to first determine whether you want to make the product yourself or outsource the work to a contract manufacturer. A contract manufacturer is a specialized manufacturer tailored to your product need that provides a lower cost option than making the product yourself.

To get in touch with a contract manufacturer and begin developing a relationship, turn to business leaders in the community for advice and referrals. Additionally, take advantage of small business centers or economic development agencies. There are also websites that attempt to bring together entrepreneurs and contract manufacturers such as Maker's Row (https://makersrow.com), Alibaba (https://www.alibaba.com), Thomas Net (https://www.thomasnet.com), and Global Sources (https://www.global sources.com). If these options do not provide success, attend a local trade show in your area to meet contractors.

Should you engage and secure a contract manufacturer, have them sign a Non-Disclosure Agreement (NDA). NDA's are standard procedure in instances where a business contracts with another party for manufacturing purposes. The NDA is a way to keep a contractor from stealing your business idea or sharing the idea with a competitor. Then, enter into negotiations with the contract manufacturer to secure a deal most suitable to your business. In the negotiation process, attempt to keep your fixed costs to a minimum and be aware of your cash flow.

Regarding location, keep in mind access to the resources your will need to do business. Attempt to pick a location that is easy to access for both the public and your suppliers. If customers do not visit your location, consider working from home or in an inexpensive warehouse.

There are several options at your disposal for distribution purposes. One option may be to contract with a company like Amazon to do your marketing and distribution for you. While this option takes away some responsibilities and allows more time for administrative duties, it is a high cost option. For a lower cost, however, you could use Amazon as a marketing provider that sells your products on its website and handle orders for you. Under this option, you will be responsible for distributing the product to the customer. You can accomplish delivery by using drop shipments or using an outbound distributor.

The larger your sales become, the more negotiating power you will have for supply and delivery contracts. If your business grows exceedingly, you may need to consider a full load trucking service contract. This option will avoid the fixed costs of owning a truck, maintenance, insurance, and other road expenses.

In sum, developing relationships that help you build your supply chain in a cost-effective and cash flow-positive manner will make a tremendous impact on your company's success. The supply chain is the foundation upon which your business will grow and a strong supply chain will most certainly lead to a prosperous business venture.

F. MANAGEMENT TEAM

It has been said that investors prefer an A team with a B idea than a B team with an A idea. Simply put, investors are more concerned with the team running your business than the type of idea you are presenting. With this thought in mind, it is important to consider that a great business idea will not go far if your team does not know how to properly execute the idea. The management team section of your business plan is your opportunity to showcase that you have assembled the right people, with the right skills, to create and build your business.

In this section you should attempt to make an impression on bankers and investors by showing that you provide something unique to your industry, and that your team is more equipped than the competition to carry out your idea. It is crucial to show investors that you have the knowledge, drive, and discipline to successfully execute your proposed idea. The management team section provides an opportunity to convince your audience that you and your team are the right people to make your business idea into reality.

This portion of your business plan should explain what the organizational structure of the business will be and explain who will comprise your management team. By providing this information, you are beginning the process of building credibility and legitimacy for your business. Seek to describe who will be running the business and why they are qualified to do so.

The management team section is not a complicated section to created, but it is one that should be treated seriously and given maximum effort, because it is a section that bankers and investors take special interest in when reading your plan.

The first step is to lay out the structure of your company. This is accomplished by creating an organizational structure portion within this section. The most effective way to approach organizational structure is to create an organizational flow chart. An organizational flow chart is a simple diagram that lists and describes all the key roles and positions within the business. This chart should list all essential positions necessary to execute the day-to-day operations of running the business. As you create your flow chart, include specific names and basic credentials of the people who will be fulfilling the roles within the company. The following is an abbreviated example of an organizational flow chart:

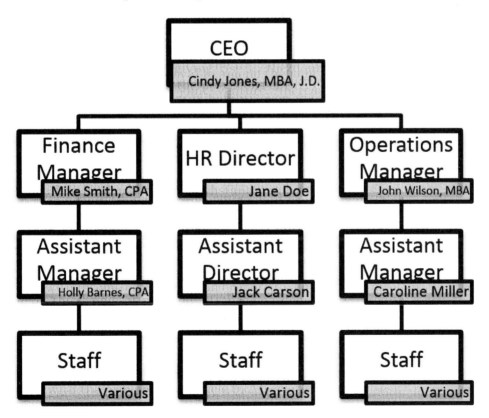

Next, describe each department in detail, including positions within the department and what functions they serve. Additionally, include information about the individuals who are going to oversee and manage these departments.

Tell the reader about yourself and your management team, what experience you have, what skills you have, and other basic information that relates to the business. Include any special skills you may have such as:

- A record of past success.

- Quantitative results of achievements.

- Time worked for previous companies.

- Management experience.

- A record of increasing revenues as a business manager.

Provide hard facts about yourself and your management team. Do not be afraid to sell yourself or your team. Tell a story of why you will be successful, why your team is the team to back, and what you bring to the table that others do not.

In this section of your business plan, attempt to be concise yet convincing. Focus on spending one paragraph to describe each person in the businesses, while giving a small amount of additional attention to the president or CEO. Make this section a quick snapshot of the key highlights of each person and save the full resumes of team members for the Appendix.

As you compile your team, seek to add people who have a proven track record of building, growing, or managing a company. Having people with this type of experience will go a long way towards reassuring investors about your business venture.

The next portion of the management team section should provide ownership information and information about the structure of the business. First, describe the legal structure of your business (sole proprietorship, partnership, corporation, LLC, etc.). Next, provide ownership information, such as the name of the owners, percentage amount that each owner owns, level of involvement of each owner, and how each owner owns the business (stockholder, or general or limited partner). This ownership information is crucial because investors will want to know how the shares of your business are divided and what their investment in your business will provide for them.

Once you have compiled an organizational flow chart and provided ownership information, you will have successfully completed the management team section of your business plan.

As you attempt to write this portion of your plan, keep the following tips in mind:

- Start by examining yourself, by determining your personal strengths and weaknesses. Have confidence in yourself but be careful to also acknowledge your weaknesses.

- Take the weaknesses you identify and hire people to compensate in areas where your skills may be lacking.

- Actively seek the help of other business leaders with more knowledge and experience.

- Consider building an unpaid board of directors or an advisory board for your business. Invite successful entrepreneurs, industry leaders, or business managers to join a group to advise you as you begin your business venture. These advisers will help you think through and tackle challenges as they arise. (If you plan to employ this strategy, mention it in your business plan, as it will allow you to show that you will have access to people who can help make your business successful.)

In sum, make your goal to first build a strong team that can then work together to turn your business idea into a successful reality.

G. FINANCIAL INFORMATION

One of the best ways to showcase to investors that you understand how to run your business is to demonstrate that you have a solid grasp on the economic side of your business. In this section of your business plan, you should address how and where you plan to spend your money. This task is accomplished through financial statements, which illustrate how a business is performing financially. Financial statements closely resemble a diagnostic report of the business.

A good understanding of financial statements will help you pinpoint your weaknesses, which will allow you to make strategic decisions to improve the business.

It is likely that your business will not yet be operational as you write your plan and create your financial statements. Therefore, your financial statements will be called "pro forma" statements. Pro forma statements are predictions of how you think the business will perform financially once operational.

The financial information section makes up the backbone of your entire business plan. This section may well be the most important section you complete, as investors will likely look to this section first before deciding whether to spend their time reading the rest of the plan.

Your financial information section should be comprised of the following documents: an income statement, balance sheet, and cash flow statement. A thorough presentation of your financial documents in your business plan will put you well ahead of most other entrepreneurs seeking money from investors.

1. INCOME STATEMENT

Income statements measure a company's financial performance over a specified period. As you complete this section, seek to look ahead to the first five years of your business operation. For the first year of projected operation, include monthly or quarterly projections, and then only include annual projections for years two through five.

The income statement, also commonly referred to as a profit and loss statement, translates your revenue into net income. Revenue is defined as the total amount of money received from the sale of your product or service. Net income, or net profit, is calculated by subtracting your expenses from your revenue.

To estimate your expenses, conduct research on industry pricing and make reasonable assumptions based on that research. The better grasp you have on expenses, the more accurate your income statement will be.

The first expense you must take into consideration is the cost of goods sold. This number is generated by determining how much you spend on making a product or delivering a service. This expense takes into consideration factors such as materials cost, labor expenses, and manufacturing expenses.

The second set of expenses you must consider are operating expenses. These expenses are generally grouped into two categories: selling expenses and general/administrative expenses. Selling expenses include costs, such as sales staff salaries, commissions, fringe benefits, advertising, travel, promotional materials, rent, utilities, postage, and office supplies, related to the sales department. General/administrative expenses include costs such as salaries for accountants, lawyers, management personnel, and human resources, as well as office supplies, rent, utilities, and postage related to the running the business.

The next step in preparing an income statement is to examine depreciation costs. Depreciation refers to the estimated useful life of your fixed assets. Fixed assets include items such as vehicles, buildings, building improvements, machinery, office equipment, computers, furniture and fixtures, computer software, and any other property or plant that you may own. Each fixed asset that you own has a different estimated useful life expectancy, so be certain to carefully evaluate each asset.

Lastly, take into consideration the payment of taxes, any interest owed, and insurance costs. Once you have taken these steps, you will be well on your way towards completing a thorough income statement. While most entrepreneurs compute rough calculations of expenses, many do not take into consideration all of the potential expenses listed above. Therefore, it is important to have good financial oversight to ensure that your entire business venture is successful.

In addition to the income statement, include any supplemental statements you may have, such as a list of the cost of goods sold, salaries, wages and payroll related expenses, amortization chart, inventory list, and any bank loan information you may have.

In this section of the business plan, it is also important to include a breakeven analysis. This is an analysis that seeks to determine when your business will be able to cover all of its expenses and begin to make a profit. To complete this analysis, identify your fixed costs, which are expenses that you will incur regardless of how many sales you make. Divide the total of your fixed costs by the price of your product, and then subtract the total of your variable costs. This will provide you with the number of units you must sell to break even.

The following is an example of what your Income Statement might look like:

YourBusiness, Inc.

Income Statement

For the Year Ended December 31, 2018

Revenues:

Sales:	$	1,200,000.00
Rental Income:	$	50,000.00
Total Revenues:		**$1,250,000.00**

Expenses:

Payroll:	$	475,000.00
Supplies:	$	20,000.00
Utilities:	$	75,000.00
Mortgage:	$	185,000.00
Depreciation:	$	20,000.00
Cost of Goods Sold:	$	100,000.00
Total Expenses:		**$875,000.00**
Net Income:		**$375,000.00**

2. BALANCE SHEET

The balance sheet is a financial statement that reports the financial position of a business at a specific point in time by listing the business's assets, liability, and owner's equity.

There are two types of assets: current and fixed. Current assets can be liquidated quickly—generally less than a year—and include cash, accounts receivable, inventory, and prepaid expenses. Fixed assets are those that remain with the company for an extended amount of time and are more difficult to liquidate. Common fixed assets include land, building, and equipment.

Liabilities are claims that creditors may have against the business. Like assets, there are current liabilities and long-term liabilities. Current liabilities are obligations due and payable during the next year or the current operating cycle. Current liabilities often include debts such as accounts payable, notes payable, taxes payable, and loans payable. Long term liabilities are obligations due and payable after at least one year and outside the current operating cycle, such as a bank loan.

Owner's equity refers to the amount of capital the owner, or owners, initially contributed towards the company, with the addition of any retained earnings. Contributed capital is the value of the owner's, or owners, stock in the business while retained earnings is the sum of the net income of the business.

The main purpose of a balance sheet is to describe where a business stands financially, what the business owns, and what the business owes to creditors.

Following is a sample balance sheet:

YourBusiness, Inc.
Balance Sheet
As of December 31, 2018

Assets:

Current Assets:

Checking Account:	$ 1,200,256.89
Savings Account:	$ 1,650,899.76
Petty Cash:	$ 15,850.00
Total Current Assets:	**$ 2,867,006.65**

(cont'd on next page)

Fixed Assets:

Vehicle Fleet:	$ 400,000.00
Office Furniture & Fixtures:	$ 150,000.00
Office Computers & Printers:	$ 100,000.00
Total Fixed Assets:	**$ 650,000.00**

Inventory:

Stock on hand:	$ 267,837.22
Total Inventory:	**$ 267,837.22**

Total Assets:	**$ 3,784,843.87**

Liabilities:
Current Liabilities:

Accounts Payable:	$ 875,000.00
Total Current Liabilities:	**$ 875,000.00**

Long Term Liabilities:

Mortgage:	$ 1,567,843.87
Total Long Term Liabilities:	**$ 1,567,843.87**

Total Assets:	**$ 2,442,843.87**

Equity:

Common Stock:	$ 575,000.00
Retained Earnings:	$ 767,000.00

Total Equity:	**$ 1,342,000.00**

3.   CASH FLOW STATEMENT

To build a cash flow statement, it is important to have a basic understanding of accounting concepts.   In accounting there are two primary methods of tracking income and expensed: the accrual method and the cash method.

The accrual method of accounting records income when it is earned and records expenses when they are incurred, without recording whether cash actually changed hands. This method utilizes the concepts of accounts payable and accounts receivable. The cash method, on the other hand, records income when it is actually received and expenses when they are actually paid.

Income statements and balance sheets are prepared under the accrual method, while the cash flow statement is prepared under the cash method.

A cash flow statement focuses specifically on converting the accrual method to a cash basis. While documents like an income statement showcase whether you made a profit, a cash flow statement showcases whether you generated any cash. In essence, the cash flow statement shows the effects of the company's operating, investment, and financial activities on its cash balance.

The operating activities section measures the cash inflows and outflows generated by the core operations of the business. These activities include those related to the production, sale, and delivery of your product. These activities generate costs for raw materials, inventory, marketing, advertising, salaries, and shipping.

The investment activities section tracks the cash flow in relation to your long-term investments such as land, building, equipment, and vehicles. This section examines how much cash you expended on these investments and any cash brought in by selling investments.

The financing activities section lists the selling of any stocks or bonds, discloses any money borrowed from a bank, payments of dividends to shareholders, and any repurchasing of company shares.

Overall, the cash flow statement should attempt to answer the following:

- Is the company generating sufficient positive cash flow from its operations to remain viable?

- Will the company be able to repay its debts as they come due?

- Will the company be able to pay dividends to shareholders or distributions to members?

- To what extent will the company have to borrow money in order to make necessary investments?

As you think about these questions and compile this section, it is important to demonstrate that you fully understand your working capital, which is determined by subtracting your current liabilities from your current assets.

Additionally, examine your returns by determining your return on assets (ROA) and your return on investments (ROI). ROA is calculated by dividing your net profit by your total assets. ROI is calculated by subtracting your investments from your earnings and dividing that number by the amount of your initial investment.

The following is a sample Cash Flow Statement:

YourBusiness, Inc.
Cash Flow Statement
For the Year Ended December 31, 2018

Cash Flows from Operating Activities:

Operating Income:	$ 489,000.00
Depreciation Expense:	$ 112,400.00
Loss on Sale of Equipment:	$ 7,300.00
Gain on Sale of Land:	− $ 51,000.00
Increase in Accounts Receivable:	− $ 84,664.00
Decrease in Prepaid Expenses:	$ 8,000.00
Decrease in Accounts Payable:	− $ 97,370.00
Decrease in Accrued Expenses:	− $ 113,860.00

Net Cash Flow from Operating Activities: $ **269,806.00**

Cash Flows from Investing Activities:

Sale of Equipment:	$ 89,000.00
Sale of Land:	$ 247,000.00
Purchase of Equipment:	− $ 100,000.00

Net Cash Flow from Investing Activities: $ **136,000.00**

Cash Flows from Financing Activities:

Payment of Dividends:	− $ 90,000.00
Payment of Bond Payable:	− $ 200,000.00

Net Cash Flow from Financing Activities: −   **290,000.00**

Net Change in Cash:	$ **115,806.00**
Beginning Cash Balance:	$ **319,730.00**
Ending Cash Balance:	$ **435,536.00**

---

4.   CONCLUSION

Since you are likely in the process of building your business as you construct your business plan, generate these statements as pro forma documents to make projections for the future of your business. Constructing these statements should help you determine if launching your business makes sense, while also showing investors that you have thoroughly thought through the financial and economic side of your business.

Building a solid financial information section in your business plan will likely mean that investors will take you seriously, and have confidence that you understand the language of business: finance.

H. RISK ANALYSIS

The risk analysis portion of your business plan is designed to demonstrate your ability to survive in adverse conditions and to outline your plan of how you plan to deal with such situations. All business ventures involve some percentage of risk. Therefore, preparing a thorough risk analysis will show investors that you are capable of handling and prepared for any challenges you may face.

The first step in compiling your risk analysis is to address your critical risks. This portion serves as a simulation of how you plan to approach critical situations and should demonstrate that you are reasonably prepares to handle whatever risks may come your way. By addressing potential critical risks, you can engineer solutions to minimize their impact, should they arise, and offer creative and effective solutions to your problems.

The next step in risk analysis is to apply the Porter Five Forces Model, developed by Harvard Business School Professor Michael Porter. The Porter Model attempts to gauge the dynamics of the industry and helps analyze the risks inherent within the industry. The Porter Model examines the following five forces present in any industry:

1. The threat of new business entering the market.

2. The threat of substitute products or services.

3. The threat of customers gaining bargaining power over you.

4. The threat of suppliers gaining bargaining power over you.

5. The threat of intense competition.

The Porter Model is helpful to most entrepreneurs because it makes business owners focus intensely on barriers to entry into the industry. It also helps entrepreneurs to decide whether they have what it takes to show consumers they have a product that is superior to the competition. While thinking about these competitive issues may be difficult, it will allow you to make well-informed decisions about your business, based on market research.

The final step in risk analysis is to conduct a SWOT analysis. The acronym SWOT stands for strengths, weaknesses, opportunities, and threats. This technique is widely used throughout the business world, especially among start-up companies.

Consider approaching a SWOT analysis in the following way:

- Compile a group of diverse stakeholders connected to the business, such as owners, the management team, future customers, employees, suppliers, distributors, and investors or bankers.

- Have this group identify critical risks the business may face. Attempt to capture as many ideas as possible during this process.

- Next, examine your strings by identifying your core competencies. Core competencies are strengths that can help your offset or address the risks your company may face. The strengths you identify will help to distinguish your company from the competition and help to mitigate future risks.

- Ask the group if they have any ideas on how to address the previously identified weaknesses. The goal here is to develop innovative solutions that other in the industry have not yet discovered.

- Consider a variety of lesser risks you may face like market, financial and competitive risks.

- After identify potential risks, turn them into "what if" statements, then answer these questions. Think also about any strategic alliances you can make to mitigate risks, such as partnering with another business to fulfill an area in which you exhibit a weakness.

As you write the risk analysis portion of your business plan, research the common risks in your industry and study how your competition has handles similar risks in the past. Look for patterns and innovative solutions to avoid these risks altogether. Give the risk analysis portion your best effort so that you can demonstrate to investors that you have a plan to face risks, to handle them effectively or avoid them, and to move forward with a successful business venture.

I. HARVEST STRATEGY AND MILESTONES

The harvest strategy and milestones section of your business plan sets forth your intentions and goals for your business in the future. For most entrepreneurs, selling their business is a major component of this section. Selling a business is a landmark event for a business owner because it is a payoff for all of the hard work and dedication to cultivating the business from ground level.

The first portion of this section should focus on establishing a harvest strategy for your business. Like a farmer who harvests his or her crops at the end of growing season, so too does an entrepreneur harvest the rewards of building a business by selling it one day. A harvest strategy is simply a plan which describes if and how you plan to sell your business.

Investors focus closely on this section because they may wish to get a large return on their original investment, or they may want to know how a successor might take over management should you end your involvement with the business. Investors want to know if you plan to run your business long-term or if you plan to start your business with the intention of selling it at a future time for a lump-sum payment or a stream of payments.

One of the main purposes of a harvest strategy is to show investors that your business is healthy to insure them that they will not lose money and to show them how and when they will be repaid.

In this section of your business plan, you should attempt to demonstrate the soundness of your business by discussing revenue projections, gross and net profit margins, your income statement, and your cash flow statement. Additionally, attempt to describe what an investment in your company will be worth because the more return an investment will bring the more interest an investor will have in your business.

The next step in this section is to value your business. Business valuation is the process that estimates the economic value of an owner's interest in a business. A common method to calculate this value is the discounted cash flow method. This method looks at three forecasts: future cash flows, the window of time in which you project the cash flow, and the discount rate.

A future cash flow projection can be created by estimating how much cash the business will generate per year, over a specified period. These numbers are primarily drawn from your financial statements in the financial information section of your business plan.

The discount rate is the process by which future dollars are translated into today's dollars. The discount rate is based on two factors: 1) the fact that the dollar is worth more in present than it will be in the future, and 2) the riskiness of the business. For the first component, one might start with the current rate of interest on the 10 year U.S. Treasury Bill as a proxy for the "risk free" rate of interest. For the second component, the risk premium, anywhere from 7% to 20% is typical, based upon an estimate of the risk of failure of the business. The discount rate indicates that, since future cash flow projections are not guaranteed, the business is reducing its projection to account for the time value of money and any future risks.

A thorough business valuation stems from successfully accomplishing your business goals, or milestones. Each time you achieve a milestone for your business, you are making your business more successful, reducing risks, and increasing the valuation of your business.

The milestones portion of this section should include events that you wish to occur during the projected future of your business. Some common milestones include:

- Completing initial product design
- Building your first prototype
- Manufacturing the product for the first time
- Making your first sale
- Reaching your break even point
- Opening multiple locations
- Begin franchising
- Qualify for additional funding
- Increase revenue by 20%, each of the first five years

In an ideal setting, you should attempt to meet some of these early milestones before presenting your business plan to prospective investors to showcase that you are serious about your business venture. In developing your milestones portion, create a timeline of major events, incorporating a brief discussion of each one. Provide specific start and end dates, and monitor your progress towards achieving your goals. It may prove beneficial to assign someone within the company to be accountable for overseeing the business's progress toward each goal.

J. APPENDIX

The appendix should be the final section of your business plan. This section should demonstrate all of your research, as well as add details about your product, customer, operations, location, team members, and financials. Include references throughout your business plan to the appendix to provide readers with additional information regarding the topic they are reading. This section should also include a bibliography, which sets out resources for all of your research within the plan.

As you prepare the appendix and wrap up your business plan, be sure to put just as much time, effort and thought into this section as previous sections. Doing so will be beneficial because investors will rely heavily on this section to find further information on specific points in your plan.

K. CONCLUSION

A thoroughly prepared business plan should read well, tell a compelling story, highlight the business's key points, be free of any inconsistencies, and be backed by solid research in the appendix and bibliography.   If your business plan is well written, presents a good opportunity for investors, and shows investors that the business idea is well researched, it is very likely to get the attention you desire and put you on track to a successful business venture.

CHAPTER 3

CHOOSING THE APPROPRIATE BUSINESS ENTITY

∎ ∎ ∎

A. INTRODUCTION

According to a 2014 Pew Research Center Analysis[1] of U.S. Census Bureau data, approximately 14.6 million people in the United States are self-employed, accounting for roughly 10% of the U.S. workforce. Approximately 29.4 million workers are hired by the self-employed. All total, 44 million, or 30% of the U.S. workforce is made up of self-employed workers and those they hire.

According to 2014 data from the IRS, there were 23 million sole proprietorships, 7.4 million partnerships and S corporations, and 1.7 traditional C corporations. These entrepreneurs range from specialty trade contractors to professional, technical, and scientific services. These small businesses (less than 500 employees) account for around half of the GDP and more than half of the employment in the United States. The bottom line is that an ever increasing segment of the American economy is dependent on the creation of small businesses.

It follows that the market for legal services focusing on the needs of small businesses will only grow in the future. In addition, some of these small businesses will grow into the Microsofts and Apples of the future, businesses that were started on a shoestring by inspired entrepreneurs and subsequently turned into public multinational corporations. While these entrepreneurs may have a business idea, the drive, enthusiasm, and appropriate business or technical knowledge to start a business, they often need assistance from attorneys who have the background to understand the legal consequences of their business decisions. Because the small business owner is typically very optimistic, they often need attorneys to help them think through all the risks and downsides potentially associated with their venture.

Entrepreneurs taking advantage of attorneys' expertise can add value to the enterprise. Working with the small business person, the attorney can carefully review all aspects of the potential new business and counsel

---

[1] Kochhar, Rakesh. 2015. "Three In Ten U.S. Jobs Are Held by the Self Employed and the Workers They Hire: Hiring More Prevalent Among Self Employed Asians, Whites and Men." Washington, D.C.: Pew Research Center, October.

the principals on a range of issues including choosing the appropriate business entity, aspects of entering into contractual agreements, protection of intellectual property, and financing the operations of the business. This chapter addresses the attorney's role and related considerations in advising entrepreneurs on choosing the appropriate form of business entity.

B. DETERMINING THE NATURE AND GOALS OF THE BUSINESS

While some business people are very sophisticated in financial, tax, and business planning matters, most have not had the requisite education and experience in the legal aspects of business to make the most out of their venture. Many small business owners often form their views on the choice of entity type based upon advice from magazines, friends, family, accountants, or business consultants, rather than based on the advice of an attorney. Attorneys, however, can best advise the business owner as to the choice of entity, explaining that it depends on the nature and goals of the specific business. Attorneys should initially ask entrepreneurs whether they have developed a business plan. Many small business owners may not necessarily have a formal plan (as described in Chapter 2) when they first contact an attorney, so, in the absence of such a plan, attorneys should be prepared to ask questions to help the entrepreneur think through the critical business issues which have legal ramifications. Examples of such questions include:

- What products and services will be sold?
- Who will the customers be?
- What is the competition for these products and services?
- What are the financial projections for the business?
- Who will supply the financial resources?
- Who will manage the business?
- Who will provide the services, employees, or contractors?
- Will facilities be required and will they be purchased or leased?
- Will the business involve the use of intellectual property or proprietary information?

This list of questions is not exhaustive and there are many other questions that may be raised depending upon the type of business and the individual entrepreneurs. But, in essence, the attorney should interview the business owner to obtain the information that should be contained in a formal business plan.

C. THE PROPER MANAGEMENT AND GOVERNANCE OF THE ENTERPRISE

After establishing the entrepreneur's goals and objectives for the new business, the first issue that should be explored is what management and corporate governance structure is most suitable. Attorneys must discuss the various forms of business entities with the entrepreneur, including their associated benefits and draw-backs. This section will provide a brief explanation of some of the most common forms of business entities.

1. SOLE PROPRIETORSHIPS

A sole proprietorship is a type of business entity that is owned and run by one individual and in which there is no legal distinction between the owner and the business. Only one person can own and operate a sole proprietorship. The owner receives all profits and has unlimited personal responsibility for all losses, debts, and other liabilities, including taxes. There is no entity holding the assets and operations of the business separate and apart from the owner. All operations are actually conducted by the owner, directly or through one or more agents, even though the business may operate under a business name. Because only one person will finance and operate the business, management by definition will be concentrated in that individual. Sole proprietorships are easy to own and operate; all that needs to be done is to obtain any necessary business licenses and permits from the city, county, or municipality where the business exists.

2. GENERAL PARTNERSHIPS

A general partnership arises when two or more persons associate as co-owners of a business. Absent an agreement to the contrary, the default terms of the partnership are that all owners have an equal voice in the conduct of the business, have the power to bind the partnership, share equally in the profits and losses of the business, and are personally responsible for all operations and liabilities, including taxes. Although a general partnership does not require legal documentation or filings, the management and governance of the partnership is typically documented in a partnership agreement. This is prudent from a legal point of view as friendships and alliances may change over time, along with the memories of the partners as to the business terms they originally agreed upon. This partnership agreement s outline the partners' roles and responsibilities in the management and governance of the partnership. In the event that the partnership chooses not to have such an agreement, the statutory law of the state in which the partnership is operating will dictate the default rules under which the partners must conduct themselves. Each partner, as an agent of the partnership, has power to bind the partnership either by transacting business as authorized by the partners (actual authority) or by appearing to act as an agent of the partnership from the perspective of third parties (apparent authority). Partners owe fiduciary duties to each other to act in good faith with due care and undivided loyalty.

Partners must be able to trust and rely upon those partners managing the partnership to promote the best interests and success of the partnership. Typically, the general partners in a general partnership participate in the daily operation and supervision of the business and as such are viewed as having fiduciary duties. Under this standard, partners must act with honesty and show good faith and fairness to each other in their partnership interactions. The duty of loyalty requires relevant partners to place the success and interests of their partnership above their own personal or other business interests. Partners should avoid any conflicts of interest between their partnership duties and their other personal and business activities. As part of the duty of loyalty, one must properly hold partnership property in trust for the benefit of the partners and not use it for one's own personal advantage. Under the duty of care, partners are expected to act in a reasonably prudent manner in managing and directing the partnership. Partners involved in managing partnership affairs are expected to comply with a duty of disclosure and candor to other partners. In order to make informed decisions, participating partners should make full disclosures about reasonably known risks and potential benefits of a particular action. Fiduciary duties are spelled out in the state's statutory law or through judicial determinations where the general or limited partnership is formed. Depending upon the particular state of formation, partners may limit, expand, or eliminate fiduciary duties by agreement, provided that these changes are reasonable under the circumstances. Under state law, certain fiduciary duties cannot be eliminated by agreement. It is important for the partners to discuss with an attorney the relevant fiduciary duties and to see if they may alter or do away with certain fiduciary obligations in the partnership agreement.

3. LIMITED PARTNERSHIPS

A limited partnership is similar to a general partnership, except that in addition to one or more general partners, there are one or more limited partners (LPs). Limited partnerships must make appropriate filings with the state under which they are organized to ensure that they will be treated as a limited partnership. Failure to do so results in the entity being treated as a general partnership, exposing all partners to personal liability.

Only one partner is required to be a general partner. The general partners are, in all major respects, in the same legal position as partners in a general partnership. They have management control, share the right to use partnership property, share the profits of the business in predefined proportions, and have joint and several liabilities[2] for the debts of the partnership. General partners owe fiduciary duties to other general partners as well as the limited partners. As in a general partnership, the general partners have actual authority as agents of the firm to bind all the other partners in contracts with third parties that are in the ordinary course of the partnership's business. As with a general partnership, an act of a general partner that is not apparently in the ordinary course of the limited partnership binds the limited partnership only if the general partner had actual authority, i.e., the act was actually authorized by all the other partners.

A limited partnership allows general partners to raise capital by granting non-management ownership interests—limited partnership interests—to investors in exchange for money, property, or other assets. Like shareholders in a corporation, LPs have limited liability, meaning they are not liable for debts incurred by the firm beyond the extent of their investment and have no management authority. The general partners pay the LPs a return on their investment, which should be defined in the partnership agreement. LPs may have voting authority over specified matters but cannot bind the limited partnership in dealings with third parties. If however, they act as if they do have such authority, they may be recharacterized as general partners and be treated as such, exposing themselves to personal liability to third parties.

Business owners need to consider federal and state securities laws when setting up limited partnerships. Although a general partner's interest is not usually considered a security under state and federal securities laws, an LP's interest usually is considered a security due to the passive nature of the LP's investment. Therefore, the general partners and the partnership must comply with the Federal Securities Act of 1933 and state corporate securities law unless the prospective limited partner fits within an exemption from these laws. These securities laws generally require a security registration statement to be filed and cleared by the appropriate agencies before the LP interests are issued. This process can be time consuming and costly, taking up to several months. There are, however, a number of state and federal exemptions to these requirements, which should be taken advantage of whenever possible. Securities laws and their exemptions are covered in more detail in the last chapter of this book.

---

[2]   Joint and several liability exists when two or more parties can be held liable for the same event or act and be fully and independently responsible for the entire amount of liability. Under this doctrine, the injured party could be awarded damages and collect from any one, several, or all of the liable parties. (Wex Legal Dictionary)

4.   LIMITED LIABILITY PARTNERSHIPS

A limited liability partnership (LLP) is a more formal partnership than a general partnership or limited partnership. This form of organization requires a written partnership agreement and annual reporting requirements. Like a general partnership, all partners can participate in the management of an LLP. While an LLP is very similar to an general partnership, the LLP form gives all partners some limited personal liability.

Liability within an LLP varies by state. Some states limit personal liability like that of shareholders of corporation, while others only limit personal liability for the negligence of a partner. Other states limit liability for negligence as well as other contracts and debts.

An LLP requires at least two or more owners. One of the main advantages of an LLP is that all partners are protected by some form of limited liability, but also have influence in how the business operates. Additionally, in an LLP, no partner is responsible or liable for another partner's misconduct or negligence. Although found in many business fields, the LLP is a popular form of organization among professionals, namely lawyers, accountants, and architects. In some states, such as California, New York, Oregon, and Nevada, LLPs can only be formed for such professional uses.

Formation of an LLP typically requires filing certificates with the county and state offices in which the business is located. Although specific rules vary from state to state, all states have passed variations of the Revised Uniform Partnership Act in an attempt to streamline and unify the application process. As in a partnership or LLC, the profits of an LLP are allocated among the partners for tax purposes, avoiding the problem of double taxation found in most corporations

5.   CORPORATIONS

The corporation, like a limited partnership, has a centralized management structure that separates those who invest in the business from those that manage it, although management can include (and typically does include) equity holders. Shareholders in a corporation, like limited partners in a limited partnership, have limited liability, meaning they are not liable for debts incurred by the firm beyond the extent of their investment and have no management authority by reason of their share ownership. Ownership interests in a for-profit corporation are represented by shares of stock. The shareholders meet at least annually to elect a board of directors and to make decisions on major matters, although notice of written consent in lieu of a meeting is common in small to medium sized corporations.

The directors typically meet as a board under the leadership of a chairman. The board of directors oversees the business affairs of the corporation and meets from time to time to plan and approve corporate actions. The board also selects corporate officers, who are management agents for the corporation and carry out the policies of the board on a day-to-day basis. This management scheme is defined in the corporate charter, bylaws, and board resolutions. The charter is the basic organic document that is filed with the state in which the corporation is organized. It is usually very general and omits any information not required by the state's corporate statutes that the corporation would not want in the public record. The bylaws are more detailed and set out the basic structure of the corporation, including the rights, powers, and duties of shareholders, directors, and management; they are generally not filed with the government and become part of the public record only in limited circumstances. Corporate resolutions are passed by the board of directors according to the rules set out in the bylaws. They are fact intensive, specific directions to management or rules that will govern the corporation in the future. Resolutions cannot supersede the bylaws and bylaws cannot supersede the charter. Corporate directors and officers owe fiduciary duties of care and loyalty to the corporation and, in some circumstances, to the shareholders.

People organizing corporations, like those forming limited partnerships, need to consider federal and state securities laws. Shares issued to passive investors need to either comply with federal and state registration requirements or fit within an exemption from the securities laws.

6. LIMITED LIABILITY COMPANIES

The limited liability company (LLC) is a flexible enterprise that blends elements of partnership and corporate structures. An LLC is created with the filing of the articles of organization, which are analogous to a corporation's charter, in the state under whose law the LLC is formed. Some LLC statutes require there be at least two members, but single member LLCs are increasingly recognized and popular.

LLCs can be member-managed, manager-managed, or director-managed. The member-managed LLCs are most appropriate for start-up businesses in which only a few people, all active in the business, hold ownership interests. Members in a member-managed LLC have the authority to bind the LLC just like general partners in a general or limited partnership. In a manager-managed LLC, members elect managers that have authority similar to that of a general partner in a limited partnership. The director-managed LLC has a board of directors and officers like a corporation.

An LLC's operating agreement is an agreement between the LLC members governing the LLCs business which outlines the member's financial and managerial rights and duties.   It is analogous to a corporation's bylaws.   While many states require an LLC to have an operating agreement, absent an agreement, the LLC is governed by the state's statutory default rules.

Members and managers of LLCs have fiduciary duties of care and loyalty to the membership and each other depending on the form of the LLC. In a member-managed LLC, fiduciary duties are similar to that of a general partnership. In a manager-managed LLC, only the manager has fiduciary duties, and members who are not a manger do not have fiduciary duties. In a director-managed LLC, directors and officers have fiduciary duties to the membership, and members who are not managers or directors do not have fiduciary duties to other members. Membership interests in an LLC can be represented by a membership certificate.

7. NON-PROFIT CORPORATIONS

A non-profit corporation is one specifically formed for purposes other than operating a profit-seeking business. They are also referred to as 501(c) corporations, named after the section in the Internal Revenue Code for the designation of non-profit organizations. Many non-profits want to obtain 501(c) status to avoid paying federal income taxes and other types of state taxes. The purpose of the organization and the structure of the organization will determine whether a not-for-profit corporation will qualify for tax exemption status under § 501(c). In order to qualify for tax-exempt status as a non-profit, the overall purpose of the corporation must fit one of the 28 categories listed in section 501(c). Some of the most common examples of non-profit companies are ones with "charitable, religious, education, or scientific purposes"—so-called § 501(c)(3) non-profits. The non-profit must file an application and submit a filing fee. Filing of the application alone is not sufficient. The IRS must receive and approve the application before the corporation can receive 501(c) status.

The following is a list of the different subsections of 501(c) and the types of non-profit entities that they provide for:

501(c)(1) — Corporations Organized Under Act of Congress (including Federal Credit Unions)

501(c)(2) — Title Holding Corporation for Exempt Organization

501(c)(3) — Religious, Educational, Charitable, Scientific, Literary, Testing for Public Safety, to Foster National or International Amateur Sports Competition, or Prevention of Cruelty to Children or Animals Organizations

501(c)(4)	—	Civic Leagues, Social Welfare Organizations, and Local Associations of Employees
501(c)(5)	—	Labor, Agricultural, and Horticultural Organizations
501(c)(6)	—	Business Leagues, Chambers of Commerce, Real Estate Boards, etc.
501(c)(7)	—	Social and Recreational Clubs
501(c)(8)	—	Fraternal Beneficiary Societies and Associations
501(c)(9)	—	Voluntary Employee Beneficiary Associations
501(c)(10)	—	Domestic Fraternal Societies and Associations
501(c)(11)	—	Teachers' Retirement Fund Associations
501(c)(12)	—	Benevolent Life Insurance Associations, Mutual Ditch or Irrigation Companies, Mutual or Cooperative Telephone Companies, etc.
501(c)(13)	—	Cemetery Companies
501(c)(14)	—	State-Chartered Credit Unions, Mutual Reserve Funds
501(c)(15)	—	Mutual Insurance Companies or Associations
501(c)(16)	—	Cooperative Organizations to Finance Crop Operations
501(c)(17)	—	Supplemental Unemployment Benefit Trusts
501(c)(18)	—	Employee Funded Pension Trust (created before June 25, 1959)
501(c)(19)	—	Post or Organization of Past or Present Members of the Armed Forces
501(c)(21)	—	Black Lung Benefit Trusts
501(c)(22)	—	Withdrawal Liability Payment Fund
501(c)(23)	—	Veterans Organization (created before 1880)
501(c)(25)	—	Title Holding Corporations or Trusts with Multiple Parents
501(c)(26)	—	State-Sponsored Organization Providing Health Coverage for High-Risk Individuals
501(c)(27)	—	State-Sponsored Workers' Compensation Reinsurance Organization
501(c)(28)	—	National Railroad Retirement Investment Trust

For purposes of incorporating, setting up a non-profit is similar to setting up a regular for-profit corporation. Non-profit corporations are formed by filing a charter in the state in which they expect to operate and paying the appropriate filing fee. The act of incorporating creates a legal entity enabling the organization to be treated as a corporation by law and to enter into business dealings, form contracts, and own property. A non-profit enjoys some of the same common features as a for-profit corporation such being a separate legal entity and providing its incorporators with limited liability protection. However, a non-profit corporation is distinctive in two ways: first, the non-profit corporation cannot be organized for any person's private gain; second, should it dissolve, the company must distribute its assets to a similar tax-exempt non-profit corporation.

Non-profits can have members but many do not. The non-profit may also be a trust or association of members. The organization may be controlled by its members who adopt bylaws and elect the Board of Directors, Board of Governors, or Board of Trustees. Non-profits may have a delegate structure to allow for the representation of groups or corporations as members. Alternatively, it may be a non-membership organization and the board of directors may elect its own successors from time to time as provided in the charter or bylaws.

The two major types of non-profit organization are membership and board-only. A membership organization has members that elect the board, which has regular meetings, and has the power to amend the bylaws. A board-only organization typically has a self-selected board and a membership whose powers are limited to those delegated to it by the board. A board-only organization's bylaws may state the organization does not have any membership, although the organization's literature may refer to its donors as members. Even though the name non-profit implies that the entity will not turn a profit, it is a mistaken belief that non-profits cannot and do not make money. Many actually do make money—positive net profit after deducting expenses—from their own charitable activities or from ways unrelated to non-profit purposes. The main structural component that distinguishes profit from not-for-profit corporations is that, in a non-profit corporation, all the profits go back into the organization—they are not distributed to members or shareholders, although they may be used to compensate directors, officers, and employees. In addition to how profits are distributed, the overall purpose of the organization will determine whether a corporation will qualify as a 501(c) not-for-profit corporation under one of the particular subsections listed above.

The 501(c) status affects the requirement of the non-profit corporation to file income taxes; however, it does not exempt the requirement of the non-profit to pay employment taxes associated with payment of wages or salaries to its employees. Depending on the rules in the jurisdiction where the not-for-profit corporation is organized, the corporation may be required to submit additional applications with the state for tax exempt status. The mere fact that a company is organized under a non-profit corporation law does not mean that contributions to it are necessarily tax deductible. For donations to be tax deductible, the charity must file an Application for

Recognition of Exemption (IRS Form 1023) with the IRS. The application must be approved by the service.

D. DETERMINING RISKS AND LIMITING LIABILITY

The next step is for the entrepreneur and the attorney to discuss the importance of limiting risk. An attorney can provide a valuable service by helping entrepreneurs determine the nature of the risks the business will face and the associated liability exposure of the company, its owners, directors, and managers. The four main areas of personal liability, aside from taxation, are:

- liability on operating contracts such as leases and franchise agreements;

- liability on long-term debt (owed to banks, financial institutions, and individual debt investors);

- liability on short-term debt owed to creditors on accounts; and

- liability for injuries and damages (torts) to third parties.

While a sole proprietorship is easy to start and operate, it may not be the most desirable business entity to form if the nature of the enterprise exposes the sole proprietor and the proprietor's assets to potential liabilities. If the business owes money, voluntary creditors of a sole proprietorship like landlords, suppliers, employees, and the like have recourse against the proprietor's personal assets, as do those involuntary creditors such as tort claimants injured during the course of business by the sole proprietor or by agents (employees) of the sole proprietorship.

General partners have unlimited personal liability for partnership obligations in both general partnerships and limited partnerships. Furthermore, liability is generally joint and several, each general partner is fully responsible personally for the debts of the partnership (there may be rights of contribution and indemnity as between the partners, but this would not affect the joint and several nature of their liability to third parties). This means that if one partner enters into a contract on behalf of the partnership, the contract is enforceable not only against the partnership, but against each individual general partner as well, even if the other general partners were not consulted or involved in the transaction. In addition, the partnership is liable as is each individual general partner for injuries caused by any partner or their agents or employees while on partnership business.

Limited liability partnerships are available under some state partnership statutes and vary from state to state as to the amount of liability protection offered. Where enacted, limited liability partnership statutes are added to the general partnership statutes, allowing limited liability partners to avoid personal liability for involuntary partnership obligations like negligence or malpractice. As a result, the LLP structure may be attractive for accountants, lawyers, doctors, and other professional service providers. Typically a partner in an LLP is personally liable only for his or her own negligence or malpractice, or that of an employee working under the partner's supervision; the partner is not personally liable for negligence of anyone else in the partnership. A partner in an LLP is still personally liable for a variety of obligations owed by the partnership to voluntary creditors such as those the partnership contracts with or from whom it obtains debt financing.

Obtaining state sponsored limitations on liability for any business entity has its limitations. Since most banks and other major financial institutions grant small business loans only with personal guarantees from business owners and others with significant financial assets, the limitation on liability offered to the entity does little to protect the entrepreneur from this sort of liability. It is useful, however, in shielding them from claims of suppliers and customers, who generally do not obtain personal guarantees. It also remains useful in protecting the equity participants from liability for torts (such as personal injury) that the business—but not the individual—has caused. Further, the limited liability of a business does not insulate the business owner for his or her own tortious acts (running down a pedestrian while driving a corporate vehicle, for instance).

In a limited partnership, at least one partner must be a managing general partner who is an agent of and has the power to bind the limited partnership. The general partners that exercise control over business operations have unlimited liability to third parties for all business obligations. Limited partners are only liable to the extent of losing their investment as long as the limited partner does not participate in the control of the business. When a limited partner participates in the control of the business, however, the limited partner may be treated as a general partner for personal liability purposes, making the limited partner personally liable for all partnership obligations. Modern statutes clarify what activities are not recognized as participation and control. Limited Partners do not lose their limited liability by virtue of being officers, directors, or shareholders of a corporate general partner, voting on major issues, voting on major business matters, or advising the general partner. However, a limited partner who participates in the control of the business is personally liable for the obligations to anyone who transacts business with the partnership and reasonably believes, based on the limited partner's conduct, that the limited partner is a general partner under the doctrine of apparent authority.

A corporation shields its shareholders, directors, and officers from personal liability for the obligations of the corporation. Shareholders do not risk personal financial resources beyond their investment in the stock of the corporation. This is also true for directors and officers working on behalf of the corporation. However, when entering into contracts, officers and directors should fully understand that they are acting as agents of the corporation, and that they should sign documents or checks only in their official corporate capacity, as agents of the corporation, otherwise the director or officer may incur personal liability. Signature blocks on contracts should reflect this capacity, and payments should be made through checks and other instruments and mechanisms in the name of the corporation, not the individual. The so-called corporate veil protects shareholders from liabilities and other obligations of the corporation for which the shareholders are not otherwise responsible in their individual capacities. Shareholders that personally guarantee debt or independently commit a tortious act are responsible for those individual actions and will remain subject to personal liability. Adequate insurance for the corporation, its officers, and the shareholders should always be maintained.

A limited liability company provides its members with limited liability just like a corporation. Although each member is an agent and has the power to bind the LLC, in a member-managed LLC, the entity's obligations are solely its own. Therefore, LLC members, like corporate shareholders, enjoy limited liability, protecting personal money and assets not invested in the business. A member in the LLC, like a limited partner in a partnership or a shareholder in a corporation, only risks their capital investment. In addition, both manager-managed and director-managed LLCs provide owners with limited liability.

The sole proprietorship, partnership, and limited partnership expose their proprietors and general partners to unlimited personal liability. Keep in mind however, that all these entities can and, should protect against this liability by carrying adequate liability insurance. In fact, in some instances, adequate insurance will accomplish the desired level of protection from liability to involuntary creditors like tort victims, with no need to resort to the corporate, LLC, or other entity form unless there is a real risk that the policy limits may be exceeded.

E. ANALYZING SHORT AND LONG-
TERM CAPITAL NEEDS

To secure financing for a new business, potential investors/lenders will want to gain a clear understanding of what they are investing in. In addition to the business idea or concept, they will want to know how the financial resources they invest/lend will be used by the business to insure that the investment/loan will yield both the principal investment and a competitive return on that investment/loan. In addition, lenders will also want some security, in the form of a collateral interest in a valuable asset or a personal guaranty to look to in the event that the business fails.

A well-prepared business plan, which includes a cash flow analysis, an income statement, balance sheet, and a statement of owner's equity, will appeal to investors/lenders. These financial statements should provide, as completely as possible, a picture of the business's present and predicted financial condition. They should discuss the expected date for reaching the break-even point and profitability. The financial statements should make clear what the largest expenses are likely to be over the next five years. The precise form of financing—debt or equity—and its amount should be abundantly clear and consistently described throughout the business plan.

In preparing these statements, rules of financial accounting should be used because these statements are being prepared for outside sources. Be aware that different rules and guidelines apply to financial accounting and tax accounting. Five basic rules should be followed when preparing or interpreting financial statements:

- Be comparable and consistent: Once a method is chosen, use only that method so that comparisons in subsequent years will be possible. If methods are changed, such changes should be highlighted in the financial statement footnotes.

- Materiality: When a financial statement is presented, the statement must not be incorrect by a material amount.

- Conservativism: Assets or income should not be overstated.

- Full Disclosure: Financial statements represent a full disclosure of everything that has happened to the business, from the starting date of the statements through the ending date. Failure to disclose or the misstatement of material facts can have very serious civil and criminal repercussions, including fines and civil damages that are not dischargeable in bankruptcy.

- Cost versus Benefit: Do not present anything that suggests that any of the business's costs outweigh their benefits. If that is the case, the cost needs to be reduced or eliminated.

The following overview will assist the entrepreneur in understanding how to effectively use financial statements.

1. "CASH FLOW" PROJECTIONS

There is no magical formula that will accurately gauge the amount of operating capital that a new business will need; however, prudent attorneys should advise entrepreneurs to include a "cash flow statement" based upon several month's to a year's worth of cash flow projections as part of the development of their business plan. "Cash flow" is a term that refers to the difference between the movement of money in and out of the business over a period of time. Cash flow does not equal sales or profits. Simply, cash flow determines the business's ability to pay bills as they come due. Including cash flow in the plan can prove valuable in arriving at a reasonable estimate.

Begin by calculating "starting cash" (or starting balance) for each month for which projections are made. "Starting Cash" is the money that the business will have on hand. "Cash in" includes all sources of cash received this month, including cash sales and paid receivables. "Paid Receivables" are made up of previously invoiced sales for which payment was received. When projecting paid receivables, estimate with as much accuracy as possible the lag time between the sale and collection of payment. "Cash in" also includes interest payments and other sources of cash, such as bank loans, stock sales, and the sale of a company asset (like equipment). A total of the above sources equals the "cash in" total.

Next, estimate "cash out." Money leaves the business in essentially two ways, either as fixed or variable expenses. Fixed expenses arise regularly and are rarely flexible. They include rent, payroll, payroll taxes, utilities, loan interest and principal repayment, and insurance payments. Variable expenses change from month to month, and frequently vary with seasonal changes, sales volume, or production. Supplies, advertising expenses, legal expenses, consulting, and commissions are some examples of variable expenses. Add fixed and variable expenses together to calculate the "cash out."

Adding "starting cash" and "cash in" together, then subtracting "cash out" from that total equals "ending balance." The cash that the business will have at end of the month is the cash the business has on hand for next month's projection. It becomes the "starting cash" entry for the next statement. To get the businesses cash flow, which simply measures the amount of net cash that flowed into the business that month, subtract "cash out" from "cash in."

By creating a cash flow projection, the business will be able to determine the amount of capital necessary to get started. For the initial projections, a zero balance should be used for "starting cash," and then the month-to-month projections should continue until the ending balance is positive. At that point, review the monthly statements and find the largest negative balance. The largest negative balance tells how much money is needed to cover the expenses until the break-even point. This amount is the amount of the necessary initial investment—what the business must have to get started. This is true if sales and collections go as planned and unless there are unforeseen expenses. If the largest negative balance is plugged in as "starting cash," the cash flow numbers will remain the same.

This is so because cash flow simply measures what goes out and comes in during any given month. What will change in those statements is that there will not be negative balances at the end of any given month. Therefore, the business can pay its bills and make payroll.

Projections about start-up needs are only as good as the estimates. Start-up estimates should include not only initial start-up expenses but working capital as well. Entrepreneurs can often make the mistake of underestimating their needs, in part due to their optimism. Attorneys should help encourage entrepreneurs to consider drawing up three different cash flow projections: best case, worst case, and somewhere in between. This will provide a better sense of the possible scenarios. It will probably take longer than expected to start generating good sales numbers. Engaging in cash flow exercises can also encourage the entrepreneur to come up with creative ways to keep costs in control or suggest alternate paths for entering their business.

2. BALANCE SHEETS

A balance sheet is a picture of a business's financial position at a specific point in time, much like a snapshot. It consists of three major categories: assets, liabilities, and owner's equity. The basic balance sheet formula is Assets = Liabilities + Owner's Equity. Assets are things of value that the business owns and can be measured in dollar amounts. Assets include cash, inventory, equipment, land, prepaid insurance, prepaid rent, buildings, and accounts receivable. Accounts receivable represent money that the business has earned but has not yet received. Each of these is a separate line item in the assets section of the balance sheet. Liabilities are the amounts that the business owes to someone else. For example, accounts payable represent money the business owes to creditors and suppliers. Owner's equity is the residual excess of value of assets over liabilities.

A statement of owner's equity (O/E) is a separate statement that must be prepared prior to preparing the balance sheet. A statement of owner's equity is an analysis of capital invested in the business. Basically this statement shows what the business has accumulated minus what it has used. To prepare an O/E:

(a) start with beginning capital;

(b) add net income (revenue − expenses = net income);

(c) add investment (*e.g.*, interest earned); and

(d) subtract any dollar amount the owner withdrew for personal use.

The final number will be used as O/E on the initial balance sheet. For a start-up business, this number may simply be the beginning capital amount if no net income, investments, or withdrawals exist. Remember that an owner's investment in the business is considered capital in the equation, not an investment.

If balance sheets are like snapshots for a particular point in time, income statements are like videos of the entire year. Income statements report net sales minus costs and expenses. Income statements are made up of two accounts: revenue and expenses. Determining revenue depends upon which accounting method your business uses, accrual or cash. Most businesses use the accrual method. Using the accrual method, revenue is not what your business has received in cash, but what it has earned. Small businesses and some nonprofit organizations use the cash method, which recognizes revenue as it is paid—not when it is earned. Expenses are the amounts the business incurs to generate the revenue. Expenses include rent, utilities, salaries, advertising, tax expenses, and depreciation.

3. SOURCES OF FUNDING

It does not require an advanced business degree to understand the fundamentals of corporate finance as they apply to starting a small business. Assets come to the business entity in the form of either debt or equity. Basically, equity financing means that an investor puts assets into the entity in return for an ownership interest in the business. Whether it is a partnership interest, a limited partnership interest, a membership interest in an LLC, or stock ownership in a corporation, the investor will obtain ownership interests in the business. Money is the most common medium of exchange for obtaining equity in the business. One may also invest by contributing physical assets, like real estate, equipment, intellectual property, or services (this last item is often referred to as "sweat equity").

The other major way to fund a business is with debt financing, i.e., borrowing the money. Attorney should advise business people that, when approaching a bank for a loan, it is likely to be granted on personal credit history or on the strength of a relative's or friend's credit, not on the strength of the business. Expect the bank to require a personal guarantee of repayment and possibly require another person to guarantee repayment as well rather than just relying on the business entity for repayment.

Contrary to popular belief, banks and venture capitalists are not the most common sources of capital for start-up businesses. Institutional sources of money regard start-up firms with skepticism as they are unproven commodities. Even if they are willing to extend credit or make an equity investment in a business, they will want to see evidence of personal and family confidence by assessing how much of the entrepreneurs' own funds are invested in the business. In addition, a business loan and/or the participation of a venture capitalist carries a heavy price, either in the form of high interest rates, a significant ownership interest, or both. A business's small size makes it less attractive to banks as well as venture capitalists because there are significant transaction costs associated with striking a deal. The entrepreneur's financing needs simply may not be large enough to interest a traditional banker or venture capitalist. Venture capitalists are looking for proven management skills and big returns on their investments over short periods of time.

The most common sources of funding for entrepreneurial start-up costs are those closest to home: personal resources and those of family and friends. From one perspective it would be nice to use other people's money, but relying on personal resources has its value. If an idea seems too risky to stake one's personal resources on, then it probably needs to be reworked or even abandoned. That does not mean that it makes sense to stake all the resources one has on her idea, because even the most carefully planned and executed business ventures sometimes fall prey to circumstances beyond the control of the entrepreneur.

When looking for start-up money, consider the following personal sources and the advantages they offer. Personal savings, including retirement funds and profit-sharing plans, are frequent sources of start-up capital. Tax penalties are associated with using such sheltered money, as well as the sacrifice in financial security. The entrepreneur may also choose to finance their start-up costs with personal borrowing.

Life insurance could also be used to fund a new business in two ways. First, the entrepreneur could use the surrender or cash value of their whole life insurance policy. However, to use the surrender or cash value one would have to cancel the policy and then the insurance company would pay out the equity that has been built up through payment of premiums over the years. While this is a new source of cash for the business, it will leave the entrepreneur without any life insurance. A second, and perhaps a more prudent, option is to borrow against the life insurance equity. The money belongs to the insured so qualifying for a loan would be unnecessary. Further, these loans offer low interest rates and very flexible repayment plans. If the insured defaults on the loan principal, it would be deducted from the benefit paid to the beneficiaries upon the insured's death.

Many entrepreneurs use credit card financing as a source of start-up capital. Credit cards are a convenient way to arrange for short-term financing because they are so easy to use. However, the interest rates are usually very steep, and, should they default, the cardholder can ruin their credit rating making it doubly hard to obtain additional financing in the future.

A personal loan, rather than a business loan, is another source of potential borrowed funds. This kind of borrowing is only available to entrepreneurs with significant collateral such as stock, life insurance, real estate, or savings accounts. These loans may incur the possibility of forced early repayment of part of the principal if the value of the pledged asset declines or if the bank has good reason to doubt the continued ability to pay. However, personal loans make it possible to use the strength of the entrepreneurs' assets without liquidating them. This advantage may be important when the liquidation of a particular asset, like stocks, results in a heavy tax burden.

When borrowing money, it is important to know the difference between the terms secured debt and unsecured debt. Secured debt refers a loan secured by specific collateral (items of personal or real property). The collateral will be lost if the entrepreneur fails to fulfill the obligation to repay their loan. Unsecured debt simply means that the obligation to repay is not secured by any collateral. An unpaid unsecured creditor will have to pursue collection, perhaps including a lawsuit and judgement enforcement, to collect the amount owed. Credit cards are a good example of unsecured debt.

A second mortgage, or home equity loan, on a home is another frequently used source of capital and the interest rates will usually be lower than those on a credit card. All or part of the interest paid may be tax deductible as well. Homeowners often have significant equity in their property, so the amount that can be borrowed is potentially large. Home equity is the difference in a home's market value (what it is worth) and the principal (what is still owed on the mortgage). However, defaulting on a mortgage in the event that the business is unsuccessful can result in foreclosure and the forced sale of the entrepreneurs' residence to satisfy the outstanding debt. Second mortgages are heavily advertised and aggressively marketed, and the application process may be shorter and easier than other loan arrangements, but do not make the mistake of thinking those banks and other financial institutions do this for charity. Rates on second mortgages are generally higher than first mortgages because of the greater risk for lenders.

If the entrepreneur is currently employed and participates in a retirement savings plan such as a 401(k) program, this could also be a possible source for borrowing money for a new business. Borrowing from a retirement plan is similar to borrowing against a life insurance policy. The terms for borrowing from a retirement plan include low interest rates and a repayment period of up to five years. The downside of a retirement plan loan is that while one is using the funds for the business, they will not be growing in one's retirement plan, which will decrease its growth rate. It is unwise to borrow from a traditional IRA plan. Borrowing from a traditional IRA is considered a distribution and will require paying immediate taxes as well as being assessed a substantial penalty.

Another way that entrepreneurs can borrow against their own money is by going on margin or margin agreement. Rather than selling their stocks or bonds and incurring taxes, and possible losses, these stocks and bonds can be used as collateral for a loan from a brokerage firm. As with home equity loans, the borrower will not be able to get the full amount of their collateral's current value because of the risk, but they offer relatively low rates and flexible repayment plans.

However, margin loans can be subject to unexpected consequences. One example is the possibility of a margin call. Should the underlying value of the stocks and bonds decrease in one's portfolio, one could experience a margin call and be forced to pay off all or part of the loan or see your stocks and bonds liquidated involuntarily to cover the debt.

Obviously, none of these options come without risk or cost, and many may not be available to everyone. Regardless of the type borrowing one might choose, cash flow projections have to take principal and interest payments into account. Moreover, the degree to which the business is leveraged (i.e., the amount of debt that has been incurred) can seriously affect its ability to respond to changes in the future. Those interest and principal payments are serious obligations, tied not only to the business, but also in some circumstances to the individual entrepreneur's creditworthiness and security through guaranties and pledges. Entrepreneurs should be advised to not undertake them without due consideration to the consequences that can follow, including personal bankruptcy, loss of a home pledged as collateral, loss of retirement savings, and the like.

In addition to using the credit strength of a family or friend to secure a loan from a bank through co-signing or guaranteeing a loan, many entrepreneurs rely on direct funding from relatives and friends. There are real dangers associated with borrowing money from and/or granting ownership interests to family and friends, but this approach does make it possible to overcome some of the risk aversion obstacles that the entrepreneur might face in getting a loan from more traditional sources. Only the participants can decide if they are willing to accept the baggage that comes with the mix of love and money, but there are ways to minimize the risk of fallout should the business or the relationship sour.

The most common problem with this kind of funding is the tendency for both parties to avoid defining the nature of the transaction out of a misguided sense of delicateness. It is irresponsible from both a personal and business standpoint not to spell out the nature of the obligations ahead of time. Lawyers can be useful in forcing this discussion and documenting its results. The terms of the agreement should be put in writing by signing a promissory note. The promissory note is a legally binding document that sets out the terms of the loan including the loan balance, the interest rate, the repayment schedule, and the rate of repayment. Any form should only be used as a template; add the specific negotiated terms for the agreement by filling in the blanks and otherwise modifying the document to reflect the terms of the deal. It may also be wise to also include a security agreement in conjunction with the promissory note.

To receive a commercial loan, an entrepreneur should expect a lengthy application process. Businesses generally must provide collateral to secure the loan, assets that the bank can foreclose upon to recover its losses in case of default, preferably real estate or other assets that depreciate slowly over time. Most start-up businesses do not have many assets that can be used as collateral. As a result, banks typically require a personal guaranty and personal assets of the founders as collateral, even if a separate entity is formed to house the business and protect the investors from personal liability. Essentially, the entrepreneur will have to secure the loan with other valuable personal or real property to get funding. Keep in mind that if there is a default on the loan, all the personal property pledged can be lost.

There are two general types of commercial loan, term and seasonal. A term loan is a fixed asset loan, meaning that it is used to purchase fixed assets like real estate and equipment. The assets purchased serve as the collateral for the term loan. Usually the loan is an installment loan, which is paid monthly. The second type, a seasonal loan, is used to satisfy a business's need for working capital. Because most businesses face a lag or delay between when it must pay expenses (such as when purchasing inventory) and collecting income (such as when selling inventory), a working capital loan or line of credit is used to bridge the gap. These loans allow the purchase of inventory, the payment of rent, wages, and the like. Many lenders require that the borrower grant a blanket lien on all their assets, or, at a minimum inventory and receivables, to secure the seasonal loan. A seasonal loan generally allows small businesses to repeatedly draw and pay down the loan over the course of the year. Essentially, the seasonal loan works like a secured credit card arrangement.

Another potential source of financing is through the United States Small Business Administration (SBA). The SBA administers loan guarantee programs throughout the United States. The SBA guarantees loans to finance small businesses for the long term and loans for short-term cyclical working capital needs. SBA guaranteed loans are granted for up to 25 years for fixed assets and 10 years for working capital. Loans are granted based on the borrower's ability to repay the loan, the loan's purpose, and the useful life of the assets financed. Financial institutions/ lenders usually request a guarantee from the SBA.

The SBA and lenders favor entrepreneurs with management expertise and sufficient funds and cash flow to operate the business and pay back the loan. The entrepreneur should be able to demonstrate that they have adequate equity or investment in the business and sufficient collateral, as well as a strong showing of commitment to success. The SBA and lenders approve loans based upon how well the entrepreneurs present themselves, the business, and its financial needs. It is essential to present a well-written and well-thought out business plan to support the loan application, regardless of whether it will be SBA guaranteed.

The SBA offers loans and lease programs to encourage banks and other financial institutions to lend money to small businesses. The SBA does not make the loans itself, rather it guarantees a high percentage of the loan amount, thereby encouraging banks to make loans that they might not normally make.

The SBA Micro Loan Program also provides funding to nonprofit intermediaries who then make loans to entrepreneurs. The loans are typically small, ranging from under $500 up to $35,000. Also, the SBA offers special programs for women, minorities, and the disabled. These programs help to develop viable loan application packages. Socially or economically disadvantaged individuals may also benefit from some SBA licensed Specialized Small Business Investment Companies.

For those small businesses that are founded on the basis of specialized knowledge or technological expertise, financial resources in the form of grants to support the startup and of research and development efforts are available through the federally-funded Small Business Innovation Research (SBIR) program.

United States small businesses who meet all of the following criteria are eligible to participate in the SBIR program:

- Organized for profit, with a place of business located in the United States;

- At least 51 percent owned and controlled by one or more individuals who are citizens of, or permanent resident aliens in, the United States, or

- At least 51 percent owned and controlled by another for-profit business concern that is at least 51% owned and controlled by one or more individuals who are citizens of, or permanent resident aliens in, the United States; and;

- No more than 500 employees, including those of affiliated companies.

All federal agencies with research and development budgets over $100 million allocate 2.5 percent of their R&D budgets to the SBIR program. Eleven federal agencies, including the Department of Agriculture, Department of Defense, and Department of Education currently participate. Phase I grants, typically limited to $150,000 within 6 months, may be awarded to small businesses to assess the potential of proposed efforts and the quality of the awardee's performance. A continuation of Phase I support is possible via Phase II grants, which provide up to $1,000,000 total costs for 2 years. SBIR awards generally do not fund the commercialization objectives associated with Stage III.

The Small Business Technology Transfer (STTR) program also provides federal funding to support research and development efforts by small businesses. STTR awards are designed to facilitate cooperation between U.S. small business concerns and research institutions. All federal agencies with extramural research and development budgets that exceed $1 billion reserve an additional 0.3% of those research budgets for STTR. STTR program criteria require that United States small businesses engage in formal cooperative research and development efforts with a U.S. research institution. A minimum of 40% of the research must be conducted by the small business concerns with at least 30% conducted by the U.S. research institution. Eligible research institutions include colleges/ universities, nonprofit research organizations and federal research and development centers. A formal intellectual property agreement between these parties is required to allocate research responsibilities and resulting property rights.

Two key differences distinguish SBIR from STTR support. SBIR awards generally require employment of the principal investigator by the recipient small business concern. The STTR program does not include an employment requirement; however, STTR support requires the small business concerns to partner with a research institution. The Small Business Administration serves as the coordinating agency for both SBIR and STTR programs.

The alternative to debt financing discussed above is equity financing. Equity investors actually buy a piece of the business. They become co-owners and share in the fortunes and misfortunes of the business. If the business goes badly and fails, there is no obligation to repay the investors. If the business is successful, the investor will continue to benefit from their investment throughout the life of the entity. This co-ownership can take many forms. The equity investors can be either active or passive investors. An active investor will want to take a direct and active role in overseeing the operations of the business and may become a partner in a partnership, a member of a limited liability company, or an officer of a corporation. Alternatively, the investors may want to take a passive role perhaps as a shareholder of a corporation or a limited partner in a limited partnership. In these roles, the investors' participation would be established through the corporate charter or certificate of limited partnership and any subsequent bylaws or partnership agreement that may apply. Equity financing will be explored in greater detail in a following section, Benefits and Uses of the C Corporation.

F. PROVIDING FOR CONTINUITY OF THE FIRM

When attorneys advise those who are forming a new business, they must first get a clear understanding of the identity of the owners, their objectives, issues, and concerns and assist them in crafting an entity which best suits the needs of all the parties. Often one individual will meet with an attorney and discuss a plan for a business in which several different individuals will participate. In such circumstances it is wise make sure all of the individuals who will be investing or working in the business meet with the attorney for a joint interview. Just because they have a common interest in starting a new business together does not mean that their personal circumstances are the same or that they all share the same vision of future outcomes. Whether it is a new business venture or a business that has successfully operated for years, the respective owners can benefit from a guided discussion concerning matters of providing for continuity of the business going into the future.

For example, imagine that Sam has run a successful convenience store as a sole proprietor near a college campus for over thirty years. He is now concerned with the transition of the business's ownership to his children. One of his children, Elisha, has been very active in the business and Sam envisions her taking over business operations when he retires. While Sam would like to retire because of failing health, he is concerned that if he does not share some of the economic benefit of the business with his other two children, the family will have a conflict over the business operations disrupting relationships with customers, suppliers, and employees.

There are a number of ways of accomplishing Sam's objectives. One possibility would be to create a corporation with two classes of stock, one voting and one nonvoting and transfer all of the business's assets to the corporation. The business would then have a legal existence of its own, separate from Sam. Contracts with suppliers could be maintained with the corporation. Sam's death would not cause the business to dissolve. Elisha could have the voting stock as she would be operating the business, while the other two siblings that are not active in the operation of the convenience store could have the nonvoting stock. Elisha could receive a salary and also share in the dividends from the profits of the business along with her siblings. Another alternative would be to establish a limited partnership with a limited partnership agreement establishing Elisha as the general partner and the other two siblings as limited partners. Through the agreement Elisha would be granted a salary, and the limited partnership agreement could outline how the profits of the business would be split. The siblings would have limited liability and Elisha would have the authority and fiduciary duties that go along with being a general partner in a limited partnership.

Consider another scenario where a graduate student approaches an attorney for advice on establishing a limited liability company to market and sell a medical health care records management software package. During the discussion it is disclosed that he has been working with three professors in this effort and they will all be participating in the business. However, after a thorough discussion with all of them, one gains an understanding that the professors want to continue teaching and do not want to take an active role in the management and operations of the business. In fact, they would like to get the business to a point where they can sell it, because their major interest is teaching and research not running a business.

While the LLC may be a workable entity given these facts and circumstances, a corporate structure might be viewed as a more favorable entity for obtaining the necessary investment capital necessary to get the business up and running. Venture capitalists look for opportunities to invest in businesses in which they can make an investment, and in a short period of time, either bring the business public or sell the business or its assets to an existing business. For a number of reasons, the corporate form is best-suited to achieve these goals.

G. TAX CONSIDERATIONS

Tax treatment of the various kinds of business entities is perhaps the single most important factor in selecting one form of business over another (both state and federal). With regard to federal income tax, IRS check-the-box provisions allow unincorporated businesses with two or more owners including general partnerships, limited liability partnerships, limited partnerships, and limited liability companies to be taxed as partnerships or corporations. Unincorporated businesses with two or more members are automatically taxed as partnerships but can elect to be taxed as corporations by making an entity classification election on IRS Form 8832. An unincorporated business with one owner (such as a single-member LLC) is not recognized for tax purposes as an entity separate from its owner.

Like sole proprietorship income, partnership income is treated as the personal income of the partners. Income and losses pass-thru the partnership to the partners, who pay tax on their share of the partnership's taxable income at the partners' individual tax rates. Generally speaking, the partners may decide how to allocate the partnership's income among themselves although the IRS may disregard allocations that lack "substantial economic effect." Substantial economic effect is a term of art that is defined through a very complex set of Treasury Regulations. Though a partnership itself is not subject to federal income tax, the partnership must file an informational income tax return with the IRS using IRS Form 1065. On Form 1065, the partnership reports both its taxable income and how those earnings are allocated to each partner using its Schedule K-1, a copy of which is furnished to each partner for use in preparing the partner's personal federal income tax return. The partnership's taxable income is taxed only once for federal income tax purposes at the partner or member level. Each partner's personal federal income tax return will show the partner's share of the taxable income or taxable loss (although the partner's ability to deduct partnership losses may be limited). Accordingly, each partner is responsible for the associated taxes on that partner's allocated share of the partnership income (whether or not the partnership actually distributes or pays this income to the partner). Individual partners may be required or elect to remit quarterly estimated tax payments.

The business entity will also have to decide if it wants to file Form 8832 (Entity Classification Election) with the IRS, often referred to as "check the box." For most unincorporated entities, there is no need to file the form. This is because of the manner in which the default mechanism operates. By doing nothing, most unincorporated entities will be taxed as pass-thru entities. If, for example, the entity is created as an LLC or partnership, doing nothing (not filing Form 8832) will, by default, cause the business to be taxed as a partnership. The Regulations begin the choice-making by defining essentially what constitutes a corporation. If the entity is a corporation, then it will be taxed as such (unless an S election is filed). Any entity that is not a corporation (or considered to be one) is an eligible entity. The choices on the form relate to three types of domestic eligible entities. These choices allow a domestic eligible entity (i.e., an unincorporated entity) to elect to be taxed as a corporation or as a partnership, while a single-owner eligible entity (such as a one-person LLC) can elect to be taxed as a corporation or be disregarded as a separate entity (i.e., sole proprietorship).

Importantly, partners are required to pay tax on their share of the partnership's taxable income as it is earned by the partnership whether or not it is actually distributed to the partners. For this reason, partners may require the partnership to make so-called tax distributions, which are distributions of cash from the partnership that the partners use to pay their tax liability.

Of particular importance for these individuals is the problem of phantom income. Phantom income is income that is treated as having been earned even though no monies flowed into the entity, as is the case when previously-deducted depreciation is disallowed or recaptured or when entity-level debt is forgiven in a restructuring. In such cases, the entity will report this phantom income and allocate it to the partners or members who will report it and owe tax on it, despite there having been no accompanying distribution of money or other assets with which to fund the tax payment. Needless to say, investors do not like phantom income, even when it is generated by recapture or reversal of previously distributed tax benefits, like losses, that they have already enjoyed.

A corporation is considered a separate taxable entity and, as such, files its own federal income tax return, Form 1120, to pay federal income tax on its taxable income. After the corporation pays federal income tax on its earnings, the shareholders and employees must pay tax on their dividends (and other corporate distributions) and wages. The IRS code effectively taxes the corporation's earnings twice—once at the corporate level on the entity's taxable income and once again at the shareholder level to the extent that the corporation distributes that income to shareholders in the form of dividends. This is referred to as double taxation. One way that corporations can eliminate the effects of double taxation when transferring funds from the operations to the employee/shareholder is by making payments to these employee shareholders as wages (compensation), rather than as dividends. Wages are an expense to the corporation, and generally are deductible for federal income tax purposes. Thus, paying reasonable compensation may lower corporate taxable income and, thus, corporate income tax due. This effectively means that the funds are taxed only at the individual and not the corporate level. There are limits to this practice—primarily the reasonableness of the wages or salary paid. The advice of a tax professional can be indispensable in structuring the corporation to minimize the total federal income tax paid.

If businesses incorporate, the owners will have to decide what sort of corporation the business will be for IRS purposes. Businesses need not be a C corporation. It is possible to be an S corporation and avoid double taxation altogether while still enjoying the limited liability that incorporation provides. Federal income tax laws allow for the S corporation as a means of encouraging small business development. The S corporation is a corporation that elects to be taxed under subchapter S (rather than subchapter C) of the Internal Revenue Code. For the most part, the S corporation passes its income, losses, deductions, and credits through to its shareholders for inclusion on their individual tax returns, as if the business were a partnership, and its income is taxed at the individual rate instead of the corporate rate. Therefore, in many cases, shareholders benefit during the early years of a business, when losses are likely, and earnings avoid double taxation. There are limitations on the ability of shareholders to deduct losses of S corporations and partnerships (including LLCs). To be eligible for S corporation treatment, the corporation must:

(a) be a domestic corporation with only one class of stock with identical rights to operating and liquidating distributions though different voting rights are permissible;

(b) have no more than 100 shareholders, all of whom must be individuals or certain trusts or estates;

(c) have only citizens or legal residents of the U.S. as shareholders; and

(d) gain the agreement of all its shareholders.

For some start-ups, S corporation status is more desirable than C corporation status if the corporate form is chosen because losses will not be trapped in the entity and income won't be subject to two levels of tax. However, the S corporation limitations on the number and kind of shareholders and classes of stock may be unachievable with certain investor bases and may reduce venture capitalist interest, although as a practical matter these issues can be easily resolved by conversion to C corporation treatment.

A corporation files Form 2553 with the IRS to elect subchapter S status. Although an S corporation does not generally pay income tax, it is required to file its own informational tax return, Form 1120S. Each S corporation shareholder pays tax on his or her share of the corporation's taxable income by reporting that taxable income on his or her individual income tax return. Unlike entities taxed as partnerships, S corporation income must be allocated pro rata based on stock ownership. Like partnerships, S corporation shareholders must pay tax on their share of S corporation income as it is earned whether or not it is actually distributed.

The new corporate tax rate and new deduction for qualified income in the Tax Cut and Jobs Act of 2017, Pub. L. No. 115-97, 131 Stat. 2054, is likely to change the choice-of-entity analysis in terms of potential tax consequences. Perhaps the most significant change in the new law relates to the corporate tax rate. Starting in 2018, the law replaces a series of tax brackets for C corporations with a flat 21% tax rate for all of the corporation's taxable income. This change will result in less taxes for C corporations that have taxable income of more than $90,385 compared to 2017 tax rates. Below that figure, the corporation will owe more taxes than the previous year. However, most small and medium size businesses are sole proprietorships, S-corporations, and LLCs, which will not be subject to the new corporate tax rate. As mentioned above, these entities pass through the businesses profits and losses to the owner's individual tax return. The new law provides for the deduction of 20% of the qualified income from the entity on their individual tax returns. For example, if an individual receives pass through income from their business in the amount of $100,000, they would get a deduction of $20,000 on their personal tax return, the remaining $80,000 would then be taxed at their individual tax rate. This example is very simplistic, and there are many thresholds, limitations and definitions that apply to this deduction, which add to the complexity in calculating this deduction. The owners of these types of entities should be advised to proactively consult with a competent tax professional such as a Certified Public Accountant to determine how these provisions apply to the their particular business and the resulting effect it will have on their individual tax return.

All 50 states tax general partnerships, limited liability partnerships, limited partnerships limited liability companies and corporations in a variety of ways. A detailed analysis of the consequences of such state taxation effect on entity business formation is beyond the scope of this book.

H. BENEFITS AND USES OF THE C CORPORATION

In a previous section of this chapter, Analyzing Short- and Long-Term Capital Needs, equity financing was briefly discussed. Equity investments can be made in:

- General partnerships and limited liability partnerships in the form of a partnership interest;

- Limited partnerships in the form of either a general or limited partnership interest;

- Limited liability corporations in the form of a membership interest; and

- Stock ownership in an S or C corporation.

While there are advantages to each of these forms of business entities because of their pass-thru taxation attributes, each has its limits for attracting certain types of equity financing. The C corporation is often considered the most attractive entity to some investors, such as angel investors and venture capitalists. Unlike the S corporation, which is limited to 100 shareholders and one class of stock, there is no limitation on the number of shares in a C corporation and it also allows for creation of preferred stock.

The C corporation is particularly attractive to venture capitalists and angel investors who are willing to invest in early stage, high-growth, start-up companies. Preferred stock is an attractive feature of the C corporation in that it can attract major investors who want additional security and the opportunity to achieve above-average returns on their investment. Preferred shares can be structured so that the investor can convert the preferred shares into common stock (convertible preferred stock) at some time in the future at an advantageous rate, in the event that the company is purchased or goes public. Eventually, incorporating a business as a C corporation is not only advantageous, but it is essential if the owners hope to attract additional investors through a public stock offering. However, the entity could initially be formed as a pass-thru entity such as a partnership, S corporation, or LLC and then incorporate prior to a public offering.

Preferred shares can provide a level of protection for the investors by providing priority over the common shareholder in the liquidation of any residual assets of the company in the event that it fails. Also, priority is typically given to preferred shares for any dividend that might be issued from profits of the corporation. In the event that the corporation pays out any dividends, the preferred shareholders would receive payment before common shareholders. While preferred shareholders do not have the same voting rights as common shareholders, these shares can include voting provisions on such matters as raising corporate debt, thus protecting the investment of the preferred shareholders. Often, angel and venture capital investors will also request to be appointed to the board of directors so they can closely monitor and participate in the direction of the corporation.

Another benefit of the C corporation is its ability to issue employee stock options. An employee stock option is a call option on the common stock of a company, issued as a form of non-cash compensation. Restrictions on the option (such as vesting and limited transferability) attempt to align the holder's interest with those of the business's shareholders. If the company's stock rises, holders of options generally experience a direct financial benefit. This gives employees an incentive to behave in ways that will boost the company's stock price.

Employee stock options are mostly offered to management as part of their executive compensation package. They may also be offered to non-executive level staff, especially by businesses that are not yet profitable, insofar as they may have few other means of compensation. Alternatively, employee-type stock options can be offered to non-employees including suppliers, consultants, lawyers, and promoters for services rendered. Employee stock options are similar to warrants, which are similar to call options issued by a company except the proceeds of the issuance is retained by the company.

One way C corporations can eliminate the effects of double taxation when transferring funds from the operations to the employee-shareholder is by making payments to these employee-shareholders as wages rather than as dividends. Providing reasonable compensation may lower corporate taxable income and, thus, corporate income tax due. The same effect can be achieved through the provision of substantial health and medical benefits and other fringe benefit programs for things like education, life insurance, retirement, and transportation costs. These are direct benefits to the employee-shareholder, but can be included in overhead costs to the corporation, thus reducing the tax liabilities to the corporation and providing little if any effect on the tax liability of the employee-shareholder. While other types of business entities can deduct the cost of many fringe benefits as a business expense, the owners of the business will ordinarily be taxed on their fair value. For tax purposes, an individual is self-employed if they are a sole proprietor, a partner in a partnership, a member of an LLC that is taxed like a partnership, or an owner of more than 2 % of the shares of an S corporation. A shareholder-employee of a C corporation is not taxed as a self-employed person and therefore has a unique advantage when it comes to taxation of fringe benefits.

Another advantage of the C corporation is that, unlike pass-through type entities, it can retain earnings for use for future growth of the corporation without any adverse effect on the individual shareholders' tax liability because the shareholder-level tax is imposed only on C corporation income that is actually distributed. This provides an incentive to the owners to delay their immediate gratification in order to spend financial resources to build the business, with the promise of even larger returns down the road.

I. STEPS IN THE FORMATION AND ORGANIZATION OF THE BUSINESS ENTITY

1. SELECTING THE JURISDICTION IN WHICH TO FORM THE ENTITY

When selecting the jurisdiction in which to create a business entity, keep in mind that cost, taxation, and laws vary from state to state, making some states advantageous for certain small business owners. Obtaining limited liability for a business in the state where the company is physically located is called home-state incorporation. It is important to consult an attorney in selecting the jurisdiction in which to incorporate, so that they can explain the advantages and disadvantages of filing in jurisdictions outside the home-state.

No matter if the business is a C corporation, S corporation, LLC, LLP, LP, or nonprofit corporation, filing fees must paid to the state when incorporation documents are filed. The entity will be subject to ongoing requirements and fees imposed by that state. Many states also have filing requirements for individuals (sole proprietorships and partnerships) that are doing business under an assumed name, requiring a filing for a certificate for a Fictitious or Assumed name.

Although intuition may guide business owners to think they will save money by incorporating in a state with low fees, regardless of whether their company is located or conducts business in that state, this is not necessarily true. Keep in mind that companies incorporated in one state but doing business in other states must still register or qualify to transact business in those states.

When deciding a company's state of incorporation, business owners should consult their attorney concerning those states' statutes to determine if there are advantages:

- Consider how sole proprietorships, partnerships, and limited liability entities are taxed by each state and the taxation requirements imposed on foreign-qualified businesses, if foreign qualification is necessary. Does a state impose an income tax on corporations and LLCs? Does it have a minimum tax or a franchise tax?

- The added costs of fulfilling the ongoing taxation requirements imposed by the state of incorporation and state(s) of foreign qualification often outweigh the perceived benefits of incorporating outside the home state.

- Try calculating the company's projected revenue for its first few years of existence and then evaluate states in terms of the true amount of taxes required, to see if there may be an advantage.

Delaware and Nevada are two states in which many small business owners opt to incorporate their businesses. They offer unique advantages for certain types of businesses. Some potential advantages of incorporating a business in Delaware include:

- Delaware's business code is one of the most flexible in the country and is generally perceived of as being management and director friendly.

- The Delaware Court of Chancery focuses solely on business law, using experienced judges instead of juries.

- For corporations, there is no state corporate income tax for companies that are formed in Delaware but do not transact business there (although there is a franchise tax).

- Taxation requirements are often favorable to companies with complex capitalization structures and/or a large number of authorized shares of stock.

- There is no personal income tax for non-residents.

- Delaware does not require director or officer names (for corporations), or member or manager names (for LLCs) to be listed in formation documents, affording a level of anonymity and privacy.

- Shareholders, directors, and officers of a corporation or members or managers of an LLC are not required to be residents of Delaware.

- Shares owned by persons outside Delaware are not subject to Delaware taxes.

Some potential advantages to forming a corporation or LLC in Nevada include:

- Nevada has no state corporate income tax and imposes no fees on corporate shares.

- There is no personal income tax or any franchise tax for corporations or LLCs, but initial and annual statement fees and business license fees apply.

- Shareholders, directors, and officers of a corporation or members-managers of an LLC are not required to be residents of Nevada.

- Nevada does not require director or officer names for corporations, or member-manager names for LLCs to be listed in formation documents, affording a level of anonymity and privacy.

Remember, if an entity is formed under the laws of Delaware or Nevada but business is transacted in another state, the entity likely will have to qualify to do business in that state. In addition, if the entity is incorporated in one state and is doing business in another state, there will be tax obligations in the state in which business is conducted. If the business incorporates in a state other than its home state, legal actions against the corporation may require officers and directors to travel to the state of incorporation to mount the defense.

2. RESERVING THE DESIRED ENTITY NAME

In some instances, businesses may want to reserve a corporate name before actually incorporating. Most states (but not all) will allow entrepreneurs to reserve a corporate name for a period of time, usually 30 to 120 days, for a small fee. Information about reserving a corporate name is available on the Secretary of State's website for one's chosen state, or can be found by calling the Secretary of State.

There is no requirement to reserve the corporate name. A corporate name can be reserved before the would-be business owners are ready to form the entity, but after they have decided on a name. If it is going to take some time to get the papers in order to proceed with the incorporation or to gather the resources needed to capitalize or operate the business, it may be a good idea to go ahead and reserve the name. If the incorporation papers are ready to go and all the entrepreneur is waiting for is finding the perfect name, and the name is available, then incorporate immediately without reserving the name. Remember, a corporate name is not the same thing as a trade name or a trademark. In fact, a corporate name can be quite generic, such as one that incorporates the address of the headquarters or a major asset, like 2312 Wilshire, LLC.

A good trade name or trademark, which can include the corporate name, may be critical to a business's future success. Corporate branding is the practice of using a company's name as a product brand name. It is an attempt to use corporate brand equity to create product brand recognition. It is a type of family branding or an umbrella brand. Think of Microsoft Windows and Microsoft Office and Heinz 57 Sauce. This strategy contrasts with individual product branding, where each product has a unique brand name and the corporate name is not promoted to the consumer.

Most states require that that a business use certain words in the corporate name to indicate corporate status, such as Incorporated, Corporation, Company, or Limited or their abbreviations Inc., Corp., Co., or Ltd. In addition, many states have certain words that cannot be used in a corporate name. For example, in California, "National," "United States," and "Federal" are prohibited. The best way to learn which words are required or prohibited is to contact the appropriate state office where articles of incorporation are filed, typically the Secretary of State.

Most states will reject a corporation name that is the same as one already on file or one that would cause confusion in the market place because of its similarity to one already in use. Even though the Secretary of State accepts one's corporate name, or indicates that it is available pre-filing, this does not guarantee a legal right to use it. An unincorporated business may already be using it as a trade name, trademark, or service mark.

3. SELECTING THE REGISTERED AGENT/OFFICE

Most jurisdictions in the United States require that any business entity that is formed or doing business within their borders designate and maintain a registered agent. This person may be known as the resident agent or statutory agent, depending on the laws of the individual jurisdiction in which the business entity is registered. The purpose of a registered agent is to provide a legal address (not a P.O. Box) within the state where there are persons available during normal business hours to facilitate legal service of process in the event of a legal action or lawsuit. Generally, the registered agent is also the person to whom the state government sends all official documents required each year for tax and legal purposes, such as franchise tax notices and annual report forms. It is the registered agent's job to forward these suit documents and notices to the entity itself. Registered agents generally will also notify business entities if their state government filing status is in "Good Standing" or not. The reason that these notifications are a desired function of a registered agent is that it is difficult for a business entity to keep track of legislative changes and report due dates for multiple jurisdictions given the disparate laws of different states. Penalties for not maintaining a registered agent generally will cause a state to revoke a business's status and in some cases assess additional penalty fees on the entity.

If a registered agent fails to perform their function, it can have dire consequences for the business entity. For example, if a customer of a business is damaged in some way and the registered agent is served with legal process initiating a lawsuit but fails to notify the business entity of a summons to appear in court to respond to the lawsuit, nobody will appear to defend the business and the customer will win by a default judgment. Additionally, the business will likely be unable to get the judgment overturned on appeal because they had been properly served. This is one of the most common reasons that business entities generally utilize a third party as their registered agent be it a commercial service company, an attorney, or in some cases, a CPA. The business entity typically maintains contact with the registered agent through its corporate secretary or governance officer.

States have differing requirements for registered agents. Typically, the agent must be a legal resident of the state in question or, in states that allow entities to serve as registered agents, an entity authorized to do business in the state. All states allow a corporate officer of the corporation to serve, and all allow the corporation's lawyer to serve. Most allow business entities to serve as registered agents for other entities. In some states, a business entity is legally allowed to act as its own registered agent, but other jurisdictions require that a business entity designate a third party as its registered agent. Because most states permit one business entity to serve as a registered agent for others, some businesses exist to serve that exact function, charging a fee to act as the registered agent for hundreds or thousands of businesses in a given state.

Some advantages of designating a third-party registered agent are:

- As the registered agent's name and address is one of public record, generally, the registered agent's legal address will be the one listed in all official public documents.

- An outside registered agent allows business entities to freely change their location at any time, without being required to file costly changes of address within the state they are registered each time they move.

- Designating a third-party registered agent allows the business owner to travel freely without the risk of a default judgment because of a missed lawsuit.

- Commercial registered agents generally have systems to keep track of filing, notification, and publishing requirements of business entities, which can save businesses hundreds or even thousands of dollars by ensuring that they do not incur penalties for missed payments or required government filings. These are referred to as Compliance Managers, Tax Calendars, and/or Compliance Calendars.

- Most commercial service providers have form libraries of forms and other documents required to file business entities in different jurisdictions or to keep the business entity in compliance or "Good Standing."

- Some commercial registered agents provide real-time notice of any litigation and forward all official documents directly to the companies they represent.

- Having service of process delivered to a company's primary place of business can spark rumors among customers and employees. Designating a separate address for receiving service of process avoids this issue.

Almost any person or business entity may legally act as a registered agent. Smaller businesses, such as business entities owned by one person who is also the corporate management, typically will name themselves as registered agent. Some states require the registered agent, if an individual, to either be a member of the board of directors or the entity's attorney. The service of being a registered agent can be provided by professionals, for example, attorneys or CPAs, but is most often performed by one of the national registered agent services companies like CT Corporation (CT), Corporation Service Company (CSC), National Registered Agents, Inc. (NRAI), InCorp Services, Inc. (InCorp), Northwest Registered Agent LLC (NWRA), Registered Agent Solutions, Inc. (RASI), Business Filings Incorporated (BizFilings), United States Corporation Agents (LegalZoom), Paracorp Inc., National Corporate Research Ltd., and Capitol Corporate Services, Inc.

The registered agent for a business entity is generally assigned in the formation documents when the entity is originally created. For example, a person forming a corporation in the State of Nevada would designate the registered agent along with the agent's address on the articles of incorporation filed with the Nevada Secretary of State. If the agent cannot sign the articles personally, some states such as Nevada provide that the registered agent may be designated using a separate "Registered Agent Acceptance" with the appropriate acceptance and signature. A representative of the business or the individual accepting responsibility as registered agent must sign to accept the responsibility of acting as agent. In most states it is a crime to knowingly file a false document with the office of the Secretary of State, although the penalties vary widely. For example, in Nevada it is a Class D felony to forge this signature, but in Michigan it is only a misdemeanor.

Information about persons or entities that may be willing to act as registered agents/resident agents by state is usually maintained by the Secretary of State. Most states also offer free access to their databases to find a business entity's registered agent.

4. DRAFTING AND FILING THE DOCUMENTS WITH THE SECRETARY OF STATE

Some states require sole proprietorships and general partnerships to register when operating under an assumed name or a name that is different from their owners. This is typically accomplished through a filing with the appropriate state or local governmental office where the business is headquartered or conducting business. In contrast, all limited liability entities must register with the state in order to obtain limited liability status. When forming a partnership or limited liability entity, the attorney is representing the entity and not the individuals involved. An attorney acting in such a capacity should first consult with the parties about the loss of the attorney-client privilege and obtain each party's informed consent in an engagement agreement.

The first step in forming a corporation is to prepare the articles of incorporation, in some states called a charter or certificate of incorporation. These documents may be regarded as a contract between the organizers and the state under authorization of the prevailing statute for the benefit of the shareholders. The state corporate statute will contain what provisions must be included in the articles, as well as any optional provisions that may be desired by the incorporators. The articles typically must state the corporation's complete name, including a reference to its corporate status. The articles must include the corporation's registered agent for service of process and for receiving official correspondence. It requires the name and address of each incorporator as well as the address of the corporation's principal office. It will also include the number of securities the corporation has the authority to issue. In the event that there are different classes of stock authorized, it will state the number of shares of each class, the privileges, rights, limitations, and preferences of each class. The corporation cannot issue more shares than are authorized without amending the articles. While it was once customary for articles to include a par value (an initial minimum amount of capitalization paid for the stock), this requirement is no longer prevalent in the United States, and thus no share price needs to be stated. The articles may contain a corporate purpose but in most instances it is preferable to state that "the corporation will engage in any lawful act or activity for which corporations may be organized under the corporate statue" of that given jurisdiction.

Most modern state statutes no longer require that the articles of incorporation contain the names and addresses of the initial board of directors. Delaware makes an exception to this general rule, requiring the names and addresses of the directors when the power of the incorporators terminates upon the filing of the certificate of incorporation. In addition, most modern statutes have discarded the requirement that the board be composed of at least three directors.

Beyond the statutorily required provisions, most state statutes allow the corporation to tailor provisions necessary to provide certain protections for its participants. Examples of such permissible provisions include:

- Special voting provisions can be included which provide for super majority approval for certain corporate actions such as charter amendments protecting minority shareholders;

- Shareholder approval for matters typically reserved by the board of directors such as determining executive compensation;

- Shareholder's preemptive right to purchase a proportionate share of any new issue of stock;

- Limitations on the personal liability of a corporate director for monetary damages for breach of the director's fiduciary duty; and

- Expanded directors' or officers' indemnification, specifying under what circumstances the corporation will pay for the liability, settlement, or cost of defense if the directors or officers are sued in their corporate capacity.

The processes of forming limited liability partnerships, limited partnerships, and limited liability companies, are very similar to the process for forming a corporation. In forming a limited liability partnership, the partners need to file an application for registration of limited liability partnership and the required fee with the Secretary of State. The name must include "Registered Limited Liability Partnership" or the abbreviation LLP or L.L.P. In addition, it must list the address of its principal office and the name and address of its registered agent. Typically, one or more authorized partners need to sign the registration.

An application for certificate of limited partnership must be filed with the required fee with the Secretary of State. Its name must include the words Limited Partnership or the abbreviation L.P. It must list the address of its principal office and the name and address of its registered agent, as well as, the name and address of each general partner. Since limited partners generally cannot participate in the management of the partnership, and rely on the efforts of others to manage their investment returns, their limited partnership interests are deemed to be securities. As a result, the limited partnership would either have to issue the interests pursuant to federal and state securities laws exemptions or register the interests as securities with the Securities and Exchange Commission and the Secretary of State which regulates securities as discussed in chapter 5.

An LLC is formed by filing articles of organization and the required fee with the Secretary of State. Its name must include Limited Liability Company or the abbreviation LLC or L.L.C. It must list the address of its principal office and the name and address of its registered agent and each organizer. The articles should contain a statement as to whether the LLC will be member-managed, manager-managed, or board-managed. There are a number of other provisions that may be included in the articles to supplement or amend the limited liability statutes default rules depending on the jurisdiction. Examples of such provisions include:

- Limitations on directors' personal liability in a board-managed LLC;

- Conflict of interest waivers for managers and directors for certain designated transactions;

- Standards of conduct for members, managers, and directors, which reflect the understanding of the parties;

- Methods for determining the amount of and terms for payment to a withdrawing or terminating members;

- Specifying certain events will trigger dissolution of the LLC; and

- Terms for expulsion of a member by the remaining members.

Once the above entities have drafted and filed the appropriate documents along with the required fee with the Secretary of State, they will be date stamped and a copy will be returned to the registered agent. The entity is deemed to be in existence upon filing, unless stated in the filing documentation that it will become effective at a later date. Once filed, they become public documents and anyone interested in confirming the existence of the entity can obtain a certificate of existence. In most instances the certificate of existence should be filed with appropriate local governmental body where the entity's principal office is located.

5. DRAFTING AND ADOPTING THE INTERNAL ORGANIC DOCUMENTS FOR THE ENTITY

There are three primary internal documents that need to be considered when creating business entities: the partnership agreement, corporate bylaws, and the LLC operating agreement. All three of these documents should be considered a contract between the participants on how responsibilities and authorities will be allocated between the parties.

These documents do not have to be filed with any office and are used internally to govern the entity's operations.

a. For the Partnership

Although a legally valid partnership (general partnership, limited liability, and limited partnership) can be created in the absence of a formal written agreement, a well thought-out partnership agreement developed with full collaboration between all the partners is the best way to realize shared expectations, uncover potential problems, and set up a mechanism for resolving disputes. By discussing potential controversial issues upfront, many management and ownership issues can be mitigated if not eliminated. In the event that there is no written agreement, the laws of the state in which the partnership operates will dictate how the partnership must conduct itself. Every state except Louisiana has adopted either the Uniform Partnership Act (the "UPA") or the Revised Uniform Partnership Act (the "RUPA"). While most states have adopted changes to these uniform laws, there is still significant consistency between the states. While it is possible that the provisions contained in the state statutes governing partnerships are acceptable to the partners, it is more likely that the partners will want to alter these default provisions through a partnership agreement. Some of the provisions that should be considered when drafting the partnership agreement include a description of the financial contributions of each partner. The amounts of the contributions may be equal but need not be. However, if one partner invests more than others, they may feel entitled to more control over partnership decisions. In addition, rather than cash contributions, the contributions may be in the form of services or property. Contributions of services for capital interest (as opposed to a profits interest) may be taxable. The partners should quantify the value of the property and services to be contributed at the outset and the terms should be clearly delineated in the partnership agreement. When transferring property to the partnership, such contributions often raise questions about what tax basis will be assigned to the property being transferred. The IRS will look at the tax basis in determining how much profit has been realized when the property is later transferred or sold, as well as the amount of losses that are realized in the event that the business is not profitable.

Another key issue that should be addressed in the partnership agreement is how and when the partners will be compensated. The partners need to determine who will receive a salary for work performed in the business in addition to how and when payments will be made for each partner's respective share of the profits. Management responsibilities of the partners should be clearly defined. Often in a small business, all partners are involved in the management and supervision of the partnership. Of particular importance is the designation of a tax matters partner, establishing the tax year, the election of how the partnership should be taxed, and necessary citations to U.S. Treasury Regulations regarding how non-recovery debt will be allocated to the partners. However, in situations where all partners will not be directly involved in management, determinations need to be made as to the authority any particular partner has when making purchases or undertaking obligations. This can be achieved by limiting the dollar amount of any transaction that an individual partner can enter into without a unanimous decision of all the other partners.

The partnership agreement should also address how the partnership will deal with the departure, disability, or death of a partner. A provision can be included which allows the remaining partners to purchase the partnership interest before transferring or selling it to outsiders. One major issue with such a buy-out clause, however, is determining how the partnership interest is valued. There are a number of ways that a partnership interest can be valued, but the method should be determined up front in the partnership agreement. For example, the partners can agree to a set dollar amount or to obtain a post-departure independent appraisal to determine the value of the partnership. The value can also be established through the book value, asset value, or capitalization of earnings methods. Each of these methods have their strengths and weaknesses in terms of accurately determining the true market value of the partnership interest, but it is critical that the partners to adopt the methodology at the outset to avoid any disputes after the fact. Finally, the parties should consider how the buy-out will be funded. Life insurance on each partner with the partnership as the beneficiary is an option.

b.   For the Corporation

Corporate bylaws delineate the rights and authority of the shareholders, directors, and officers of the corporation. In a few states, bylaws must be adopted by the incorporators and in others states by the directors. Bylaws are drafted under the authority of the controlling state statute and the corporation's articles of incorporation. In the event that the bylaws are silent as to a particular matter, the prevailing state corporate statute will govern. State law does not require that the bylaws be filed with the Secretary of State or other public office.

Typically the bylaws describe such matters as the functions of each corporate office, how shareholders' and directors' meetings are called and conducted, the formalities of corporate and special meetings of shareholders, how much notice needs to be provided for meeting, and what constitutes a quorum for an effective vote. They spell out the qualifications for the directors, how they are elected and what authority they have, how they will be compensated, and the functions of board committees (such as executive and audit committees). Generally, the titles of corporate officers such as the President, Secretary, and Treasurer are listed in the bylaws. In addition, the bylaws should include procedures for and restrictions on issuing shares, the fiscal year of the corporation, and how the bylaws can be amended. A common mnemonic device for remembering the typical articles in bylaws is NOMOMECPA, pronounced "No mommy, see pa!" It stands for Name, Object, Members, Officers, Meetings, Executive board, Committees, Parliamentary authority, Amendment. Bylaws generally cannot be amended by an organization's Board of Directors. A super-majority vote of the membership, such as two-thirds present and voting or a majority of all the members, is usually required to amend the bylaws.

c.   The Limited Liability Company

The operating agreement serves a function similar to partnership agreements and corporate bylaws. It is an agreement among limited liability company members governing the LLC's business and the member's financial and managerial rights and duties. Many states require an LLC to have an operating agreement. LLCs operating without an operating agreement are governed by the State's default rules contained in the relevant state statute and developed through relevant case law. In single-member LLCs, an operating agreement is a declaration of the structure that the member has chosen for the company and sometimes used to prove in court that the LLC structure is separate from that of the individual owner and thus is necessary so that the owner has documentation to protect himself from potential liability.

While most small businesses tend to operate as member-managed LLCs, rather than manager-managed or director-managed LLCs, if the business chooses one of the other two options, the operating agreement will need to include a special section outlining how the managers or directors will be chosen and removed and what authority they will have. Regardless of the type of LLC, the operating agreement will typically contain provisions addressing the following issues:

- How will the member's capital contributions be made to the LLC and what additional contributions can be made in the future?

- How will the members' percentage interest in the LLC be determined?

- How will the members vote? Is it based on the amount of capital contributions made? Will decisions be made by simple majority vote or will some decisions require a greater majority vote?

- How will membership interests be transferred in the event of death, disability, or withdrawal?

- How will the interest of the departing member be valued? Can the departing member transfer ownership of their membership interest to outside parties, or will they be required to sell the interest to the remaining members?

- How will profits and losses be allocated to the members? Who will determine if and when distributions will be made? (This issue is important for tax purposes too.)

Keep in mind that in the absence of an operating agreement indicating otherwise, most statutes deem the LLC to be member-managed. In this situation, each of the members is an agent of the LLC and has the authority to bind the business when entering into routine transactions.

6. HOLDING THE FIRST ORGANIZATIONAL MEETING

Whether the business is a partnership (general, limited, or limited liability), corporation, or limited liability company, it should hold a formal organizational meeting to take additional steps that are either legally required or are a matter of good business practice. One of the first matters that all entities need to address is the establishment of a bank account. The bank will require that the business provide them with a copy of their organizational documents so that they can verify that the individuals establishing the account have the authority to do so. The bank will want to know who has the authority within the organization to sign checks and/or borrow money and whether any counter signatures will be required. It will also request the business's Employee Identification Number (the "EIN") so that they can report interest income to the Internal Revenue Service.

Although an initial partnership meeting is not legally required, it is a good business practice to hold such a meeting and have a general discussion of the terms of the partnership agreement along with the formalities of signing the document. It should also include a discussion of the creation of capital accounts for each partner and how and when profits will be distributed and losses assessed. This is especially true with limited partnerships. As managers of the business, the general partners owe fiduciary duties to the limited partnership. As a practical matter, the general partners will have drafted the limited partnership agreement, including provisions for management fees, overhead expenses, and the percentage profit the general and limited partners receive, typically, a 20/80 split). These issues should be clearly explained to the limited partners along with the limited partnership's investment strategy and return expectations.

The initial corporate directors meeting should begin with the adoption of the bylaws. While this is often viewed as a formality, if the bylaws have not been distributed, discussed, and tentatively approved in advance of the meeting, the process can be very time-consuming. Keep in mind that the shareholders have the power to adopt, amend, and repeal the bylaws. The board only has this power if it is included in the articles. The meeting may also entail adopting a shareholders' agreement. In closely held corporations, the owners often agree not to transfer their shares and usually include mandatory purchase obligations, as an outsider who gains an ownership interest can disrupt the smooth flow of the business. While such restrictions can be included in the articles of organization or bylaws, a separate shareholder's agreement focusing specifically on shareholder transfer rights is recommended.

The designation and approval of corporate officers is also a critical early step. Most corporate transactions are not specifically approved by the board of directors, rather the board delegates authority to corporate officers for certain types of transactions. The board's delegation of authority to an officer allows that officer to bind the corporation. Typically, the president or Chief Executive Officer is given the authority to bind the corporation in all matters in the ordinary course of business. This position should be distinguished from that of Chairman of the Board, who presides over board meetings, but does not have any administrative authority to bind the corporation. A vice president should only bind the corporation as to matters within their management authority. The secretary normally does not bind the corporation but merely maintains and certifies corporate records. The treasurer normally does not have the authority to bind the corporation but is responsible for keeping the corporate books, receiving payments, and making authorized payments.

The directors should also approve any future contractual transactions that they anticipate such as employment agreements, purchase agreements, and leases; and ratify any transactions entered into prior to incorporation. If an officer's action taken on behalf of the corporation was not binding against the corporation when it was made, the board can authorize the transaction retroactively by ratifying the transaction. Ratification creates an agency relationship that relates back so that the prior transaction it is treated as being authorized from the start.

The board should also authorize the issuance of stock. Although the articles of incorporation enumerate the number of shares that are authorized for sale, the board must authorize the issuance of such shares in order for them to be distributed. Those shares that have been authorized but not issued are referred to as treasury stock. The board may authorize this stock sometime in the future when additional equity is needed for the corporation.

Since the limited liability company shares attributes of both a partnership and a corporation, the initial meeting of the members will take on attributes of both. Like the partnership agreement and corporate bylaws, the operating agreement should be distributed for review and comment prior to the meeting so that it can be formalized and executed by the membership. Although the default rule is that all members are entitled to participate in the control of a limited liability company, as a practical matter only one member, or a committee of members, will actually be responsible for managing the day-to-day business operations. In fact, the members may choose an individual to be responsible for management and operations who does not hold an equity stake in the LLC. Under such circumstances, the members or board must establish appropriate management reporting systems so that all of the members can monitor performance of the business on a periodic basis. Such detailed reporting systems would not be included in the operating agreement, but are an essential first step in establishing operational expectations and objectives and in measuring progress against those milestones.

7. DOCUMENTING ENTITY ACTIONS

No matter what form a business entity takes, all actions taken at the initial meeting, annual meeting, or special meetings should be documented to ensure that all participants have a historical record of the actions and decisions that the entity has made. Typically this is done through the taking of minutes which are an instant written record of the meeting. They describe the events of the meeting, starting with a list of attendees, a statement of the issues considered by the participants, and related responses, decisions or votes for the issues.

Minutes may be created during the meeting by a typist or court reporter, who may use shorthand notation and then prepare the minutes to be issued to the participants afterwards. Alternatively, the meeting can be audio-recorded or a group's appointed or informally assigned secretary may take notes, with minutes prepared later. Usually the minutes are drafted in a terse fashion, including only a summary of topics discussed and decisions made; more detail is only fodder for litigation should conflict arise. The minutes of the corporate board of directors and limited liability membership meetings are important legal documents and must be kept on file.

Generally, minutes begin with the name of the entity or committee holding the meeting, place, date, list of people present, and the time that the chair called the meeting to order. The minutes then summarize what was actually said at the meeting, either in the order that it was actually said or in a more coherent order, regardless of whether the meeting follows any written agenda. A less-used format may record the events in the order they occur on the written agenda, regardless of the actual chronology.

Since the primary function of minutes is to record the decisions made, all official decisions must be included. If a formal motion is proposed, seconded, passed, or not, then this is recorded. The voting results may also be included. The part of the minutes dealing with a routine motion might indicate merely that a particular motion was moved by an individual and passed unanimously. It is not necessary to include the name of the person who seconds a motion. Where a tally is included, it is sufficient to record the number of people voting for and against a motion (or abstaining), but requests by participants to note their votes by name may be allowed. If a decision is made by roll call vote, then all of the individual votes are often recorded by name. If it is made by general consent without a formal vote, then this fact may be recorded. Tallies may be omitted in some cases (*e.g.*, a minute might read "After voting, the Committee agreed to. . .").

Minutes typically include whether a report was presented, a legal issue was discussed (such as a potential conflict of interest), if a particular aspect of an issue was considered, or that a person arrived late (or left early). The minutes may end with a note of the time that the meeting was adjourned. Minutes are generally submitted by the secretary at a subsequent meeting for review. The traditional closing phrase is "Respectfully submitted," followed by the officer's signature, his or her typed (or printed) name, and his or her title. If the members of the committee or group agree that the written minutes reflect what happened at the meeting, their approval is recorded in the minutes of the current meeting. If there are significant errors or omissions then the minutes will be redrafted and submitted again at a later date. Minor changes may be made immediately and the amended minutes may be approved "as amended." It is normally appropriate to send a draft copy of the minutes to all the members in advance of the meeting so that the meeting is not delayed by a reading of the draft. Once the minutes have been approved, they should be maintained in a record book, and perhaps maintain a PDF backup, for review if necessary at a later date.

Minutes are also used to record corporate resolutions detailing decisions made during the board meeting. The resolution is a written statement made by the board of directors detailing which officers are authorized to act on behalf of the corporation. The resolution could be on any subject and takes the form of a legal document to be used in a variety of matters. One common subject, because it is required by banks and securities firms to open accounts, is to define which individuals are authorized to act on behalf of a corporation. This form of corporate resolution is also required by title agencies when selling corporate owned real estate. The form and structure of this document varies depending on the state in which the corporation is organized. Although resolutions are customarily thought of in connection with corporations, if properly structured, they can be used in the context of other business entities as a legal document to grant organizational authority to take actions.

Occasionally, urgent board action is required yet it is not possible or practical to conduct a formal board meeting. In such cases, most states permit the board members to conduct official business by taking action by written consent. Unlike directors voting at a meeting, which may require only a majority of the directors to approve any board action, most states that permit action by written consent require unanimous approval. Once an action by written consent is signed by all of the directors, the written consent will have the same effect as a resolution that gained a unanimous vote of the Board.

In such cases, an action by written consent will be sent to each individual director by mail, e-mail, or fax for his or her signature. To streamline the signature gathering process, the written consent document can permit counterpart signatures. This means that each director can sign the signature page of his or her copy and the signed signature pages, when taken together, are considered a validly executed document.

In the case of direct mail or fax, the director will sign his or her approval and submit the signed copy to the secretary for filing. When written consents are conducted through e-mail, some questions of legality can arise. It is best to print and sign the action taken by written consent and then fax or e-mail a copy and mail the original to the secretary. In the case of consents that will be relied upon by a third party, such as a bank or title company, it is best if the records contain the signed original consents rather than copies or e-mails approving the transaction to ensure the signatures will be accepted.

Generally, the action is considered to be taken on the date the last director signs the consent. For recordkeeping purposes, the signed consents must be kept by the secretary in the corporate minute book. Additionally, the resolution should be entered into the minutes of the next board meeting and made part of the official record of the corporation. Like the corporate resolution, most states allow limited liability companies to use actions taken by written consent. State statutes should be consulted to determine if the charter or articles of organization are required to contain a provision allowing actions to be taken by written consent. At the very least, the process should be clearly outlined in the bylaws or operating agreement.

The following items should be kept in the corporate record book: the articles of corporation; the bylaws; minutes of meetings; resolutions; consent actions; and stock certificate stubs or a ledger of when and who received stock certificates.

8. BUSINESS PERMITS, INSURANCE, TAXES, AND REGULATION

Depending on the nature of the business and its location, it may be required to have various types of state and/or municipal licenses, certificates, and/or permits. As different licenses are administered by various agencies, it is best to check with the County Clerk in the county in which the business is located and with the appropriate state taxing agency.

Prudent business owners should carry business insurance to protect the business against fire, theft, flood, and other losses. Many types of insurance exist including property, liability, business interruption, worker's compensation, group health, life, disability income, keyman insurance, and others. The most common insurance mistake is not carrying enough liability coverage. It is unwise to believe that a judgment or accident cannot potentially hurt the owners or business because the business has little revenue or assets. At a minimum, a business needs property insurance, liability insurance (including motor vehicle insurance on all business vehicles), and, if the business has the state required number of employees, worker's compensation insurance. Workers compensation is a form of insurance that provides wage replacement and medical benefits for employees who are injured in the course of employment, in exchange for mandatory relinquishment of the employee's right to sue his or her employer for the tort of negligence. Workers compensation laws vary slightly from state to state. If the business has a loan, banks will typically require keyman insurance, which protects key individuals in the business. Keyman insurance helps the lender ensure that the bank will get its money back if something happens to the key individual responsible for making the business generate a profit.

It is also a good idea to secure business interruption insurance (also known as business income insurance). It differs from property insurance in that a property insurance policy only covers the physical damage to the business, while the additional coverage allotted by the business interruption policy covers the profits that would have been earned. In the event the business is the victim of fire, flood, or other specified catastrophes, business interruption insurance will provide money to compensate for the period the business does not operate (other forms of casualty insurance compensate for the property that suffered the catastrophic loss). Also, if the business provides products for public use, it should also carry products liability insurance. Products liability insurance indemnifies claims from third parties who claim the business's product injured them. It will also provide benefits for the defense of the legal action.

In most instances, a business must file IRS Form SS-4 to obtain a Federal Employer Identification Number (an "EIN"). An exception is found in the case of single-member LLCs. They use the social security number or EIN of the sole owner. Obtaining an EIN allows the new business to comply with federal income tax regulations, as well as with Social Security and Unemployment Insurance regulations. States also require that most businesses apply for a Tax Registration Number. This number is different from the EIN; it requires a separate application which must be filed with the state revenue agency to register the business for state tax purposes.

An individual business owner is responsible for paying self-employment tax. However, 50% of the self-employment tax can be deducted from the individual owner's personal tax return. Also, limited partners and certain LLC members are not subject to self-employment tax. The self-employment tax should be calculated and reported on Schedule SE of Form 1040. If the estimated annual tax on self-employment income is less than $1,000.00, estimated payments are not required. Also, business owners are not responsible for Federal Insurance Contributions Act (the "FICA") tax—self-employment tax replaces it.

Many states require the taxation of sales, use of tangible personal property, and certain services. After the business files for registration with the appropriate state taxation agency, the state will issue a State Tax Number to use when filing all state taxes. If a business is subject to any tax, the business must collect and then remit the tax to the State. The State will then remit the local or county portion of the tax to the appropriate local or county agent. If the business is exempt under any particular exemptions to the Sales and Use Tax, it should maintain file copies of the appropriate documentation, such as the resale or tax-exempt certificate of the purchaser in both the attorney's and business's files. The business will also likely be subject to various local taxes. Information on these particular taxes can be gained from the local tax assessor's office.

If the business hires even one employee, state and federal guidelines apply that must be followed. Attorneys and business people should be familiar with the Fair Labor Standards Act (the "FLSA"), which establishes guidelines for minimum wage, overtime pay, child labor standards, and record keeping. The FLSA guidelines apply to employers of both full and part-time employees. Each state also has an agency that handles labor matters, and additional information should be available from these sources.

The business's management should also be familiar with Title VII of the Civil Rights Act of 1964 and any other state anti-discrimination laws that apply to employers. Management should also be aware of the Occupational Safety and Health Act (the "OSHA"), and any state counterpart, which require employers to provide safe workplaces for employees. Also, the National Labor Relations Act (the "NLRA") regulates labor practices by defining the rights of employees and employers. It is enforced by the National Labor Relations Board (the "NLRB").

As an employer, the business must be certain to fulfill its responsibility to withhold income tax from its employees' paychecks. This withholding is based upon each employee's filing status, the number of dependents he or she has, and the amount of wages or salary the employee is due. Federal law also requires that the business withhold each employee's share of Social Security tax and Medicare tax. The business must also pay the employer's share of the FICA tax. The Internal Revenue Service's Publication 15 explains federal withholding and SSI in detail.

The business must pay State and Federal Unemployment taxes (the "SUTA" and the "FUTA"). The federal unemployment rate is equal to 6.2% of gross compensation, but normally nets to 0.8% because the employer is allowed to take a credit up to 5.4% of compensation for state unemployment taxes paid by the employer. This is true if the employer is eligible for the maximum credit. A sole proprietor or a partnership is not responsible for paying FUTA on the compensation of the sole proprietorship or the partners. If a business is subject to FUTA payment, use Form 940 for calculation and payment of the tax. Each state has a different unemployment tax rate. Businesses will have to consult the state agency that administers the unemployment insurance program for the requirements for their particular state regarding tax rates and maximum wage base. A new business will be required by many states to have an average starting rate until an employment history is created and established.

9.   PROCEDURES FOR STOCK ISSUANCE

Before shares of stock can be issued, the articles of incorporation must authorize the number, class, and type of shares of stock to be issued. The board of directors then needs to act through a formal resolution to name the individual and the consideration given for the shares. Although the modern trend is that shares of stock can be exchanged for any benefit to the corporation, there are a number of states that limit the types of consideration that can be used to purchase stock. Some state statutes prohibit a corporation from issuing shares in consideration for unsecured promissory notes or promises of future performance by a shareholder. When property or services are contributed instead of cash, the board of directors' valuation of the consideration is conclusive unless actual fraud can be proven. Under such circumstances, the board should adopt a resolution determining the cash value of the property or services being contributed to the corporation in exchange for the shares, as future evidence of the integrity of the boards' valuation decision.

Although the corporation is technically formed upon filing of the articles of incorporation with the Secretary of State, if stock is not issued at an initial organizational meeting, the business is potentially at risk of losing its limited liability protection and corporate tax status. While not a decisive factor when determining alter ego liability, the non-issuance of stock is a solid indication that there is a fundamental failure to follow corporate formalities drawing a distinction between the business owners and the corporate entity.

Not all of the stock that is authorized in the articles of incorporation need be issued. Those shares that are not issued to shareholders are kept in the company's treasury, to be used to raise additional cash in the future. Such shares do not pay dividends, have no voting rights, and are not included in the calculation of shares outstanding. Alternatively, treasury stock can be created when a company completes a share buyback or purchases its shares on the open market. This can be advantageous to shareholders because it lowers the number of shares outstanding. Another reason a company may maintain a supply of treasury stock is to keep a controlling interest within the treasury to help ward off hostile takeovers.

Common stock represents the basic ownership and control rights of the corporation's shareholders. Common shareholders are often characterized as the owners of the corporation. Common stock is usually voting shares, although the organizers can issue non-voting shares in situations where equity investors are willing to invest in the corporation without having voting rights on corporate decisions. Such voting limitations must be clearly outlined in the articles of incorporation.

Holders of common stock are able to influence the corporation through votes on establishing corporate objectives and policy, stock splits, and electing the company's board of directors and auditors. Some holders of common stock also receive preemptive rights, which enable them to retain their proportional ownership in a company should it issue another stock offering. There is no fixed dividend paid out to common stock holders and so their returns are uncertain and are contingent on earnings, company reinvestment, and efficiency of the market to value and sell stock. In the event of dissolution or bankruptcy, common stock investors receive their funds after preferred stock holders, bondholders, and creditors.

Preferred stock is a class of stock often viewed as a hybrid between debt and common stock. Similar to bonds, preferred stocks are rated by the major credit-rating companies. The rating for preferred stock is lower since preferred dividends do not carry the same guarantees as interest payments from bonds and they are junior to all creditors. Preferred stock is a special class of shares that may have any combination of features not possessed by common stock. Preferred stocks offer a company an attractive alternative form of financing. In most cases, a company can defer dividends paid to preferred shareholders by going into arrears without much of a penalty or risk to their credit rating. With traditional debt, payments are required and a missed payment would put the company in default.

Some argue that a straight preferred stock, being a hybrid between a bond and a stock, bears the disadvantages of each of those types of securities without enjoying the advantages of either. Like a bond, a straight preferred does not participate in any future earnings and dividend growth of the company and any resulting growth of the price of the common. But the bond has greater security than the preferred and has a maturity date at which the principal is to be repaid. Like the common, the preferred has less security protection than the bond. But the potential of increases in market price of the common stock and its dividends paid from future growth of the company is lacking for the preferred. One big advantage that the preferred stock provides its issuer is that it gets better equity credit at rating agencies than traditional debt, since it is usually perpetual.

In general, preferred stocks have preference in dividends payments. A preference does not assure the payment of dividends, but the company must pay the stated dividend rate to preferred stock prior to paying any dividends on common stock. Preferred stock can either be cumulative or noncumulative. A cumulative preferred stock requires that if a company fails to pay any dividend or any amount below the stated rate, it must make up for it at a later time. Dividends accumulate with each passed dividend period, which can be quarterly, semi-annually, or annually. When a dividend is not paid in time, it has passed and all passed dividends on a cumulative stock are dividends in arrears. A stock that does not have this feature is known as a noncumulative or straight preferred stock and any dividends passed are lost forever if not declared.

Convertible preferred stock allows the holders to exchange preferred shares for a predetermined number of the company's common stock. This exchange can occur at any time the investor chooses regardless of the current market price of the common stock. It is a one-way deal so one cannot convert the common stock back to preferred stock. This feature is particularly attractive to venture capital investors who desire to make equity investment in a business. Holding preferred stock that allows the investor to receive a dividend if the company earns a profit, receive priority over common shareholders in the event of liquidation, and the ability to convert the preferred shares into common shares to fully participate in the growth of the company if it is sold or goes public, is extremely desirable.

While preferred shareholders typically do not have the voting rights of common shareholders, investors in a new business may negotiate voting rights in corporate decisions that may affect the preferred shareholders investment. In more mature companies that have established financial track records, the corporation may have greater bargaining power and can limit or exclude the voting authority of the preferred shareholder. In fact, under such conditions, the corporation may carry a call provision, enabling the issuing corporation to repurchase the preferred shares at its (usually limited) discretion.

Once the number and type of shares is decided upon by the board of directors, the company needs to determine if it will issue paper certificates. A stock certificate is a legal document that certifies ownership of a specific number of stock shares in a corporation. Stock certificates are generally divided into two forms: registered stock certificates and bearer stock certificates. A registered stock certificate is normally only evidence of title and a record of the true holders of the shares will appear in the stockholder's register of the corporation. A bearer stock certificate, as its name implies is a bearer instrument, and physical possession of the certificate entitles the holder to exercise all legal rights associated with the stock. Bearer stock certificates were a way to transfer beneficial title to assets held by the corporation with perceived confidentiality, but are very uncommon and rarely seen in practice today. While companies are no longer required to issue paper certificates, businesses can obtain them from office supply stores or on the Internet.

CHAPTER 4

TRANSACTIONAL DOCUMENTS, NEGOTIATION, AND DRAFTING

■ ■ ■

A. INTRODUCTION

This section of the book provides an overview of the issues and processes involved in the negotiation and drafting of contracts and transactional documents. It should enable you to analyze the basic structure of contracts and other deal documents and develop the macro and micro techniques used to efficiently create those documents with precision and clarity.

Contracts often govern ongoing relationships. It is therefore important to understand how applicable law affects the parties' private dealings and what can be done to limit or expand this relationship. You should verify that the substantive laws referred to in the text are applicable in your jurisdiction and, if not, tailor your documents accordingly.

Transactional documents are an opportunity to structure a relationship while preventing and planning for future litigation. You should think about how to integrate concepts from other courses and experiences into contracts. Transactional lawyers draft to fall within or to avoid the ambit of particular statutory or case law. What contract remedies would be available under the law if the contract makes no provision for them? How can this result be altered in the contract? What is the evidentiary significance of various parts of the contract in later litigation? What can be done to render these portions admissible evidence? How can they be drafted so that they are favorable evidence for either party? Contract drafting provides an opportunity to use and reinforce a full range of substantive legal skills.

Good contracts are not solely the product of legal knowledge and skill. They are also the product of business and practical knowledge. This business and practical knowledge will be used to interpret the contracts, especially in jurisdictions where a weak form of the parol evidence rule is in force. This business and practical knowledge is needed to draft a good contract. It is critical that counsel understands the client's business, its goals, and the forces and events that drive the enterprise and its industry to produce practical, precise documentation of a deal that will properly allocate risk between the parties, provide a legal mechanism for exchange, redress for short falls in performance, and stand up to interpretation and enforcement in the litigation or other dispute resolution process when everything has broken down.

Remember, legal drafting, like so many things, is subject to the whims of fashion. Reasonable minds may differ on many of these matters. As with all legal writing and drafting, the point is communication. It is easier to tailor the form of your message to your audience than to try to force your audience to enjoy the form of your message. Use the rules, principles, and methods in this book as a default guide to contract drafting—but modify them to fit your audience and surroundings.

B. FUNDAMENTAL CONSIDERATIONS IN CONTRACT DRAFTING

This chapter discusses the context of transactional documents in terms of the deal timeline, a chain of events that characterizes most transactions, and then discusses the drafting process and its major, overarching components.

1. THE CONTEXT: THE DEAL TIMELINE: BIG OR LITTLE, DEALS FOLLOW A PATTERN

A transaction generally follows a standard timeline or chain of events. First, the parties make contact and negotiate. A preliminary agreement is reached and they contact their lawyers, if they have not done so already. Although the key business issues have probably been addressed by the parties, there will often be significant issues left open, some of which will only become apparent to the client after consultation with counsel.

If possible, it is helpful for clients to meet with counsel prior to negotiating the basic business deal to explore the possible issues and structures for the contemplated transaction. A well prepared client can then bargain for an issue or structure with the other party from the beginning. This may result in key issues being resolved in your client's favor with little or no discussion or quid pro quo. This might not be the case if the opposing party was just as prepared, left the issue open, followed up with her own counsel, and then negotiated the point.

As the parties proceed with formal documentation, due diligence (detailed factual and legal investigation) begins. Usually one party will produce documents and information relevant to representations and warranties that are being negotiated.

The definitive transactional documents are finalized and signed and further due diligence and other pre-closing activities take place. Then, the closing occurs. A closing checklist typically will be prepared to ensure that details are not overlooked. This is the point at which the majority of the consideration changes hands.   Payments or deliveries may be made directly, party-to-party, or through an escrow, the preferred route for all but the most basic transactions.   Escrows provide the parties with the security of knowing that although they have parted with their consideration, it will not be delivered to the other party until that party's deliveries are complete. In case of a dispute, the escrow agent can hold all consideration already delivered and maintain the status quo pending the dispute's resolution.   There may be a post-closing adjustment period as well.

For simple transactions, this timeline is condensed and one or more steps may be omitted. On the other hand, in major business transactions, the timeline can extend over a year or more. The middle ground of 90 or 120 days is the length of an average residential home purchase and sale transaction. It is also the typical period in which a small to medium commercial lease or corporate transaction might take place.

Keep this timeline in mind when drafting.   Know where your transaction is on the timeline and where it is going. Your relative position on this chain of events will affect the pace and the level of detail with which you draft.

Early in the drafting process, have a frank discussion with your client about your role in this process. Some clients prefer to have the lawyer take the lead in all negotiation, documentation, and due diligence activities. Many prefer to take the lead in all matters and see the lawyer's role as that of a scrivener. Others fall in between these extremes. Clarify your client's expectations of your role early in the process to avoid confusion and client dissatisfaction.   Both the costs and benefits of your activities should be evaluated.

Contract negotiation and documentation is an exercise in selling. In the process, you are selling three things. You are:

1.   Selling the parties on executing the documents now;

2.   Selling the parties on voluntary performance after execution; and

3.   Selling a later court (or other entity) on enforcement after voluntary performance has ceased.

These three sales goals undermine each other to some extent. Consider the tension between selling the parties on execution, which tends to imply vanilla documentation with few, if any, teeth, on the one hand, and selling the parties later on voluntary performance, which is furthered by fairly detailed documents that contain both carrot and stick provisions tailored to the particular parties. Balanced documents that accomplish all three sales goals require careful consideration before and during the negotiating and drafting process.

2. THE DRAFTING PROCESS—STEP BY STEP

1. Investigate the facts (including related documents);

2. Investigate applicable law as needed;

3. Develop a contact list and task schedule according to deadline date and responsible party;

4. Check exemplars and other resources;

5. Prepare initial drafts;

6. Circulate drafts for comments—which may lead the drafter back to earlier steps in the process before moving ahead;

7. Negotiate and document the final, definitive documents;

8. Execution (signing) of the final, definitive documents;

9. Preparation for closing and closing; and

10. Post-closing adjustments and clean up

3. THE GOAL: PRACTICAL, PRECISE DOCUMENTS

The goal of the drafting process is to produce precise documents that are understandable to both the legal and lay audience involved in the project. The words of the transactional document will govern the parties' relationship, rights, and duties. They will be considered to be the primary, and often only, evidence of the parties' intentions. Thus, precise documentation that clearly communicates its meaning to the parties, their counsel, and enforcing courts is the goal of the drafting process.

As the discussion of plain English later in this chapter indicates, legal precision does not have to be sacrificed to achieve plain English. Avoid being a drafter that relies on less-than-plain language to achieve transactional ends. The plainer the language and the clearer the drafting organization, the more likely it is that the parties will not have differing interpretations of the contract. This should minimize the potential for litigation, or at least the risk of loss in litigation caused by a court adopting a different interpretation.

Contractual precision has at least four elements:

1. It is accurate, meaning that it correctly expresses the deal.

2. It is complete, meaning that all possibilities have been addressed. Look down the road, determine the range of different contingencies, and provide your client with rights and remedies to address contingencies if they occur. Focus on what could occur if one party fails to perform and is insolvent, injured, or dead. Include protections for your client addressing these possibilities.

3. It is exact, meaning that it lacks both vagueness and ambiguity. These are two different concepts. What is the difference?

4. Finally, it is able to withstand hostile, critical review. More likely than not, after the contract is executed, the next thorough review of its provisions is likely to be by someone trying to break the contract or sue over the transaction. That person will focus on interpreting the document in a vacuum, ignoring any evidence of the parties' intent not found within the four corners of the document. Edit your contract with an eye to identifying and fixing unclear pronoun references, modifiers that may relate to one or all of the terms in a series, conjunctions that make list conjunctive or disjunctive, introductions that make the list exclusive or inclusive, and classification or categorization systems that do not accurately reflect hierarchical relationships.

To address these elements, some drafters tend to be long and wordy. They use overlays of multiple synonyms, qualifying phrases, and arcane or legalistic prose in an attempt to be accurate, complete, and exact. All too often, the work product collapses under the weight of these techniques. It becomes filled with ponderous, repetitive sentences, paragraphs, and sections. Rather than using as many words as possible—the shotgun approach—strive to find the right word or words. This will involve considering the level of detail and generality of the words involved as well as their potential multiple meanings and connotations.

Contractual precision is also achieved through good organization. Within a document, each section should address a specific subject or aspect of the transaction. Within each section, each subsection or paragraph should carry out one function. Within each subsection, each sentence should perform one subtask. Do not hesitate to subdivide sections, subsections, paragraphs, and sentences as needed to break them into meaningful, digestible chunks.

There are many rules of construction and interpretation and a host of equitable maxims, many of which you may have encountered in your contract law class. While lengthy discussion of these principles is possible, the key point is that they are often used by courts to justify decisions that have been reached for other reasons. For a tabulation of the contrary doctrines of interpretation, see Llewellyn, *Remarks on the Theory of Appellate Decision and How the Rules or Canons about How Statutes Are to be Construed*, 3 VAND. L. REV. 395 (1950). Rather than taking comfort in the thought that ambiguity in a document could be resolved in your client's favor under the doctrine of some such, realize that the ambiguity is more likely to allow a reviewing court to rearrange the parties' relationship according to its own perception of the correct outcome.

* * *

One often used technique that greatly increases clarity, precision, and overall readability is a tabulated or tabular form, which uses indented subparagraphs to format lists and set out items and terms. Here is an example of the tabular form used for part of an indemnification provision:

9.12 *Participating in or Assuming the Defense*

The indemnifying party may participate in the defense at any time or it may assume the defense by giving notice to the other party. After assuming the defense, the indemnifying party:

    (1)   must select an attorney that is satisfactory to the other party;

    (2)   is not liable to the other party for any later attorney's fees or for any other later expenses that the other party incurs, except for reasonable investigation costs;

    (3)   must not compromise or settle the action without the other party's consent (but the other party must not unreasonably withhold its consent); and

    (4)   is not liable for any compromise or settlement made without its consent.

For tabular form to be effective, all items in each level of subparagraphs, indicated by successive indents, must be part of the same hierarchical rank or class. Each item in the list must be structured so that, if read immediately after the introductory language, it would be grammatically correct. This also means that each of the list's items must be grammatically similar or parallel. The same is true for sentences that continue beyond the list.

Finally, either:

    (A)   each item in the list should be followed by the appropriate conjunction ("and" and "or" are the most common), or

    (B)   the second-to-last item should be followed by the appropriate conjunction, which is applicable to the whole list. Form B—used in the indemnification provision above—is most common.

Remember how important it is to listen to what your client says she desires, then translate this into legal terms and discuss or mirror your understanding back to her until both of you are satisfied. Do this first, before putting ink on a page, or fingers to keyboard, to avoid wasting your time or your client's money.

4. PLAIN ENGLISH

The Securities and Exchange Commission (the "SEC") has issued plain English guidelines for disclosure documents filed under the Securities Act of 1933, and companies filing registration statements under the Securities Act of 1933 must:

- write the forepart of these registration statements in plain English;

- write the remaining portions of these registration statements in a clear, understandable manner; and

- design these registration statements to be visually inviting and easy to read.

The principles of the SEC's plain English rule can and should be applied to almost any legal document.

Characteristics of Plain English

1. Short sentences;

2. Definite, concrete, everyday language;

3. The active voice;

4. Tabular presentation of complex or multi-factor information;

5. Separate paragraphs and sections, with headings for separate concepts;

6. The absence of legal jargon or highly technical business terminology and use of Latin or other foreign terms; and

7. The absence of double or multiple negatives.

Closely related to the virtues of plain English is the goal of drafting provisions that are clear and conspicuous to non-lawyers.

5. THINKING LIKE A TRANSACTIONAL LAWYER

Being a transactional lawyer involves a mode of analysis that is different from the litigation model that traditionally dominates law school, especially the first year. In the litigation model, one extracts rules of law from a treatise, cases or statutes, examines a given set of facts, spots the issues, applies the law to the facts, and reaches a conclusion. (IRAC: Issue, Rule, Analysis, Conclusion). At every step of the way, one is dealing with givens, facts that have already happened, or laws that have already been made by legislatures and courts (even when one is arguing for a change in law). This is not to say that they cannot be argued, emphasized, or shaded in the advocacy process—but at bottom they are fixed.

Transactional lawyering is different. It involves understanding the parties' deal and translating the business terms into a transactional structure that uses contract, commercial, and other business law principles to govern the parties' relationship. It also involves making an appropriate record along the way as negotiations and documentation continue so that, should the deal break down and litigation ensue, litigation attorneys can present the case in the light most favorable to your client. The key here is that nothing, or at least very little, is a given. There are notions of what is customary or what is the market approach or rate and regulatory systems may affect what it is possible to achieve with a given transactional structure, but the attorney is creating the structure and the provisions along the way in a manner that creates the most benefit for the client by harnessing applicable law and allocating risk and reward. This means determining what facts or states of nature should form the basis of conditions precedent to the transaction moving forward, what factual matters should be the basis for representations and warranties, when and how the transaction should terminate, if needed, and what sources of recovery should be available in the event of loss.

This is not to say that the same attorney cannot serve as a transactional lawyer and a litigator. Rather, the attorney should be conscious of her current role and adjust her mode of thinking accordingly. Too often, especially with new attorneys, there is a tendency to look at transactional law and deal documents with the eyes of a litigator rather than a transactional planner. The transactional focus is on constantly improving the structure and utility of the documents. But the transactional lawyer needs to be mindful that there can be a tendency to become too much of a formalist and believe that whatever the deal documents say will be reliably enforced every time in every court. This is not always true and the flexible standards of modern contract law, like mistake, misrepresentation, unconscionability, impracticability, can lead to a different result.

C. THE FORM OF TRANSACTIONAL DOCUMENTS

This chapter discusses macro issues relating to the form of transactional documents and includes some overall rules for successful structuring and drafting. You should refer to the contracts in the appendices for examples of these concepts as needed.

1. GENERAL OUTLINE

1. Title

2. Introductory paragraph, including the parties and the date of agreement

3. Recitals or a Statement of Background Facts

4. Definitions

5. Core substantive provisions, including consideration, conditions, and closing

6. Representations, warranties, covenants, indemnities, guaranties, and releases

7. Events of default and remedies

8. Boilerplate

9. Signature Blocks

10. Exhibits and Attachments

The overall organization of a transactional document or group of transactional documents follows a group of rules:

- General provisions before specific ones.

- Important, central provisions before others.

- Rules before exceptions.

- Separate provisions or subsections for each concept.

- Technical, boilerplate, housekeeping, and miscellaneous provisions located last, before the signature blocks.

Each contract should cover the following five major categories of issues:

1. Parties: who are they, exactly, and in what capacity are they acting?

2. Pertinent Background Information:
   - What is the intention of the parties?
   - Definitions
   - List of appendixes, exhibits, and schedules
   - List of documents incorporated by reference

3. The Exchange:
   - What is each party to do and receive?
   - Rights and duties
   - Assurances
   - Performance—duties, orders, and conditions
   - Consequences of nonperformance and defective performances

4. Providing for the Future in Ongoing Relationships:
   - Duration and termination
   - Change of parties
   - Change of obligation
   - Severance of unenforceable provisions
   - Dispute resolution
   - Other boilerplate

5. Concluding Provisions:
   - Entire Agreement/Integration Clause
   - Effective date
   - Signature blocks

2. TRANSACTIONAL DOCUMENTS MEMORIALIZE A DEAL

Transactional documents speak as of one particular time (in the case of most, the date of their execution). This means they are intended to capture the agreements of the parties, to set out their respective rights and obligations, and to establish rules that will govern future dealings. They must provide for substantially all of the details of the parties' future dealings or they fail in their job.

3. THE DOCUMENT'S TITLE AND INTRODUCTION

Generally, the first page of any transactional document begins with a title in all caps, centered, and underlined. The title should identify the type of contract using a generic term, such as "Lease," "Prenuptial Agreement," or "Asset Purchase Agreement."

The introduction paragraph is not numbered. It should be in the form:[1]

> *This [Agreement, Lease, etc. as appropriate] ("the [Defined Term]") dated [as of], 20xx, is between, [a Corporation, Limited Liability Company, General Partnership, an Individual, etc., as appropriate] ("[Defined Term]")[2] and, [a Corporation, Limited Liability Company, General Partnership, an Individual, etc., as*

---

[1]   Note the form used to define a term. It should be used consistently throughout the document. For ease of future use of this agreement as an exemplar for future transactions, choose generic defined terms like "Buyer," "Seller," "Landlord," "Tenant," etc. This allows a change of party name in the first paragraph to ripple or flow through the document automatically when the document is used as an exemplar in a subsequent matter.

[2]   Bracketed—[ ]—text in examples is optional language or language needing replacement when drafting a specific provision. Brackets should be deleted when using these provisions.

appropriate] ("[Defined Term]") [add additional parties as needed].

For example:

This asset purchase agreement (the "APA") dated September 21, 2003, is between Mayfield & Associates, LLC, a Delaware limited liability company (the "Buyer") and Bronson Construction, Inc., a California Corporation (the "Seller").

The first paragraph of the agreement identifies the parties and the type of transaction they are documenting, establishes defined terms for the parties, and provides a reference date for the document. Ensure that all parties' names and other information (such as state of incorporation) are correct—using defined terms means they will not come up again until the signature blocks. Beyond these items there is no need for further detail. Leave that for the recitals and the body of the contract.

4.   PREAMBLES, RECITALS, AND TRANSITIONING INTO THE AGREEMENT

Preambles or recitals set the context for the agreement and are useful in later interpretation. They also provide a place to list related transactional documents and other things that may be part of the transaction as a whole but are otherwise not referenced in the particular agreement. Preambles or recitals do not need to be preceded by the word "whereas" and it is not necessary to title the section, Recitals, although you will no doubt run into those forms (and those who aggressively adhere to them) in practice.

Each recital should be written in plain English and should be preceded by a capital letter, numbering, or ordinal system (just like this section of this text). In the recitals, include facts that will help a later reader grasp the nature, purpose, and basis for the agreement.

Examples of appropriate facts for recitals include: (i) the relationship and goals of the parties, (ii) the nature of the transaction, and (iii) other transactional documents and things associated with the transaction. Take care to be accurate and not to include unnecessary facts in the recitals—they may be used later in litigation to prove that which they state. When in doubt, be more general than specific in the recitals. Avoid the temptation to recite everything.

Immediately after the recitals, you will want to draft a transition to begin the substantive portions of the agreement. One useful formulation is:

The parties agree [as follows]:

It is not necessary or desirable to draft a lengthy transition using archaic phrases, such as:

> *Know all men by these presents: Now, THEREFORE, and in consideration of the premises and the mutual promises, terms, and conditions stated herein, the parties do now AGREE as follows:*

If your recitals are stated prior to a section of the document that is labeled "agreement" or could be construed as the real agreement, as distinct from the mere recitals, then the accuracy of the recitals should be addressed in the real agreement section. This can be done by including a provision stating that the parties represent and warrant to one another that the recitals are accurate, perhaps with a "to the best of their knowledge" limitation. Alternatively, the parties may desire to disclaim any implication that they are representing or warranting that the recitals are accurate. This can be accomplished by introducing the subject recital with *"[specify party] asserts that [state recital]."* In either case, a provision regarding the accuracy of the recitals should be expressed clearly in the main agreement section of the document to avoid any implication that the recitals are not part of the agreement.

5. DEFINITIONS AND DEFINED TERMS: A POWERFUL TECHNIQUE TO ENHANCE MEANING AND READABILITY

When an agreement's definitions are numerous or complicated, the defined terms should be set out alphabetically in a separate section located near the beginning or end of the agreement. If the document is a short one, if definitions are not numerous, or if it makes sense for some other reason, definitions can be introduced the first time they occur, including in the preamble, the introductory paragraph, or the recitals. For example:

> *This ASSET PURCHASE AGREEMENT AND ESCROW INSTRUCTIONS (the "Agreement") is entered into and effective as of [date], at [city], [state], by and between _____ (the "Seller"), and _____ (the "Buyer"), on the basis of the following facts and constitutes (i) a contract of purchase and sale between the parties and (ii) escrow instructions to _____ (the "Escrow Agent"), the consent of whom appears at the end of the Agreement.*

> —or—

> *THIS LEASE, made at _____, _____, on the__ day of _____, 20__, between _____ a _____ _____ (the "Landlord"), and _____, a (the "Tenant").*

> *1. Premises. Landlord hereby leases to Tenant, and Tenant hereby hires and takes from Landlord, upon the terms and conditions below, the premises containing approximately____*

square feet located in _____ and outlined in red on Exhibit "A" attached hereto, which are located on the _____ _____ floor(s) of the building (the "Building") located at _____.

2. Term. The term of this lease shall be for_____ _____ (__) years and shall commence on the _____ day of _____, 20__ (the "Commencement Date"), and end on the ___ day of ___ ___ ___, 20__, (the "Termination Date").

Defined terms used in only one section may be defined when used. If defined when used and a definitions section is included, the term should be included in the definition section as well, stating "defined as stated in section ___" for its definition. The idea is to ensure that, if the definition is changed, the change will ripple through the document automatically to avoid ambiguity that could be caused by revising one appearance of the definition and not another.

Defined terms are powerful tools that can decrease the length and increase the readability of substantive provisions. They are the solution that allows you to draft to avoid leaving out a concept while not cluttering your provisions with litanies of near-synonymous terms. They enable you to retain the list of necessary terms. At the same time, they increase the readability of your document by unpacking your provisions. In the same way that nicknames can make it easier to refer to a person, defined terms simplify references to longer, more detailed concepts.

For example, one definition of the word "claim" might be: "Any right to payment, whether or not such right is reduced to judgment, or is liquidated, fixed, contingent, matured, disputed, legal, equitable, or secured, or a right to an equitable remedy for breach of performance whether or not such right to an equitable remedy is reduced to judgment, fixed, contingent, matured, disputed, or secured." 11 U.S.C. § 101(5) (bankruptcy code definition of "claim"). If this definition is provided for separately in the document, the single word "claim" can be used when needed in the contract's substantive provisions and its broad meaning is included without need for the litany.

Beware: Overly broad or narrow definitions can inadvertently introduce ambiguity or reallocate beliefs and burdens. Defined terms can also be used to intentionally cloud meaning. The less than careful reader will often assume that a term has its ordinary, lay meaning and will not refer to a definitions section for clarification. Consider a contract that provides that refund claims submitted to a local company "will be Paid In Full within 90 days of Receipt." The initial-capped terms are defined, many pages away, as meaning "compensated in lawful money of [name of non-domestic country or state], calculated at the then prevalent exchange rate" and "when received by the Claims Processor [itself defined as a company in China]," respectively. Consider the ethical implications of using defined terms to obfuscate or mislead. Does it matter to these considerations if the contract is a form, once prepared by a team of lawyers that is distributed by non-lawyers to commercial clients? To consumers? Beyond ethics, what about the morality of that conduct? Is there a standard to judge when elegant, persuasive drafting of a contract crosses a line and is criminal, tortious, unethical, or immoral? What is that standard?

But be careful—if you define a term, it must only be used in the defined sense in the document. If not, ambiguity crops up. This is directly opposed to the practice of elegant variation from English composition classes. Those courses often encourage the use of different words for the same concept to avoid repetitive prose. The rule is different in legal drafting. Repetitive prose is the order of the day if expressing the same concept. Use the same words for the same meanings every time.

To protect against inadvertent use of defined terms that may create ambiguity, many drafters adopt a standard form of defined term that varies the normal rules of format, capitalization, and the like. Examples include: Initial Caps, ALL CAPS, *italics*, **boldface**, or <u>underlining</u>.

Initial capitalization drapes the defined term in the mantle of a proper noun. This is appropriate because, within the document, the term essentially becomes a proper noun. This book places the defined term in parentheses and quotes when it is defined, with an appropriate article, if any, outside the quotes but inside the parentheses, *e.g.*,:

> . . . June 7, 2005 (the "Due Date").

When the defined term is later used, it is in initial capitals (also known as Initial Caps), *e.g.*,:

> . . . on the Due Date, the Payer shall. . .

Finally, take care to make the definition either inclusive or exclusive. Consider, for example, whether trade secrets constitute Intellectual Property under each of the following definitions:

> Inclusive: *"Intellectual Property" means intellectual property as that term is generally used and includes all patents, copyrights, and trademarks.* (Yes).

> Exclusive: *"Intellectual Property" means patents, copyrights, and trademarks.* (No).

> Ambiguous: *"Intellectual Property" means and includes patents, copyrights, and trademarks.* (Maybe?).

6. INFORMATION SCHEDULES

Certain sections of agreements are designed to elicit information from the parties to the agreement, such as lists of existing indebtedness, contracts, subsidiaries, etc. Those items should be included as a schedule to the agreement or identified as having been delivered under the agreement. Identification of the schedules can be by sequential numbering or lettering or may correspond to the numbers of the sections addressing this information in the agreement. Rather than leaving the form of schedules as an open issue to be resolved after the parties have signed the main transactional documents, negotiate and agree to them up front. This will avoid later disputes when one party will have gained or lost negotiating leverage. This establishes that everyone knows what is expected and helps to avoid later, disruptive disputes.

7. INFORMATIONAL DOCUMENTS

Where an agreement requires the delivery of existing documents or certificates, copies of the documents do not need to be attached to the agreement as long as it states that the documents will be delivered prior to closing. Often, the attorney will also want the representations and warranties of the party to apply to these documents. The documents should be accurately identified and incorporated into the agreement with a specific reference in the representations or warranty section.

8. SUPPLEMENTAL DOCUMENTS

Where an agreement calls for the execution and delivery of other, related documents (notes, employment agreements, security documents, etc.), consider attaching forms of these documents as consecutively numbered or lettered exhibits ("in substantially the form of Exhibit A to this Agreement"). As with schedules to an agreement, it is the best practice to negotiate the form of supplemental documents up front rather than leaving them for negotiation and preparation after execution of the main agreement. Among other things, this will force the parties and counsel to really think through all aspects of the deal and make appropriate arrangements for all foreseeable contingencies. This practice can make for bulky documents; however, the benefits generally outweigh the extra work and paper expended on the front end to prevent later disputes.

9. SUBSTANTIVE PROVISIONS AS EXHIBITS

Consider including complicated provisions dealing with special aspects of the transaction (complex valuation or pricing formulas, for example) as exhibits. This is common practice in real estate transactions, where a metes and bounds description of property can be long and cumbersome. It is often used in purchase contracts, where pricing formulas and worksheets can be complex, but its use can be expanded into many other areas of practice.

10. THE TABLE OF CONTENTS

Include a table of contents listing all major sections and all schedules and exhibits in any agreement of more than ten pages. Consider doing so even with shorter documents.

11. CROSS-REFERENCES AND PARAGRAPH REFERENCES

Cross-referencing can help cut down on otherwise repetitive provisions. It is generally better to cross-reference to articles, sections, and paragraphs rather than pages, as pages change in the drafting process. A good general rule is to use the word "section" to refer to separate provisions of a formal agreement and the word "paragraph" to refer to separate provisions of an informal letter or letter agreement. The key is to be specific and consistent. Remember to proofread cross-references at the very end of the drafting process to make sure they remain accurate. Some drafters prefer to leave the section or paragraph reference blank until the last draft, *e.g.*, "section ___", essentially forcing themselves to proof the cross-references.

12. HEADINGS

Each major section of a transactional document should have a heading. The heading describes the substance of that portion of the document at a high level of generality. Headings enable readers to quickly skim through the document or the table of contents and find the provision that she wishes to consult.

Writing good headings can be difficult. The heading should not be over-inclusive or under-inclusive. Having a heading that refers to matters not touched on in the provision itself can give rise to contextual ambiguity at a minimum and may render the provision legally ineffective, for example in the case of a disclaimer of warranties that is not clear and conspicuous because it is not referenced in the provision's heading.

Although many, if not most, contracts will feature boilerplate provisions stating that the headings are inserted for convenience and are not part of the contract itself, one should not rely upon such a provision. However, courts have often looked to the headings of a contract (or a statute) in order to interpret it, notwithstanding such provisions.

13. SUBSTANTIVE NUMBERS

It is common practice that numbers used in legal agreements are both spelled and represented in numerals to avoid confusion, ease proofreading, and make later alteration more difficult. For example, the sum of five thousand, five hundred dollars ($5,500) will be paid at closing. The only justification professed for this practice that makes any sense today is that it makes later alteration or forgery more difficult. Using the written-out and numerical format makes it harder to slip in an extra zero or delete one.

Recognizing that large numbers are difficult to read when expressed in words, drafters long ago began placing numbers in parentheticals to aid the reader. This makes reading easier and the form has stuck. Because drafters continued to express the number in words also, discrepancies between the two sometimes occurred. This made it necessary to develop rules governing how to resolve the ambiguity. *See, e.g.,* U.C.C. § 3–114 (contradictory terms; typewritten terms prevail over printed terms, handwritten terms prevail over typewritten or printed terms, and words prevail over numbers).

Leading commentators on modern formal use of English disfavor writing out numbers as words. Unless concerns about alteration of the document are strong, drop the double form of expression and use numerals exclusively. Alternatively, write out the numbers one through ten in words and use numerals for 11 and up. Either system makes documents easier to proofread and prevents the opportunity for words to conflict with numerals, eliminating another source of ambiguity. As with other matters of style, be sensitive to your audience. If that audience is willing to embrace modern plain English drafting styles, use them. If, however, your client expects numerals and words to be used to express numbers, by all means take that into account. Whatever you do, be consistent. Where concerns regarding alteration of the document are strong, use the double format, as in the case of checks and other negotiable instruments. Read and proofread substantive numbers carefully—mistakes can be costly to fix.

14. EXEMPLAR CONSIDERATIONS

The term "exemplar" rather than the word "form" is used in the title of this section because, except for the most basic documents, there are no real forms in the sense of "fill in the blanks and it is done." Most true forms will be more cost-effectively prepared by counsel's assistant or paralegal. Counsel should think of the documents used as precedent for new documents as examples or models of what was done in the last, similar deal and proceed to modify the entire document to fit the new transaction. You may also describe exemplars as precedent documents—a formulation that highlights their use in prior, somewhat analogous transactions, and the need to apply precedent to the new and different matter at hand. When using an exemplar, analyze each provision and whether it is appropriate for the current transaction. Do not include unnecessary provisions or ones that you do not understand just because they are in the exemplar.

To save time and expense, maintain exemplars from prior deals, or exemplars that otherwise cross your desk or desktop so that they can be accessed and tailored for a new transaction quickly. This is most easily accomplished by maintaining files in word processing format in separate folders in your computer system along with an index listing file names, document title, and comments (*e.g.*, LeaseLL.wpd, Lease of Real Property, Landlord Oriented). When a similar matter arises, you will be able to consult the index, pull up the exemplar, and proceed to tailor the document to the specifics of the new deal. This technique will greatly speed your revision of the document if your agreements use generic defined terms for parties and other deal specifics. You can then change these items in the preamble and definitions sections and proceed to review and modify the substantive provisions. Remember, laws and practices change; exemplars do not. Always understand what substantive provisions and legal phrases mean. Do not simply parrot a document. It may be outdated.

Finally, remember that an exemplar from a prior transaction was right for that transaction, not the current one. It represents a negotiated compromise of issues that were in play in that prior deal. Said another way, it represents an allocation of risk and reward, benefit and burden, between those parties at that time. This being the case, it is best to view the exemplar with a critical, not an accepting, eye and reset the provisions to a neutral position or one that favors your client before proposing the document to the other side. Another way to address this situation is to start with an exemplar from a deal in which the party on your client's side of the current deal had the most leverage. In such a situation, most of the provisions should be slanted in favor of your client from the beginning.

D. DRAFTING RULES

This section presents a detailed list of general rules for contract drafting. In contrast to the prior chapter, these rules focus on the micro level of the contract or transactional document—the sentence and word level. Skim the list and use it as a reference on points where guidance is needed.

1. THE ACTIVE VOICE—WHO DOES WHAT, TO WHOM, WHEN

The active voice of English grammar is characterized by a sentence structure in which an actor (the subject) performs an action (the verb) on or in relation to another thing (the object). Contract clauses should be drafted in the active voice whenever possible. Test your clauses by looking for the Subject-Verb-Object (SVO) structure. To be complete, each clause should specify who is doing what, to whom (or what), when to be complete.

2. HEREIN

If you are trying to say "in this document," say that—name the document (using a defined term—this Agreement, this Lease, etc.—can be helpful here). If you are trying to say "in this paragraph/section/etc.," just say it.

The same applies to all the here-, there- and -said words like hereby, hereinafter, therefore, therein, aforesaid, etc. Similarly, "same," and "such" should be avoided if at all possible. They are weak substitutes for proper pronouns and good defined terms. They can also create ambiguous references.

3. AND/OR—AMBIGUITY ALERT

"And" is generally inclusive. To draw on tort language, it is joint and several. "And" can mean A and B, together (jointly), and each separate and apart (severally). But there are times when "and" needs to be restricted to its joint sense (when "A and B" means only both together). "Or" can be exclusive (A or B but not both) or inclusive. *See* American Surety Co. v. Marotta, 287 U.S. 513, 53 S.Ct. 260, 77 L.Ed. 466 (1933) (holding that "or" includes "and"); 11 U.S.C. § 102(5) (accord).

A partial solution may be the use of "and" only jointly, "or" only severally, and "and/or" to indicate joint and several relationships. This could be accomplished by use of a provision defining the terms. This would require one to carefully and consistently use the defined terms appropriately. Because 100% consistency is the exception rather than the rule, this may be unworkable in the rigors of actual practice. Many commentators recommend strongly against the use of "and/or," finding it ambiguous and/or a sign of hasty, sloppy drafting although this author does not find it objectionable to show a joint and severed relationship between items on a list. One can also use constructions such as "A or B or both," "A or B but not both," or "A and B together but not separately" and the like. Confront the issue, adopt a workable solution, and apply it uniformly to your drafting.

4. SHALL, WILL, MUST, AND MAY

The key problem here is that "shall" is commonly (mis)used for all four words, causing ambiguity. "May" is permissive—meaning the actor has an option of taking an action or receiving a benefit—it expresses a right. "Shall," on the other hand, means the actor has no choice, he has a duty.

At or before the closing, the Seller shall *deliver the Purchase Price to the Escrow Agent.*

Buyer may *waive any of the conditions to Buyer's performance in its sole and absolute discretion.*

Differentiate between rights (permissive) and duties (mandatory). Rights are "may" phrases (tenants may landscape the area adjacent to the patio); duties are "shall" phrases (tenants shall clean and maintain the area around their front doors in good repair). If the word "must" could be substituted, "shall" is appropriate. It is best to use shall—which is fairly archaic English—only to refer to duties.

"Will" is predictive but is otherwise similar to "shall," as it may refer to a duty. When indicating a duty, it is best to stick to "shall" (or "must") and eliminate "will" to avoid the implication of different meanings. "Will," being predictive, is appropriate when speaking of future events.

> *If the bill passes as it is, the President* will *veto it. At the end of this session, the Legislature* will *adjourn. At that time, Contractor* shall *begin installation of new carpet in the Assembly Chamber.*

> *The closing will take place at [address].*

If the name of a party does not appear before the word "shall" in an apparent shall/duty clause, it is probably an incorrect use of the imperative tense. For example, agreements often state that they "shall" be governed by the law of a particular state. This is incorrect. Rather, the agreement should state the choice of law clause as a present tense actual circumstance, i.e., using "is."

> *This agreement is governed by the laws of [state].*

If the provision is a declaration of a future fact, use "will" in its predictive sense instead of "shall."

> *Final approval or disapproval will occur no later than June 1, 2008.*

Note that this same phrase, cast in the active voice to identify the actor, becomes a "shall clause":

> *The Buyer shall approve or disapprove performance no later than June 1, 2008.*

Drafters should also include consequences of a failure to perform the duty, either by listing it as an event of default that may trigger a remedy or by specifying that failure to, for example, approve or disapprove performance by a set date, will not be deemed to be approved.

5. DOUBLETS, TRIPLETS, AND OTHER FORMS OF SYNONYMOUS REPETITION

Avoid legal doublets and triplets unless each has an independent purpose that cannot be served by increasing the level of generality.

These are those famous repetitious chains of words that are part of the hoary legal chant that has come down through the ages. Examples: null and void; settlement and compromise; swear and affirm; right, title, and interest; etc. Ask yourself, do I really need each of these terms? Will fewer do? Will listing these terms leave the provision vulnerable to the doctrine of *expressio unis et exclusio alterius*? If so, consider using a more general term that contains within its meaning all desired alternatives.

Further, tucking a general reference such as "etc." or "and the like" at the end of a list to cure the *expressio unis* problem may invoke the dangers of the doctrine of *ejusdem generis*. When using a general reference, look back at the specific examples previously given. They establish the scope of the general reference, limiting its effectiveness in expanding the scope of the list. This discussion illustrates the contradictions within the canons of construction and the equitable maxims. There is usually a canon or maxim that counters another canon or maxim.

Examine lists of synonymous terms and rank them in a hierarchy. Are they all of the same rank? If not, this is an indicator that *expressio unis* and *ejusdem generis* problems may be lurking in the list. Consider eliminating lower rank words and using fewer words of a higher rank. Consider the list "carrots, peas, and other vegetables." Why not replace all three words with one, "vegetables." Similarly, the list "tigers, lions, and other animals" can be reduced to "animals." Legal terms can be similarly arranged and the term or terms at the correct hierarchical level can be chosen.

On the other hand, do not indiscriminately delete pairs or triplets. Although they may have similar meaning, pairs or triplets may still function as more than simply a list of synonyms. For example, in a land sale agreement, the seller should be under a duty to execute and deliver the deed to the property. Execution without delivery (and vice versa) is ineffective to transfer title.

6. OMIT NEEDLESS WORDS

The statements made in this section are general ones, and you must evaluate, in each instance, whether the general advice should be followed. In drafting agreements, concentrate on whether your chosen word has the correct level of specificity. Underlying these rules is the belief that overdressing one's writing makes it harder to read and does not demonstrate education or sophistication. Rather, education and sophistication are shown by elegant drafting that makes its meaning clear with little effort on the reader's part. Of course, reasonable minds can differ on matters such as word choice. Use the following suggestions as a guide, but, as with most legal drafting, it is best for you to make up your own mind as to what is appropriate under particular circumstances.

Avoid compound prepositions:

Avoid	Use Instead
the question as to whether	whether (the question whether)
all of the issues	all the issues
at that point in time	then
in the nature of	like

Avoid overly showy words:

Avoid	Use Instead
additionally	also
adequate number of	enough, sufficient
adjacent	next to (specify distance?)
aforesaid	previous, prior
any and all	any
at the time	when
approximately	about
at [the] present [time]	now
by means of	by
cease and desist	stop, cease
circumstances in which	when, where
commence	begin
contained in	in
contiguous	next to
due [to the fact that]	because
eventuates	occurs, happens
facilitate	help, assist
has a negative impact	harms
including but not limited to	including
inquire	ask
null and void	void
notify	tell, inform
permit	let, allow
penultimate	second to last
request	ask

retain	keep
ultimate	last
utilize	use

7. USE FAMILIAR AND CONCRETE WORDS; AVOID LAWYERISMS

"Witnesseth," "Now, Therefore," "Know all men by these presents," "Based on the above premises," "In consideration of the following covenants and conditions," and the like can all be eliminated. Use common English in their place:

Accordingly, the parties agree:

"Witnesseth" in particular, and "Now, Therefore" and "Know all men by these presents" reflect what contract drafting is all about: providing an accurate, objective written record of a transaction that can be referred to by the parties or others, now or later. It is making a record of the deal struck, to borrow a phrase from litigation practice. These terms thus make historical sense, but they can be avoided safely when drafting modern transactional documents.

8. USE NORMAL WORD ORDER AND INVERSIONS FOR EMPHASIS

The normal, active voice, word order in English is subject, verb, and object. If you wish to change this order for emphasis, remember that the strongest places in the sentence are the beginning and the end. Generally, stick to the subject, verb, object (SVO) order. The best contract clauses follow this order and tell the reader who, is to do what, to whom, when.

9. HYPHENS

Limit your use of hyphens. Generally, hyphens should be used to form compound adjectives.

The short-term loan agreement contained a cross-default clause.

There are exceptions. Nonpayment, intercompany, and pro rata should all be written without hyphens. Even if omitting a hyphen results in a double letter, a hyphen should generally not be used to attach a prefix to a word. However, if the result would cause confusion or mispronunciation (such as in the case of co-op or re-lease), a hyphen is justified. GARNER § 1.61, at 36.

In some cases, hyphens are helpful in distinguishing between use of a word as a verb (no-hyphen) or a noun (hyphen). Verb: *". . . the bank is entitled to set off any deposit . . ."* Noun: *". . . the bank is entitled to a set-off in the event . . ."* But the same effect can be generated with the use of an article to indicate the noun, as is also done in this example with the indefinite article "a."

When in doubt as to the use of a hyphen, write the word as one unit without a hyphen.

10.   PARENTHESES

A sentence containing a parenthetical expression is punctuated outside the parenthesis exactly as if the parenthetical expression were absent. The parenthetical expression itself is punctuated as if it stood by itself, except that the final or terminal punctuation mark is omitted unless it is a question mark or an exclamation point.

> *Payments of interest should be made quarterly (on the first business day of each quarter), but will be compounded daily.*

> *The defendant protested (and why should we doubt his word?) that he had delivered the goods as specified.*

(When a wholly detached statement is contained in parentheses, the final punctuation comes before the closing of the parenthesis, as here.) Garner reminds writers that "[i]f the writer's purpose is to make the parenthetical content stand out rather than hide, a pair of dashes is probably the better tool." GARNER § 1.33, at 21.

11.   SOME BASIC RULES OF GRAMMAR RELEVANT TO DRAFTING CONTRACTS

a.   Forming the Possessive

i.   Form the possessive singular of nouns by adding " 's" even if the singular noun ends in "s."

James's case. The judge's ruling.

Note that the possessive is *not* used when specifying a time period, such as for a notice period. For example it is "20-days notice" (compound adjective form) rather than "20 days' notice" or worse, "20 day's notice" (incorrect possessive forms).

An apostrophe followed by an "s" is often used to form the plural of letters, single-digit numbers, and symbols. While this form looks like possessive form, it is merely plural. It is incorrect to pluralize names with an apostrophe followed by "s". For example, "the Brown's" is the incorrect plural form. The correct plural form is "the Browns" with no apostrophe. GARNER § 1.79, at 42.

ii.   Form the possessive plural by adding an apostrophe

The lawyers' presentations

iii. Its, it's, his, and hers

"Its" is the possessive form of "it."

"It's" is a contraction for "it is."

"His" and "hers" are possessive and take no apostrophe.

b. Use of the Semicolon Versus the Colon

i. The Semicolon

When joining two or more grammatically complete (independent) clauses without a conjunction, use a semicolon.

The attorney's argument was compelling; he persuaded the jury.

Apart from being used to separate items in a list that are themselves long or compound, this punctuation mark has limited relevance to contracts and transactional documents. If you find that you are using semicolons in transactional documents other than as part of a list, examine your use carefully.

ii. The Colon

A colon directs the reader to what follows. It usually follows an independent clause and can be used to introduce a variety of related statements: a list of particulars, a quotation, an appositive, an illustration, or an amplification. Even two independent clauses can be joined with a colon if the second interprets or amplifies the first.

A list can have only one item.

It is not necessary to use a colon every time a list is introduced. For example, "The model you like is available in red, blue, white, and ochre" takes no colon. Overuse of a colon with lists is cumbersome.

The first letter of the word that follows a colon is capitalized unless that word is the first in a list of multiple items, in which case each item begins with a lower case letter.

iii. Slashes

The slash should not be used in legal writing because of the ambiguity involved. The slash could indicate "and" (conjunctive) or "or" (disjunctive), thus creating unnecessary ambiguity. The only acceptable uses for a slash in legal writing are for dates and fractions.

c. The Series Comma and Semicolon

i. In a compound sentence composed of a series of short independent clauses the last two of which are joined by a conjunction, commas should be placed between the clauses and before the conjunction:

The attorney presented his closing argument, the judge instructed the jury, and the jury retired to consider the case.

ii. In a series consisting of three or more elements, the elements are separated by commas. When a conjunction joins the last two elements in a series, a comma is used before the conjunction:

Small, Nelson, and Lee attended the conference.

The owner, the agent, and the tenant were having an acrimonious discussion.

iii. Although not technically correct, increasingly, writers often delete the last comma in the series: "Payments should be made to the bank, the payee[,] or the agent." The technically correct method is to include that last comma. Using the last comma will never be wrong, but omitting it may cause confusion. Whichever method you choose, be consistent throughout the document and examine your result carefully to ensure your intended meaning is clear and legally precise.

iv. In a series consisting of three or more elements that are themselves either clauses or subseries, use a semicolon in place of a comma for the highest level of the list. For example, "the available color combinations are red, white, and blue; yellow, green, and tan; gold, red, and purple."

d. Subject and Verb Must Agree in Number

i. The number of the subject determines the number of the verb. This is true even if other nouns are connected to it by "with," or "no less than."

The statute, as well as the regulation, favors a strict construction.

The statutes favor a strict construction.

ii. Plural Versus Singular Nouns

A. Remember—forum, memorandum, datum, and criterion are singular; fora, memoranda, data, and criteria are plural.

B. Singular verbs should be used with "either" and "any" and, in its usual form, "neither . . . nor."

12. QUOTATION MARKS

Proper English grammar requires quotation marks to close after the terminal punctuation of a sentence.

"Oh, no."

The parties exclaimed, "We have a deal!"

Many lawyers, however, place the quotes before the terminal punctuation in order to avoid the implication that the punctuation has itself been quoted. The same effect can be generated with the use of square brackets to indicate the inclusion of the punctuation.

The first word of the sentence is "help[.]"

The recommended method is to use proper English grammar—quotes after terminal punctuation—unless there is substantial concern about confusion. In that case, the square bracket method should be used to indicate that the terminal punctuation is a modification of the quoted language.

If you are only quoting one word, you have some discretion. Periods and commas should be included inside the quotation marks. Question marks and exclamation points may be either inside or outside the marks at the drafter's discretion. Colons and semicolons should be placed outside the quotation marks.

13. SPACING AFTER SENTENCES

Two spaces are used after a sentence's terminal punctuation and the first word of the next sentence. This aids the reader when skimming or speed-reading the document by providing the eye with a double space to identify the beginning of the next sentence.

E. DOCUMENT REVIEW AND COMMENTS

Before discussing contract drafting further, a few remarks are in order regarding the process that takes place after you have initially drafted a contract or other legal document: review by others and the inevitable comments and criticism that you will receive.

F. COMMENTS AND MARK-UPS INDICATE INTEREST IN YOUR WORK

When someone reviews your work and proceeds to mark it up or otherwise make comments, this is not a sign of failure. In fact, to the extent that the reviewer, be it client, supervising attorney, or opposing counsel, makes any comments at all, this expresses interest in the document and shows that you have the reviewer's attention. When given a document to review, most lawyers reach for a pen, knowing that they will use it. Receiving comments and mark-ups of your work is par for the course. You should get used to it as soon as possible to avoid unnecessary pain and anguish.

G. DIFFERENT CONSIDERATIONS FOR DIFFERENT REVIEWERS

Who will be doing the review and providing the comments?

1. YOUR COLLEAGUES AND SUPERVISORS

Especially when starting out, the first group to review your documents will probably be your colleagues and supervisors in a firm. These comments will be designed to improve the documents and your client's position. As such, you should receive them as what they are: constructive commentary from a different perspective, produced with the benefit of different experiences and knowledge that are meant to improve the final work product. They are not a personal indictment of your failure to grasp what needs to be done.

First, make any suggested changes that improve the document, then make the other ones that do not harm the document (this is much easier than explaining why you do not think they are necessary). Disregard, with explanation, the ones that harm the document. Even if you are in the unfortunate position of receiving comments that appear designed to undermine your confidence and sense of self-worth (which does happen from time to time), you should look for the constructive, beneficial points hidden within what may appear to be venom. Even comments that seem minor or purely stylistic are important. They should be internalized so that the next project involving that commentator incorporates the feedback from the last project in its first draft. Do not incorporate these changes into all your projects in the future, unless (a) you like them or (b) you are working with another client, or colleague, with similar style.

A very effective technique to minimize your reviewer's time and effort and to focus attention on the areas that most require review is to use black lining, also known in modern parlance as track changes from its name in the Microsoft Word™ user interface. Knowing how to use track changes and the comment function in Word™ has become just as much a required skill for attorneys as touch typing.

In a black-lined document, revisions are indicated by using ~~strikeout~~ text to indicate deletions from a prior draft and <u>underlining</u> to indicate additions. The beauty of black lining is that, when reviewing successive generations of drafts, the reviewer knows exactly what is new and needs to be reviewed, the other material presumably having been approved earlier. Black lining may even be appropriate at the first draft stage if you are basing the document on an exemplar, especially one prepared by your reviewing attorney.

If you use black lining it must be accurate and complete. Inaccurate black lining will establish your reputation as sloppy within your firm and with your client. With opposing counsel it is likely to create distrust and concern about your ethics.

It is also valuable to communicate to the reviewer what you need reviewed, when you need it back, and other contextual matters. Find out how they like to get this information, what information they like to get, and the best method for getting it to them.

To minimize comments about your work that may negatively impact your reputation, take great care to make your document as good as you can before turning it over for review. Attorneys and clients are busy people for whom time and effort are valuable resources. Skilled practitioners can spot a misspelled or misused word, a grammatical mistake, or even an extra space from a mile away. These distractions impede their review of the substance of your prose—they feel compelled to scratch in a correction with their pen.

Learn the drafting rules of your supervising attorney and follow them slavishly before turning in work for review. Although most supervising attorneys will clean up your grammatical and typographical mistakes, this is not their job. Forcing them to do so is not good for your career. Develop your eye for detail as early as possible.

Finally, especially for new attorneys, it is easy to find yourself in a cycle of endless revisions that are rather pointless. After a certain point, polishing results adds no further material increase in quality. If you bill your client for the time spent on these rounds of revisions, your work product will be overpriced. If you do not bill for the time, you will be working without compensation. If you find yourself making endless rounds of nonsubstantial changes, such as changing all instances of "Seller's" to "of the Seller" or vice versa, and are making no meaningful changes—stop.

2. CLIENT REVIEW

The next category of reviewer is your client. The degree of depth of this review depends upon your client representative's level of interest and training. Inside counsel and accountants can be expected to give the document a relatively thorough reading and rarely require much in the way of explanatory cover letters. For those without such detail-intensive backgrounds, you may want to enclose a cover letter highlighting the most important points in the documents or this round of revisions to ensure that the client is on notice of these items and will pay attention to them during the review.

Some clients will not want to review the documents at all, or will be happy to review them at the same time that the other side reviews them. In such a case, the documents should be transmitted with a cover letter to opposing counsel stating that the documents have not yet been reviewed by your client and are therefore subject to modification. It is a good idea to make sure that your client reviews the documents at least once prior to the final draft. You should take note of their comments and modify the documents accordingly. This ensures that you really do understand the directions your client has given to you.

Remember, clients rarely care if you fail to incorporate comments from the other side. They do mind when their comments—however minor, inconsequential, or wrongheaded they may seem to you—are not incorporated or at least discussed with them and discarded after that discussion.

3. REVIEW BY OPPOSING COUNSEL

You have transmitted the documents to the opposing counsel—is your review over? *No.* Take a break, so that your next review of the document will be conducted with fresh eyes. Then, without waiting for opposing counsel to get back to you, review the document one more time and note any corrections that appear. Things will be apparent to you at this stage that you could not see earlier. You will be prepared to raise them in your first conversation with opposing counsel, thus avoiding protests based on notions of waiver, closure, or re-opening negotiations. Your changes will provide you with a selection of trading points to use as consideration for changes requested by opposing counsel.

Encourage opposing counsel to provide you with a marked-up copy of the document showing specific line-edits that are desired, not vague comments like "we need an indemnity here" or "this will not work." It is usually a waste of time for this mark-up to be accompanied by lengthy commentary in the cover letter explaining and justifying each change, and those letters are costly. They should be generated only when it is important to make a detailed record of the negotiations beyond what marked-up drafts would show. This may be the case in extremely large multi-party transactions where one attorney is collecting and synthesizing the comments of many lawyers; in situations when negotiations are going badly and may fall apart, perhaps precipitating lawsuits; or when they are required by clients who wish to receive this sort of costly narration and entertainment.

Comments from opposing counsel fall into one of four categories and should be responded to as follows:

Beneficial to all parties or to the document and the deal. Make the changes, perhaps thanking opposing counsel for insight and contribution in the cover letter.

Matters of style of opposing counsel and changes that do no harm to the documents or your client's position. Consider making the changes. It is less expensive than trying to negotiate out opposing counsel's pet peeves. But also consider how acquiescence across the board can affect the way you are viewed by opposing counsel and your colleagues. Acquiescence can be perceived as a sign of weakness. Sometimes you have to put your foot down and say no to a change that would not really matter to maintain your authority and credibility.

Harmful to either your client's position or the smooth operation of the document. Reject the changes, with an explanation of the problem that they cause. If the effect that opposing counsel was aiming for is evident, and you believe the effect may be desirable or merely neutral, consider suggesting an alternative method of reaching the same end without doing violence to your client's interests or the document.

Valid points for future negotiation. Consider what, if anything, you would request in exchange for the change. You could also be tentative about making the change, perhaps inserting the requested change into the document as an alternative to the original provision, which is also retained. Make reference to the trade off, if any, or to keeping the issue open in your cover letter. Do not acquiesce without receiving something in return unless you and your client have run out of points, issues, and comments. Once you give something away it is difficult or impossible to come back and try to charge for it.

For each comment you receive from opposing counsel, or anyone else, think: what is the point of this comment? What substantive effect are they trying for? Then determine if that effect is acceptable to your client. This may require checking with your client and gaining authority for the change. If acceptable, ask yourself, "Is this the best way to gain this effect?" If it is not, respond with an alternative change that has the same effect, pointing out that it addresses the same issue, but is better because it is more elegant, will take less time to institute, will not affect other issues, is less costly, etc.

For example, a landlord's counsel may demand a large cash security deposit from a start-up tenant with little or no track record. This may be unacceptable or impossible for your client—but your client could obtain a letter of credit from a reputable bank or provide a guaranty from a well-heeled shareholder. Either of the alternatives should satisfy the landlord's legitimate desire for some form of credit support. But, unlike the security deposit, they do not require your client to part with cash at the present time. If the effect is unacceptable, you will have to respond by rejecting the comment or change and, if necessary, explaining why it is unacceptable.

H. CONTROL OF THE DOCUMENT, MAKING REVISIONS, AND SUBSEQUENT DRAFTS

Assuming that your client has the resources and is willing to expend them, the best possible strategy is for you to control the drafting and revision process. This allows you to craft the document's nuances. If you perform the unglamorous word processing services, you will have the opportunity to be the master of the document's intricacies and will be in the best position to protect your client at every opportunity. Indeed, you will likely be the attorney who knows the document the best.

After you have made the changes you and your client are willing to make in response to the opposing counsel's comments, go over the document one more time, looking for conforming changes. If the same language that was changed appears in other locations and it is appropriate to make the changes in those location, do so.

I. REVIEWING DOCUMENTS— A TEN POINT CHECKLIST

When reviewing documents drafted by others and when critically examining your own drafting, use the following questions to focus your review:

1. Parties, Dates, Dollar Amounts, and Interest Rates

    Does the document identify the correct parties in their proper capacities? Are the dates correct? Are all currency amounts and interest rates correct and complete? Never assume that any factual statement is correct. Trust, but verify.

2. Appropriate Structure

    Does the document and the overall structure of the transaction suit your client's needs? Do you understand the deal that is at issue? Is there an alternative structure that is more desirable for your client, perhaps for reasons outside the immediate transaction, such as accounting and tax treatment? Does the document match your client's expectations? Does it match your client's earlier description of the deal to you?

3. Clear, Mandatory Duties, and Optional Rights

    Does the document contain clear mandatory duty provisions regarding all performances by other parties? Are mandatory duties specified using the words "shall" or "must?" Are rights or options expressed in terms of "may?" Do these provisions clearly state who does what, to or for whom or what, when?

Timing of performance is essential; do not neglect to specify the "when."

4. Representations and Warranties

Does the document contain representations and warranties running in favor of your client regarding all facts, statements, and assurances upon which your client is relying? Are any qualities (knowledge, material, thresholds, etc.) appropriate? If these representations and warranties prove false, is there a mechanism (perhaps a covenant coupled with an indemnity, an event of default coupled with a remedy, or a covenant and third party guaranty) for recovering from a credit-worthy entity, for rescinding, or for otherwise modifying the transaction? Does the document require your client to make broad or unnecessary representations and warranties? Can these be estimated, narrowed, or limited in temporal or geographic scope? Can a materiality threshold limiting the representation to things over a certain amount (*e.g.,* claims in excess of $25,000) be added to limit the breadth of the statement? Can a knowledge limitation be inserted so that a representation, especially as to the lack of something, is limited to the knowledge of a specific individual at a specific time? Are those representations and warranties that your client is making factually correct? How about those of the other side? Are there any that you know to be false?

5. Internal and External Consistency

Does the document fit the desired structure? Is it complete and consistent internally and with any other documents involved in the transaction? Defined terms and boilerplate should be consistent across all documents in a transaction to avoid confusion and potential ambiguity. Do all the documents contain a non-severability clause? Are they governed by the same integration, merger, choice of law, choice of forum, and alternative dispute resolution provisions?

6. Substantive Understanding

Do you understand each provision of the document? Review each of them until you understand them completely and their interaction with the other sections of the document and related documents.

7. Hypothesize Performance

Think through the life of the transaction and the document under various fact patterns. What will happen, moment by moment, if the parties comply with all the terms in a timely manner? Sometimes it is useful to think this life cycle through in reverse to determine if the final product is supported in all respects by the agreement's provisions. Are performances required in the proper order?

8. Hypothesize Non-Performance and Default

What if one or both parties fail to perform all or part of the agreement? Are the consequences of failure to perform stated and closely linked to the performance required? Does the document address other issues and problems that are likely to arise in the course of performance? Resolve issues and problems now, at the drafting stage, rather than waiting for the parties to reach the problem. It is likely that the parties will never be more amenable to working out details than they are at the inception of the deal. Capitalize on the opportunity to prevent trouble before it occurs.

9. Address Bankruptcy Risk

Analyze what will happen if one of the parties files a bankruptcy petition or becomes subject to a receivership. Will property or rights that are important to the other party become property of the estate under 11 U.S.C. § 541? Will performance be stayed or affected by the automatic stay of 11 U.S.C. § 362? Will the document be considered an executory contract subject to assumption or rejection under 11 U.S.C. § 365? If so, will this assumption or rejection be possible independently from assumption or rejection of the other documents in the deal? If so, is there a way to structure the transaction so that this property or these rights are held by a third party that is unlikely or unable to be the subject of a bankruptcy case? Can the document incorporate or be incorporated into other documents from which it should not be divisible? Do the recitals in the contract make clear what performances and property rights are important to each of the parties and what injury and damage they may suffer if they are deprived of them? Can you provide for a lien, security interest, or third party credit support, such as a guaranty or letter of credit, to secure the opposing party's payment and performance obligations?

10. Consider the Worst Case Scenario

Assume that the document is executed and the parties become openly hostile, seeking to undermine each other at every opportunity. Will the document provide sufficient guidance to govern the relationship? Will it provide sufficient guidance to a court interpreting the document or imposing remedies if the parties are locked in mortal combat with no thought to the opportunity or litigation costs involved? Although this may be a worst case scenario, that is the appropriate test for a well-drafted transactional document.

J. CONSIDERATION AND THE TERM OF THE AGREEMENT

1. CONSIDERATION

With limited exceptions, to be enforceable, a contract must be supported by mutual consideration. There must be a benefit conferred or a detriment suffered by each party to the contract. Consideration takes a number of forms including cash, promissory notes, letters of credit, transfers of property, services, transfers or surrenders of rights, assumption of another's duty or liability, or mutual promises.

Generally, lack of consideration is not an issue in real life (as compared to in law school), especially as the modern conception of consideration focuses on the bargain test rather than on notions of sufficiency or adequacy, yet it bears remembering. In some jurisdictions there are presumptions of consideration that arise when a written contract recites that consideration has been "had and received" or similar formulations. *See, e.g.,* CAL. CIV. CODE § 1614. Do not forget that not acting, by forbearing or surrendering a right, is consideration just as much as is affirmative action. CAL. CIV. CODE § 1614.

Perhaps the time that consideration comes up the most is when contracts are modified, especially when the modifications amount to a decrease in the duties owed by a single party. A contract to modify an existing contract must generally be supported by mutual consideration. It is good practice to make sure this is the case by providing for consideration on both sides of the deal (the one-dollar-had-and-received formulation of yore), even if your jurisdiction has done away with the common law pre-existing duty rule (requiring more than a pre-existing duty to support a contract). *See, e.g.,* U.C.C. § 2–209(1) (pre-existing duty rule repealed by UCC for sales of goods).

Consideration is also an issue when one party's contractual obligations are supported by a third party's guaranty of payment or performance. In such a circumstance, the guarantor may not appear to be receiving consideration for the guaranty as the only parties receiving benefits are those to the contract being guaranteed; the guarantor appears merely to be gratuitously sticking its neck out for another. Some transactional lawyers put their minds at ease over the guaranty/consideration issue by ensuring that the guaranty states that it is being given by the guarantor to induce one or both of the parties to enter into the primary transaction and having the guarantor sign the guaranty before the parties execute the primary transactional documents.

Most contracts include a statement of consideration near the beginning of an agreement. Examples of statements of consideration include the following (which range from archaic and legalistic to plain English):

> *NOW, THEREFORE, premises considered and in consideration of the mutual covenants and agreements hereinafter set forth and in consideration of one dollar ($1.00) paid by Seller to Buyer, the receipt and adequacy whereof is hereby acknowledged, the Seller and Purchaser hereby covenant and agree as follows:*

—or—

> *NOW, THEREFORE, in consideration of the mutual promises set forth in this Agreement, the parties agree [as follows]:*

—or—

[Accordingly] The Parties agree:

The second formulation is preferable to the first as it retains the notion of agreement and bargain and transitions a reader from the recitals to the main body of the agreement. Further, it strips out all the excess verbosity that seems to elevate form over substance by suggesting that this recital of consideration will make the contract enforceable even if it is not true. Although this may be correct in limited circumstances—option contracts (Restatement (SECOND) OF CONTRACTS § 88), for example—the law is not uniform in this area and the lengthy chant about consideration may give false courage, a sort of whistling in the dark while walking by a graveyard. Better is the short statement of agreement that follows recitals that describe the transaction, including the bargained-for nature of the exchange of covenants and other provisions that can aid in interpretation or demonstrate consideration.

2. ALLOCATION OF CONSIDERATION

This issue is most important in the purchase and sale context, where allocation of the purchase price will affect the buyer's tax basis in the items acquired and the seller's gains and income. Buyers generally favor allocating as much of the price as is reasonably possible first to noncapital assets such as accounts receivable, notes receivable, inventory, and work in progress so as to minimize income later when those items are collected or sold. Then, they allocate the price to assets that can be quickly expensed or depreciated so as to quickly recover the cost. Sellers typically have the reverse preferences, although they may not object to allocations favoring non-capital assets if the capital assets involved have been subject to substantial appreciation over the buyer's holding period (*e.g.,* land held over long periods).

Clauses allocating purchase price often refer to an attached schedule to cut down bulk in the body of the contract. The parties' duties are often phrased in terms of committing to report the transaction to tax and other authorities either "as stated" in the schedule or "in a manner not inconsistent" with the schedule.

3. VARIABLE CONSIDERATION

Provisions for variable consideration are appropriate when the consideration will depend upon future events. Such provisions can include formulas (*e.g.,* percentage of rent provisions which are common in leases and licenses), as well as adjustments to base consideration depending upon the amount of assets, such as receivables or inventory on hand, when a sale transaction closes. It is crucial that the drafter think through all possible outcomes for the formula. On the opposite side of the deal, it is also important to understand the formula proposed by the drafter and any potential impact upon your client. It is often useful to include an example to illustrate the workings of a complex formula or adjustment provision.

Because businesses are not static and because most accounting data and reporting is not yet generated on an instantaneous, dynamic, real-time system, if the contract does not provide a post-closing adjustment mechanism to change the purchase price when the data are reported, one party to the transaction may receive an unintended windfall. Examples include sellers that have unanticipated positive earnings in the period between contract signing and closing, as it is common for the contract to prohibit distributions to owners during this period. Alternatively, if the unexpected financial events are negative, the buyer would suffer the loss. The buyer might be protected by a no-material-adverse change condition to closing, but that is a crude tool that only provides a walk-away right. Post-closing purchase price adjustment provisions can adjust the consideration so that the contract represents the real economic deal that the parties struck without having to engage in brinksmanship and renegotiation after a threat to walk away.

Further, adjustment provisions in sale agreements provide an incentive for the seller to continue to actively manage the business to keep the numbers up rather than sitting back and neglecting things pending the closing. They also provide a mechanism to remedy any misrepresentations or breached warranties.

The forms of adjustment provisions are many. They mirror the way businesses are valued and purchase prices set. Commonly they involve comparison of working capital, net worth, income, or cash flows as of the contract signing (or another date) and the closing date based upon audited financial statements available only after closing. The adjustments can be dollar-for-dollar or a step-function based upon ranges or even just simple pro rating of expenses. To ensure the availability of the funds to make the adjustment, at least on the part of the seller, a purchase price hold-back or payment into escrow is generally recommended.

4. THE TERM OF THE AGREEMENT

1. *The Effective Date.* A contract is generally in force as of its execution, and in the case of execution on different dates, upon the later date. This can, however, be varied by the parties through use of an effective date, either a date certain (*e.g.,* June 22, 2xxx), or a date variable (*e.g.,* 30 days after execution of this contract by both parties).

2. *The Termination Date.* Contracts can continue indefinitely or terminate upon a fixed or variable date and can be extended or terminated by the parties. Extension or early termination can be the subject of an agreement external to the original contract or can be built into the initial contract. It may even be appropriate to define termination by reference to what effect termination has on the rights and obligations of the parties. Termination can be a multifaceted concept, embracing different modifications of the parties' rights, such as termination for or without cause, termination by failure of condition precedent, or termination by condition subsequent. Each of these forms of termination can leave different provisions in force. As you are drafting, identify provisions that need to survive termination to achieve their purpose. For example, confidentiality, non-disclosure, return of trade secrets, and covenants not to compete are provisions that are needed after the termination just as much, if not more than, before termination.

3. *Termination and Renewal; Continuation and Cancellation.* A contract can be drafted so that it regularly terminates and must be renewed by both parties or so that it continues until canceled by one or both parties. These two structures produce different relationships, motivations, and incentives for the parties. Cancellation and renewal, common in real property leases, forces the parties to regularly contemplate whether to renew the contract, providing a regular reminder and opportunity to renegotiate. This is an advantage for the party with the most leverage and power. It also limits bankruptcy risk, as a contract or lease that is extinguished automatically by its own terms is not extended when one of the parties files a bankruptcy petition. The bankruptcy estate takes the debtor's rights subject to the terms of those rights.

On a practical note, however, many clients will be unable to administer an automatic contract cancellation and renewal program, especially if there are many such contracts or the initial terms are short. Remember: no matter how legally exquisite a structure may be, it has to be workable for the client. Otherwise, conduct that does not conform to the contract's terms may produce defenses to enforcement of the contract as written such as waiver, laches, modification by conduct, and the like.

K. CONDITIONS

Besides remedies, if there is one topic that is really useful in the practice of law, which is taught typically in a first-year law school contracts course, it is express conditions. Express conditions are the mechanisms that control how a transaction progresses. When the condition relates to the occurrence of an event outside the control of the parties (death, calamity, effectiveness of a government regulation, a cost of living change, etc.), the condition adjusts the transaction to the change in the outside world. For example, a lease may contain a rent escalator clause that increases the rent based upon increases in the cost of living (the condition).

When the condition is satisfaction of one party's covenant, the condition ensures that each party's duties arise and ripen at precisely the time they are needed to ensure that the other party is able to perform or does not need to perform until it is clear that the second party is ready, willing, and able to perform. For example, a construction contract may provide for periodic payment to the contractor as work progresses based upon submission of a ploy application to the project architect who is to certify that the job is x% complete and that payment (usually partial payment to allow for retainage) is appropriate. The contractor's work and the architect's certification are express conditions to the owner's duty to make payment.

Conditions must be carefully drafted and integrated into the rest of the contract. First, you must take care to clearly draft the condition so its terms are clear. Conditions generally trigger duties ("shall" clauses) or rights ("may" clauses). The reader must be able to determine when the condition is satisfied and, if not, what consequences follow. Word choice is key.

In most contract negotiations, one party will seek to include many conditions, especially conditions to closing or other events when they must part with consideration, and the other will want only a few. For example, in a purchase and sale agreement, the seller will try to limit the conditions to closing to as few objective conditions as possible, such as any needed third party approvals and the lack of any prohibitory injunction or other adverse ruling by governing bodies. By doing so, the seller is seeking to lock the buyer into the deal.

The buyer, on the other hand, will want to build in as many conditions and to keep these conditions as subjective and dependent upon the buyer's own judgment as possible. By doing so the buyer can more easily walk away if due diligence reveals that things are other than as expected, or enjoy the opportunity to later renegotiate terms in exchange for a waiver of the condition. For example, a buyer may seek to include as a condition that its due diligence will conclude with satisfactory results (as judged by the buyer in its sole discretion). This sort of condition can also be framed as "lack of material adverse change" condition to closing. *See generally In re* IBP, Inc. Shareholders Litig., 789 A.2d 14 (Del.Ch.2001) (refusing to allow party to invoke a material adverse change provision to cancel merger and discussing case law regarding such provisions).

Pay careful attention to what "lack of material adverse change" means and who determines whether the condition has been met. Buyers should keep it as subjective as possible and attempt to maintain control over the determination that the condition has been met, while sellers should keep it as objective as possible. Parties may also consider including a materiality threshold to define a material adverse change.

A materiality threshold is a minimum measurement hurdle that must be met for the event to count for purposes of triggering other provisions of the contract. Examples include minimum levels for inventory, receivables, and the like; limiting a "no undisclosed claims or lawsuits" condition, representation, or warranty to those "where the amount in controversy exceeds $100,000;" or a requirement in a financing commitment that the potential borrower have submitted financing applications "to no less than 3 federally chartered financial institutions."

One specific condition should be mentioned: time is of the essence. Generally speaking, the law is that time is not of the essence and delayed performance will be found to constitute substantial performance rather than material breach unless the parties make time for performance an express condition. Thus, the inclusion of the venerable time is of the essence clause, often is the boilerplate section of the contract. Those magic words seem to fix the problem, right? No. Cases are legion in which the courts have found that they are mere boilerplate and are contradicted by other words in the contract or the parties' actions. However, drafters have overcome this challenge by making it clear that the parties agreed that time of performance was material to their deal. To this end, a contract should reference to the time of performance, and perhaps the reason for its importance belongs in the recitals of the contract. A covenant of timely performance also belongs in the consideration section along with all the important economic terms. Finally, an argued consequence of untimely performance such as notice, an opportunity to cure (or not), and a remedy should be provided. One cannot handcuff a determined judge or jury, but one can make it harder for them to dismiss a boilerplate five-word statement of such an important condition.

Another common condition is that of one party obtaining financing and final written approval by all internal and external entities with any jurisdiction over the transaction. Again, the buyer is motivated by two desires: (a) the ability to back out of the deal if it is no longer interested in proceeding for whatever reason and (b) the ability to threaten to back out in order to gain more favorable terms.

Consider the benefits of linking your client's material duties to the condition that the other party use its best efforts to perform either all or an enumerated list of duties under the contract. This is especially worthwhile in the case of parties with unequal economic or bargaining power in which the weaker party's success is dependent upon the stronger party's performance. In those circumstances, a best efforts clause is to the weaker party's advantage. Examples include construction agreements, distribution agreements, and intellectual property agreements. *See, e.g., Polyglycoat Corp. v. C.P.C. Distribs., Inc.*, 534 F. Supp. 200 (S.D.N.Y. 1982) (distributor violated best efforts clause when it chose to promote competing product rather than one manufactured by the plaintiff); *Van Valkenburgh, Nooger & Neville, Inc. v. Hayden Publishing Co.*, 30 N.Y.2d 34, 330 N.Y.S.2d 329, 281 N.E.2d 142 (1972) (publisher breached best efforts clause to promote author's book). Case law demonstrates that inclusion of a best efforts clause may give rise to an almost fiduciary level duty on the part of the burdened party. *Bloor v. Falstaff Brewing Corp.*, 454 F.Supp. 258 (S.D.N.Y.1978) (retailer breached a best efforts clause when it allowed plaintiff's beer brand sales to plummet while retailer implemented a business strategy to maximize its own profits). Even without a best efforts provision, one may be implied into an agreement like an exclusive license. *See Wood v. Lucy, Lady Duff-Gordon*, 222 N.Y. 88, 118 N.E. 214 (1917) (best efforts to market designer's clothing implied in exclusive license per Cardozo, J.). Inclusion of a "best efforts" clause should cause some concern unless the contract defines "best efforts" and provides an objective measure (such as dollars or time spent) for when the standard is met. George W. Kuney, *Best Efforts and Reasonable Efforts Clauses: Couldn't You Try Just a Little Bit Harder*, CAL. BUS. LAW. PRACT. (CEB 2006).

You must confront the fact that parties and courts often ignore or waive conditions. Contracts are often full of clauses providing that a party's failure to act or enforce a right shall not be deemed[3] to be a waiver of that right, and that any waiver of a current right shall not be a waiver of any other right or a future incidence of the same right. The litany continues: time is of the essence; non-severability; no amendment or waiver by conduct; all amendments and waivers must be in writing; recitations that both parties have been represented by counsel, or at least had the opportunity to consult with counsel, have read the agreement, and understand it.

---

[3] "Deeming" something to be the case is what lawyers and judges do when something is not truly the case, but they want it to be.

All these provisions are the parties' attempts to avoid a court's later finding that a provision was waived by conduct, was unconscionable, would otherwise lead to a forfeiture, and the like. A determined court can often find some way to excuse a failed condition and can usually do so in a ruling that is so fact-based that it is largely immune on appeal. (Why are fact-based decisions more immune on appeal than purely legal determinations? Consider the applicable standard of review, generally abuse of discretion (factual findings) or de novo (legal conclusions). The drafter can best guard against this result by

- drafting the consequences of failure of a condition into the condition, thus removing it from the preview of the default and remedy provisions of the agreement;

- employing good boilerplate to document the parties' intention that all the terms of the document be strictly construed; and

- explicitly stating the reason that the condition was included and that the condition was a fundamental inducement for one or more of the parties to enter into the transaction.

When reviewing conditions, focus on what is likely to occur if the condition is not met. Does your client have an appropriate course of action to pursue under the terms of the contract? If not, provide for one. Also, consider whether this test is met for the opposing party. If not, is it better for your client if this remains the case? Or is it better to attempt to fix the potential problem and fill the void? Answers vary enormously depending on context.

L. REPRESENTATIONS, WARRANTIES, COVENANTS, GUARANTIES, AND INDEMNITIES

Contracts frequently use representations, warranties, covenants, releases, guaranties, and indemnities. Each is a different type of provision, and it is important to select the proper type to generate the proper legal effect. Perhaps more than any other set of provisions, those described in this chapter highlight the litigation or default planning aspects of transactional practice and contract drafting. Each of these provisions gives rise to a particular set of causes of action in the event of breach or error.

In particular, representations, warranties, covenants, guaranties, and indemnities are interrelated and reinforce each other. A represented fact will induce a party to enter into negotiation and documentation of a transaction. If a representation is false, a misrepresentation action will support rescission or damages. That representation will likely also be a warranty that survives closing, which would then provide a breach of warranty action that can support an award of damages. A covenant may be used to produce a duty on the part of the warranting party to make the facts as they were warranted. Finally, to the extent that the non-warranting party has been damaged by the breached or incorrect warranty, an indemnity or a guaranty can create a route for damage recovery.

Unlike the way you were probably taught to analyze a set of facts for tort, contract, or property claims—element by element, starting with duty and concluding with damages or other remedies—when thinking as a drafter, you should approach the problem from the desired remedy first. For example, if certain facts are misstated, what remedy do you want? Possibilities include pre-closing rescission, post-closing rescission, or consequential or liquidated damages from the other party or from a creditworthy third party. Then draft the type of provision that will produce a cause of action for your client that is ripe when needed, lies against the appropriate defendant, and provides the desired remedy.

M. GENERAL RULES FOR REPRESENTATIONS, WARRANTIES, AND COVENANTS

1. REPRESENTATIONS

Classically, a representation is a statement of presently existing facts that is intended to induce reliance and action by a party, such as entering into a contract. Statements about future conditions do not qualify as representations because no one can know the future. An incorrect representation will support an action for rescission or damages sounding in contract, and tort, if fraud is present. Tort claims for fraudulent misrepresentation require a showing of

(a)   scienter (knowledge of falsity or conscious ignorance of its truth or lack thereof),

(b)   intent to induce reliance, and

(c)   reasonable or justifiable reliance.

A party that discovers a misrepresentation pre-closing can either seek to rescind the contract and receive restitution for any funds expended in reliance on the misrepresentation or can elect to affirm the contract and seek damages. The rescission remedy is not available for breach of a warranty, which is why representations are so important in transactional practice in which many months of due diligence may take place between signing the documents and the closing of the deal. If due diligence uncovers unsatisfactory information, rescission provides a party, usually a buyer, with a way out of the deal.

Unless otherwise specified, the representation speaks as of the execution of the document in which it is contained. The cause of action is, therefore, generally ripe as of that time, which may be pre-closing. Pre-closing representations may terminate at closing by operation of law unless the contract specifies that they survive the closing. Check governing law in your jurisdiction on this point and, best of all, address the matter specifically in the contract with survival and no-merger clauses. A survival clause specifies that the representation in the agreement survives the closing. A no-merger clause is one that defeats the common law doctrine of merger in a real estate transaction, whereby the land sale contract's provisions are said to merge into the deed, thereby being destroyed and replaced by the common law covenants of seizen, right to convey, against encumbrances, general warranty, quiet enjoyment, and further assurances in the case of a general warranty deed, or nothing at all if a quitclaim deed is used.

Representations are meant to give one party some reassurance that the other party's statements of fact are true. In this sense, they shift the risk that a stated fact is untrue to the representing party. Typical subjects for representations include the accuracy of financial statements, due formation of a business entity, compliance with laws, the existence or non-existence of adverse claims, breached or defaulted contracts, liens, encumbrances, and legal actions.

Representations are also used to shift the burden and cost of investigation and disclosure in the due diligence process. For example, assume that your client wishes to purchase a business but wants to know if there are any claims or lawsuits against the business. You and your client could search relevant court records, perhaps nationwide. You could also dig through all of the business records looking for evidence of claims. These are burdensome and expensive activities. Alternatively, you could insert a representation and warranty into the purchase agreement in which the seller states that, except as disclosed on an attached schedule, no claims or lawsuits have been asserted against the company. This sort of blanket statement is known as a flat or unqualified representation. It shifts the burden of investigation and disclosure back to where it belongs— on the seller—which is the entity that is the least-cost-provider of the information.

Typically, the seller's counsel would respond with the suggestion that the representation be qualified, often by narrowing it to relate to claims or lawsuits of a certain type or over a certain size—a materiality threshold— or known to certain specific individuals—a knowledge limitation. Depending on the circumstances, this may be acceptable to your client. If so, make sure that either limitation is not overbroad. Materiality thresholds should be set at levels that sound appropriate alarms, but filter out the noise generated by immaterial claims. Knowledge limitations should specify persons who are likely to know the details involved; rarely will it be sufficient to limit knowledge to that of the uppermost tier of management. In this way, the burden of necessary investigation and disclosure can appropriately be shifted to the sellers.

The inclusion of a knowledge qualifier has the effect of shifting the representations from those based on the existence of the facts themselves to ones based on awareness of the facts. A party may justify its need to include a knowledge qualifier by arguing that it should not be required to make an assertion that it does not know to be the truth. If a party has incomplete knowledge or if the truth of a fact is fairly immaterial and difficult or costly to obtain, a knowledge qualifier may be appropriate. On the other hand, if the statement of fact is based upon something within the party's control or is one that the other party wishes to rely upon in deciding whether to proceed with the transaction, a knowledge limitation is inappropriate.

Representations are generally drafted in the form:

[Buyer, Seller, other defined term] represents [representation carefully stated as to scope and substance].

Representations should almost always be drafted in the present or past tense, not the future tense, to prevent them from being interpreted as covenants.

A representation is often combined with a warranty, in which case the form is:

[Buyer, Seller, other defined term] represents and warrants [representation and warranty carefully stated as to scope and substance].

This combination ensures that a cause of action will lie post-closing if the representation has terminated as of closing but the warranty survives or as part of an overall belt and suspenders approach.

For a good case illustrating representations and warranties in action, *see Linden Partners v. Wilshire Linden Assocs.*, 62 Cal. App. 4th 508; 73 Cal. Rptr. 2d 708 (1998).

For a good discussion of the operation of warranties in transactional documents, *see CBS Inc. v. Ziff-Davis Publishing Co.*, 75 N.Y.2d 496; 553 N.E.2d 997; 554 N.Y.S.2d 449 (1990).

2. COVENANTS

A covenant is a promise to act or not to act in the future. It is essentially a single contractual duty within a document. Breach of a covenant will support an action for damages or specific performance sounding in contract (or tort under the theory of promissory fraud), and the cause of action is generally ripe at the time the covenant was to be performed. However, doctrines such as anticipatory repudiation, impossibility, prospective inability to perform, and voluntary disablement may accelerate the accrual of the cause of action.

Covenants are generally drafted in the form of a "shall clause," an active voice statement that identifies the party making the promise and states that promise directly.

"Seller shall indemnify and defend Buyer from all adverse claims to title."

Test all of your covenants for the active voice, asking: "do they clearly state who is to do what to or for whom, when, and in what manner, quality, or quantity?"

A final consideration when drafting covenants, similar to the decisions faced when drafting representations and warranties, is: what degree of performance will be required? Some covenants are unqualified and provide that a party shall do something, period. Other times they are drafted in terms of best efforts, commercially reasonable efforts, or reasonable efforts. When drafting or reviewing covenants, consider whether language qualifying the obligation is appropriate and whether it really adds any certainty by reference to an objective measurement or statement.

A duty to use best or reasonable efforts to obtain that result usually arises in one of three ways in contracts cases. First, the contract itself may specifically require that the promisor put forth his or her best efforts. Second, the contract might expressly or implicitly specify a result, and this may be interpreted as imposing a duty of best efforts. Finally, a court may impose a duty of best efforts based simply on the facts and circumstances surrounding a contract. Either of these last two theories explains the result in that staple of first year law school contract law classes, *Wood v. Lucy, Lady Duff-Gordon*, 222 N.Y. 88, 118 N.E. 214 (1917), in which Judge Cardozo implied a duty to use reasonable efforts into a distribution and marketing arrangement in order to hold a fashion designer to the contract rather than allowing her to escape her implied obligations to the man she had hired so that she could market her designs through Sears-Roebuck.

There appears to be no firm rule as to what constitutes adequate or sufficient best efforts. In general, each case turns on its particular facts. Some cases suggest that best efforts requires the same amount of effort under a contract as that expended under other, similar contracts where the quality of effort has not been questioned. Others imply that the promisor should merely avoid manifestly harmful conduct. The duty to act reasonably, like a duty to employ best efforts or to act in good faith, is not reducible to a fixed formula—unless the contract itself provides the formula or an objective measure.

A duty of best efforts is separate and distinct from the duty of good faith. Good faith is a standard with a moral component that has honesty and fairness at its core and that is imposed on every party to a contract. A best or reasonable effort is a standard that focuses on diligence in performance or attempted performance. One method to address the uncertainty of best or reasonable efforts clauses is to provide for a specific dollar limit on expenses to be incurred on account of specific best effort covenants or for all similar covenants together.

Parties in preliminary negotiations, either oral or written, may intend to bind themselves to negotiate further in good faith. Some may even promise to use their best efforts to do so. Doing so can elevate what may have been an unenforceable agreement to agree into an enforceable agreement to negotiate in good faith, which is a somewhat vague, and thus troublesome, duty. *See, e.g.,* Cable & Computer Technology Inc. v. Lockheed Sanders, Inc., 214 F.3d 1030 (9th Cir. 2000). Take care to avoid this trap.

3. THE UCC APPROACH

In a sale of goods contract covered by the Uniform Commercial Code, however, any "affirmation of fact or promise made by the seller to the buyer which relates to the goods and becomes part of the basis of the bargain creates an express warranty that the goods shall conform to the affirmation or promise." U.C.C. § 2–313. This approach blurs the distinction between classic definitions and distinctions between representations, warranties, covenants, and even conditions. These UCC warranties also survive the closing of the sale.

4. GENERAL RULES AND TECHNIQUES: TYPICAL REPRESENTATIONS AND WARRANTIES

Each of the general rules regarding representations, warranties, covenants, and conditions can be altered by language of the contract itself, so none can be drafted or interpreted in a vacuum.

Typical representations and warranties include assurances that

1. the party is duly organized, in good standing, and authorized to enter in the transaction;

2. the transaction is not a breach of any other agreement and does not violate the law;

3. a seller or lessor has good title to all assets being sold or leased, and those assets are free of liens and encumbrances; and

4. all material facts have been disclosed.

Each is often phrased as "except as disclosed on schedule X to this agreement, [representation or warranty]." As noted above, this structure makes the provision more than just a representation or warranty—it becomes a due diligence tool that shifts the burden of finding and discussing exceptions to the statement to the representing and warranting party. Representations and warranties of this type are often combined with a covenant to defend against claims that are adverse to any of the representations and warranties and an indemnity against losses caused by inaccurate representations or warranties.

That combination of provisions resembles deal insurance in that one party makes a representation and warranty and then agrees to indemnify and defend the other party from claims that render the representation or warranty incorrect. Remember, however, that insurance is only as good as the insurer when the claim is made. Do not take too much comfort in unsecured, unregulated insurance-like provisions—circumstances change and parties die, are dissolved, and become insolvent or judgment-proof. Due to the use of blanket and purchase money security interests to support business financing, the sale and securitization of rights to payments and payment streams, and the use of limited liability entities to separate assets and retained earnings from liability-creating operations, many, if not most, businesses are judgment-proof beyond whatever insurance coverage they have. This does not mean clients should not contract with these businesses, just that counsel must focus on ensuring that their clients understand the risks involved and whether there is a creditworthy payor or other source of funds to look to if a representation, warranty, or other provision is incorrect or breached.

An important method of reducing the scope of a representation or warranty, and any covenant or indemnity linked to it, is a knowledge limitation. For example, "the representations and warranties of section X below are limited to facts of which $a, b,$ or c [people] have actual knowledge on the date of this agreement." This is a fair limitation, as long as the appropriate persons are specified: those who would naturally have the knowledge sought. Do not stop at the senior executive level—as knowledge there is generalized—but delve down to cover the knowledge of middle management and even the operations level of a business, as appropriate.

5. TIME LIMITATIONS

One way to avoid the uncertainty caused by issues such as merger, the collateral promise rule, and survival is to include a time limits provision for claims by each party. A time limits provision should first disclaim post-closing liability broadly, and then specify exceptions to this general rule. For example:

12.4 Time Limits; Buyer's Claim.

If the closing occurs, the Seller will have no liability under this Agreement except for claims arising under [specific sections] that are asserted by the Buyer against the Seller by no later than one year after the date of closing, written notice specifying the factual basis of the claim in reasonable detail, given under section 12.5 of the Agreement.

6. GUARANTIES, INDEMNITIES, AND RELEASES

a. Guaranties

A guarantor is one who promises that, if another party does not perform a duty, the guarantor will. A guarantor is not a party to the primary contact. The guarantor stands behind the primary obligor, promising to perform those obligations if the primary obligor does not do so.

The word guarantee, when used in the colloquial sense of a warranty (on your microwave oven, for example) has one spelling and guaranty, when used in its formal legal meaning (a promise to perform a third party's obligation) has a different spelling. There should be no double-e guaranties in your contracts.

If the beneficiary of the guaranty wants a right of direct action against the guarantor without first needing to pursue the primary obligor, the drafter should use a guaranty-of-payment provision, rather than a guaranty-of-performance provision. The following is an example of guaranty-of-payment language:

> *In consideration of the sale of goods and the extension of credit to the Buyer, [name of guarantor] ("Guarantor") hereby guaranties to Seller payment of the balance of the purchase price on the terms stated above. Upon default in payment of any or installment of the credit extended or in the performance of any requirement or provision contained in the security between Buyer and Seller, Guarantor shall, upon demand, pay the full amount of the unpaid purchase price with accrued interest.*

Contrast it with the following guaranty-of-performance language:

> *This guaranty is conditional and is guaranty of collection only. Guarantor shall not be obligated to make any payment under this guaranty until all attempts to collect from obligor, with due diligence and using reasonable legal means, have failed.*

Further, the creditor should negotiate a waiver of the guarantor's exoneration rights which may arise by operation of law from events such as a change in the principle obligation without the surety's consent. Typically, this sort of waiver language is in the form:

> *Notice of acceptance of this guarantee, notices of non-payment and non-performance, notices of amount of indebtedness outstanding at any time, protests, demands, and prosecution of collection, foreclosure, and possessory remedies are hereby expressly waived.*

It is understood and agreed that the liability of Guarantor shall not be affected by any settlement, extension, or variation of terms of the security agreement or by the discharge or release of any obligation of the buyer or any other interested person, by operation of law or otherwise.

b. Indemnities

An indemnity is a collateral contractual obligation where one party, the indemnitor, engages to hold another, the indemnitee, harmless from losses to third parties. A common indemnity is one that covers any losses from a breach or inaccuracy of any representation or warranty in the agreement. The indemnitor need not be the other party to the contract. Like guaranties, indemnities are only as good as the indemnitor.

The basic issues that arise with indemnities are related to scope. Scope of indemnification is defined or limited by

    (i)   the time period during which claims can be asserted;

    (ii) the time period during which the event underlying the claim occurred;

    (iii) the minimum and maximum amount of any claim or of all claims in the aggregate, or over a particular period of time;

    (iv) the damages covered (actual pecuniary loss to third parties, consequential damages, punitive damages, liquidated damages); and

    (v) the mechanism for presenting claims and solving disputed claims.

But, unlike guarantors, an indemnitor is usually a party to the primary contract. Typically, the indemnity arrangement provides that A agrees that if B becomes liable to a third person, A will pay B the amount of B's liability to the third person.

c. Releases

A release of a right, claim, or privilege is a cancellation of the right to assert a right, claim, or privilege. A similar result may be achieved by assignment of the claim, which can have other different effects that are useful in creatively structuring a transaction, such as maintaining the subordinate priority of other claims or one party's judgment-proof status.

7. CAUTIONARY PROCEDURES

At the outset, consider including a master provision that eliminates or disclaims, as far as legally possible, all express or implied representations, warranties, covenants, indemnities, and releases except as expressly provided in the contract. This is an attempt to wipe the slate clean of common law and statutorily implied provisions such as the UCC's warranty of merchantability or fitness for intended use provisions. *But see* U.C.C. § 2–316(1) (disclaimers of express warranties in conflict with apparent warranty will be inoperative if that construction is unreasonable); U.C.C. § 2–316(2), (3) (disclaimer of implied warranties with specific disclaimers, general disclaimers, buyer inspections, and course of performance). A disclaimer of warranties may be subject to different, peculiar drafting requirements that seem to indicate the potential judicial hostility to overreaching disclaimers and releases obtained by economically dominant parties. Include a merger or integration clause to trigger the parol evidence rule to exclude evidence of any statements that could be construed as agreements, representations, warranties, covenants, etc. made during negotiations or earlier rounds of documentation.

The use of the incorrect type of provision can result in the provision working in unintended ways, limiting a party's rights or giving rise to unintended defenses or consequences. For example, because warranties concern the present existence of facts, the characterization of a covenant as a representation or warranty may prevent the covenant from applying to a future breach of the obligation. Likewise, the characterization of a covenant as a representation or warranty may create fraud or misrepresentation tort liability, including potential punitive damages for the promisor's breach, although that breach should only be a contract claim (limiting damages to compensatory ones, not punitive damages), if a true covenant is used.

Claims of breach or inaccuracy accrue and statutes of limitations run at different times depending on the type of provision used. A claim for misrepresentation can arise at the time of signing a purchase and sale or other agreement, when the representation was first made, and again at closing if a condition to closing is the subject of a bring down certificate, which renews the representation as of that time. A breach of warranty claim generally arises at the time of the closing or sale. A breach of covenant claim accrues when the party does not honor the covenant, which may be in the distant, post-closing future.

Failing to recognize a guaranty as a guaranty may lead to failing to include a waiver of the guarantor's suretyship defenses, exoneration rights, notice, presentment, exhaustion of claims against the primary obligor, or unique state law provisions, such as the anti-deficiency or one-form-of-action statutes of a minority of states.

> Anti-deficiency and One Form of Action Laws
> Anti-deficiency statutes typically provide that a lender secured by a lien on real property may only look to that

> property to satisfy the debt upon default. *See, e.g.,* CAL.
> CIV. PROC. CODE § 580b (anti-deficiency provision
> applicable to so-called seller-takeback financing for one-
> to-four unit dwelling occupied by borrower). One form
> of Action or One Action Rule laws limit a lender to first
> proceeding judicially against the collateral in a judicial
> foreclosure action and then, in that same action,
> obtaining a deficiency judgment against the borrower or
> electing to waive the result to seek a deficiency
> judgment by proceeding non-judicially against the
> collateral, such as by a deed of trust. *See, e.g.,* CAL. CIV.
> PROC. CODE § 726.

If an indemnity is used to cover a warranty claim, the indemnitee may
not have a claim if the indemnitor can limit its liability to true indemnitor
liability, which includes only reimbursement of the indemnitee for its
liabilities to third persons. Self-sustained and remedied damages are not
included. This limitation can be drafted around in many jurisdictions by
expressly including otherwise excluded damages.

An indemnity against liability becomes collectible immediately when
the indemnitee becomes liable to a third person. An indemnity against
anything else (such as claims or damages) becomes collectible only after
the indemnitee has paid the third person. This distinction is similar to the
guaranty of payment or performance distinction discussed above.

Finally, an indemnity may not be effective if the indemnitee's own
negligence contributed to its obligation to a third party. Generally, an
indemnitee can recover in these circumstances only if the indemnity
expressly provides for recovery under those circumstances. Draft carefully.

N. EVENTS OF DEFAULT AND REMEDIES

Notes, leases, and other contracts that govern continuing relationships
feature specific sections that delineate events of default, procedures for
declaring a default, and the remedies available to a non-defaulting party
upon declaration of default. These provisions are the special concern of
lawyers because, at the front end of the deal, clients are primarily focused
on performance, not on default.

In contracts courses, law students study common law rules regarding
remedies, from limits on damages to the availability of specific performance
and other equitable remedies. As a contract drafter, you need to plan your
way into or around these legal rules to allow your client to recover as much
as possible in the event of the other party's breach. Good transactional
lawyers know the substantive law applicable to their transactions and then
plan and structure transactions to take advantage of favorable law (*e.g.,*

tax effects, validation of liquidated damages provisions, etc.) and to avoid, or draft around, unfavorable law.

Default is a broader concept than breach of contract. The default and remedy section of a contract should begin with a listing of what actual events are events of default. Although the enumerated events of default generally include events that would be a breach of the contract under the common law without a specific default section (for example, non-payment of rent under a real property lease), they can also include many things that would otherwise not be considered a breach, such as changed financial status as measured by financial ratios, a failure to maintain casualty insurance for collateral, and other insecurity provisions. Events of default or a declaration of default under one contract can also be a default or an event of default under another agreement, including an agreement involving a completely separate transaction and completely different parties. This is known as a cross-default.

Events of default are selected for each transaction. Common events of default include:

- failure to perform an obligation;

- failure to pay monies when due;

- failure to maintain a certain status (membership, financial condition, etc.);

- breach or inaccuracy of a representation or warranty;

- bankruptcy and similar insolvency-related conditions and proceedings (although these are generally unenforceable if the contracting party is the subject of a bankruptcy case);

- default under another agreement; and

- general insecurity of the other party.

The contract can make the occurrence of an event of default an automatic default under the contract entitling the non-defaulting party to exercise its remedies. It may require the non-defaulting party to give notice that the event of default has occurred and declare a default. The latter form gives the non-defaulting party more flexibility, but also requires more careful monitoring of the other party, especially if non-monetary defaults are involved. As a practical matter, every jurisdiction will require some form of notice of the default prior to exercise of remedy. Remember, a notice of default or termination will generally not be effective if the defaulting party has filed a bankruptcy petition before the proper notice is given of an event of default. *See generally* 11 U.S.C. § 362(a) (prohibiting taking action against a debtor or a debtor's property after a bankruptcy case is commenced and the order for relief is entered); *but see* 11 U.S.C. § 362(b) (listing exceptions and unstayed types of acts).

Many default provisions include the concept of a right to cure, or fix the default and avoid application of the remedies provided in the contract. Different cure periods can apply to different events of default, and the contract should specify when the cure period begins to run. In drafting, one of two approaches is used to provide for cure rights. One either drafts a separate provision addressing the right to cure or builds the cure right into each event of default provision.

The provisions that establish a default are generally followed by provisions that specify:

(i)   remedies;

(ii)   whether those remedies are automatic or elective on the part of the non-defaulting party;

(iii) how the election of remedies, if any, is to be made; and

(iv)   whether the remedies are mutually exclusive or cumulative.

Consider the legality and enforceability of remedies as well. The most effective ones that you can imagine are often unenforceable or of limited enforceability.

The mutual foreseeability test of *Hadley v. Baxendale*, 9 Exch. 341 (Court of the Exchequer 1854), would limit liability unless the draftsperson used, among other provisions, a liquidated damage clause and a prevailing party attorneys' fee clause. Alternatively, the drafter could include recitals showing what damages were reasonably foreseeable by all parties. Similar issues arise in other areas, including provisions for acceleration of payment obligations, post-judgment attorneys' fees, interest, default interest, prepayment fees, or calculation of interest based upon an actual year or a 360-day accounting year. The drafter needs to assess all applicable issues, the limiting or expanding effect of otherwise applicable law, and possible draft-arounds available to serve the client's interests.

A final note about default and remedies: when an event of default has occurred and it is time to declare the default, the notice of default (generally in the form of a letter) should be drafted in unequivocal language and should track the language and requirements of the contract exactly. There is no need to be overly kind or insulting in tone. A neutral description of the contract, the pertinent provisions, the event of default that has occurred, a declaration of the default, an election of remedies, if needed, and any demand for action will suffice. The notice of default should be transmitted exactly as specified in the contract. Failure to strictly adhere to the contractual requirements will afford the defaulting party a defense to enforcement and may allow additional time to cure and reinstate the agreement.

O. THE IMPORT AND SCOPE OF BOILERPLATE

Boilerplate is the term used for those standard provisions inserted at the end of almost every transactional document. The term makes them sound routine and unimportant. Nothing could be further from the truth. These provisions commonly come into effect when there is a problem or disagreement between the parties, so they must be carefully considered and drafted to ensure that they work correctly when they are needed most. They represent another opportunity for prelitigation planning, something that every business lawyer must keep in mind when drafting transactional documents.

The term boilerplate is derived from the word for flat-rolled steel used to make steam engine boilers and the hulls of ships. In the early days of newspaper syndication the term was also used to describe the plates of non-movable type that publishers delivered to local newspapers and which contained the syndicated text and advertising that the local paper would adopt in full, adding its own stories and advertising to supplement the syndicator's standard material.

Applied to contracts, boilerplate refers to an assortment of standard provisions that cover issues common to most contracts such as choice of law, choice of forum, severability, integration or merger, execution in counterparts, notice, and the like. These provisions are routine, but, like real boilerplate making up a boiler in the hull of a ship, or for a local paper, they are very important. Without good boilerplate, the boiler explodes, the ship sinks, and the paper consists only of local interest stories and farm reports. They are also called "housekeeping provisions." Like the term "miscellaneous," this term tends to denigrate their importance.

If you think about it you will see that boilerplate provisions often address or trigger fundamental, important bodies of contract law. As an example, consider a merger or integration clause which, if well drafted and given effect by a court, will bar admission of evidence regarding prior or contemporaneous agreements or discussions to prove what constitute the terms of the contract. The term boilerplate, when understood, reflects the fundamental importance and the routine nature of those sorts of provisions.

Never take boilerplate for granted or simply incorporate standard provisions without thought and analysis. When reviewing contracts drafted by others, do not just skim the boilerplate—much mischief can be hidden there. Students and lawyers that do not have a transactional practice sometimes claim that this advice is hypertechnical and exaggerated. But transactional lawyers confirm the import and potential mischief of boilerplate again and again. Just as beginning litigators are advised never to agree to the standard stipulations in a deposition without knowing what those stipulations are, transactional attorneys are cautioned against accepting the other side's boilerplate without critical analysis.

P. CERTIFIED VERSUS REGISTERED MAIL

Certified letters travel with regular mail; you get a receipt certifying that you sent it. Unless you also request return receipt requested (the little green card they attach) you cannot prove that the recipient ever received it. Most people pay the small additional cost for the return receipt.

Certified is cheaper than a registered letter, which travels outside the regular mail flow and is signed for and individually handled at every stop in the process. It therefore takes more time to be delivered and is more expensive. Because it is considered more secure, valuables are often sent registered rather than certified. If lost, there is a log book record of the travels of the registered letter (or package) at every stop, making recovery more likely (just like the tracking records on the Internet for United Postal Service, Federal Express, and DHL Courier).

Certified mail is not insured unless you buy extra insurance from the post office at additional cost. Registered mail may be insured up to $25,000 or more with the purchase of additional insurance.

A certified letter will be delivered to anyone at a particular address if they sign for it (a secretary at an office, for instance), but a restricted certified letter will be delivered only to the person whose name appears on the envelope.

Lawyers generally use certified mail with return receipt to prove that their documents were both mailed and received.

Regular first class mail is the cheapest, followed by certified, with registered being the most expensive.

A Note Regarding Boilerplate: Integration Clauses

We hear a lot about frivolous tort claims, but bogus contract claims are probably an even bigger problem. The facts of the contract cases aren't as interesting, so you don't read about them in the newspapers, but they are a constant problem for American business. They typically arise when one party can't perform. The builder can't get the project done on time, or even more commonly, the buyer can't pay for whatever it is they've bought. The nonperforming party then comes up with some alleged promise to give additional time to perform or some oral warranty that was breached and lets the buyer out of its duty to pay for the goods.

Here's the way it plays out. The case of the cash-short buyer is a good illustration. The buyer typically doesn't complain when the product is delivered. It just hopes that today is the day the big infusion of cash is going to come in. When the seller pushes to get paid, it is put off with promises that the money is coming in. Only when the seller finally gets frustrated and files a lawsuit do these claims of breaches of oral warranties appear. The seller will of course move for summary judgment, but if the judge takes a wishy-washy position on things like merger clauses and the parol evidence rule, the case will drag on for as long as it takes to get to trial in that particular jurisdiction. In some jurisdictions, it can take as long as five years to get to trial. However long it takes, the buyer has that long to turn itself around or file a Chapter 11. You can guess which is the more likely scenario. Of course, if the seller has a bulletproof merger clause, the seller can get a summary judgment (and its money), and the buyer has to find someone else to stiff, someone whose lawyer isn't as thorough. So even when we teach a case where the contract's drafting is ultimately upheld, we need to talk about ways it could have been done better, so that the transaction never resulted in a trial, let alone an appellate opinion.

Robert M. Lloyd, *Making Contracts Relevant: Thirteen Lessons for the First-Year Contracts Course*, 36 ARIZ. S. L. J. 257, 259–60 (2004) (entertaining footnotes omitted).

Q. ARBITRATION AND OTHER ALTERNATIVE DISPUTE RESOLUTION PROVISIONS

All businesses hope to avoid the cost and expense of litigation. One possible solution is arbitration, a form of alternative dispute resolution. Although arbitration has its adherents, it can be dangerous or inappropriate and should only be included in a contract after careful consideration. According to a variety of studies cited by the National Arbitration Forum, arbitration can significantly reduce attorneys' fees and in unemployment and financial services contexts, individuals fare at last as well in arbitration as they do in lawsuits. *Arbitration vs. Lawsuits, White Paper, National Arbitration Forum*, http://www.adrforum.com/ (2003). This may or may not mean that arbitration is favored by a particular business; reasonable minds can differ on the pros and cons of the process, often based upon past experience.

Virtually all contracts can provide that disputes between the parties must be settled through arbitration. Courts routinely enforce such provisions and will grant motions to dismiss against parties that seek to litigate rather than arbitrate. Since the early 1980s when the ADR movement gained momentum, arbitration has been considered to be beneficial, featuring more privacy, less cost, and more speed than traditional litigation, and eliminating the wildcard decision-maker that is a civil jury. *See* Keating v. Superior Court, 31 Cal. 3d 584, 183 Cal. Rptr. 360, 645 P.2d 1192 (1982) (recognizing arbitration in the "commercial context is quite common, and reasonably to be anticipated." As such, franchisees are not in a position to claim that an arbitration clause did not "fall within [their] reasonable expectations.")

In fact, the mere elimination of the jury is often enough to allow for early settlement of a dispute. Without a jury, the parties are faced with the cold, hard facts of their cases and can be more certain of the relative strengths of the legal arguments involved, and thus have less incentive to roll the dice with a lay jury that may be swayed by theatrics, passion, rhetoric, and prejudice. This has led to contract provisions that stop short of arbitration but eliminate the jury wildcard—waivers of the right to a jury trial. These waivers are particularly appealing to banks, insurance companies, and large institutions, which benefit from the procedures and opportunities for review afforded by the court system, but feel unfairly vulnerable to juries that may be bent on redistributing wealth and resources. Note that such waivers are not enforceable in all jurisdictions. *See, e.g.*, Grafton Partners v. Superior Court, 36 Cal. 4th 944, 32 Cal. Rptr. 3d 5, 116 P.3d 479 (2005); Bank South N.A. v. Howard, 264 Ga. 339, 444 S.E.2d 799 (1994).

It is important to recognize that arbitration can have its negative aspects. Its flexibility, if not addressed by the drafter, can lead to undesired results. In many states, the decision of an arbitrator acting under a binding arbitration clause is final and cannot be reviewed by a court unless the decision violates fundamental public policy or the arbiter is shown to be deranged or incompetent. These are high standards to meet. Even a clear mistake of law on the arbitrator's part is generally not grounds for review and reversal. The lesson to take from this state of affairs is that, while arbitration may be useful or appropriate in many circumstances, careful thought should occur before it is adopted, and any arbitration provision should be carefully drafted to control the resulting process.

There are several concerns to take into account when drafting an arbitration clause. First, an arbitration provision drafted to favor one side may be challenged as unconscionable and, thus, the provision should be drafted to pass a test of fundamental fairness. Stirlen v. Supercuts, Inc., 51 Cal. App. 4th 1519, 1520, 60 Cal. Rptr. 2d 138 (1997) (a compulsory arbitration clause in a contract of adhesion ("a standardized contract, which, imposed and drafted by the party of superior bargaining strength, relegates to the subscribing party only the opportunity to adhere to the contract or reject it") is deemed unconscionable.) Engalla v. Permanente Medical Group, 15 Cal. 4th 951, 985, 64 Cal. Rptr. 2d 843, 938 P.2d 903 (1997) (unfairness found in an arbitration requirement because the insurance company established the arbitration system with a bias toward giving itself the advantage (taking advantage of its repeat-player status)). In this vein, the agreement to arbitrate should be mutual; that is, all parties should be required to arbitrate, not just one party or group of parties.

Second, since the right and duty to arbitrate is created by the agreement, it is the agreement that governs the procedures. Parker v. Babcoc, 37 Cal. App. 4th 1682, 1687, 44 Cal. Rptr. 2d 602 (1995) ("[p]rivate arbitration [as opposed to judicial arbitration] occurs only pursuant to agreement, and it is the agreement which determines the details of the process . . . [t]ypically, those who enter into arbitration agreements expect that their dispute will be resolved without necessity for any contact with the courts."). The drafter may incorporate the rules of a specific arbitrating body, such as the American Arbitration Association (the "AAA"), may incorporate federal or state rules or procedures, or may make up a procedure out of whole cloth. The last is rare. The danger of the first approach is that it is very easy to simply adopt the rules and procedures of the AAA or other organization without even knowing what they are and which side they might benefit in your particular situation. Arbitration groups often have different sets of rules for different types of disputes, which could result in application of a procedure other than the one intended. Before incorporating rules and procedures into a contract, the prudent attorney will know what procedure is being incorporated and the relative costs and benefits of that particular procedure. It may also be a good idea to include the stipulation that the rules will be the rules in effect on the date of the contract; not some future set of rules that could be adopted after the contract is signed but before the incident resulting in arbitration arises.

Issues that need to be addressed in any arbitration provision, either by explicit drafting or by knowing the procedures of an outside arbitration service include the following: How does a party start the arbitration process? Where will the arbitration be conducted? How is an arbiter selected? How will the parties present their cases? Will there be discovery or disclosure of facts? Do rules of evidence apply? What substantive law will apply? Is there an opportunity to challenge the arbiter's ruling and if so, how? Is the ruling binding or merely advisory?

Other considerations that should be taken into account include:

- How much power should the arbitrator have? Should all possible remedies be available, or only a specified few?

- How broad should the scope of the clause be? Are all disputes between the parties to be arbitrated or only a select few? For example, are validating and formation defenses like fraud in the inducement, misrepresentation, and mistake to be arbitrated or just issues of enforcement, performance, and breach?

- Will a fast or slow process benefit your client? What time periods and other procedural rules can you eliminate or invoke to affect this dimension of the arbitration?

- Do you want to provide for narrow or broad judicial review? As discussed above, narrow review means all but certain confirmation of the arbiter's award.

- How expensive should the process be and should the party initiating the arbitration be required to make a deposit to cover the arbitrator's fees in whole or in part?

- Should the arbitrator be an expert or a generalist?

- Which party is likely to initiate the arbitration? In other words, is your client likely to be prosecuting or defending the action?

- Are non-signatory parties—such as parent, subsidiary, or affiliate companies, employees and agents—subject to the arbitration clause?

- Should the arbitration clause allow or prohibit class action arbitration? After *Green Tree Financial Corp. v. Bazzle*, 539 U.S. 444, 123 S.Ct. 2402, 156 L.Ed.2d 414 (2003), permitted class action arbitration and the American Arbitration Association adopted special class action rules, this potential cannot be ignored. In *Ting v. AT&T*, 319 F.3d 1126 (9th Cir. 2003), the court struck down a ban on class action arbitration as unconscionable.

Finally, if you or your client is unwilling to give up the procedural and substantive rights afforded by the court system, but wish to provide for some chance of resolution short of a lawsuit, a mediation provision may be adopted. Drafting mediation provisions involves considerations similar to arbitration provisions. How does a party instigate the mediation process? Who is to serve as the mediator? What will the process be for educating the mediator about the parties, the contract, and the dispute? Are only certain types of disputes suitable for mediation? How and when can the parties determine that the mediation is fruitless and seek redress in the court system? What portions, if any, of the mediation are confidential, non-discoverable, and inadmissible in later court proceedings? Consider including submission of a reasonable settlement offer as a condition precedent to the duty to mediate in an effort to encourage the settlement process along. Since settlement is often an incremental process, front-loading the procedure can facilitate getting to eventual compromise. For those seeking to create disincentives for litigation, a waiver of a jury trial coupled with a pre-suit mediation provision may accomplish this goal without subjecting the parties to the potential dangers of binding, non-reviewable arbitration.

R. SIGNATURE BLOCKS

1. INTRODUCTORY LANGUAGE FOR SIGNATURES

Before the signature blocks at the end of the body of the agreement where the parties sign, there is usually some introductory language. Like other standard provisions in agreements, there is a tendency for this language to become ossified and exhibit dated legalese. It is better to delete phrases such as "In Witness Whereof" and "as of the date that first appears above" and use a modern, plain English provision. It should simply establish that, by signing the document, the parties are agreeing to its terms.

> *To show that they have agreed to the terms of this agreement, the Parties have executed this Agreement below on [the date stated on page 1* or *the date(s) indicated below].*

—or—

> *The Parties agree to the terms of this Agreement above.*

—or—

AGREED:

To avoid inconsistent dating of documents, the introductory language to a signature block often refers to a date appearing on the first page or paragraph of the document. This is fine, as long as that date is filled in. Too many times, in the heat of closing, the parties simply flip to the last page of the agreement (which they have reviewed many times before in negotiations, so why read it again?) and fail to note that the date on page 1 has been left blank. In another form that is common in practice, the agreement is dated "as of" a date contained on the first page (filled in early in the drafting process) and the signature blocks are undated or contain the dates of execution by the parties. In such a case, it is a good idea for the contract to specify which date is the effective date.

2. TRADITIONAL SIGNATURE BLOCKS

Signature blocks accomplish two purposes if properly drafted. First, as the place where the parties will sign the agreement when executed, they indicate mutual assent to the contract. Second, they establish the formal identity and capacity of the entities that are parties to the agreement and the individuals expressing that assent.

Signature blocks for an individual person, look like this:

Form	Example
[defined term for the party] [party name, typed], [capacity if other than self] [if the party's address does not appear elsewhere, include it here to assist in identification, Social Security numbers are also used but take into account privacy and identity theft concerns]	Seller John W. Doe 1234 W. Willow Way. Wonderland, Wyoming

Signature blocks for an incorporeal entity (LLC, Corp., Partnership, etc.) look like this:

Form	Example
[defined term for the party] [name of party entity]	Buyer International Drain Systems, LLC, a Delaware Limited Liability Company
[name of signing person], [title]	By[4] Mary Ann Vortex, President

For either of these forms, following the name of party or capacity, include any information relevant to or qualifying that capacity, such as "subject to approval of the [bankruptcy or probate] court [give details of court and case or other identifying information]," or "as trustee for Joan Jenrett, a minor child," etc.

A complex signature block may result if one is dealing with multi-level incorporeal entities.[5] For example:

---

[4]   There is some variance in practice as to whether or not to use a colon after the word "By," "Its," "Title," and the like. One convention is to use the colon when the document is prepared as a form or when the signing party is unknown at the time of drafting and will be filled in at the time of execution. If the identity of the signing person is known when the documents are prepared, no colon is necessary. Conventions like this vary jurisdiction to jurisdiction, firm to firm, and attorney to attorney.

[5]   Multi-level corporate structure is used to, among other things, isolate income and liability producing assets from other assets, including profits previously drawn off of these assets, to diversify ownership and risk in particular economic activities among various investors, and to realize tax advantages.

Portofino Properties, LLC

_____

By   Floorboard Associates, LLP,
     Its Managing Member

_____

By   Wainscott Investments, LLC
     Its General Partner

_____

By   General Interiors, Inc.
     Its Managing Member

_____

By   Assiduous Perry,
     President

In this style, Mr. Perry would sign on all lines as the authorized representative of the entities indicated. Alternatively, the intervening signature lines are omitted, and he only signs once, as President of General Interiors, and the authority of that signature flows through the corporate structure to Portofino Properties, as shown below:

Portofino Properties, LLC

_____

by Floorboard Associates, LLP,
Its Managing Member
       By Wainscott Investments, LLC
       Its General Partner
              By General Interiors, Inc.
              Its Managing Member
                     By Assiduous Perry, President

Styles like this vary from region to region and firm to firm. The key is (a) to identify the proper chain of authority through the incorporeal entities to the actual person signing the document, and then (b) ensure that the signature block you create accurately reflects this chain of authority.

Take care with party names and make sure you get them exactly right. Issues of punctuation, such as commas and periods, and descriptors of limited liability status, such as LLC or Inc. are especially easy to miss. For example, Allen Bates & Lebowitz LLP could be a limited liability partnership that is the successor to Allen, Bates & Lebowitz and is legally distinct from the former entity, a general partnership including professional corporations. Many jurisdictions do not prohibit the formation of entities with very similar names, which might differ only by a comma or spelling out the word "and" rather than using an ampersand (&). Train your eye to notice details of this nature. It is embarrassing when the client catches the mistake at the closing. It is even worse when the error is not uncovered until subsequent litigation has ensued.

Witness signature blocks and notary jurats are related to signature blocks of the parties. Witness and notary requirements vary from state to state and transaction to transaction. It is important to research and comply with the applicable requirements. *See, e.g.*, Simon v. Chase Manhattan Bank (*In re* Zaptocky), 250 F.3d 1020 (6th Cir. 2001) (invalidating mortgage as second witness required by Ohio law not proven to have attended closing). Local counsel and the law digests in the Martindale Hubble legal directory can be useful sources of information as to these forms and other local requirements.

Even the most seemingly mundane portions of a transactional document are driven by detail and require review with a keen eye to avoid mistakes.

3. E-SIGNATURES AND RELATED MATTERS

a. The E-Signature Act

The Electronic Signatures in Global and National Commerce, 15 U.S.C. §§ 7001 to 7006, 7021 and 7031, validates the practice of recognizing either a clicked "I accept" button on an Internet site or a faxed or e-mailed signature for contract law purposes. The E-Signature Act provides that:

> Notwithstanding any statute, regulation, or other rule of law. . . , with respect to any transaction in or affecting interstate or foreign commerce: (1) a signature, contract, or other record relating to such transaction may not be denied legal effect, validity, or enforceability solely because it is in electronic form; and (2) a contract relating to such transaction may not be denied legal effect, validity, or enforceability solely because an electronic signature or electronic record was used in its formation.

15 U.S.C. § 7001(a). The act defines an electronic signature as "an electronic sound, symbol, or process, attached to or logically associated with

a contract or other record and executed or adopted by a person with the intent to sign the record." 15 U.S.C. § 7006(5).

Complying with E-Signature Act will negate a statute of frauds defense based on federal law and state law statute of frauds defenses if the state in question has not enacted The Uniform Electronic Transactions Act (the "UETA").

The E-Signature Act preempts any state law that invalidates signatures, contracts, and records solely because they are in electronic form, unless the state has enacted the UETA, in which case the UETA preempts the E-Signature Act. 15 U.S.C. § 7001. All other substantive requirements of state contract law remain in place.

The act includes a number of restrictions on contracts related to consumer transactions. A consumer is "[a]n individual who obtains, through a transaction, products or services which are used primarily for personal, family, or household purposes." 15 U.S.C. § 7006(1). As to consumers, the act mandates that a business may only use electronic records if the consumer

(1) has affirmatively consented to their use;

(2) has not withdrawn their consent; and

(3) is given a clear and conspicuous statement informing them of the right to have the record provided in a non-electronic form, informing them of their right to withdraw consent and notifying them of the technology and software requirements needed to access the electronic documents.

15 U.S.C. § 7001(c). Moreover, the consumer must consent to the electronic records in a form that reasonably demonstrates that the consumer can access the information in electronic form. These consumer restrictions do not apply to business-to-business transactions. 15 U.S.C. § 7006(1).

The E-Signature Act contains a number of exceptions to its enforcement that may limit its effect. The act does not apply to contracts or records governed by the Uniform Commercial Code (other than sales, leases, waivers, and the statute of frauds). 15 U.S.C. § 7003(a)(3). Thus, the act does not apply to negotiable instruments (Article 3), bank deposits (Article 4), fund transfers (Article 4a), letters of credit (Article 5), documents of title (Article 7), investment securities (Article 8) or secured transactions (Article 9). The act does apply to sales (Article 2) and leases (Article 2a). Thus, one may be able to enter into a valid electronic contract for the sale of goods or the lease of commercial property, but the financing documents for transactions will have to be in hard copy and bear actual signatures. The act also does not apply to:

(1) wills, codicils, or testamentary trusts;

(2) state statutes or regulations (actual hard copy thereof);

(3) court documents and notices;

(4) notices of cancellation or termination of utility services;

(5) default, foreclosure, or eviction notices on a primary residence;

(6) notices canceling or terminating health or life insurance;

(7) product recalls; or

(8) any document required to accompany the transportation or handling of hazardous or toxic materials.

15 U.S.C. § 7003(a), (b).

In areas where the E-Signature Act does not apply, state and local law must be consulted to determine the effectiveness of e-mail signatures, "I accept" buttons, and fixed signatures.

b. The Uniform Electronic Transactions Act

Many states have enacted or are considering enactment of the Uniform Electronic Transaction Act (the "UETA"), which supplants and is broader than the E-Signature Act. The National Conference of State Legislatures maintains a website listing the various states that have enacted a version of the UETA, the year of enactment, and a link to the statute. The UETA has been widely criticized by consumer groups and technical computer groups that are not associated with pro-business sentiment. The main feature of the UETA is section 5(b) which provides that a party's consent to engage in transactions by electronic means is determined in "the context and surrounding circumstances" of the transaction and the conduct of the parties. This is a looser and less well-defined standard than those of the E-Signature Act, and has been the focus of critics concerned with consumer interests. Supporters, on the other hand, characterize the standard as a more flexible one that can better adapt to a variety of circumstances.

If issues involving electronic transactions and signatures arise in a transaction, counsel will be well advised to consult not only the E-Signature Act but applicable local laws, including any enacted version of the UETA, for current requirements and regulations. Non-conforming versions of the UETA have been enacted in some jurisdictions, so carefully checking the actual text of the applicable state statute is critical.

4. CONTRACTING ON THE INTERNET

a. Clickwrap and Browsewrap Contracts

Today, not only are contracts drafted and transmitted via electronic means—as they have been since at least the 1980s—signatures are commonly generated electronically, and, in some cases, a signature is not even needed to enter into an agreement—assenting to a one hundred plus page contract is as "simple" as a mouse click or a finger tap on a touch screen. From "apps" to websites, there are various new ways for consumers and businesses to enter into contracts—some of which have absolutely no historical analogues. New laws have been enacted to keep up with the changing of the times, and any attorney practicing today would be wise to, in the least, gain a working knowledge of the "buzz" words and laws relevant to electronic commerce issues.

Attorneys and entrepreneurs must often be intimately involved in the presentation and flow of the contract. All of the elements of an old-fashioned, paper contract must still be present and accounted for. So much of the assent process rides on making sure that the individual accepting the contract knows, or at least has the opportunity to know, what he or she is really agreeing to by typing their name in the box or clicking "I Accept." Also bear in mind that these contracts may have no geographical bounds and may be subject to the laws of countries around the globe.

A "clickwrap" contract is an agreement in which a software vendor requires the customer to click or tap on an "I accept" icon, button, or check box for the agreement to take effect. A "browsewrap" contract, on the other hand, refers to an agreement covering access to a website or downloadable product. In a browsewrap contract, the terms and conditions of use for a website or other downloadable product are provided, typically as a hyperlink at the bottom of the screen. Unlike a clickwrap contract, a user does not need to take action to affirm his consent to be bound. Instead, the agreement typically states that use of the website is deemed as acceptance of the agreement.

The terms "clickwrap" and "browsewrap" evolved from the body of law that developed around the cellophane wrapping that sealed the boxes of mass-marketed, store-bought software—commonly called a "shrink-wrapper." Underneath the shrinkwrap or inside of the box there was a software license agreement (or "end-user agreement") which becomes effective when the buyer tears away the plastic from the box.

b. Enforceability of Clickwrap and Browsewrap Contracts

Courts consistently have found consumer assent to these agreements because it is typically impossible for the customer to accomplish his or her goal (*e.g.*, downloading software or gaining access to other information) without clicking the "I accept" button. *See generally* Davis, *Note: Presumed Assent: The Judicial Acceptance of Clickwrap*, 22 Berkeley Tech. L.J. 577 (2007). Courts appear to have a three step process for evaluating assent to clickwrap agreements:

- First, did the user assent to the terms that were proffered?

- Second, are there any meritorious defenses to assent based on failure to read, appreciate, or understand the contract?

- Third, do doctrines such as unconscionability or violation of public policy provide a reason not to enforce the terms in question?

The case law in this area is overwhelmingly federal, presumably because arbitration clauses under the Federal Arbitration Clauses Act (FAA) (9 U.S.C. §§ 1–16) or forum selection clauses (which implicate diversity jurisdiction) are often the ones at issue.

Typically, clickwrap agreements have been held sufficient to put a user on notice while browsewrap agreements require a more thorough analysis of whether notice of the terms of the agreement was sufficient. The focus on whether the user was "on notice" is central to the courts' analysis in all subsequent cases. *See, e.g.,* In re Zappos.com, Customer Data Sec. Breach Litig., 893 F Supp 2d 1058, 1064 (D. Nev 2012), collecting cases and stating:

> Without direct evidence that Plaintiffs click on the Terms of Use, we cannot conclude that Plaintiffs ever viewed, let alone manifested assent to, the Terms of Use. . . . No reasonable user would have reason to click on the Terms of Use, even those users who have alleged that they clicked and relied on statements found in adjacent links, such as the site's "Privacy Policy."

In Nicosa v. Amazon.com, Inc., 834 F.3d 220, 236 (2d Cir. 2016), the court was faced with a situation in which a user "was asked to click on a 'Place your order' button after being told elsewhere on the page that 'By placing your order, you agree to Amazon.com's privacy notice and conditions of use,' with the latter phrase hyperlinked to the 2012 Conditions of Use." Nicosa argued that the 2012 Conditions of Use were a browsewrap agreement, while Amazon argued that it was neither browsewrap or clickwrap, but rather a hybrid of the two. The court was faced with the question of whether a reasonably prudent person would understand that the 2012 Conditions of Use governed her actions, such that her purchase manifested implied assent to additional terms. Ultimately the court found that Nicosa was not on notice, stating:

> "In a seeming effort to streamline customer purchases, Amazon chose not to employ a clickwrap mechanism. While clickwrap agreements that display terms in a scrollbox and require users to click an icon are not necessarily required, *see Register.com*, 356 F.3d at 403 (an offeree need not specifically assent to certain terms by clicking an "I agree" icon so long as the offeree "makes a decision to take the benefit with knowledge of the terms of the offer"), they are certainly the easiest method of ensuring that terms are agreed to, *see Starkey*, 796 F.3d at 197 n.3 (noting that it would have been "simpler to resolve" this question had a

clickwrap mechanism been used). To be clear, we do not hold that there was no objective manifestation of mutual assent here as a matter of law. . .We therefore hold that Amazon has failed to show that Nicosia was on notice and agreed to mandatory arbitration as a matter of law." 834 F.3d at 237–38.

In Lima v. Gateway, Inc., 886 F. Supp. 2d 1170 (C.D. Cal. 2012), the federal district court found that the plaintiff's purchase of a computer monitor was subject to Gateway's limited warranty, which was posted on Gateway's website, because the plaintiff assented to its terms. The sales receipt indicated that the warranty applied and could be viewed on Gateway's website. In addition, a printed copy of the warranty was enclosed in the box shipped to the plaintiff. The plaintiff, however, was not bound by other terms and conditions posted on Gateway's website. Although the plaintiff had visited Gateway's website, he had no actual knowledge of those other terms and did not make the purchase online but instead by telephone.

In Hines v. Overstock.com, Inc., 668 F. Supp. 2d 362 (E.D.N.Y. 2009) aff'd, 380 F. App'x 22 (2d Cir. 2010), the court found that the plaintiff had no actual or constructive notice of Overstock.com's terms and conditions—or of the arbitration provision included in those terms—when she filed a class action concerning the restocking fees charged by Overstock.com in connection with product returns. The terms were only referenced in a hyperlink in small type on the bottom of the Overstock.com website; plaintiff "was never advised of the Terms and Conditions and could not even see the link to them without scrolling down to the bottom of the screen." 668 F. Supp. 2d at 367.

In Berkson v. Gogo LLC, 97 F. Supp. 3d 359, 365 (E.D.N.Y. 2015) plaintiffs argued that "defendants improperly increased their sales and profits by misleading customers into purchasing a service that charged a customer's credit card, on an automatically-renewing continuing monthly basis, without adequate notice or consent." Defendants argued that "the terms plaintiffs consented to not only clearly provided for automatic renewal, but that they included mandatory arbitration and waiver of venue protection." 97 F. Supp. 3d at 365. The court found that:

> "Gogo's sign-in contract of adhesion is not binding on Berkson. The design and content of the website, including the homepage, did not make the 'terms of use' readily and obviously available to Berkson. The hyperlink to the 'terms of use' was not in large font, all caps, or in bold. *Id.* Nor was it accessible from multiple locations on the webpage. *Id.* By contrast, the 'SIGN IN' button is very user-friendly and obvious, appearing in all caps, in a clearly delineated box in both the upper right hand and the lower left hand corners of the homepage. *Id.* The importance of the 'terms of use' was obscured by the physical manifestation of assent, in this case clicking the 'SIGN IN' button, expected of a

consumer seeking to purchase in-flight Wi-Fi. Once Berkson clicked 'SIGN IN,' the 'terms of use' did not appear in a new screen or in a pop-up window on the same screen. *Id.* He was not required to scroll through the contract of adhesion and its boilerplate terms in order to click 'accept' or 'I agree.' " 97 F. Supp. 3d at 404.

The cases of *Swift v. Zynga Game Network, Inc.*, 805 F. Supp. 2d 904 (N.D. Cal. 2011) and *Nguyen v. Barnes & Noble, Inc.*, No. 8:12-CV-0812-JST RNB, 2012 WL 3711081, at *1 (C.D. Cal. Aug. 28, 2012), illustrate the different results that obtain from the same standard analysis for purported contracts based on assent to terms of use. Each involved enforcement of mandatory arbitration clauses. In *Swift v. Zynga Game Network, Inc.*, the plaintiff sought to bring a class action against Zynga for unfair competition in connection with certain "special offer" transactions offered by Zynga.

When users determined that they wanted to play a Zynga game, they were confronted with a disclaimer page with a large virtual button labeled "Allow," a smaller button labeled "Cancel," and a "smaller grey font stating 'By proceeding, you are allowing YoVille to access your information and you are agreeing to . . . the YoVille [blue hyperlink] Terms of Service.' " 805 F. Supp. 2d at 908. Later, Zynga changed its terms of service (which the prior version allowed it to do unilaterally) to include an expanded arbitration clause, waiver of jury trial (in all caps), a prohibition on class arbitration, and a severability clause that would allow for enforcement of all parts of the terms of service not found unenforceable. The Swift court had no trouble upholding the Zynga terms of service, including the arbitration clause. After distinguishing *Specht v. Netscape Communications Corp.* as a browsewrap case, not a clickwrap case, the court held that Zynga 's contract terms were enforceable. 805 F. Supp. 2d at 911.

In marked contrast is *Nguyen v. Barnes & Noble, Inc.*, which refused to enforce an arbitration clause in a browsewrap, rather than a clickwrap, license. There, the plaintiff responded to an advertisement for HP TouchPad tablet computers offered for sale on bamesandnoble.com for $101.95. After ordering two tablets, the plaintiff was informed the next day that his order would not be fulfilled. Disappointed, he sued to recover the difference between the advertised price and the cost of obtaining substitute products. The defendant moved to compel arbitration in accordance with its terms of use. In contrast to the facts in *Swift*, the terms of use in *Nguyen* were hyperlinked from the bottom of the Barnes & Noble ordering webpage and the plaintiff was not required to " 'affirmatively assent' because 'it [was] not necessary to click on the Terms of Use in order to make a purchase.' " Moreover, Barnes & Noble did not specifically direct consumers to its terms of use before making a purchase. 2012 WL 3711081, at *6.

The *Nguyen* court made it clear that the label, "clickwrap" or "browsewrap," was not dispositive to the outcome of the case (although case law does support this distinction, depending on the facts of particular cases). The fundamental inquiry was "whether plaintiff had constructive notice of the terms of the agreement and therefore agreed to be bound by them." 2012 WL 3711081, at *10. The court found the same essential facts present in *Nguyen*—that Barnes & Noble had not posted its terms of use where website users would necessarily see them and did not give notice (except in the terms of use themselves) that the terms applied. The court held that the plaintiff had not assented to the terms of use and refused to compel arbitration.

In a commercial context, courts may be more inclined to find terms of use to be binding on users of Internet websites, particularly if the user accessed the site by an automated "robot" or "web crawler."   In *Register.com, Inc. v. Verio Inc.*, 356 F.3d 393 (2d Cit. 2004), the court found Verio's repeated access to and use of information from Register.com's WHOIS database evidenced consent to Register.com's terms of use, notwithstanding that Verio did not see the terms of use until after it had completed using the database and never click on an "I Agree" button. Similarly, the court in *Cairo, Inc. v. CrossMedia Servs., Inc.*, No. C 04-04825 JW, 2005 WL 756610, at *1 (N.D. Cal. Apr. 1, 2005), held that the terms of use found on CrossMedia's Internet site were binding, given the defendant's actual knowledge of the terms of use and continued use of the site. The court also found that, even if Cairo had no actual knowledge of the terms of use, its repeated access to the site via "robot" resulted in imputed knowledge even though the robot was not capable of collecting, and did not collect, information on the contents of such terms.

S. AMENDING AND RESTATING AGREEMENTS

Often, contracts and other transactional documents require amendment after they have been executed. There are three basic methods of amending a contract.

The first is crude but effective. The parties manually change the provisions by hand on a hard copy version, striking out or inserting text on the original document and then initialing each change. It may be a good idea to add new signature blocks at the end of the document, or on a separate sheet, where the parties re-execute the agreement as amended.

The second method is to prepare a second document, entitled "Amendment Number ___ to [name original document]," and then to specify the amendments that are being made, perhaps including recitals that give context to the amendment for later use in understanding what went on and why the document was amended. In essence, this sort of amendment acts as an instruction sheet for later use in virtually cutting and pasting the two documents together into the new, resulting agreement.

The third method is called amending and restating the document. Using this method, the original contract terms, as amended, are written out or typed as a new contract. The contract can be prepared to reflect the original contract date, the amendment date, or both. This is the best method for situations where there are many amendments to be made at once. Sometimes, an original agreement has been amended piecemeal many times using the second method described above, and it may make sense to amend and restate the amendments. This would result in the original agreement accompanied by a consolidated amended and restated set of amendments.

In choosing the method used, consider how often the document will be referred to by the parties for guidance. If the answer is seldom, then either of the first two methods may be used effectively. If it will be re-examined often, amending and restating, or restating amendments is appropriate. The major risk in embarking on a complete restatement of a document is that it may reopen issues for negotiation that had been previously settled.

When the amendment is complete, ensure that it is distributed to all those that have or had the original document and ask them to include the amendment with their copy of the original documents. When amending documents that have been filed or recorded with governmental offices, it is probably necessary for the amendments, an amended and restated document, or, at a minimum, an abstract of them, to be filed with the same office to be perfected or "good against the world." This is generally the case with recorded deeds, encumbrances, lease abstracts, UCC–1 financing statements, and the like. In re-filing, thought must be given to the effect of intervening filings by the parties or third parties, and the effect of those filings and the new filings on lien priority and similar issues. Title policy endorsements are available to provide no loss of priority protection in some cases.

T. LETTERS OF INTENT

A letter of intent, a memorandum of understanding, or term sheet is a preliminary transactional document, generally prepared by a lawyer, which captures some or all of the key deal points the parties have agreed upon. It is usually not the final document that will govern the transaction, and the final transactional documents will generally supersede the letter of intent, usually expressly through integration or merger clauses. Here, we focus on a letter of intent. Drafting considerations for memoranda of understanding and term sheets are similar.

1. WHY USE A LETTER OF INTENT?

a. To Commit the Other Side Prior to Preparation of Definitive Documents

This is important in a deal of any real significance, as substantial time, effort, and attorneys' fees will be generated in arriving at final documentation and performing due diligence. It is often prudent to memorialize the parties' present agreement on key points as well as those areas that have not yet been agreed upon, before proceeding to incur additional transaction costs.

b. To Establish an Exclusive Right to Negotiate

Buyers (and others similarly situated) may achieve this goal with an express provision to this effect in the letter of intent. As a practical matter, however, even if the letter of intent is silent it will achieve this result to some degree. After all, what buyer would want to expend precious time, effort, and money negotiating and performing due diligence when they are second in line? Sellers should be reluctant to enter into a letter of intent for this reason alone, unless they receive separate consideration (generally a payment of money or perhaps a loan on favorable terms) from the buyer. Otherwise the seller will find that it has given the other party a free option and will have difficulty interesting third parties in negotiations. When a seller is subject to an option and can no longer use the potential of another buyer (the market) to drive the price and other terms in the seller's favor, the seller is at a significant disadvantage.

c. To Allow for Information Sharing Under a Confidentiality and Non-Disclosure Arrangement

Such provisions should be contained in the letter of intent, and it is best to provide, explicitly, specific remedies in case of breach.

d. To Outline the Basic Agreement

This can allow the parties to seek necessary financing prior to the negotiation and documentation of definitive final documents (which can be costly). It also allows the parties to seek approvals from boards of directors, loan committees, junior lien holders, and the like prior to incurring substantial transaction costs.

2. THE RISKS OF USING A LETTER OF INTENT

a. Premature Contractual Obligation

The parties may be obligated before all terms are worked out, and this may mean that a party is forced to conclude a transaction that is very different from the one it contemplated at the time of entering into the letter of intent.

b. Rigidity

The existence of the letter of intent may cause or increase rigidity in the parties' positions, which may have negative impacts upon the negotiation process.

3. ENFORCEABILITY AND DRAFTING POINTS FOR LETTERS OF INTENT

Courts can and will enforce letters of intent if they are convinced that the parties intended to be bound to the agreement, and the agreement is sufficiently definite to be enforced. *See, e.g., Arcadian Phosphates, Inc. v. Arcadian Corp.*, 884 F.2d 69 (2d Cir.1989). As a result, when deciding to use a letter of intent, the parties should determine if it is to be binding or not. They should then explicitly and unambiguously express this intent. If enforceability is contemplated, including express remedies, the letters of intent will assist a later court in concluding that the parties meant the letter of intent to be binding and enforceable and in determining the appropriate measure of damages or the equitable remedy.

Failure to address the binding or non-binding nature of the letter of intent can dramatically increase the uncertainties faced by the parties and their exposure to litigation risks. For example, the corporate oil giant Texaco was forced to take refuge in bankruptcy when a Texas jury found that a letter of intent between Penzoil and Getty Oil that was ambiguous as to its binding nature was binding and, therefore, Texaco had interfered with Penzoil's contractual advantage. The verdict against Texaco was $10.53 billion, a sum it could not bond around to obtain a stay of execution pending consideration of its appeal. Thus, it sought protection in Chapter 11. Counsel needs to carefully review the documents that are signed to ensure that their meaning will be clear to a reviewing court.

U. OPINIONS OF COUNSEL

Opinions of counsel, or opinion letters, used in transactional practice form a very important part of modern law firm practice. The opinion letters discussed here are typical of sophisticated transactional practice, and are gradually becoming part of ever more basic transactions. Opinion letters are commonly used to:

- Provide comfort that an intended course of action is legal or that certain definite legal consequences will follow;

- Provide comfort to the clients and opposing counsel by indicating that opining counsel has performed the due diligence investigation necessary to issue the opinion letter;

- Confirm the existence (or lack) of specific legal relationships; or

- Provide for undertaking a detailed review of a legal issue that bears on a transaction and to reach a legal conclusion upon which other parties can rely.

Opinion letters are the subject of much discussion, debate, and disagreement as well as local practice differences. A complete understanding of legal opinion practice is beyond the scope of this book, but there are a few key points that every lawyer involved in commercial transactions should know:

A. A legal opinion applies a body of law to a set of facts. Lawyers do not opine as to the underlying facts. They will reasonably assume certain facts, in reliance upon statements in documents, including other opinions of counsel, officers' certificates, and the like. Making unreasonable assumptions, or assumptions that are at variance with known facts, will not insulate the lawyer from liability in an action against the lawyer over an incorrect opinion.

B. A legal opinion is not a guaranty, a warranty, a representation, an indemnity, or an insurance policy. It is an opinion. If it is incorrect, the remedy is a malpractice claim, which requires a showing of damage caused by a breach of the applicable standard of care to one to whom a duty was owed. Without putting too fine a point on it, if the issuing attorney has met the appropriate standard of care in issuing it, the lawyer and his or her firm will not be liable, even if it is incorrect. This limits an opinion letter's efficacy as a protection for the client and others who rely on it.

C. Typically, opinions express legal conclusions as to

   (i)   the existence and proper formation of an entity;

   (ii) an entity's good standing;

   (iii) the attachment, perfection, and priority of liens;

   (iv) the legality and enforceability of all or part of a transactional document;

   (v)   the validity of prior transactions;

   (vi) whether a transaction contravenes or breaches an applicable law, rule, regulation, or contract; and

(vii) similar matters.

D. There are two general forms of formal opinion letters: the clean opinion and the reasoned opinion. A clean opinion states an absolute opinion as its conclusion, while a reasoned opinion states what the lawyer concludes should be the conclusion of a court or other adjudicative body faced with the same facts and law. Obviously, clean opinions are more desirable to clients and others relying upon them, such as sources of financing and rating agencies.

E. Assumptions. Opinion letters contain assumptions, but attorneys cannot rely upon a stated assumption if the attorney knows, or should know it to be untrue. In other words, the attorney must act reasonably when "assuming away" issues. Customary assumptions include:

  (i)   due organization and good standing of opposing parties,

  (ii) genuineness of signatures,

  (iii) enforceability of transactional documents against opposing parties, and

  (iv) authenticity and completeness of documents.

F. Qualifications. Opinion letters also contain qualifications on the opinion given. Typical qualifications limit the opinion

  (i)   to the laws of the state in which the opining attorney is licensed;

  (ii) to exclude the effects of bankruptcy and other similar laws; and

  (iii) to exclude future changes in law, whether by statute, rule, regulation, or court decision, particularly future court decisions.

G. A Simple Rule of Honor in Opinion Letter Practice. Never request an opinion that you would not be willing to give if you stood in opposing counsel's shoes.

Transactional documents often include conditions involving an opinion. For example, a buyer may condition closing of a sale on receiving an appropriate opinion from seller's counsel opining that the seller is duly organized and in good standing and has obtained all necessary authorizations to enter into the transaction with the buyer. Whether or not the condition describes the desired opinion generally or attaches a form as an exhibit, counsel should at least preliminarily discuss and negotiate the terms of the opinion early on. Otherwise, the parties may expend considerable time and expense documenting a transaction and conducting due diligence only to find that closing is held up or prevented because one firm refuses to issue an opinion or one in the form required by the other party. Clients are not very understanding in those circumstances.

Legal opinions are not only important; they represent a very real risk of liability for the firm and the attorneys issuing the opinion. Limit your opinions as much as possible. Follow firm procedures for issuing opinions strictly. The failure to do so can have dire consequences. *See Dean Foods Company v. Arthur J. Pappathanasi*, 18 Mass. L. Rep. 598, 2004 WL 3019442 (2004).

CHAPTER 5

OVERVIEW OF INTELLECTUAL PROPERTY ISSUES

■ ■ ■

A. INTRODUCTION

Intellectual property, which consists of property rights in innovations and creative works, is central to business and technological development in the global market. In the United States, the primary intellectual property rights are protected by state and federal trade secret law, federal patent and copyright law, and state and federal trademark law. Each body of law protects different interests and operates in different ways. Further, these areas of law undergo frequent change due to the technological innovations they foster.

Intellectual property law is something of an anomaly in American law. In our society, competition and free markets are the norm, and the law generally disfavors monopolies, at least unregulated monopolies. Yet, one group of intellectual property laws—trade secret, patent, and copyright law—grants limited monopolies to induce inventors and authors to create new inventions and works. The key word here is "limited." In addition to granting property rights, intellectual property law is concerned with limiting the intellectual property monopoly and preventing its misuse. Thus, the scope and limits of the monopoly control the extent to which intellectual property law limits competition.

The other primary group of intellectual property rights covered in this book is state and federal trademark and similar laws. These laws also grant a monopoly—but not in exchange for innovation or creation. Rather, trademark law is meant to prevent confusion about the source of goods and services in the market. These laws are more in keeping with the American conception of the competitive marketplace. Trademark law prevents confusion about the source of goods and services by allowing the goods and services to be branded. In this way, trademark law improves the information provided to market participants and lowers transaction costs associated with information gathering. Thus, trademark law promotes competition even as it grants a monopoly on the use of a particular mark.

Intellectual property law has become increasingly important and increasingly pervasive in the practice of law. Although once considered to be a narrow specialty area, it is now critical that attorneys in the practice of general business law have at least a basic understanding of intellectual property law.

B. TRADE SECRETS

- Trade secret protection is derived from state common law and recently enacted federal legislation, drawing heavily from the following four sources: the Restatement (First) of Torts § 757, the Restatement (Third) of Unfair Competition § 39, the Uniform Trade Secrets Act and most recently the Defend Trade Secrets Act of 2016.[1]

- Trade secret law protects proprietary information for as long as it remains secret (rather than for a fixed term like patents and copyrights).

- Information qualifies as a trade secret provided that it:

    (1) is not a matter of general knowledge and is not readily ascertainable;

    (2) is commercially valuable or gives the holder an economic advantage because of its secrecy; and

    (3) is guarded by reasonable means to maintain its secrecy.

- Misappropriation can be committed by: acquiring a trade secret through improper or wrongful means; disclosing or using a trade secret that was acquired wrongfully, in breach of a duty, or by mistake; or using a trade secret that was acquired wrongfully, in breach of a duty, or by mistake.

- Defenses to misappropriation include a valid licensing agreement; that the information was not actually secret; and discovery by proper means, such as independent invention, reverse engineering, discovery under a license, observation of public use, and discovery through published literature.

- Remedies for trade secret misappropriation include injunctions, damages, attorneys' fees, and punitive damages. Misappropriation might also result in criminal penalties, including prison sentences and fines as high as $5,000,000.

- Licensing allows the trade secret holder to share and profit from the information without compromising its secrecy. Licensing agreements often include provisions related to updates and technical support, renewal rights, confidentiality, and non-disclosure agreements, exclusivity of the license, and residual rights.

---

[1]   Defend Trade Secrets Act of 2016, 114 P.L. 153 | 130 Stat. 376.

- Trade secrets can serve as collateral. Security interests in trade secrets attach and are perfected as general intangibles under Article 9 of the Uniform Commercial Code.

Trade secrets allow businesses to protect proprietary information and ideas that do not qualify for protection as a patent or copyright. A business may also choose trade secret protection instead of patent and copyright protection because it does not want to be subject to the limitations of patent and copyright laws. For example, a patent applicant must enter the content of its application into the public record in order to obtain a patent, but there is no such requirement to protect an invention or idea as a trade secret. Furthermore, common law trade secret protection may be broader than the finite terms of patent and copyright protections. Trade secrets remain protected as long as their holder takes the necessary steps to keep them secret, but once the information is no longer secret, trade secret protection is no longer available. Thus, precautions against the disclosure of trade secrets are very important.

Although almost any meaningful information can be protected as a trade secret, trade secrets are often overlooked and unrecognized business assets. In fact, the value of a business's trade secrets can be greater than the aggregate value of its other intellectual property holdings, such as copyrights and patents. Perhaps the most famous trade secret is the formula for Coco-cola. Since 1891, the Coco-Cola company has enveloped the formula in a cloud of secrecy, maintaining it in a vault, and allowing only two employees to have access to the formula at any time.

American recognition of trade secret protection began as early as 1868 in *Peabody v. Norfolk*, 98 Mass. 452 (1868). In *Peabody,* a mill owner (Peabody) had been developing machinery to manufacture a certain type of cloth. He employed an engineer (Norfolk), who signed a contract promising to only use the machinery for the benefit of Peabody and to prevent other persons from obtaining information that would enable them to use their machinery. About six months after signing his contract, Norfolk made arrangements to leave Peabody's mill to build a cloth-mill for a competitor using the secret information Norfolk had learned from Peabody. The court granted an injunction restraining Norfolk from using Peabody's secret information, stating that the policy of the law is to encourage and protect invention and commercial enterprise. Most importantly, the court held that:

> One who invents or discovers, and keeps secret, a process of manufacture, whether proper for a patent or not, has a property interest therein which a court of chancery will protect against one who in violation of contract and breach of confidence undertakes to apply it to his own use or disclose it to third persons.

This remains the essence of trade secret law today.

1. DEFINING TRADE SECRETS

Trade secret law in the United States developed from state common law based on various theories and policies. Historically, some jurisdictions have adopted the position that trade secrets, like other forms of intellectual property, should be protected as a property interest. Other courts have rejected that approach, holding that trade secret protection is based on the theory of tortious breach of confidence. Later, courts and state legislatures took the view that trade secrets should be protected by prohibitions against unfair competition. As a result, courts relied on different sources of law to base their decisions when confronted with trade secret issues.

Trade secret law has evolved over time. Most states followed a combination of three approaches in classifying a trade secret. The first approach provided in the Restatement (First) of Torts § 757 cmt. b (1939): "A trade secret is any formula, pattern, device, or compilation of information used in business that gives the user a competitive advantage over others that do not know the secret." The comments to the Restatement (First) of Torts explain that a trade secret is not simply information pertaining to single or short-lived events, but rather something that is continuously used in the business. Additionally, the comments specify that a trade secret must actually be secret and cannot be a matter of public knowledge.

The Restatement (First) of Torts expressly states that the policy underlying trade secret law is protection against bad faith and breaches of confidence, not protection of property rights to reward and foster invention and innovation. This is in contrast to, for example, the temporary monopoly granted to a patent holder in exchange for disclosing an invention—a reward for taking socially desirable action. The Restatement (First) provides six factors for determining whether something is a trade secret:

1. the degree that the secret is known to others;

2. the degree that the secret is known to those involved in his business;

3. the measure taken to guard the secret;

4. the secret's value;

5. the time, effort, and money invested to develop the secret; and

6. how difficult it is for others to legitimately develop the information comprising the secret.

The Uniform Trade Secrets Act (the "UTSA"), introduced by the National Conference of Commissioners on Uniform State Law in 1979, as amended in 1985 has now become the most widely recognized authority on trade secret law, and has been adopted in some form by 48 states.[2] The UTSA § 1(4) defines a trade secret as information including a formula, pattern, compilation, program, device, method, technique, or process, that:

(A) derives independent economic value, actual or potential, from not being generally known to, and not being readily ascertainable by proper means by other persons who can obtain economic value from its disclosure or use; and

(B) is the subject of efforts that are reasonable under the circumstances to maintain its secrecy.

The following table provides citations to the various state trade secret statutes:

Alabama	Ala. Code § 8–27–1 et seq.
Alaska	Alaska Stat. § 45.50.910 et seq.
Arizona	Ariz. Rev. Stat. § 44–401 et seq.
Arkansas	Ark. Code Ann. § 4–75–601 et seq.
California	Cal. Civ. Code § 3426 et seq.
Colorado	Colo. Rev. Stat. § 7–74–101 et seq.
Connecticut	Conn. Gen. Stat. § 35–50 et seq.
Delaware	Del. Code tit. 6, § 2001 et seq.
District of Columbia	D.C. Code § 36–501 et seq.
Florida	Fla. Stat. § 688.001 et seq.
Georgia	Ga. Code Ann. § 10–1–760 et seq.
Hawaii	Haw. Rev. Stat. § 482B–1 et seq.
Idaho	Idaho Code Ann. § 48–801 et seq.
Illinois	765 Ill. Comp. Stat. § 1065/1 et seq.
Indiana	Ind. Code § 24–2–3–1 et seq.
Iowa	Iowa Code § 550.1 et seq.
Kansas	Kan. Stat. Ann. § 60–3320 et seq.
Kentucky	Ky. Rev. Stat. Ann. § 365.880 et seq.
Louisiana	La. Rev. Stat. Ann. § 51:1431 et seq.
Maine	Me. Rev. Stat. Ann. tit. 10, § 1541 et seq.
Maryland	Md. Code Ann., Com. Law § 11–1201 et seq.

---

[2] The goal of the UTSA is to make the state laws governing trade secrets uniform. This is especially important to companies who operate in more than one state.

Massachusetts	Mass. Gen. Laws Ann. ch. 93, § 42 et seq.
Minnesota	Minn. Stat. Ann. § 325C.01 et seq.
Mississippi	Miss. Code Ann. § 75–26–1 et seq.
Missouri	Mo. Rev. Stat. § 417.450 et seq.
Nebraska	Neb. Rev. Stat. § 87–501 et seq.
Nevada	Nev. Rev. Stat. Ann. § 600A.010 et seq.
New Hampshire	N.H. Rev. Stat. Ann. § 350–B:1 et seq.
New Mexico	N.M. Stat. Ann. § 57–3A–1 et seq.
North Carolina	N.C. Gen. Stat. § 66–152 et seq.
North Dakota	N.D. Cent. Code § 47–25.1–01 et seq.
Ohio	Ohio Rev. Code Ann. § 1333.61
Oklahoma	Okla. Stat. Ann. tit. 78, § 85 et seq.
Oregon	Or. Rev. Stat. § 646.461 et seq.
Pennsylvania	12 Pa. Cons. Stat. Ann. § 5301 et seq.
South Carolina	S.C. Code Ann. § 39–8–10 et seq.
South Dakota	S.D. Codified Laws § 37–29–1 et seq.
Tennessee	Tenn. Code Ann. § 47–25–1701 et seq.
Texas	Tex. Code Ann. §§ 134A.001–134A.008
Vermont	9 Vt. Stat. Ann. § 4601 et seq.
Washington	Wash. Rev. Code Ann. § 19.108.010 et seq.
West Virginia	W. Va. Code Ann. § 47–22–1 et seq.
Wisconsin	Wis. Stat. § 134.90

The Restatement (Third) of Unfair Competition § 39 (1995) employs a broad definition of trade secret, "[a] trade secret is any information that can be used in the operation of a business or other enterprise and that is sufficiently valuable and secret to afford an actual or potential economic advantage over others."

Congress has since amended the Economic Espionage Act of 1996,[3] (EEA) creating for the first time a federal cause of action for trade secret misappropriation and related disputes; thus, the provisions of the Defend Trade Secrets Act of 2016 ("DTSA") will become increasingly important—

---

[3] The Economic Espionage Act gives the U.S. Department of Justice broad authority to prosecute trade secret theft occurring both domestically and abroad, as well as over the Internet. The EEA was directed at the theft of trade secrets by foreign governments, their instrumentalities and agents. It expanded the definition of trade secrets to include information technology but it provided no private cause of action and relied solely on the Department of Justice to investigate and provide enforcement.

if not controlling—components of trade secret litigation.[4] The DTSA generally enables private civil action in federal court by the owner of a misappropriated trade secret, provided that the trade secret is related to a product or service used or intended for use in commerce.[5] Although the DTSA federalizes trade secret protection, Congress did not choose to preempt state law trade secret protections. Rather, actions will lie under both federal and state laws.

In addition to the creation of federal jurisdiction, the DTSA allows courts to grant *ex parte* orders providing for the seizure of property "necessary to prevent the propagation or dissemination of the trade secret that is the subject of the action."[6] Notably, the statute instructs courts to grant the order only in "extraordinary circumstances."[7] The statute also states that orders should be denied unless the facts clearly present that several factors[8] have been demonstrated by the moving party, showing

---

[4]   At the time of this edition, many questions regarding the contours of the DTSA have not had a chance to be fully litigated (including issues regarding preemption of state causes of action). However, Congress used the Uniform Trade Secrets Act as inspiration for the DTSA: Much of the language used in the DTSA was pulled from the UTSA, which presumably will generate similar results where courts have previously litigated a given issue under the UTSA.

[5]   18 U.S.C. § 1836(b)(1).

[6]   18 U.S.C. § 1836(b)(2).

[7]   *Id.* [1836b2].

[8]   **(ii)** Requirements for issuing order. The court may not grant an application under clause (i) unless the court finds that it clearly appears from specific facts that—

> **(I)** an order issued pursuant to Rule 65 of the Federal Rules of Civil Procedure or another form of equitable relief would be inadequate to achieve the purpose of this paragraph because the party to which the order would be issued would evade, avoid, or otherwise not comply with such an order;
>
> **(II)** an immediate and irreparable injury will occur if such seizure is not ordered;
>
> **(III)** the harm to the applicant of denying the application outweighs the harm to the legitimate interests of the person against whom seizure would be ordered of granting the application and substantially outweighs the harm to any third parties who may be harmed by such seizure;
>
> **(IV)** the applicant is likely to succeed in showing that—
>
>> (aa) the information is a trade secret; and
>>
>> (bb) the person against whom seizure would be ordered—
>>
>>> (AA) misappropriated the trade secret of the applicant by improper means; or
>>>
>>> (BB) conspired to use improper means to misappropriate the trade secret of the applicant;
>
> **(V)** the person against whom seizure would be ordered has actual possession of—
>
>> (aa) the trade secret; and
>>
>> (bb) any property to be seized;
>
> **(VI)** the application describes with reasonable particularity the matter to be seized and, to the extent reasonable under the circumstances, identifies the location where the matter is to be seized;
>
> **(VII)** the person against whom seizure would be ordered, or persons acting in concert with such person, would destroy, move, hide, or otherwise make such matter inaccessible to the court, if the applicant were to proceed on notice to such person; and

Congress' intent that the seizure of property be used as a last-resort method of securing allegedly stolen trade secrets. To date, federal courts have rarely granted orders for *ex parte* seizure of property: the applicable scope of clearly proven requirements for issuance of an order, as well as the situations that constitute extraordinary circumstances as understood by the courts is yet to be fully determined.[9]

The DTSA also grants immunity from liability for confidential disclosure of a trade secret to an attorney or government official in an attempt to report a suspected violation of the law.[10] Employees are also protected in lawsuits alleging employer retaliation for the employee's disclosure of a suspected violation, provided that the disclosure occurs under seal.[11] The most important portion of this provision pertains to notice of immunity, as the employer now has an affirmative duty to inform the employee of his or her immunity from liability under the DTSA.[12]

Given the infancy of the newly enacted DTSA, many courts still look to the Restatement (First) of Torts (1939), the Restatement (Third) of Unfair Competition, and the Uniform Trade Secrets Act of 1979, as persuasive sources of state trade secret law.

Finally, as defined by the DTSA, a trade secret means:

"all forms and types of financial, business, scientific, technical, economic, or engineering information, including patterns, plans, compilations, program devices, formulas, designs, prototypes, methods, techniques, processes, procedures, programs, or codes, whether tangible or intangible, and whether or how stored, compiled, or memorialized physically, electronically, graphically, photographically, or in writing if—

(A) the owner thereof has taken reasonable measures to keep such information secret; and

(B) the information derives independent economic value, actual or potential, from not being generally known to, and not being readily ascertainable through proper means by, another person

---

(VIII) the applicant has not publicized the requested seizure.

[9] *See* Mission Capital Advisors LLC v. Romaka, No. 16-cv-5878 (S.D.N.Y. July 29, 2016) (*wherein* the court initially denied the request for seizure of assets and thereafter partially granted a subsequent motion, allowing two files with sufficiently detailed confidentiality/importance to be seized, but denied other components of the motion because these requests lacked sufficient specificity). Note that many courts have been hesitant to grant motions under the DTSA provision, often preferring to use TRO's under Rule 65. . .my guess is that they're simply more used to dealing with these laws, and don't want to use the potentially harsher approach under the DTSA unless absolutely necessary.

[10] 18 U.S.C. § 1833(b)(1).

[11] *Id.* at § 1833(b)(2).

[12] *Id.* at § 1833(b)(3).

who can obtain economic value from the disclosure or use of the information. . . ."

18 U.S.C. § 1839.

2. CHARACTERISTICS OF A TRADE SECRET

Customarily, a trade secret generally involves information that:

(1) is not a matter of general knowledge and is not readily ascertainable;

(2) is commercially valuable or gives the proprietor an economic advantage because of its secrecy; and

(3) is guarded by reasonable means to maintain its secrecy.

The essential characteristics of a trade secret vary from one jurisdiction to another, as do limitations on the availability of trade secret protection. For example, some jurisdictions that adopt the Restatement (First) definition refuse to extend protection to ideas alone. In other jurisdictions, however, ideas may be protected as trade secrets, though protection is often conditioned on a showing that the idea is novel, sufficiently concrete, disclosed (if at all) in confidence, and actually in use.

Additionally, under the DTSA, the characteristics of a trade secret heavily mirror the characteristics under the UTSA. In fact, the definition of a trade secret under the DTSA is substantively identical to the UTSA, and the legislature even incorporated the narrower interpretation of who the trade secret cannot be generally known by or readily ascertainable to, which was originally found in the UTSA. Specifically, the DTSA substituted the concept "another person who can obtain economic value from the disclosure or use of the information" from the UTSA for "the public" from the 2015 Economic Espionage Act.[13] In fact, courts have used the similarity of the definitions under the two Acts in analyzing cases under the DTSA; additionally, courts have commented that the implementation of the DTSA was not a reaction to insufficiencies of any trade secret laws from the states, but a response for this particular area of law's need for a singular, uniform federal cause of action.[14]

Technical information, business information, and even know-how are generally protectable as trade secrets.

- Technical information refers generally to scientific information such as formulas (including chemical formulas), manufacturing techniques, and software.

---

[13] 18 U.S.C. § 1839(3)(B).

[14] *Brand Energy & Infrastructure Servs. v. Irex Contracting Grp.*, No. 16-2499, 2017 U.S. Dist. LEXIS 43497, at *1, *16–17 (E.D. Pa. Mar. 24, 2017).

- Business information generally encompasses any other commercially valuable information including financial data, market research, customer lists, vendor lists, uncompiled computer source code, and unannounced business negotiations.

- Know-how is not capable of precise description but is generally thought of as factual knowledge which gives one an ability to produce something that they otherwise would not have known how to produce and knowledge necessary for commercial success. In other words, it is knowledge of how to do something better, faster, or cheaper than a competitor.

Although technical information, as a category, generally encompasses subject matter eligible for patent protection, the Supreme Court has held that federal patent law does not preempt state trade secret protection even in regard to inventions that are clearly patentable. Rather, the Court has held that Congress's intent to use the patent law limited monopoly to encourage disclosure of genuinely novel inventions is not undermined by the availability of an alternative legal mechanism for fostering innovation, like trade secret law.

a. Not a Matter of General Knowledge or Readily Ascertainable Information

Common knowledge and readily ascertainable information cannot qualify as trade secrets. Further, if information is an industry custom or is known by even one competitor, trade secret protection may not be available. On the other hand, unlike other forms of intellectual property such as patents and copyrights, a trade secret need not be exclusive; thus multiple independent developers may have rights in the same trade secret if each develops the secret independently and each developer maintains secrecy.

Whether information is readily ascertainable is also significant in determining the availability of trade secret protection. According to the UTSA, a trade secret must not be readily ascertainable by proper means. Proper means include discovery by independent invention, reverse engineering, discovery under a license from the trade secret owner, observation of the item in public use or on public display, and obtaining the trade secret from published literature. Generally, if information is discoverable within the bounds of commercial morality and reasonable conduct, it will not be protected as a trade secret. Further, the same is true of trade secret protection under the DTSA, as the legislature directly codified the UTSA's comments regarding proper use into the statute.

Likewise, publication of information in trade journals, reference books, or even advertisements will undermine its status as a trade secret.

Publication on the Internet may also cause information to become generally known, unless the information is sufficiently obscure or is inaccessible to relevant parties, such as potential competitors.

In many instances, trade secret protection is an alternative to patent protection, but the inventor's choice is exclusive. Publication in a patent destroys the trade secret because patents are intended to be widely disclosed. Moreover, trade secret protection will ordinarily be foreclosed by a patent application even if the patent is denied, because applications are published eighteen months after filing assuming that the patent applicant does not request otherwise and does not seek a foreign patent of the same invention.

Parties under a contractual duty of confidentiality will not be relieved of that duty if a patent or application has disclosed information claimed as a trade secret.

b. Value

Under both the UTSA and the DTSA, information must be at least minimally commercially valuable to qualify as a trade secret. Actual or potential economic advantage conferred by the secret is sufficient. The Restatement (First) definition requires trade secret information to be in continuous use, but modern trade secret law recognizes value in information or processes not yet put into use and even negative information—knowledge of what will not work. Whether actual or potential, the economic advantage of keeping information secret need not be great, but must be more than trivial. Moreover, the advantage gained need not be competitive in the traditional sense, and many jurisdictions recognize economic value independent of competitors. Paralleling the value requirement, in many jurisdictions misappropriation of trade secret information is not actionable unless the information is at least minimally novel either to the world at large or to the misappropriator. Novelty shows that the idea was obtained from the trade secret holder and that the disclosure of the idea had some value.

c. Reasonable Means to Maintain Secrecy

Again, because the legislature heavily relied on the UTSA when drafting the DTSA's provisions, the interpretation of what constitutes as reasonable means necessary to maintain secrecy of a trade secret will likely be the same as it has been under the UTSA. Conventionally, information will not be protected as a trade secret unless its holder uses reasonable means to protect the information's secrecy. Proprietors must actively protect their trade secrets; merely describing information as secret is not enough. Absolute secrecy, however, is not required. Rather, secrecy is a relative term and is construed equitably, not absolutely. Although public disclosure undermines any claim of secrecy,

[t]he holder of a secret need not remain totally silent: "He may, without losing his protection, communicate it to employees involved in its use. He may likewise communicate it to others pledged to secrecy. Nevertheless, a substantial element of secrecy must exist, so that except by the use of improper means, there would be difficulty in acquiring the information."[15]

In essence, the means by which the trade secret holder protects his information need only be reasonable under the circumstances, which include the size of the company and the resources. Appropriate protections can include hiding it from any public view, placing it in a restricted access area, posting restricted access signs and requiring any company employee with access to the information to sign a non-disclosure agreement. Other reasonable protective measures include securely locking secret files, guarding facility entrances, restricting access to certain areas, issuing identification to employees, requiring confidentiality or non-disclosure agreements, with everyone privy to the secret and using passwords to protect computer software. The law does not, however, require that extreme and unduly expensive procedures be taken to protect against flagrant industrial espionage.

Holders may, without destroying trade secret protection, divulge their processes or information to a limited extent. For instance, proprietors may make controlled disclosures to their employees and licensees without destroying secrecy. Many trade secret holders use confidentiality or nondisclosure agreements to prevent employees or licensees from further disseminating secret information. These agreements typically require employees to (1) acknowledge that during the course of employment they may be exposed to confidential or proprietary information that is the exclusive property of the company and (2) agree that they will not disclose that information to third persons without first having obtained written permission from the company. Confidentiality agreements provide employers with evidence that reasonable measures were taken to preserve secrecy. In addition, violation of a confidentiality agreement may permit a breach of contract claim against an employee who discloses proprietary information.

An implied duty of confidentiality may be imputed to employees, business partners, and even parties who gain knowledge of a trade secret through unconsummated contract negotiations. For example, an implied duty of confidentiality frequently arises where employees gain specialized knowledge during their employment that may qualify as a trade secret. Under such circumstances, an employee may be enjoined from disclosing or using trade secrets to compete with their employer even where the

---

[15]   *Metallurgical Indus, Inc. v. Fourtek, Inc.*, 790 F.2d 1195, 1200 (5th Cir. 1986).

employer did not obtain a non-disclosure agreement. However, employees may always use non-secret information to compete with a former employer.

3. MISAPPROPRIATION OF A TRADE SECRET

The holder of a trade secret is entitled to recover under trade secret law only if the trade secret is misappropriated. Misappropriation of a trade secret gives rise to a variety of civil remedies and even criminal penalties. Misappropriation, under both the UTSA and DTSA, is defined as the:

(1) acquisition of a trade secret of another by a person who knows or has reason to know that the trade secret was acquired by improper means; or

(2) disclosure or use of a trade secret of another without express or implied consent by a person who:

    a. used improper means to acquire knowledge of the trade secret, or

    b. at the time of the disclosure or use, knew, or had reason to know that his knowledge of the trade secret was:

        i. derived from or through a person who had utilized improper means to acquire it;

        ii. acquired under circumstances giving rise to a duty to maintain its secrecy or limit its use; or

        iii. derived from or through a person who owed a duty to the person seeking relief to maintain its secrecy or limit its use; or

    c. before a material change of position, knew or had reason to know that is was a trade secret and that knowledge of it had been acquired by accident or mistake.[16]

Ga. Code Ann. § 10–1–761 (mirroring UTSA § 1(2)).

While some practitioners in the field have speculated that the federal cause of action under the DTSA will largely mirror the trade secret laws of California,[17] few cases have been fully litigated under the new legislation. The language of the DTSA defines theft of trade secrets as follows:

> Whoever, with intent to convert a trade secret, that is related to a product or service used in or intended for use in interstate or foreign commerce, to the economic benefit of anyone other than the owner thereof, and intending or knowing that the offense will, injure any owner of that trade secret, knowingly—

---

[16]　Ga. Code Ann. § 10–1–761 (mirroring UTSA § 1(2)); 18 U.S.C. § 1839(5).

[17]　*See, e.g.*, David Bohrer, *Threatened Misappropriation of Trade Secrets: Making a Federal (DTSA) Case Out of It*, 33 Santa Clara Computer & High Tech L.J. 56 (2017).

(1) steals, or without authorization appropriates, takes, carries away, or conceals, or by fraud, artifice, or deception obtains such information;

(2) without authorization copies, duplicates, sketches, draws, photographs, downloads, uploads, alters, destroys, photocopies, replicates, transmits, delivers, sends, mails, communicates, or conveys such information;

(3) receives, buys, or possesses such information, knowing the same to have been stolen or appropriated, obtained, or converted without authorization;

(4) attempts to commit any offense described in paragraphs (1) through (3); or

(5) conspires with one or more other persons to commit any offense described in paragraphs (1) through (3), and one or more of such persons do any act to effect the object of the conspiracy. . ." [18]

In sum, misappropriation may be committed in three ways:

(1)   by acquiring a trade secret through improper or wrongful means;

(2)   by disclosing a trade secret that was acquired wrongfully, in breach of a duty, or by mistake; or

(3)   by using a trade secret that was acquired wrongfully, in breach of a duty, or by mistake.

Where one person steals a trade secret and discloses it to another who uses the information knowing that it was stolen, three separate actions of misappropriation have occurred.

Actual misappropriation is not necessary for relief; the threat of misappropriation is sufficient. Although the requirement of misappropriation developed from law regarding breach of confidential relationships (such as information disclosed by an employer to an employee or under a confidentiality agreement), misappropriation can be committed by someone who had no confidential relationship with the trade secret holder. While the language of the DTSA closely tracks with the language of the UTSA and thus, other state trade secret laws, there are three important departures in which courts may distinguish the DTSA from the UTSA and corresponding state laws. Notably, however, the recently enacted DTSA has undergone relatively little litigation and courts are still

---

[18]   18 U.S.C. § 1832(a). The DTSA further notes that actions for theft of trade secrets may be brought against organizations, as well: "Any organization that commits any offense described in subsection (a) shall be fined not more than the greater of $5,000,000 or 3 times the value of the stolen trade secret to the organization, including expenses for research and design and other costs of reproducing the trade secret that the organization has thereby avoided." *Id.* § 1832(b).

in the process of interpreting it. Nonetheless, under the DTSA, there are three general trends forming from the current litigation: (1) a plaintiff is now able to utilize a continuing use theory for recovery; (2) there is an additional interstate commerce requirement for eligibility to invoke the act; and (3) the inevitable disclosure doctrine was explicitly limited, if not outright rejected.

Described in more detail later in the chapter, the DTSA noticeably deviates from the UTSA in its effective date provision, which allows a claim for misappropriation that occurred before May 11, 2016 (the DTSA's effective date) but continued afterwards. In concluding that the DTSA supports what has been called the "use-based" theory, many district courts have relied on the DTSA's explicit omission of a key phrase found in the UTSA: "[w]ith respect to a continuing misappropriation that began prior to the effective date, the [Act] also does not apply to the continuing misappropriation that occurs after the effective date."[19] The courts reason that, because of the legislatures access and knowledge of this provision in the UTSA and other state trade secret laws, the explicit omission of the limitation establishes the legislature's intent for the DTSA to support a continuing use theory of recovery.

Additionally, to raise a claim for misappropriation of a trade secret, the DTSA requires that the plaintiff's trade secret be used in, or intended for such use in, interstate or foreign commerce.[20] In this way, the DTSA necessitates an additional step for a plaintiff to prove a claim for misappropriation than what is required under the UTSA or similar state trade secret laws.[21]

Further, before the DTSA, courts have utilized the inevitable disclosure doctrine under the UTSA when determining whether to grant an injunction. Based on this idea, the plaintiff need only prove that the previous employee has knowledge of a trade secret and that in his new employment, he will inevitably disclose that trade secret. However, the language of the DTSA conspicuously limits injunctions when the basis of ordering one is founded on the inevitable disclosure doctrine.[22] Specifically, the DTSA states that in a civil action for misappropriation of a trade secret, a court may order an injunction

> to prevent any actual or threatened misappropriation [under the Act] . . . provided the order *does not prevent a person from entering into an employment relationship*, and that conditions placed on such employment shall be based on evidence of threatened

---

[19]   UTSA, § 11.

[20]   18 U.S.C. § 1836(b)(1)

[21]   *E.g., SPBS, Inc. v. John D. Mobley & Intermed Grp. Servs., Inc.*, No. 4:18-CV-00391, 2018 U.S. Dist. LEXIS 148881, at *1, *6–7 (E.D. Tex. Aug. 31, 2018) (noting that a plaintiff does not need to show use in interstate commerce under the TUTSA).

[22]   18 U.S.C. § 1836(b)(3)(A)(i)(I).

misappropriation and *not merely on the information the person knows.*[23]

Based on the scant litigation available, courts are mixed on whether to follow the exclusion of the inevitable disclosure doctrine. For example, in UCAR Technology (USA) Inc. v. Li, the California court held that the plaintiff's complaint alleged violations of the DTSA sufficient to survive a motion to dismiss but explicitly rejected the plaintiff's inevitable disclosure allegations.[24] By reaching its conclusion, the court strongly noted that "[t]o the extent the complaint relies on these types of "inevitable disclosure" allegations, those allegations are ordered stricken from the complaint."[25] On the contrary, an Illinois court has potentially resurrected the inevitable disclosure doctrine for DTSA plaintiffs. In Molon Motor & Coil Corp. v. Nidec Motor Corp., the plaintiff's complaint was saved based solely on the theory of inevitable disclosure.[26] In allowing the complaint to move forward, the court completely ignored the language found in the DTSA and stated that the plaintiff's allegations "are enough to trigger the circumstantial inference that the trade secrets inevitably would be disclosed by [former employee] to [competitor employer]."[27] Accordingly, we must wait for future cases to shed light on the status of the inevitable disclosure doctrine under the DTSA.

a. Acquisition by Improper Means

It is difficult to precisely determine what constitutes improper means. As broadly defined by the Restatement (First), improper means fall below the generally accepted standards of commercial morality and reasonable conduct. The UTSA and DTSA both define improper means to include theft, bribery, misrepresentation, breach (or inducement of a breach) of duty to maintain secrecy, or espionage through electronic or other means. This definition includes any tortious or criminal act as improper means. In certain circumstances, conduct that would otherwise be lawful may also constitute improper means.[28] The Restatement (Third) of Unfair Competition takes a flexible approach, defining improper means to include acquisition by "means either wrongful in themselves or wrongful under the circumstances of the case."

---

[23]   *Id.* (emphasis added).

[24]   No. 5:17-cv-01704-EJD, 2017 U.S. Dist. LEXIS 206816, at *1, *9–11 (N.D. Cal. Dec. 15, 2017).

[25]   *Id.* at *9.

[26]   No. 16 C 03545, 2017 U.S. Dist. LEXIS 71700, at *1, *12–13, 17 (N.D. Ill. May 11, 2017).

[27]   *Id.* at *17.

[28]   *See* E.I. du Pont de Nemours & Co., Inc. v. Christopher, 431 F.2d 1012 (CA 5, 1970), *cert. denied,* 400 U.S. 1024, 91 S. Ct. 581, 27 L. Ed. 2d 637 (1970). In this case, a competitor hired photographers to fly over a DuPont methanol plant during its construction to obtain pictures of DuPont's secret methanol-producing process. *See id.* at 1013. The court held that although it is otherwise lawful to fly over a plant during construction, it is improper to do so to obtain secret information of a competitor. *See id.* at 1016–17.

A party need not use or disclose improperly obtained information to be liable for misappropriation; acquisition of the trade secret is sufficient. The improper means of obtaining the secret are the basis for liability. For example, theft of a trade secret from an employee or other person entrusted with the secret is misappropriation. Additionally, to knowingly accept secret information procured through improper means is a form of misappropriation.

Improper means may even include memorization of secret information, particularly of confidential client lists, which generally qualify for trade secret protection. Some jurisdictions do not protect client lists on the assumption that the contact information contained in the list is almost certainly easily ascertainable. The value of memorization as a defense under trade secrets law is unclear. However, employees who, on their last day of work, peruse their employer's customer list with the intention of obtaining trade secret information will probably be found to have used memorization as an improper means of obtaining secret information.

b. Disclosure of Another's Trade Secret

As described above, a person who wrongfully discloses trade secret information without the proprietor's consent or who discloses a trade secret obtained by improper means can be liable to the trade secret holder.[29] In addition, persons who obtain trade secret information by mistake, but who know that the information was obtained by mistake, are liable if they disclose the secret information.[30] Likewise, a person who knowingly receives information from another who is bound by a non-disclosure agreement is liable for disclosure of a trade secret along with the person who disclosed it.[31] Thus, if an employee discloses to his present employer a trade secret of his former employer, both may be guilty of misappropriation.[32]

Disclosure of information obtained accidentally constitutes misappropriation if the disclosing party knew or had reason to know that it had accidentally or mistakenly acquired trade secret information. Thus, persons who receive trade secrets via fax to the wrong number or e-mail to the wrong address are liable for misappropriation if they disclose the secret information to a competitor of the sender.[33]

---

[29]   Unif. Trade Secrets Act § (1)(2)(ii)(B)(I)–(III).

[30]   *Id.*

[31]   *Id.*

[32]   *See, e.g.*, First Fin. Bank, N.A. v. Bauknecht, 71 F. Supp. 3d 819 (C.D. Ill. 2014).

[33]   *See* Goldine v. Kantemirov, 2006 U.S. Dist. LEXIS 44155 (N.D. Cal. June 19, 2006) (web site developer who was given access to confidential database in course of engagement allegedly offered to provide confidential and proprietary information to plaintiff's competitors).

c.   Use of Another's Trade Secret

Use of a trade secret is a broad concept with no bright-line definition. According to the Restatement (Third) of Unfair Competition § 40 cmt. c, "any exploitation of the trade secret that is likely to result in injury to the trade secret owner or enrichment to the [misappropriator] is a 'use.'" For example, use may occur by operating under an expired license, contacting another's customers from a proprietary customer list, incorporating a trade secret into a production process, advertising a product that was manufactured using another's trade secrets, or even relying on another's trade secret in developing a business model. Furthermore, unauthorized use need not extend to every aspect or feature of the trade secret; use of a substantial portion of the secret is sufficient to subject the actor to liability. However, the use must be more than minor or inconsequential, and the trade secret owner must demonstrate that the misappropriator received some sort of unfair trade advantage.

An employer may, under certain circumstances, have a "shop right" to use trade secrets or even the patented inventions of its employees. A shop right is a common law right that entitles an employer to use an invention developed by one or more of its employees without charge and without liability for misappropriation infringement when appropriate under principles of equity.

4.   DEFENSES

The chief defense to a claim of misappropriation is discovery through legitimate means, which, as stated in the comment to UTSA § 1 and broadly incorporated in the definition of "improper means" in § 1839(6)(B) of the DTSA, includes:

(a) Discovery by independent invention;

(b) Discovery by reverse engineering, which involves starting with the known product and working backward to find the method by which it was developed. The acquisition of the known product must also be by a fair and honest means, such as purchase on the open market, for reverse engineering to be lawful;

(c) Discovery under a license from the owner of the trade secret;

(d) Observation of the item in public use or on public display; and

(e) Obtaining the trade secret from published literature.

However, under the newly enacted DTSA, several other potential defenses to a claim against misappropriation may arise, including whistleblower protection, employee right to notice, and what is commonly known as the "timing defense."

Under the whistleblower provision in the DTSA, an individual will be shielded from liability only if the disclosure is in strict accordance with the provision; that is, if the individual confidentially discloses the trade secret to the government or in a court filing.[34]   Further, to satisfy the whistleblower provision in its entirety, employer's must meet certain standards regarding employee notice. For example, in any contract or agreement between the employer and the employee which governs the use of confidential information, the employer must provide notice of this immunity.[35] If an employer fails to afford an employee this notice, the employer may not be entitled to exemplary—or "punitive"—damages or attorney's fees in an action against such an employee for disclosure of a trade secret.[36]

Noticeably, the whistleblower immunity provision and the employee right to notice defenses are interrelated, as the employee's right to notice defense is specifically connected to the employer's duty to notify their employees of their right to disclose a trade secret in conformity with the statute.[37] Accordingly, the two defenses can likely be asserted together.

Further, the timing defense, specifically borne from the implementation of the DTSA, is yet another possible attack on a plaintiff's misappropriation claim—albeit with minimal success. Nonetheless, this defense is based on the statute's effective date of May 11, 2016, and stands for the idea that a plaintiff cannot allege facts based solely on misappropriation that occurred before the effective date and remain to make a claim under the DTSA. However, "[n]othing suggests that the DTSA forecloses a *use-based theory* simply because the trade secret being used was misappropriated before the DTSA's enactment."[38] In other words, if the plaintiff can plead facts that suggest that the defendant continued to use the plaintiff's misappropriated trade secret after the DTSA's enactment, her claim can survive the dismissal stage.[39]

Importantly, as a consequence of this line-drawing, a crafty plaintiff may be able to get around this defense with clever drafting at the pleading stage. To illustrate this point, consider the stark differences in the outcomes in Cave Consulting and Brand Energy. In Cave Consulting, the court made special notice of the general trend in allowing a DTSA claim if there was continued use; however, the court dismissed the plaintiff's claim, because the complaint lacked specific allegations of the defendant's use of

---

[34]   18 U.S.C. § 1833(b).

[35]   *Id.* § 1833(3)(A).

[36]   *Id.* § 1833(3)(C).

[37]   *Id.* § 1833(b)(3).

[38]   *Cave Consulting Grp., Inc. v. Truven Health Analytics, Inc.*, No. 15-cv-02177-SI, 2017 U.S. Dist. LEXIS 62109, at *1, *9 (N.D. Cal. Mar. 23, 2017) (emphasis added).

[39]   *123 Exteriors, Inc. v. N. Star Exteriors, LLC*, No. 17-4337, 2018 U.S. Dist. LEXIS 128748, at *1, *20–21 (E.D. Pa. Aug. 1, 2018).

the misappropriated trade secret *after* the DTSA's enactment.[40] Specifically, the plaintiff alleged general wrongful conduct on the part of the defendant, but the court reasoned that that allegation was not sufficient to state a claim under the DTSA.[41] In contrast, in Brand Energy, the plaintiff's claim survived dismissal, because the amended complaint successfully alleged that the defendant used the trade secrets at numerous times after the effective date of the DTSA.[42] Thus, in juxtaposition to the plaintiff in Cave Consulting, Brand Energy was able to continue with its claim under the DTSA.[43]

5.   REMEDIES

a.   Civil Remedies

A variety of civil remedies are available to the holder of a trade secret that has been misappropriated. These include damages, injunctions, accountings, and awards of profits, as well as destruction of objects embodying or incorporating the trade secret.

Injunctions are generally issued only if the trade secret remains a secret. An injunction usually lasts only as long as necessary to eliminate the commercial advantage or "lead time" obtained through misappropriation. Injunctions may be issued to prevent threatened use or disclosure of a trade secret. Further, under the inevitable disclosure doctrine, an injunction may be available to prevent former employees from performing the same job for a competitor of their former employer. The inevitable disclosure doctrine is based on the idea that in certain circumstances, trade secrets will inevitably be used or disclosed, regardless of a prior non-disclosure agreement by the employee. For example, if an employee obtained knowledge of his employer's future business plans and then left the company to work for a competitor, disclosure of the secret would be inevitable because the employee could not be forced to forget the information and would naturally consider it when making decisions for the new employer. Therefore, courts may grant injunctions to prevent the employee from working in a similar position until the information is no longer secret or has lost its value.

However, the language of the DTSA markedly limits injunctions when the basis of ordering one is founded on the inevitable disclosure doctrine.[44] Although commentators initially believed that because the DTSA limited this doctrine it would become a "dead letter," courts have since produced mixed results. Again, due to the DTSA's relative infancy, we must wait

---

[40]   *Cave Consulting*, 2017 U.S. Dist. LEXIS 62109, at *12–13 (emphasis added).

[41]   *Id.* at *13.

[42]   *Brand Energy*, 2017 U.S. Dist. LEXIS 43497, at *10–11.

[43]   *Id.* at *11.

[44]   18 U.S.C. § 1836(b)(3)(A)(i)(I).

while the courts battle to an agreement over the inevitable disclosure doctrine's relevancy under the DTSA.

Both traditionally under the UTSA and modernly under the DTSA, the court may also award damages in addition to, or in lieu of, an injunction. Damages can include both compensation for actual loss and recovery for unjust enrichment. Alternatively, the court may order an accounting and award royalties lost because of unauthorized use or disclosure of trade secret information. The court may award attorneys' fees where the misappropriation was in bad faith, and exemplary or punitive damages are appropriate in cases of willful and malicious misappropriation. Importantly, in a claim made under the DTSA, if an employer has not given the prerequisite whistleblower notice to the employee, that employer cannot recover exemplary damages or attorney's fees from the employee being sued for misappropriation of a trade secret.[45]

Arguably in the most extreme departure from the UTSA, the DTSA established an additional civil remedy, which comes in the form of an *ex parte* civil seizure. In short, this highly debated provision allows the court to "issue an order providing for the seizure of property necessary to prevent the propagation or dissemination of the trade secret . . . ."[46] Ultimately, what this new civil remedy means for future defendants is that authorities can confiscate a defendant's property without the defendant receiving notice or an opportunity to be heard by the courts—providing plaintiffs a competitive edge for the discovery and gathering of evidence. Fortunately, this *ex parte* remedy, which is granted only in the most extreme situations, has several procedural and substantive prerequisites that applicants must satisfy before the order is granted. Specifically, the court must conclude from the particular facts in the case that:

(I)   an order issued pursuant to Rule 65 of the Federal Rules of Civil Procedure or another form of equitable relief would be inadequate to achieve the purpose of this paragraph because the party to which the order would be issued would evade, avoid, or otherwise not comply with such an order;

(II)   an immediate and irreparable injury will occur if such seizure is not ordered;

(III) the harm to the applicant of denying the application outweighs the harm to the legitimate interests of the person against whom seizure would be ordered of granting the application and substantially outweighs the harm to any third parties who may be harmed by such seizure;

(IV)   the applicant is likely to succeed in showing that—

---

[45]   *Id.* § 1833(b)(3)(C).

[46]   *Id.* § 1836(b)(2)(A)(i).

(aa) the information is a trade secret; and

(bb) the person against whom seizure would be ordered—

(AA) misappropriated the trade secret of the applicant by improper means; or

(BB) conspired to use improper means to misappropriate the trade secret of the applicant;

(V) the person against whom seizure would be ordered has actual possession of—

(aa) the trade secret; and

(bb) any property to be seized;

(VI) the application describes with reasonable particularity the matter to be seized and, to the extent reasonable under the circumstances, identifies the location where the matter is to be seized;

(VII) the person against whom seizure would be ordered, or persons acting in concert with such person, would destroy, move, hide, or otherwise make such matter inaccessible to the court, if the applicant were to proceed on notice to such person; and

(VIII) the applicant has not publicized the requested seizure.[47] Additionally, the physical order granting the *ex parte* seizure must contain several "elements" in order for it to be upheld.[48]

Indeed, several plaintiffs have attempted to use this highly advantageous remedy in an action under the DTSA; however, because of the provision's extreme measures, courts have been reluctant to impose this relief mainly due to the plaintiffs' failure to prove extraordinary circumstances—that is, circumstances where temporary restraining orders or injunctions under Rule 65 would be inadequate protection for the plaintiff. Accordingly, the civil seizure under the DTSA is incredibly narrow in its application.

b. Criminal Penalties

In addition to civil remedies, several jurisdictions have enacted legislation criminalizing misappropriation of trade secrets. States that impose criminal penalties for misappropriation generally do so either by expressly criminalizing misappropriation of trade secrets or by incorporating trade secrets within the coverage of larceny or robbery statutes. For example, in Georgia, misappropriation of a trade secret is a crime punishable by one to five years in prison and a fine of up to $50,000. Ga. Code Ann. § 16–8–13 (2007). Minnesota, on the other hand, simply

---

[47] *Id.* § 1836(b)(2)(A)(ii)(I)–(VIII).

[48] *Id.* § 1836(b)(2)(B)(i)-(vi).

defines property under its theft statute to include "articles representing trade secrets." Minn. Stat. § 609.52 (2007).

Congress has also enacted federal legislation criminalizing the misappropriation of trade secrets. The Economic Espionage Act of 1996 governs the criminalization for the misappropriation of trade secrets. Although aspects of the Economic Espionage Act were amended through the implementation of the DTSA, the majority of the criminal sanctions are still in effect. The Economic Espionage Act still authorizes a prison sentence of up to ten years and a fine of up to $500,000 for any person (or up to $5 million for any "organization") who:

(1) steals, or without authorization appropriates, takes, carries away, or conceals, or by fraud, artifice, or deception obtains [trade secret] information;

(2) without authorization copies, duplicates, sketches, draws, photographs, downloads, uploads, alters, destroys, photocopies, replicates, transmits, delivers, sends, mails, communicates, or conveys [trade secret] information; [or]

(3) receives, buys, or possesses [trade secret] information, knowing the same to have been stolen or appropriated, obtained, or converted without authorization. . . .[49]

The DTSA amendments to the Economic Espionage Act include a provision that organizations can be fined "not more than the greater of $ 5,000,000 or 3 times the value of the stolen trade secret to the organization, including expenses for research and design and other costs of reproducing the trade secret that the organization has thereby avoided."[50] Where one misappropriates a trade secret with the intent to benefit a foreign government, 18 U.S.C. § 1831 provides a maximum sentence of 15 years. Under the Economic Espionage Act the prosecution must prove only that the defendant sought to acquire information which he or she believed to be a trade secret, regardless of whether the information actually qualified as such.

6. LICENSING OF TRADE SECRETS

Trade secrets, like other forms of intellectual property, may be licensed. In fact, because a trade secret is only protectable while it remains secret, licenses are particularly useful in allowing trade secret holders to exploit the value of their proprietary information while maintaining its secrecy. Without a license, trade secret holders would likely be unwilling to share their secret with others and allow it to be used.

---

[49]   18 U.S.C. §§ 1832, 3571 (1996).

[50]   *Id.*

A license is a contract and, as such, may take many forms and encompass many different groupings of rights, duties, and remedies. Trade secret licenses are no more constrained than any other type of contract. By default, any right not specifically licensed from the trade secret holder to the licensee remains with the licensor. From the licensee's perspective, it is important to think through all the steps necessary to exploit the trade secret and protect the investment that it makes in doing so by including, for example, provisions regarding the right to use subsequent versions, updates, and innovations of the trade secret; to receive technical support if appropriate; and to define the scope of renewal rights in the secret. From the licensor's perspective, covenants of the licensee to protect the secrecy of the trade secret are perhaps as important as the consideration they are to receive in exchange for the license. Confidentiality agreements, non-disclosure agreements, and covenants to turn over material derived from the trade secret at the end of the contractual term are critically important.

In the absence of patent, antitrust, or other federal law issues, state law governs the assignment and licensing of pure trade secrets. Trade secrets can form the res of a trust and pass to a trustee in bankruptcy. Moreover, courts do not generally construe the parties' obligations under trade secret licenses as contingent on the continued secrecy of the subject matter.

a.   Exclusive Versus Nonexclusive Licensing

One of the primary distinctions between types of trade secret licenses is whether they are exclusive or nonexclusive. An exclusive license is an express or implied covenant by the licensor not to use the trade secret themselves or grant others the rights contained in the exclusive license. A nonexclusive license is more limited and is treated merely as a covenant by the licensor not to bring suit to enjoin the licensee from using the trade secret within the scope of the license.

b.   Residual Rights

Residual rights involve the licensee's responsibilities regarding non-tangible information that is retained by the licensee after the term of the license expires. If a licensee uses a particular formula or method of manufacture, for instance, the licensee will probably remember all or part of the trade secret, even once the license has expired. Unlike computers, licensees' minds cannot be "wiped clean" at the end of the license. Thus, licensors and licensees should contractually specify how the licensee may use (or not use) such information. The licensee has residual rights in the trade secret insofar as the licensee may use part of the secret after the term of the license has expired. Licensors take a dim view of residual rights and tend to view them as uses of the trade secret by the former licensee beyond the scope of the license. Licensees take the opposite view, and striking a balance between these two positions is complex in most situations.

c. Hybrid Trade Secret and Patent Licenses

Problems may result from the so-called hybrid license that licenses both trade secrets and patents. A patent typically has a term of twenty years, after which the patented subject matter becomes part of the public domain and is no longer subject to the patent holder's monopoly. Licensing a trade secret and a patent together for a period longer than the patent's term constitutes a tying arrangement that violates antitrust laws. The solution is to (1) untangle the two licenses and give consideration for each so that they are separate—even if related—contracts, and (2) to provide for licensing of the trade secret alone once the patent has expired.

7. SECURITY INTERESTS IN TRADE SECRETS

A security interest is a present, usually non-possessory, interest in property that may become possessory in the future if certain contingencies occur. An example is an automobile financing company's lien on a vehicle it has financed. When granted, the lien is non-possessory—the financing company does not possess or have the right to possess the vehicle. Upon default by the vehicle's owner, however, after complying with applicable foreclosure laws, the financing company may repossess the vehicle in satisfaction of all or part of the outstanding debt.

Trade secrets, along with other intellectual property such as copyrights and trademarks, often represent a significant portion of an entity's assets, and as such can be useful sources of collateral for secured loan transactions. To maintain priority, lenders must know how to properly create and perfect their security interests in intellectual property. Security interests in intellectual property are governed by both the U.C.C. and federal law. The extent to which the U.C.C. or federal regulations govern a particular security interest depends upon the type of intellectual property used as collateral. For trade secrets, only the state's enactment of the U.C.C. needs to be considered.

Article 9 of the U.C.C., which has been adopted by all fifty states, governs the creation and perfection of security interests in intellectual property—categorized by the U.C.C. as general intangibles. A security interest in intellectual property is not enforceable (even against the debtor) and does not attach to the collateral unless:

(1) the secured party has given value in exchange for the collateral,

(2) the debtor has rights in the collateral, and

(3) the debtor has signed a security agreement that provides a
     description of the collateral.

Lenders must ensure that the debtor has rights in the intellectual property
collateral to obtain the security interest. When a security interest is
properly granted it is said to have attached and is then enforceable against
the debtor.

In a security agreement, a general description of the personal property
used as security is sufficient if it reasonably identifies what is described.
Therefore, a description of trade secret collateral in the security agreement
as "general intangibles" or "trade secrets" is theoretically sufficient.
However, it is best to also identify all important collateral as specifically as
possible to avoid subsequent disagreement over what was included. The
collateral description should, therefore, include all pending
misappropriation claims; rights to income, profits, or other rights related
to the trade secrets, including those arising under licenses; and all
inventions and improvements related to the trade secrets. In addition, the
agreement should both oblige the debtor to take all necessary measures to
protect the collateral from infringement and guarantee the secured party's
right to take any steps it deems reasonably necessary to maintain and
protect its collateral.

Perfection of the security interest is the legal status that the security
interest enjoys once the appropriate formalities have been complied with
to make it good against the world rather than only enforceable against the
debtor. Through perfection of its security interest, a secured party achieves
and maintains the highest available priority for its security interest in
collateral. In bankruptcy, the difference between a perfected security
interest and an unperfected security interest means the difference between
a full recovery as a secured creditor and no (or minimal) recovery as a
general unsecured creditor.

A security interest is perfected upon attachment if the applicable
requirements are satisfied before attachment. A security interest in most
types of personal property is perfected when a properly completed UCC–1
financing statement is filed with the appropriate state office, most often
the office of the secretary of state. The financing statement must name
both the debtor and the secured party, and must describe the collateral
covered by the financing statement. The U.C.C. no longer requires the
debtor to sign an electronically filed financial statement, although the
debtor must authorize the filing.

The relative priorities of creditors holding conflicting security interests
in most collateral are straight forward. Under the U.C.C.:

(1) if the conflicting security interests are perfected, they rank
     according to priority in time of filing or perfection;

(2) a perfected security interest has priority over a conflicting unperfected security interest; and

(3) if the conflicting security interests are unperfected, the first security interest to attach has priority.

Thus, perfecting a security interest in a trade secret is accomplished by obtaining a security agreement from the trade secret owner and properly filing U.C.C. financing statements at the appropriate state office. This perfection makes the security interest good as against other creditors and provides the creditor recourse against the trade secrets if the debtor defaults on its obligations.

C. PATENT LAW

American patent law is derived from Article 1, Section 8 of the United States Constitution and is governed solely by federal law. At its core, the US patent system is designed to promote the progress of the useful arts by granting exclusive rights to the inventor for a certain period of time.

A patent—short for "letters patent"—is the government's grant to its holder of a limited monopoly that enables the holder to exclude others from making, using, selling, importing, or offering the patented invention for sale for a fixed period of time. In return for this grant of temporary exclusivity, patent applicants must reveal information that would allow the invention to be reproduced. Patents function as compromises between the government's interest in promoting scientific and technological advances and inventors' interest in maximizing profit from their invention. The government, which normally discourages monopolies, gives inventors a limited monopoly over their inventions for a certain period of time (twenty years for most patents), and because of this temporary monopoly, inventors—who might otherwise keep their invention a (trade) secret— agree to reveal it to the public.

Implicit in this compromise is the requirement that the public has adequate notice before a monopoly is unrightfully granted with the issuance of the patent. To meet this end, the United States and most countries around the world provide notice via mandatory publication within eighteen months of the filing date of the application. When a patent expires, the invention passes into the public domain and anyone may make free use of the invention. This advances the overall goal of patent law, to stimulate and reward technological innovation, because it allows current generations of inventors to advance technology by using older technology.

D. DEFINING PATENTS

1. BASIC PRINCIPLES

From the mid-twentieth century until only recently, patent law was defined by the Patent Act of 1952, codified in Title 35 of the United States Code. Although aspects of the law remain intact, the America Invents Act made considerable changes to the prior system following its passage in 2011 (AIA).[51] Under both the old and new law, inventors may obtain patents on articles of proper subject matter—specifically, "any new and useful process, machine, manufacture, or composition of matter, or any new and useful improvement thereof." 35 U.S.C. § 101. However, patents do not issue automatically; all inventions must meet the minimum requirements outlined in the statute. The key requirements for patentability are: (1) patentable subject matter (§ 101); (2) novelty (§§ 101–102), (3) utility (§ 101), (4) non-obviousness (§ 103), and (5) adequate description and enablement (§ 112).

- To qualify as useful under § 101, an invention need only be minimally operable towards some practical purpose. As mentioned above, section 101 also provides the statutory basis for categories of patentable subject matter.

- For an invention to be considered new or novel under § 102, it must differ from previously known inventions and pre-existing knowledge in the field (prior art).

- Non-obviousness under § 103, requires that the invention must be different enough from the prior art that its creation would not be obvious to "a person having ordinary skill in the art."

- In contrast to the above substantive thresholds, § 112 imposes procedural obligations on the applicant. This section requires the inventor applicant to adequately describe the invention within the application; the description must be thorough enough to enable another to practice the invention.

An invention may only be patented once; otherwise, an inventor could extend the monopoly beyond the specified statutory term (usually twenty years from the date of the patent application). In addition, only one inventive entity may patent a particular invention. Generally this means that one inventor may receive a patent on his or her invention; however, certain instances may occur that enable multiple inventors to be listed on a single patent, such as where multiple inventors work for a single

---

[51] *See generally*, 35 U.S.C. §§ 101 et seq. LEAHY-SMITH AMERICA INVENTS ACT, 112 P.L. 29, 125 Stat. 284. For the purposes of this Chapter, unless otherwise indicated, any statutes cited may be presumed to be the current version of the law under the AIA.

company. Under the America Invents Act, the United States now follows the first-inventor-to-file rule, which harmonized US law with the approach used in most other countries. With a few exceptions, the first-inventor-to-file rule awards the patent to the first inventor to file a patent application, regardless of the date of actual invention. Particularly in light of the increasingly global nature of the US economy, the first-inventor-to-file rule is perceived to be easier to administer, more certain, and encouraging of diligent, timely patent application filings.

2. OVERVIEW OF PATENT APPLICATIONS

To obtain a patent, an inventor must file a patent application with the United States Patent and Trademark Office (the "PTO"). Section 112 of the Patent Act, as amended by the AIA, requires that the application describe the invention such that a person of ordinary skill in the particular field would be able to replicate and use the invention (this is the "enablement" requirement). A patent application must also contain "one or more claims particularly pointing out and distinctly claiming the subject matter which the applicant regards as his invention." 35 U.S.C. § 112.

The patent claims exclusively define the invention and are the most important part of the patent application in terms of receiving legal compensation and protection in litigation. A patent's claims determine the scope of the patent in legal actions regarding the validity or infringement of the patent. Thus, the patent application must contain distinct, definite claims that clearly encompass the substance of the claimed invention.

In determining whether to approve a patent, the patent examiner compares the claims with existing publications, technologies, and inventions (collectively, the "prior art") to determine the ordinary level of knowledge held by one skilled in the art. If the invention claimed in the patent application meets the § 112 requirements, is proper subject matter for patenting, and is useful, novel, and non-obvious from the perspective of the ordinarily skilled artisan, a patent will issue.

3. DURATION

The length of duration varies between the different types of patents. The vast majority of patent applications that are filed with the PTO are non-provisional, which grant patentees a monopoly over their invention for a twenty-year term, beginning on the earliest date to which the application is entitled (which in general means the date of filing). 35 U.S.C. § 154(a)(2). Provisional applications—as the name implies—are essentially a place holder for inventors. Applicants are given one year after the date of filing of the provisional to provide the PTO with a "complete" application, which will acquire the benefit of an earlier filing date by claiming reference to the provisional application.[52] The provisional filing date is not counted as part of the 20 year life of any patent that may issue with a claim to the provisional filing date.

Design patents, however, still look to the date of issue as the relevant date and expire fifteen years after they are issued.[53] The term of a plant patent is not explicitly stated, under 35 U.S.C. § 161, which states: "the provisions of this title relating to patents for inventions shall apply to patents for plants, except as otherwise provided." Thus, a plant patent's duration is the same as a utility patent's, twenty years from the date of application.

Under 35 U.S.C. § 156, the term of a patent for the substance, manufacture, or method of use of either a drug or a recombinant DNA technology (which are subject to regulatory review before they can be marketed) may be extended for up to five years for time lost due to regulatory review. However, this can be a trap for the unwary. Patent extensions are limited, and may be offset if the patent holder failed to exercise due diligence toward obtaining regulatory approval. In addition, only one patent related to a particular invention may be extended to offset the time lost due to regulatory review. 35 U.S.C. § 156.

A patent may also be extended to offset delay in the issuance of an approved patent when the delay is attributable to interference proceedings, appeals from interference proceedings, secrecy orders, or the failure of the PTO to act in a timely fashion. 35 U.S.C. § 154(b). An extension is reduced by any delay caused by the patentee's failure to exercise due diligence. Amendments, reissues, and other modifications of patent applications are retroactively limited to the date of the original patent application and expire with the rest of the patent, regardless of when they were submitted or accepted.

A patentee can shorten the term of a patent by filing a terminal disclaimer, which allows a patentee to "disclaim or dedicate to the public the entire term, or any terminal part of the term, of the patent granted or to be granted." 35 U.S.C. § 253. The terminal disclaimer is especially important where a patentee has substantially improved an earlier-patented invention, which could not be patented independently on the grounds of obviousness in light of the earlier patent. In *In re Deters*, 515 F.2d 1152 (C.C.P.A. 1975), a tool used to cut clay drain tile that had been slightly modified from the inventor's previous patent was unpatentable be-cause it was obvious in light of the earlier patent. Had the inventor timely

---

[52] Provisional patents do not vest any rights in the applicant/owner; they are merely a tool designed to promote early filing and to allow ideas to mature before filing a full patent. They will never matriculate into a "full" patent, nor are they prosecuted by the PTO.

[53] This too was a change ushered in by the AIA. While design patent terms are still determined by the date of issuance, design patent applications that were filed before May 13, 2015 are subject to a fourteen year term from the date of issuance. *See* 35 U.S.C. § 173.

filed a terminal disclaimer, he or she would have been entitled to a patent on the tool as modified. Terminal disclaimers allow patentees to extend the monopoly on their invention with a patent that covers an improved version of the earlier patented invention. The second patent expires simultaneously with the first, so the public's right to use the invention after the first patent term expires remains unimpaired. However, if the claims of the second patent application are substantially the same as those of the first, a terminal disclaimer cannot save the application.

E. PATENT TYPES

1. PATENTABLE SUBJECT MATTER

The categories of patentable subject matter, also known as patent eligibility are found in 35 U.S.C. § 101. Categories include "any new and useful process, machine, manufacture, or composition of matter, or any new and useful improvement thereof." Patentable subject matter can be defined in two broad categories: processes and products. The breadth of patentable processes and products reflects congressional intent to make patentable "anything under the sun that is made by man." However, there are limits on the scope of patentable subject matter: laws of nature, physical phenomena, and abstract ideas are not patentable.

To qualify as patentable subject matter, an invention must satisfy two criteria: one statutory and one judicial. First, the subject matter of the invention must fall within the category of process, machine, manufacture, or composition of matter. Second, the subject matter can not fall within an exception recognized by the courts, namely laws of nature, physical phenomena, and abstract ideas. Thus, new minerals discovered in the earth and new plants discovered in the wild are not patentable, Einstein could not have patented $E=mc^2$ and Newton could not have patented the laws of gravity. The rationale for this limitation is that natural things and natural laws have always existed in the environment and should not be subject to the exclusive ownership of a single person. Courts recognized the "products of nature" doctrine to limit the patentability of natural phenomenon. However, the courts have also determined that such a product of nature may be patentable if significant artificial changes are made. By purifying, isolating, or otherwise altering a naturally occurring product, an inventor may obtain a patent on the product in its altered form. For example, in *Diamond v. Chakrabarty*, 447 U.S. 303 (1980) the Court held that a bacterium genetically engineered to break down crude oil was eligible for patent protection, even though it was a living organism, because it was not naturally occurring and was created by human invention. The following broadly defined categories constitute a nonexclusive list of patentable subject matter: business methods and processes; computer software[54]; machines; sports equipment; electronics; pharmaceuticals; fabrics and useful designs; and software programs.

As technology has progressed, the administrative and judicial approach to defining patentable subject matter has evolved and continues to evolve. This evolution has caused a great deal of confusion and debate not only for inventors, but for patent attorneys as well. For many years, section 101 was rarely used to invalidate an issued patent or reject an application pending at the PTO. This situation changed over the past decade due in large part to four decisions issued by the Supreme Court since 2010 addressing patentable subject matter. In each instance the Court concluded that the invention before it was unpatentable. The four cases were:

- *Bilski v. Kappos,* 561 U.S. 593 (2010), pertaining to a business method;

- *Mayo Collaborative Services v. Prometheus Laboratories, Inc.* 566 U.S. 66 (2012), considering a method of medical diagnosis;

- *Association for Molecular Pathology v. Myriad Genetics, Inc.,* 569 U.S. 576 (2013), addressing human genes; and

- *Alice Corp. v. CLS Bank International*, 573 U.S. 208 (2014), relating to computer software.

On October 2005, the PTO issued interim guidelines for patent examiners[55] to determine if a given claimed invention meets the statutory requirements of being a useful process, manufacture, composition of matter or machine. These guidelines state that a process, including a process for doing business, must produce a concrete, useful, and tangible result to be patentable. It does not matter whether the process is within the traditional technological arts or not. Subsequently, the Court of Appeals for the Federal Circuit issued a decision concerning the patentability of business methods. The court's opinion in *State Street Bank,* which at the time established the principle that a claimed invention was eligible for protection by a patent if it involved some practical application and it produces a useful, concrete and tangible result. *State Street Bank v. Signature Financial Group*, 149 F.3d 1368 (Fed. Cir. 1998).

---

[54] Applications for software patents continue to be examined and issued by the PTO. However, as discussed below, even where the application is approved by the examiner (i.e., where the computer program produces a useful, concrete, and tangible result), recent Supreme Court decisions have greatly increased the chance of the patent being invalidated in a subsequent proceeding.

[55] United States Patent and Trademark Office, *Interim Guidelines for Examination of Patent Applications for Patent Subject Matter Eligibility*, OG Notices: 22 November 2005 (html).

On August 24, 2009, the PTO issued new interim guidelines[56] so that examination would comport with the Federal Circuit opinion in *In re Bilski*, 545 F.3d 943, 88 U.S.P.Q.2d 1385 (Fed. Cir. 2008) which held that the "useful, concrete, and tangible" test for patent-eligibility is incorrect and that *State Street Bank* is no longer valid legal authority on this point. Instead, the Federal Circuit and the new PTO guidelines used the Machine-or-Transformation Test to determine patentability for processes. Under this test of patent eligibility, a claim to a process qualifies for consideration if it:

- Is implemented by a particular machine or apparatus in a non-conventional and non-trivial manner; or

- Transforms an article from one state to another.

The Supreme Court issued an opinion on appeal two years later in *Bilski v. Kappos,* 561 U.S. 593 (2010). In this case, the patent application was for a method of hedging the seasonal risks of buying energy. The majority of the Court relied on the "Supreme Court Trilogy,"[57] of *Benson, Flook,* and *Diehr* and found that the claims at issue in the patent were abstract, given that such hedging methods have long been taught in economics and finance. The Court found that although the Machine-or-Transformation Test was a valuable tool, it is not the exclusive test for determining the patentability of process or methods claims. The Court instead resolved the case before it based on the traditional rule that abstract ideas were not patentable subject matter.

In 2012 the Supreme Court shifted focus from information technologies to the life sciences when it unanimously decided *Mayo Collaborative Services v. Prometheus Laboratories, Inc.*, 566 U.S. 66 (2012). The patents in question claimed methods for determining optimal dosages of thiopurine drugs used to treat autoimmune diseases. The Court analyzed the case with a two part test:

1. Do the patents in question claim laws of nature, natural phenomena, or abstract ideas? If so,

---

[56] United States Patent and Trademark Office, *New Interim Patent Subject Matter Eligibility Examination Instructions*, August 24, 2009.

[57] Gottschalk v. Benson, 409 U.S. 63 (1972) (The Court ruled that a process claim directed to a numerical algorithm, as such, was not patentable because "the patent would wholly pre-empt the mathematical formula and in practical effect would be a patent on the algorithm itself." That would be tantamount to allowing a patent on an abstract idea, contrary to precedent dating back to the middle of the 19th century); Parker v. Flook, 437 U.S. 584 (1978) (The Court ruled that an invention that departs from the prior art only in its use of a mathematical algorithm is patent-eligible only if the implementation is novel and nonobvious. Various judges on the panel were dramatic and not definitive); Diamond v. Diehr, 450 U.S. 175 (1981) (The Court held that controlling the execution of a physical process, by running a computer program did not preclude patentability of the invention as a whole).

2. Does the claim recite additional elements that transform the claim into a patent-eligible application of a law of nature, natural phenomenon, or abstract idea.

Essentially this two part test seeks to determine if the claim incorporate an "inventive concept" that amounts to more than just applying the laws of nature, natural phenomenon, or abstract idea to a particular technological environment.

The Court concluded that the claims were directed towards natural laws and were therefore unpatentable. Any correlation that occurs when a man-made substance, in this case a pharmaceutical, interacts with a natural substance, like human blood, also qualifies as a natural principle. This is because although it takes human intervention to trigger the correlation (in this instance administering a drug) the correlation still happens independent of human action. In support of this contention, the Court stated that the process claims merely describe a natural law combined with "well-understood, routine, conventional activity previously engaged in by researchers in the field. The Court explained that phenomena of nature and abstract concepts could not be patented because the monopolization of basic tools through the granting of a patent would inhibit innovation more than it would tend to promote it.

In 2013, the Supreme Court ruled in *Association for Molecular Pathology v. Myriad Genetics, Inc.*, 569 U.S. 576 (2013), that genomic DNA was ineligible for patenting under § 101 because of the "product of nature" doctrine. After the *Chakrabarty* decision, the PTO issued over 50,000 patents relating at least in part to DNA.[58] However, some experts had believed that the decision to patent human genes misconstrued the "product of nature" principle. In their view, the fact that scientists have isolated a gene is a "technicality" that did not allow genes to be patented.[59] The Supreme Court decision in *Myriad* reflects this position.

At primary issue in this case were several patents owned by Myriad that claim isolated human genes known as BRCA1 and BRCA2. Certain alterations or mutations of these genes are associated with predisposition to breast and ovarian cancers. As a result Myriad was the only source of genetic testing for these cancers associated with the BRAC1 and BRAC2 genes. The Court found that Myriad had not created anything, nor had they altered the genetic information encoded on the BRCA1 and BRCA2 genes. Furthermore, the Court was not persuaded by Myriad's claim that the DNA had had been isolated from the human genome by the severing of chemical bonds, with a non-naturally occurring molecule.

---

[58] Guyan Lian, "Molecules or Carriers of Biological Information: A Chemist's Perspective on the Patentability of Isolated Genes," 22 Albany Law Journal of Science and Technology 133 (2012).

[59] Eileen M. Kane, "Splitting the Gene: DNA Patents and the Genetic Code," 71 Tennessee Law Review 707 (2004).

However, the Court took a more favorable view of the second set of claims concerning "complimentary DNA". These claims were focused on synthetic DNA in which the sequence of bases is complimentary to naturally occurring DNA from which it was derived. The Court concluded that this synthetic DNA did not constitute a "product of nature" and was therefore patentable. The Court noted that it had not considered the patentability of DNA in which the order of the naturally occurring DNA nucleotides had been altered. The Court limited its holding to genes and that information that they encoded with are not patent eligible merely because they have been isolated from the surrounding genetic material.

In 2014, the Supreme Court considered the patentability of a computer-implemented financial exchange system designed to mitigate the risk that only one party to a transaction will pay what it owes. The patents at issue in *Alice Corp. v. CLS Bank International*, 573 U.S. 208 (2014) included:

1. A method for exchanging financial obligations (method claims)

2. A computer system used to carry out those methods (computer system claims)

3. A computer readable medium, such as a disc or flashdrive, containing program code for performing those methods (computer-readable media claims)

The Court applied the two part test established in *Mayo,* and found that the method claims were derived from the abstract idea of intermediated settlement, a fundamental and longstanding economic practice. Applying the second prong of the test to the remaining claims, the Court found that the they amounted to nothing more than implementation of an abstract idea on a computer. Merely using the application on a generic computer does not make a patent-ineligible abstract idea into a patent-eligible invention.

The Supreme Court cases discussed above represent the current state of the law as it pertains to whether a particular invention is eligible for patenting under § 101. The courts and PTO will first ask if the claim recites a law of nature, natural phenomenon, or abstract idea. If so, does the claim include additional, inventive elements that indicate the claim applies one of the three excluded subject matters. In addition, the Court will analyze the patent claim to determine if it preempts a field of activity. This area of the law remains in its infancy and should be expected to grow and develop more distinct boundaries on a case-by case basis over time.

2. UTILITY PATENTS

Inventions that fall into one of the four § 101 categories, "process, machine, manufacture, or composition," may qualify for a utility patent, which is the type of patent most recognized by laypersons and lawyers. A utility patent covers innovative products and processes for a twenty-year term and is the type of patent most frequently applied for. To be awarded a utility patent, an invention must meet the statutory requirements of: (1) utility, (2) novelty, and (3) non-obviousness.

a. Process

Courts have encountered some difficulty in defining the term process used in § 101, especially given the ever-increasing complexity of modern technology. The term is somewhat circularly defined in 35 U.S.C. § 100(b) as a "process, art or method, and include[ing] a new use of a known process, machine, manufacture, composition of matter, or material." In *In re Durden*, 763 F.2d 1406 (Fed. Cir. 1985), the Court of Appeals for the Federal Circuit broadly described a process as "a manipulation according to an algorithm."

Whatever definition is applied, process patents must still meet the requirements of non-obviousness, utility, and novelty. In *Durden*, the court denied a patent for a process to recombine chemical compounds for use in a pesticide, even though the process yielded a new (although expected) result, because the application of an obvious process to a novel material is still considered obvious. Similarly, an abstract mathematical formula (sometimes called a mathematical algorithm) is not useful and is therefore unpatentable subject matter; however a mathematical formula may be patentable as an integral part of patentable subject matter (such as a machine or process) if the claimed invention is "useful."

The limitation on patenting mathematical formulas and concepts is narrowly applied to preserve the patentability of useful processes that depend on formulas, because all sequential processes depend in some sense on an algorithm. This narrow application makes it possible to patent computers and computer programs. In general, novel and useful inventions created with scientific knowledge or application of abstract ideas are patentable.

The patentability of mathematical processes is a question of law decided under a two-step analysis. The court first determines whether a mathematical algorithm is recited directly or indirectly in the patent claim. If the claim constitutes a mathematical algorithm, the court then determines whether the claim is directed toward a mathematical algorithm that is not applied to or limited by physical elements or process steps. If the algorithm is merely presented and solved by the claimed invention, patent protection is impermissible. However, while a step-by-step mathematical process is not patentable, an invention that combines mathematical formulas with other discrete elements is patentable. Without a particular practical application, manipulation of an abstract idea or mathematical problem is not patentable.

b. Machine

A machine is a physical object, consisting of parts or devices. A machine's operation distinguishes it from other machines, but the machine itself is more than the abstract principles it employs. Machine includes every mechanical device that performs a function and produces a result and can be anything from a cotton gin, to a stapler, to a hovercraft. If the result is produced by chemical action, however, it is a process. For example, one who discovers that combining rubber with certain salts at a certain temperature produces a better product would be entitled to a process patent, whereas one who invents an improved furnace that can efficiently carry out this process would be entitled to a patent for the machine.

c. Manufacture

In *Diamond v. Chakrabarty*, 447 U.S. 303 (1980), the Supreme Court adopted the definition of manufacture as "the production of articles for use from raw or prepared materials by giving to these materials new forms, qualities, properties, or combinations, whether by hand-labor or by machinery." Following *Chakrabarty*, the Supreme Court in *J.E.M. Ag. Supply, Inc. v. Pioneer Hi-Bred International, Inc.*, 534 U.S. 124 (2001), held that utility patents could be awarded to genetically altered plants or seeds. The court concluded the *Chakrabarty* decision rested on the distinction between "products of nature whether living or not, and human made inventions" and determined that plants containing human made inventions were thus eligible for utility patent protection.

d. Composition of Matter

In *Chakrabarty*, the Supreme Court also adopted the construction that a composition of matter includes "all compositions of two or more substances and all composite articles, whether they be the results of chemical union, or of mechanical mixture, or whether they be gases, fluids, powders or solids." Patented compositions of matter are generally chemical compounds produced by chemists.

3.   DESIGN PATENTS

Design patents, also called ornamental patents, are available for any "new, original and ornamental design for an article of manufacture" and have a fifteen-year term from the date it is granted. 35 U.S.C. § 173. Differences between the requirements for an ornamental patent and a utility patent are subtle, but significant. The design must not be dictated by the function of the object. If the design affects the operation of the object and is not separable from its function, it is not eligible for design patent protection although it may be eligible for a utility patent. To be patentable, an ornamental design must be new, non-obvious, and original, as well as ornamental. 35 U.S.C. § 171. For a design patent to be valid, it must be:

(1) new,

(2) original,

(3) ornamental,

(4) non-obvious to a person of ordinary skill in the art, and

(5) not primarily for the purpose of serving a functional or utilitarian purpose.

In the past, courts applied either the ordinary intelligent person or the ordinary designer standards in determining whether a design is obvious. However, in *In re Nalbandian*, 661 F.2d 1214 (C.C.P.A. 1981), the predecessor court to the Federal Circuit noted that an ordinary person may have a "less discerning eye" than a trained designer, and that the ordinarily intelligent person standard made it easier to invalidate design patents. The *Nalbandian* court, recognizing the circuit split, elected to adopt the position of the Second, Third, Tenth, and D.C. Circuits, which required obviousness for design patents to be determined according to the ordinary designer standard. Although stating that the difference was basically semantics, the *Nalbandian* court found the ordinary designer standard to be more in line with the statute. Under this test, the *Nalbandian* court held that the designer's illuminated tweezers were rendered obvious by prior illuminated tweezers, and that the slight differences between the two—differing finger grips and straight rather than slightly curved pincers—were de minimis modifications. The conflict regarding the appropriate standard for determining obviousness in design patents has not yet been conclusively resolved. This may not matter in practice, as courts will continue to find designs patentable or unpatentable according to their perceptions, regardless of the phraseology of the obviousness test.

The application deadline for design patents is different than for other patents. Designers have only six months after filing a foreign patent application to apply for a United States design patent before the statutory bar—a type of statute of limitations—forecloses patentability. In addition, non-provisional design patent applications do not relate back to the filing date of an earlier provisional application. The most conspicuous difference, however, is that designs may be protected for only fifteen years[60], rather than the usual twenty for utility patents.

4. PLANT PATENTS

Plant patents are available for one who invents or discovers and asexually reproduces any new variety of plant. 35 U.S.C. § 161. Plant patents cannot cover tuber propagated plants and wild plants found in uncultivated areas. Tuber propagates like the potato and the Jerusalem artichoke were excluded because of their importance as basic food sources. As long as the plant is found in a cultivated area, it need not be the product of human work or intervention.

The basic requirements for patenting plants are slightly different than those for a utility patent. While an invention must be useful, novel, and non-obvious to be patentable, a plant need only be distinct and novel to be eligible for plant patent protection. Further, because the plant may be found in nature (as long as it is in a cultivated area), the novelty requirement is not as strict as that for a utility patent. Additionally, the patentee must asexually propagate the plant through cuttings or division rather than by seed. Otherwise, the patent provisions for other inventions apply in basically the same way to plant patents.

Characteristics that bear on whether a plant variety is distinct include habitat; immunity from disease; resistance to cold, drought, heat, wind, or soil conditions; color of flower, leaf, fruit, or stems; flavor; productivity, including ever-bearing qualities in the case of fruits; storage qualities; perfume; form; and ease of asexual reproduction. Patent protection is extended only to the direct, asexually produced progeny of the patented plant. Thus, an infringement claim depends on a showing that the alleged infringement involved the asexual propagation of the patented plant's descendants—rafting, for instance, from patented stock—it is not enough that an allegedly infringing plant substantially resembles the patented plant.

The Plant Variety Protection Act (the "PVPA") protects sexually reproduced or tuber propagate plants, but it is not actually a patent. The PVPA is administered by the Department of Agriculture rather than the PTO. The eligibility requirements, found in 7 U.S.C. § 2402, are similar to that of a plant patent: the plant must be new, distinct, uniform and stable. Additionally it must not have been sold in the United States more than one year before the filing. The PVPA protection allows the breeders of sexually reproduced plants to exclude others from selling, offering to sell, importing, exporting, or producing hybrids from their protected plant, 7 U.S.C.

---

[60]   Design patent applications filed before May 13, 2015 have a fourteen year term from the date of grant. However, any design patent application filed after May 13, 2015, are subject to a fifteen year term from the date of grant.

§ 2483(a), and this protection lasts for twenty years from the date of issue (twenty five years for trees and vines), 7 U.S.C. § 2483(b).

New varieties of plants may also be eligible for a utility patent (rather than a plant patent) if they meet the more exacting standards required to patent a composition of matter. To obtain a utility patent, a plant breeder must show that the plant is novel, useful, and non-obvious. The breeder must also include a written description that satisfies 35 U.S.C. § 112 and a deposit of seed that is publicly accessible.

Under the Orphan Drug Act, a manufacturer may receive a seven year exclusive license (which is not technically a patent) to manufacture medicine to treat a rare disease. 21 U.S.C. § 360cc(a)(2). A rare disease is one which affects fewer than 200,000 people in the United States or more than 200,000 people if there is no reasonable expectation that the cost of developing and marketing a drug for the disease can be recouped by United States sales. The purpose of the Orphan Drug Act is to encourage development of medicine to treat diseases that are so rare that it would not be profitable to develop drugs to treat them without this period of exclusivity.

F. UTILITY

The basic benefit of the patent monopoly contemplated in the Constitution and intended by Congress is the public benefit from an invention's substantial utility. To that end, § 101 of the Patent Code mandates that patents issue only to useful inventions. In reality, however, the utility requirement is rarely an obstacle to patentability. A finding of utility has long been held to require only a minimal showing that the invention is capable of practical application. The specifically claimed utility must also be reduced to practice, a requirement intended to ensure that a patent does not "block off whole areas of scientific development" by asserting a claim that is too general.

To be patentable, an invention's utility must be more than purely speculative. The utility requirement is satisfied when an inventor has learned enough about the product to justify the conclusion that it is useful for a specific purpose.

The required utility may be commercial rather than practical, and the fact that one product can be altered to make it look like another may itself be a specific benefit that satisfies the statutory utility requirement. For example, cubic zirconium simulates diamonds, imitation gold leaf imitates real gold leaf, and synthetic fabrics simulate expensive natural fabrics.

To be useful, the subject matter of the claim must be operable. This operability requirement is closely related to the § 112 enablement requirement. If the claim results in an impossibility, the invention as described is inoperable, not useful, and lacks enablement. Examples include perpetual motion machines and processes that prevent a person from aging.

G. NOVELTY

The novelty requirement requires that to qualify for a patent, an invention must differ from other inventions in the field which are known as prior art. A patent for technology already known to the public would limit competition and raise prices on known devices and methods. Thus, the novelty requirement preserves information already in the public domain by preventing individuals from appropriating it for their exclusive benefit through a patent monopoly.

To avoid losing novelty, an inventor should avoid disclosing or selling the invention prior to filing her patent application. Although there can be a one-year grace period in the United States between first disclosure or commercialization and the deadline for filing for a patent, this is not the case in most other nations and disclosure or commercialization prior to filing will bar patentability in those countries.

In determining whether an invention meets the novelty requirement, a patent examiner makes two distinct inquiries. First, the examiner determines which references (sources in the universe of available knowledge) are relevant to the novelty inquiry. The references are cumulatively known as prior art. Second, the examiner determines whether the described invention is equivalent to any of the prior art. If the invention is equivalent to any reference, patent protection will be unavailable because the invention lacks novelty, but if the invention differs from the relevant prior art, the examiner will proceed under 35 U.S.C. § 103 to determine whether the invention is obvious in light of the prior art.

For many inventors and patent owners the most important changes to the U.S. patent system ushered in by the America Invents Act[61] center on novelty and priority. The AIA has changed the patent system from a first-to-invent system under the 1952 Act to a first-proven-inventor-to-file system under the AIA. The new Act has simplified the novelty rule from the structure that was created by the 1952 Act by providing one novelty rule, and then a list of exceptions to it, in the form of the grace period provision. The new structure adds clarity to the one-year grace period by establishing that a disclosure made one year or less before the effective filing date is not considered prior art if certain conditions are met. Under

---

[61] *See generally*, 35 U.S.C. §§ 101 et seq. LEAHY-SMITH AMERICA INVENTS ACT, 112 P.L. 29, 125 Stat. 284.

the AIA the two distinct concepts of novelty and statutory bars contained in the 1952 Act are eliminated.

As a practical matter the new regime makes the following fundamental changes:

- The date a patent application is filed is the critical date for most purposes;

- Prior art relevant to a particular patent claim is comprised of all references included in the statute from the date of filing rather than the date of invention (subject to the one-year grace period);

- There are no geographic restrictions on prior art. Foreign patents, publications and sales meet the definition of prior art for U.S. patent law consideration, no matter where they occur.

- Priority challenges between competing inventors are determined almost entirely by when the patent application is filed.

The best way to understand the decision logic of the novelty rule is to read the new language of § 102:

(a) **Novelty; Prior Art.**—A person shall be entitled to a patent unless—

(1) the claimed invention was patented, described in a printed publication, or in public use, on sale, or otherwise available to the public before the effective filing date of the claimed invention; or

(2) the claimed invention was described in a patent issued under section 151, or in an application for patent published or deemed published under section 122(b), in which the patent or application, as the case may be, names another inventor and was effectively filed[62] before the effective filing date of the claimed invention.

(b) **Exceptions.**—

(1) **Disclosures made 1 year or less before the effective filing date of the claimed invention.**—A disclosure made 1 year or less before the effective filing date of a claimed invention shall not be prior art to the claimed invention under subsection (a)(1) if—

---

[62] The "effective filing date" includes an application filed first in the United States and also certain applications filed first in foreign patent systems that are granted the benefit of U.S. filing by virtue of compliance with international treaties.

(A) the disclosure was made by the inventor or joint inventor or by another who obtained the subject matter disclosed directly or indirectly from the inventor or a joint inventor; or

(B) the subject matter disclosed had, before such disclosure, been publicly disclosed by the inventor or a joint inventor or another who obtained the subject matter disclosed directly or indirectly from the inventor or a joint inventor.

(2) Disclosures appearing in applications and patents.—A disclosure shall not be prior art to a claimed invention under subsection (a)(2) if—

(A) the subject matter disclosed was obtained directly or indirectly from the inventor or a joint inventor;

(B) the subject matter disclosed had, before such subject matter was effectively filed under subsection (a)(2), been publicly disclosed by the inventor or a joint inventor or another who obtained the subject matter disclosed directly or indirectly from the inventor or a joint inventor; or

(C) the subject matter disclosed and the claimed invention, not later than the effective filing date of the claimed invention, were owned by the same person or subject to an obligation of assignment to the same person.

(c) Common Ownership Under Joint Research Agreements.—Subject matter disclosed and a claimed invention shall be deemed to have been owned by the same person or subject to an obligation of assignment to the same person in applying the provisions of subsection (b)(2)(C) if—

(1) the subject matter disclosed was developed and the claimed invention was made by, or on behalf of, 1 or more parties to a joint research agreement that was in effect on or before the effective filing date of the claimed invention;

(2) the claimed invention was made as a result of activities undertaken within the scope of the joint research agreement; and

(3) the application for patent for the claimed invention discloses or is amended to disclose the names of the parties to the joint research agreement.

(d) Patents and Published Applications Effective as Prior Art.—For purposes of determining whether a patent or application for patent is prior art to a claimed invention under subsection (a)(2), such patent or application shall be considered to have been effectively filed, with respect to any subject matter described in the patent or application—

> **(1)** if paragraph (2) does not apply, as of the actual filing date of the patent or the application for patent; or
>
> **(2)** if the patent or application for patent is entitled to claim a right of priority under section 119, 365(a), 365(b), 386(a), or 386(b), or to claim the benefit of an earlier filing date under section 120, 121, 365(c), or 386(c), based upon 1 or more prior filed applications for patent, as of the filing date of the earliest such application that describes the subject matter.

As described above, the novelty rule first defines all categories of references that qualify as prior art and then describes the situations in which prior art appearing before the inventors effective filing date deprives the inventor of patentability under § 102(a)(1) and (2). Section 102(b) identifies the grace period (disclosures made 1 year or less before the effective filing date of the claimed invention) as an exception to the general rule that prior art appearing earlier that the inventor's filing date prohibits patentability for the claimed invention. The grace period has the effect of excluding prior art from the examination process if the inventor by filing a patent application or provisional within a year of the date the prior art appears. The remainder of subsection 102(b) further delineates situations in which an inventor might file a valid patent application even after invalidating information exists in the prior art.

The categories of prior art documents and activities are set forth in 35 U.S.C. § 102(a)(1) and the categories of prior art patent documents are set forth in 35 U.S.C. § 102(a)(2). These documents and activities are used to determine whether a claimed invention is novel or nonobvious. The documents upon which a prior art rejection under 35 U.S.C. § 102(a)(1) may be based are an issued patent, a published application, and a non-patent printed publication. The documents upon which a prior art rejection under 35 U.S.C. § 102(a)(2) may be based are U.S. patent documents. Evidence that the claimed invention was in public use, on sale, or otherwise available to the public may also be used as the basis for a prior art rejection under 35 U.S.C. § 102(a)(1). A printed publication that does not have a sufficiently early publication date to itself qualify as prior art under 35 U.S.C. § 102(a)(1) may be competent evidence of a previous public use, sale activity, or other availability of a claimed invention to the public where the public use, sale activity, or other public availability does have a sufficiently early date to qualify as prior art under 35 U.S.C. § 102(a)(1).[63]

Section 102(b)(1) grace period only removes disclosures made by the inventor from the prior art. If a third party performs an act that constitutes prior art before the inventor files a patent application, the inventors 102(b)(1) grace period does not apply. Nevertheless, § 102(b)(2) allows an inventor to file a valid patent application even when a third party's prior art event occurs, if the inventor makes a public disclosure before that prior art event is made. The courts however have yet to define what constitutes public disclosure under AIA § 102. Currently the PTO is treating the term "disclosure" as a generic expression intended to encompass the documents and activities enumerated in AIA 35 U.S.C. 102(a) (i.e., being patented, described in a printed publication, in public use, on sale, or otherwise available to the public, or being described in a U.S. patent, U.S. patent application publication, or World Intellectual Property Organization (WIPO) published application).

The PTO provides further guidance on how 35 U.S.C. § 102(a) and (b) is to be applied through the Manual of Patent Examining Procedures (MPEP). Section 2152 of the MPEP provides a detailed discussion of the rules that patent examiners and attorneys should follow in determining whether an invention is novel.

H. PRIORITY

The distinction between novelty and statutory bars contained in the 1952 Act have been eliminated under the AIA. Section 102, now combines the two related but distinct concepts of novelty and priority together, reducing the complexity of determining patentability. Novelty focuses on the relationship between the inventor and prior art. If an inventor files a patent application before relevant prior art enters the field which would invalidate a claim, the patent will be granted. Priority on the other hand focuses on which inventor should receive a patent for an identical invention. The AIA first-inventor-to-file rule eliminates the need to determine which of the inventors actually invented first, the first to file wins. The only exception to this rule is where a competing inventor learned of, or misappropriated the invention from another patent applicant. Under such circumstances, the PTO can undertake a derivation proceeding under § 135 to determine the rightful owner of the invention. Derivation proceedings allow an inventor to assert that he or she actually invented the patent in question. Petition for derivation proceeding must be filed within one year of patent publication, must be supported by evidence, and petitioner must file a patent for the invention (otherwise the inventor lacks standing).

---

[63]   See *In re Epstein*, 32 F.3d 1559 (Fed. Cir. 1994).

I. STATUTORY BAR

The statutory bar of 35 U.S.C. § 102 ensures that a patent will not issue if, 1 year or less before the effective filing date of the claimed invention, any of the following disclosures are made:

(1) patent,

(2) described in a printed publication,

(3) publicly used,

(4) sold,

(5) or otherwise available to the public.

35 U.S.C. § 102(a). The AIA eliminates geographic distinctions for all categories of prior art. No matter where an activity or event occurs, it is considered prior are for purposes of U.S. patent law.

The critical date is set at 1 year or less before the effective filing date of the claimed invention. The effective filing date includes both provisional and full patent applications. The statutory bar is triggered if any prohibited activity occurs before this effective filing date. For purposes of the statutory bar, it is irrelevant whether the prior prohibited activity was authorized by the inventor. In other words, an inventor who is the victim of misappropriation is in the same position as one who has permitted the use of his process.

J. PUBLICATION BAR

The bar against patenting an invention disclosed by printed publication was designed to prevent an inventor from patenting an invention already in the public domain. Publication sufficient to trigger the statutory bar is minimal. The inquiry turns on whether a perceptible description of the invention was available to the "pertinent part of the public" more than twelve months before the application was submitted. In *In re Wyer*, 655 F.2d 221 (C.C.P.A. 1981), a patentee filed for a patent in Australia over a year before filing in the United States. Because the Australian Patent Office published the application and copies were available upon request, the court invoked the statutory bar to block patentability.

Claims disclosed in an earlier patent application (whether foreign or domestic) do not trigger the statutory bar unless (1) they share substantial identity with the claims disclosed in the earlier application and (2) the new invention is substantially the same invention as the old one described in the prior application.

K. PUBLIC USE BAR

The effective filing date and statutory bar encourages prompt filing of patent applications so that delay cannot be used to artificially extend a monopoly on an invention. The public use bar to patentability is triggered if an invention was used publicly 1 year or less before the effective filing date of the claimed invention. The bar is triggered if the invention is used publicly by anyone—the inventor, their agent, or even an unauthorized third party—prior to the effective filing date. The use does not have to be broad or even overt; a single use of an invention for commercial purposes is enough. In other words, a commercial use is considered a public use, even if the use is kept secret.[64]

L. PRIOR USER RIGHTS

The prior user rights defense under 35 U.S.C. § 273 was originally created in 1999 by the American Inventors Protection Act,[65] as Congress' response to *State Street Bank & Trust Co. v. Signature Financial Group Inc.*[66] In that case, the U.S. Court of Appeals for the Federal Circuit held methods of doing business to be eligible subject matter for patenting. The patentability of business methods meant that a corporation's continued use of trade secret business strategies could infringe a patent held by a later inventor. Section 273 was intended to offer trade secret holders a prior user rights defense so that they could continue to use a business method despite a later patent.

Although the general intent of § 273 remains the same, the AIA made four significant changes to the scope of the defense. Section 273 (Defense to infringement based on prior commercial use) expanded both the categories of persons who may assert the defense and the applicable subject matters. It also raised the level of proof required to successfully assert the defense and created the § 273(e)(5) "university exception," which removes prior-user rights to certain patents from certain institutions of higher education and their technology-transfer organizations.

Under the AIA version of § 273, the defense is no longer limited to the direct user of the invention or trade secret. Under 35 U.S.C. § 273(e)(1)(A) it extends beyond "the person who performed or directed the performance" of the use as well as to "an entity that controls, is controlled by, or is under common control with such person," Furthermore, there is a "good faith" provision under § 273(a)(1) where a party charged with induced or

---

[64] The new act allows some private, commercial use (or at least allows a defense of it). Section 273 of the new patent act expands prior user rights. Under this new provision, if a person or entity made use of the claimed device or process more than one year before filing, he can continue the use to the same extent.

[65] Pub. L. No. 106-113, § 4302 (1999).

[66] 149 F.3d 1368, 1375 (Fed. Cir. 1998).

contributory infringement may also be able to assert the defense. However, this defense is only available to defendants in the United States.

Although prior-user rights cannot be assigned, licensed or transferred to other parties, a third party may obtain the right "as an ancillary and subordinate part of a good-faith assignment or transfer for other reasons of the entire enterprise or line of business to which the defense relates." *Id.* § 273(e)(1)(B). However, for successors-in-interest, subsection (e)(1)(c) limits the defense to sites where the alleged infringing use was "in use before the later of the effective filing date of the claimed invention or the date of the assignment or transfer of such enterprise or line of business." The term "site" is undefined, leaving open the question whether the business at the acquired site can be expanded and covered by the defense or whether sites owned before acquiring the defense may be covered. Hence, the defense may be of limited value to expanding enterprises.

M. ON SALE BAR

The statutory bar is also triggered if the invention is sold or merely offered for sale by anyone (whether the inventor, their agent, or an unauthorized third party) prior to the critical date. Even free distribution of a prototype may raise the on-sale bar if the distribution is intended to solicit a sale.[67]

Whether a communication amounts to an offer to sell rests on the inventor's "present intent to sell" once the invention has been reduced to practice. If the circumstances show that the inventor intended to sell the invention in patentable form and prior to the critical date, the statutory bar is triggered, regardless of whether the sale was actually consummated.

What is sold (or offered for sale) must disclose and also *embody* the claimed invention in order to trigger the on sale bar. The question is not whether the sale discloses the invention at the time of the sale, but whether the sale relates to a device that embodies the invention. Contract law principles apply in order to determine whether a commercial sale or offer for sale occurred.

The Federal Circuit, in Helsinn Healthcare S.A. v. Teva Pharmaceuticals USA, Inc.,[68] found that the term "on sale" means the same thing under the AIA that it did under the 1952 Act. The U.S. Supreme Court affirmed the Helsinn case on appeal holding that a commercial sale to a third party who is required to keep the invention confidential may place the invention "on sale" under § 102(a). The Court further concluded that when Congress reenacted the same "on sale" language in the AIA, it

---

[67]   This is also amended slightly with § 273's prior user rights. Prior users are allowed to sell the invention, though only privately. However, generally, the on sale bar is the same, only with a new critical date.

[68]   855 F.3d 1356 (Fed. Cir. 2017), aff'd 139 S. Ct. 628 (2018).

adopted the earlier judicial construction of that phrase established under the 1952 Act.

N. EXPERIMENTAL USE EXCEPTION

Under 35 U.S.C. § 271(a), anyone who uses a patented invention without authorization is liable for patent infringement However, there is a longstanding common-law exception to this provision. The "experimental use exception" allows for de minimis use of a patented invention when the purpose is experimental.

Over the last twenty-five years, the Federal Circuit has addressed numerous experimental use issues and its decisions have made the common-law experimental use exception inoperable in most practical situations. In *Roche Products, Inc. v. Bolar Pharmaceuticals Co.*[69] Roche, a brand-name pharmaceutical company, sued Bolar, a generic drug manufacturer, for using Roche's patented chemical. Bolar used Roche's patented active ingredient in experiments to determine if its generic product was a bioequivalent. The Federal Circuit held that the experimental use exception did not apply because Bolar intended to sell its generic product in competition with Roche's product after patent expiration and thus conducted experimentation solely for business interests. It also concluded that experimentation conducted in pursuit of FDA approval was an inherently commercial purpose in furtherance of a business agenda.

In 2002, the Court of Appeals for the Federal Circuit further limited the scope of the research exemption in *Madey v. Duke University.*[70] The court did not reject the defense, but left only a very narrow and strictly limited experimental use defense for amusement, to satisfy idle curiosity, or for strictly philosophical inquiry. The court also precludes the defense where, regardless of profit motive, the research was done "in furtherance of the alleged infringer's legitimate business. In the case of a research university like Duke University, the court held that the alleged use was in furtherance of its legitimate business—namely increasing the status of the institution and luring lucrative research grants, and thus the defense was inapplicable.

In reaction to Roche, Congress enacted the Drug Price Competition and Patent Term Restoration Act of 1984[71] ("Hatch-Waxman Act") that passed an amendment codified as § 271(e)(1) termed the "Safe Harbor Provision. This rule exempts from infringement use of a patented invention solely for "uses reasonably related to the development and submission of information under the Federal Law which regulates the manufacture, use, or sale of drugs or veterinary biological products. The

---

[69]   733 F.2d 858 (Fed. Cir. 1984).

[70]   307 F.3d 1351 (Fed. Cir. 2002).

[71]   Pub. L. No. 98-417 (1984).

Safe Harbor Provision is seen as a reversal of Roche. This allows generic drug companies to experiment with patented brand name drugs to make bioequivalencies, but actual submission of the data to the FDA would constitute an act of infringement. The exception expands over everything submitted to FDA, including medical devices.

The U.S. Supreme Court determined the scope of § 271(e)(1) in *Merck KGaA v. Integra Lifesciences I, Ltd.*[72] The Court held that the research must be "reasonably related" to the pursuit of information that would be used in FDA applications to qualify for the § 271(e)(1) exception, even if the research at issue was ultimately not submitted to the FDA. It is important to note that neither § 271(e)(1) nor the common-law exception were addressed by the Leahy-Smith America Invents Act (AIA) or its legislative history. Consequently, the USPTO has not taken a stance on whether the AIA changes the applicability of these exceptions.

O. NON-OBVIOUSNESS

Under § 103 of the America Invents Act, a patent for a claimed invention:

> may not be obtained, notwithstanding that the claimed invention is not identically disclosed as set forth in section 102, if the differences between the claimed invention and the prior art are such that the claimed invention as a whole would have been obvious before the effective filing date of the claimed invention to a person having ordinary skill in the art to which the claimed invention pertains. Patentability shall not be negated by the manner in which the invention was made.

The non-obviousness requirement is one of the most significant hurdles to obtaining a patent. It allows the PTO to deny a patent and the courts to invalidate a patent even if the claimed invention has never been made or the claimed process has not previously been performed. Section 103 requires courts and PTO examiners to decide whether an inventor's work product differs enough from the prior art to be patentable.

According to § 103, patentability is not affected by the manner in which the invention was made. Accidental discoveries may yield non-obvious inventions, and unexpected beneficial results are evidence of non-obviousness. No weight is given to whether the claimed invention was derived at by experimentation rather than inventive genius.

Under the AIA, § 103 changes the time for determining obviousness from the date the invention was created to the effective filing date of the

---

[72] 545 U.S. 193 (2005).

patent. This change is tied to the definition of novelty under § 102 and the change to the first inventor to file rule.

1. PRIMARY CONSIDERATIONS

To evaluate the non-obviousness of an invention, courts and PTO examiners apply a three step analysis similar to the novelty inquiry:

(1) identify the relevant prior art;

(2) ascertain the differences between the prior art and the claims at issue; and

(3) resolve the level of ordinary skill in the art.

The standard for determining non-obviousness is the knowledge possessed by one with ordinary skill in the art, i.e., a scientist or engineer in the relevant field. Secondary considerations such as commercial success, long felt but unsolved needs, and the failure of others are also relevant to the obviousness inquiry.

The patent examiner bears the burden of establishing a prima facie case of obviousness if denying a patent application for non-obviousness. Similarly, because issued patents are presumed valid, and any challenger bears the burden of proving the invention's obviousness by clear and convincing evidence.

Prior art relevant in determining an invention's non-obviousness will usually be the same as prior art relevant to the question of its novelty. However, several prior art references may be combined to show obviousness if the inventor combined the prior art references with a reasonable expectation that the combination would succeed. The fact that—in hindsight—each aspect of the invention was present in other patents does not defeat the new invention unless the examiner shows that there was some motivation to combine the references that would have been apparent to one with ordinary skill in the art.

Essentially, an invention is unpatentably obvious where differences between the invention and the prior art are such that the invention would have been obvious to a person having ordinary skill in the art at the time the invention was made. However, an analysis based upon intuition is inappropriate, and the complexity of an invention does not necessarily affect obviousness.

Unawareness at prior art does not allow a prior for an obvious invention. Inventors are presumed to have knowledge of all relevant prior art both in their field and in all reasonably pertinent fields.

In comparing an invention to relevant prior art, the legal issue is not the obviousness of differences between the invention and the prior art, but the obviousness of the invention as a whole.

The scope of relevant prior art is determined based on the nature of the invention and the knowledge that a skilled person in the field would be expected to have. Prior art from analogous fields may also be relevant. However, the more distant the prior art is from the patent's subject matter, the less persuasive or relevant it is. If inventors combine knowledge from multiple widely diverse fields, their inventions will likely survive the obviousness inquiry.

Slight structural variation from prior art may yield a novel result. An invention should be evaluated not only by the degree of change from a prior art reference but also by the purpose of the invention.

To determine the level of ordinary skill in the art, as stated in *Environmental Designs, Ltd. v. Union Oil Co. of California*, 713 F.2d 693 (Fed. Cir. 1983), the court may consider factors including:

(1) the educational level of the inventor;

(2) the type of problems encountered in the art;

(3) the prior art solutions to those problems;

(4) the rapidity with which innovations are made;

(5) the sophistication of the technology; and

(6) the educational level of active workers in the field.

For design patents, the hypothetical standard is that of the ordinary designer. The ordinary designer differs from an ordinary person because their specialized knowledge brings more prior art into consideration. The obviousness determination in design patents is not simply a regrouping of prior art; it involves analyzing primary references to determine what modifications would have been obvious given knowledge of the prior art.

2. SECONDARY CONSIDERATIONS

In *Graham v. John Deere Co.*, 383 U.S. 1 (1966), the Supreme Court stated that secondary considerations such as "commercial success, long felt but unsolved needs, failure of others, etc.," may be relevant as "indicia of obviousness or non-obviousness. . ." While *Graham* is one of the most influential cases for § 103 purposes, the application of secondary considerations remains split. Though some courts treat secondary considerations as a strong fourth factor of the *Graham* test, other courts treat these secondary considerations as merely relevant.[73] These courts

---

[73] *See Stratoflex, Inc. v. Aeroquip Corp.*, 713 F.2d 1530, 1538 (Fed. Cir. 1983) (*stating* that secondary consideration evidence must always be considered in a determination of obviousness); *see also Simmons Fastener Corp. v. Illinois Tool Works, Inc.*, 739 F.2d 1573, 1575 (Fed. Cir. 1984) (*outlining* the *Graham* test as four part—the three traditional elements (scope and content of prior art; level of ordinary skill in the pertinent art; and differences between the prior art and the claims at issue), as well as evidence of secondary considerations.); *but see Leapfrog Enters, Inc. v. Fisher-Price, Inc.*, 485 F.3d 1157, 1162 (Fed. Cir. 2007) (*holding* that substantial evidence of secondary considerations are not enough to overcome a final conclusion that a patent claim is obvious.);

give little weight to secondary factors that do not directly relate to the patent claims.

3. SYNERGISM

Some courts have held that synergism is a prerequisite to patentability for inventions that simply combine obvious elements.   Synergism is achieved when the combination of known elements as a whole exceeds the sum of its parts.   However, some courts have rejected a separate requirement of synergism, holding that the requirement is inconsistent with the non-obvious standard set forth in § 103 and is not a proper test to measure the patentability of combination inventions.

P. PROPERTY INTEREST IN PATENTS

The inventor or assignee named in the patent instrument is the initial owner. Where more than one inventor is named, each owns an undivided interest in the patent and each joint owner may exploit the patent without the consent of any other owner. However, courts have held that a joint owner of a patent must obtain permission from all other owners before commencing a patent infringement suit.

Patentees may assign (i.e., sell) or license their patent to others. 35 U.S.C. § 261. Pending patent applications and rights to future inventions are also assignable. It is common for employers to require employees to assign rights to inventions created within the scope of their employment as a condition of employment. Patentees may also use their patent as collateral in a secured transaction.

In contrast to an assignment, a license does not transfer ownership of the patent; rather, it permits a third party to use the patented invention, usually in exchange for royalties. The patent owner contractually specifies the specific rights granted under the license. A patent license agreement is simply a promise by the licensor to not sue the licensee. Regardless of the terms of the license, the licensor cannot convey an absolute right to the patent because their patent right is merely one of exclusion.

The most important distinction between a patent assignment and a patent license is that an assignee is the sole owner of a patent and can bring suit for patent infringement under 35 U.S.C. § 281, but a licensee usually cannot enforce a licensed patent. A licensee has only a promise that the licensor will not sue the licensee for patent infringement. Licensees can protect themselves by obtaining a covenant in their licensing agreement that requires the licensor to enforce the patent.   Another

---

Richardson-Vicks Inc. v. Upjohn Co., 122 F.3d 1476, 1483 (Fed. Cir. 1997) (*finding* that evidence of secondary considerations does not control the obviousness analysis, it is merely relevant to the analysis).

distinction is that an assignment must be in writing, but a license need not be. 35 U.S.C. § 261.

A license may also be implied. The Federal Circuit established a two part test to determine the existence of an implied license. First, a patent holder must have sold a product that had no non-infringing uses. Second, the circumstances of the sale must "plainly indicate that the grant of a license should be inferred." Met-Coil Systems Corp. v. Korners Unlimited, Inc., 803 F.2d 684 (Fed. Cir. 1986).

A valid license may also provide an affirmative defense to a suit for patent infringement.

Cross-licensing is becoming an increasingly important mechanism for preventing patent litigation. A cross-licensing agreement allows two or more parties to grant a license to each other for use of the subject matter claimed in a patent (or patents) each of the parties own. Such cross-licensing may be seen in the telecommunications field. For example, while Apple may sell the final telecommunication product, internally there are several patented components that are necessary for the final product to function. Cross-licensing inhibits companies to build onto these inventions for commercialization. More importantly, a cross-license allows a means for addressing blocking patents. Cross-licensing allows for these blocking inventions to be brought to market, rather than being allowed to sit dormant and prevent society from reaping the benefit of the inventions.

Q. SECURITY INTERESTS IN PATENTS

Patents, along with other intellectual property such as copyrights and trademarks, often represent a significant portion of an entity's value, and can be useful sources of collateral for secured transactions. To maintain priority, lenders must properly create and perfect their security interests in intellectual property. Security interests in intellectual property are governed by both the Uniform Commercial Code and federal law. The extent to which the U.C.C. or federal regulations govern a particular security interest depends upon the type of intellectual property used as collateral. For patents, both state and federal law must be considered.

Article 9 of the U.C.C., which has been adopted by all fifty states, governs the creation and perfection of security interests in intellectual property, which is categorized as a general intangible. A security interest in intellectual property is not enforceable (even against the debtor), and does not attach to the collateral unless:

(1) the secured party has given value in exchange for the col-
     lateral;

(2) the debtor has rights in the collateral; and

(3)   the debtor has signed a security agreement that provides a description of the collateral.

Lenders must ensure that the debtor has rights in the intellectual property collateral prior to obtaining the security interest. When a security interest is properly granted it is said to have attached and it is then enforceable against the debtor.

In a security agreement, a general description of personal property used as security is sufficient if it reasonably identifies the property. Therefore, a description of patent collateral in a security agreement as general intangibles or patents should be sufficient. However, it is best practice to identify all patents by number, country, issuance or filing date, and expiration date. The collateral description should also include all pending patent infringement claims; rights to income, profits, or other rights related to the patents; all inventions and improvements described in the patents; and all continuations, divisions, renewals, extensions, substitutions, and reissuances of the patents.

A security agreement for which patents serve as collateral should address several additional issues. Because patents expire after twenty years and lapse unless maintenance fees are paid, 35 U.S.C. § 154(a)(2), a security agreement should require the debtor to make timely payments of all applicable fees prior to their due date and permit the lender to do so and recover reimbursement from the debtor should the debtor fail to pay the fees. The security agreement should also require the debtor to notify the secured party of patents acquired after the execution of the security agreement and to execute perfection of its security interest so that the secured party achieves and maintains the highest available priority for its security interest in collateral. An unperfected security interest may be effective against the debtor, but it is of little value against third parties. In bankruptcy, the difference between a perfected security interest and an unperfected security interest means the difference between full recovery as a secured creditor and little or no recovery as an unsecured creditor.

A security interest is perfected when it attaches if the applicable requirements are satisfied before attachment. The process of perfecting a security interest in most types of personal property is accomplished when a properly completed UCC–1 financing statement is filed with the appropriate state office, most often the office of the secretary of state. The financing statement must name both the debtor and the secured party and must describe the collateral covered by the financing statement. The U.C.C. no longer requires the debtor to sign an electronically filed financial statement, although the debtor must authorize the filing.

The relative priorities of creditors who hold conflicting security interests are straightforward under the U.C.C.:

(1) if the conflicting security interests are perfected, they rank according to priority in time of filing or perfection;

(2) a perfected security interest has priority over a conflicting, unperfected security interest; and

(3) if the conflicting security interests are unperfected, the first security interest to attach has priority.

However, under § 9–109(c)(1), Article 9 does not apply to the extent that it is preempted by federal law.

Filing a financing statement is neither necessary nor effective to perfect a security interest in collateral that is subject to a separate federal filing requirement. In such cases, compliance with such a federal requirement is equivalent to filing a properly completed UCC–1 financing statement, and compliance with federal law is the only means of perfection. U.C.C. § 9–311(b). However, even in cases where federal law governs the perfection of security interests, Article 9 governs the relative priorities of conflicting security interests unless federal law also establishes separate priority rules. Sections 9–109 and 9–311 of the U.C.C. raise distinct issues. Under § 9–109, federal law preempts Article 9 where federal law governs ownership rights in the property secured as collateral. Under § 9–311, the U.C.C. defers to federal law regarding perfection if federal law has defined a filing requirement. The practical distinction between these sections is unclear and it is equally unclear whether security interests in intellectual property rights governed by federal law must be perfected in accordance with federal law or the U.C.C. Because of this uncertainty, security interests in patents, trademarks, and copyrights should be filed with both state and federal agencies.

Federal law provides that "[a]n assignment, grant or conveyance shall be void as against any subsequent purchaser or mortgagee for a valuable consideration, without notice, unless it is recorded in the Patent and Trademark Office within three months from its date or prior to the date of such subsequent purchase or mortgage." 35 U.S.C. § 261. This statute does not clearly satisfy the Article 9 preemption provisions and therefore does not displace the U.C.C. for purposes of perfecting security interests in patents. The case law in this area suggests that the U.C.C. controls the perfection of security interests in patents. Nevertheless, filing with the PTO provides important protections to the holder of a security interest. See *In re* Transportation Design & Technology, Inc., 48 B.R. 635 (Bankr. S.D. Cal. 1985); *In re* Cybernetic Services, Inc., 252 F.3d 1039 (9th Cir. 2001); *In re* Tower Tech, Inc., 67 Fed. App'x 521 (10th Cir. 2003).

In sum, a security interest in a patent is perfected by properly filing U.C.C. financing statements at the appropriate state office, at least as against lien creditors and hypothetical lien creditors such as a trustee in bankruptcy. However, filing with the PTO may be necessary to protect against subsequent bona fide purchasers and mortgagees who properly record. No statute or case law specifically addresses the rights of a subsequent bona fide purchaser for value or of a mortgagee who has properly filed with the PTO, so secured parties should make appropriate filings under both U.C.C. Article 9 and Title 15.

R. ACQUIRING PATENTS

1. PATENT PROSECUTION

Patent rights, unlike other types of intellectual property rights, arise only after a formal application process and government review. Patent prosecution is the administrative process by which an inventor acquires a patent from the Patent and Trademark Office, or PTO, a federal administrative agency within the Department of Commerce.

a. The Patent Applicant

Only natural persons may qualify as inventors. Inventors are presumed to own the patent application and patents issued for their invention unless they previously assigned their patent. To prosecute a patent, the patent's assignee must become an assignee of record by filing a copy of the executed assignment with the PTO.

Special restrictions apply when a patent is granted for an invention conceived by multiple inventors:

> When an invention is made by two or more persons jointly, they shall apply for a patent jointly and each make the required oath, except as otherwise provided in this title. Inventors may apply for a patent jointly even though (1) they did not physically work together or at the same time, (2) each did not make the same type or amount of contribution, or (3) each did not make a contribution to the subject matter of every claim of the patent.

35 U.S.C. § 116. Rather than defining joint inventorship, this provision defines a joint invention as the product of collaboration between two or more persons. The existence of joint inventorship is a question of law determined in view of the underlying facts.

Every joint inventor must join in the patent application if possible, but if a joint inventor refuses to join or cannot be reached after diligent effort, then the missing joint inventor need not join in the application and the patent may issue in the name of all the inventors. Should an inventor be accidentally omitted from the application, the Director of the PTO may authorize an amendment to the application. 35 U.S.C. § 116.

Even if the inventors did not contribute equally to the invention, each co-inventor owns an equal undivided interest in the entire patent unless they have contracted otherwise, and each joint owner may exploit the patent without the consent of any other owner. However, 35 U.S.C. § 281, which grants patent holders a civil remedy for patent infringement, has been interpreted to require a joint owner to obtain permission from every other joint owner before bringing a patent infringement suit.

b. Patent Applications

The patent application describes the claimed invention and should include drawings (or diagrams) as necessary. Applicants are required to declare to the best of their knowledge that they are the original inventor of the invention they seek to patent. 35 U.S.C. § 115. An applicant also has a duty to disclose any prior art known to be material to the patentability of the claimed invention. 37 C.F.R. § 1.56. The required elements of a patent application are listed in 37 C.F.R. § 1.77.

Under 35 U.S.C. § 122, patent applications are initially confidential, subject to limited exceptions. However, confidentiality is temporary; all applications must be published eighteen months from the filing date unless they are: no longer pending; subject to a secrecy order; provisional applications; or applications for design patents. Patent applicants may also request that their application not be published if they certify that the application will not be filed in a foreign country.

A patent application must include a specification, a drawing, and an oath and be accompanied by the appropriate fee and signed by the inventor. 35 U.S.C. § 111. In a patent application, the specifications must include one or more distinct claims about the invention. 35 U.S.C. § 112. Applicants must testify under oath that they believe themselves to be the first inventor of the invention that they are seeking to patent. 35 U.S.C. § 115.

Patent applicants may instead file a provisional application to gain the benefit of the provisional filing date for priority purposes under a relation-back theory, provided they later file a non-provisional application. A provisional application must include a specification and drawing, but need not include claims, inventors' oaths or declarations, or any information disclosure statement. 35 U.S.C. § 111(b). They are slightly less expensive to file than traditional, non-provisional applications. 37 C.F.R. § 1.16(a)–(d). Provisional applications are not examined or published by the PTO and are considered abandoned if the applicant takes no further action within twelve months of filing. One popular use of a provisional application is to document and lock in potential patent rights while attempting to obtain funding for further development or to pursue the more expensive patent application. The earliest filing date of a provisional application may also be very important where for example a statutory condition of patentability is about to expire and there is insufficient time to generate a complete non-provisional application.

c. Specifications

The first paragraph of § 112 requires that the patent application disclose the invention. The specification or description called for by the first paragraph of § 112 is perhaps among the most difficult legal instruments to draft. The specification is subject to the three statutory requirements of 35 U.S.C. § 112:

- First, it must contain a written description of the invention sufficient to enable a skilled artisan to make and use the invention. This is often referred to as the enablement requirement.

- Second, the description must show that the inventor had accomplished the invention at the filing date.

- Third, the specification must detail the best mode contemplated by the inventor for carrying out his invention. That is, it must state the best way to work the invention claimed in the patent application. The best mode requirement restrains inventors from applying for a patent while concealing preferred embodiments of the invention.[74]

d. Claims

Section 112 also requires that the specification "conclude with one or more claims particularly pointing out and distinctly claiming the subject matter which the inventor or joint inventor regards as the invention." While claims are technically part of the specification, patent practitioners commonly refer to the specification and claims as distinct portions of the patent instrument because claims are independently important. Claims both define the scope of the patent and distinguish the invention from prior art.

e. Claim Drafting

Claims define the scope of the protected invention. They must be adequate and definite as to the extent of legal protection afforded by the patent. A claim is adequate and definite if an expert in the field would understand all the language of the claim when read in light of the specification. The terms used in the claims are construed to have the ordinary and customary meaning as understood by a person of ordinary skill in the art unless the patent holder devises specific definitions or terminology in the application, in which case assigned meanings will be applied rather than the customary meanings. Applicants may phrase the

---

[74] The AIA has largely removed the consequences associated with failure to disclose the inventors best mode. Pre-AIA the failure to disclose the best mode of the invention led to the invalidation of the claim for failure to comply with any requirement of § 112. Post-AIA § 282 states that failure to disclose best mode is not a basis for invalidity. 35 U.S.C. § 282(b)(3)(A).

claim however they wish, provided that the form and language precisely and distinctly claim the invention.

Claims are particularly important and must be drafted with great care, as they define the absolute boundaries of the invention which are not claims will not be protected.

Because poor drafting can result in forfeiture of an invention's features an invention should be described with many claims of progressively broadening scope that differ by only one aspect or term so that, if challenged, some of the claims may be stricken without damage to the remainder.

f.   Types of Claims

There are three types of claims: independent, dependent, and multiple dependent claims. Independent claims are integrated claims drafted to stand alone. Dependent claims incorporate by reference, build upon, or otherwise depend upon another claim. Multiple dependent claims are the same as dependent claims, but reference, build upon, or otherwise "depend" upon multiple other claims.

Independent claims are organized into three parts: a preamble that generally describes all the non-novel or obvious elements of the claim, a transitional phrase (such as "wherein the improvement comprises")[75], and a description of the "elements, steps and/or relationships" actually claimed as the subject of the invention. 37 C.F.R. § 1.75(e).

The patent application must also include drawings that further describe and define the invention when needed to understand the invention claimed in the patent application. 35 U.S.C. § 113. Drawings supplement and give meaning to claims (i.e., they illustrate claims) but do not expand claims or other aspects of the patent.

g.   Claim Construction

A patent is construed in light of its claims and its file wrapper, the patent's prosecution history in the PTO. A file wrapper is the complete record of all PTO proceedings regarding a particular patent, including all representations and limitations made by the applicant during the approval process. In prosecuting their patent application, applicants may accept limitations on their claims to circumvent a prior art-rejection by the examiner. If a claim has been narrowed, the doctrine of file-wrapper estoppel (also called prosecution history estoppel) will bar the patentee

---

[75]   There are three widely used transitions: "comprising" is the 'open' transition, meaning the invention *at least* has the elements listed after the transition (i.e., could be made of other things, as well); "consisting of" is the 'closed' transition, meaning that the invention is *limited to the elements listed* immediately following the transition—and nothing else; and "consisting essentially of" is an intermediate transition; it means that the invention contains essential elements (like those in the 'consisting of' group), as well as non-essential elements.

from later advocating a construction of that claim that is broader than the construction presented to the PTO. For example, an examiner may refuse to issue a patent on an invention as it is described in the claims, but may be willing to do so if the inventor agrees to narrow the claims. If the inventor agrees to narrow the scope of the claims, file-wrapper estoppel will prevent him from later claiming that his patent covers the forfeited features.

h. Duty of Candor

Given the non-adversarial *ex parte* nature of patent prosecution, the public interest is best served when the PTO is aware of and evaluates all information material to patentability. 37 C.F.R. § 1.56(a). Thus, every party associated with the filing and prosecution of a patent application—including inventors, attorneys, agents, and anyone else substantially involved with the application—is required to disclose all material information throughout the prosecution with "candor and good faith in dealing." The duty of candor ceases when the claim is withdrawn from consideration or the application is abandoned. Compliance is ensured by the policy that no patent will be granted for an application involving fraud or attempted fraud on the PTO or a violation of the duty of disclosure through bad faith or intentional misconduct.

The Federal Circuit has defined materiality to mean a substantial likelihood that a reasonable examiner would have considered the information important in deciding whether to issue a patent. Molins PLC v. Textron, Inc., 48 F.3d 1172 (Fed. Cir. 1995). Full disclosure of even adverse facts is prudent, since a breach of the duty of candor will render the patent unenforceable.

i. Rejection and Appeal

Under 35 U.S.C. § 134, an applicant whose claim has been twice rejected—whether for lack of novelty, lack of utility, or obviousness—may appeal the examiner's decision to the Patent Trial and Appeal Board (PTAB). The PTAB replaces the pre AIA Board of Patent Appeals and Interferences and consists of three person administrative patent judge panel. The Federal Circuit has exclusive jurisdiction over all appeals from the Patent Trial and Appeal Board regarding the denial of a patent application or the determination of a derivation proceeding.[76] However, by appealing to the Federal Circuit, the applicant or patent owner waives the right to bring a civil action to compel the PTO to issue a patent or decide a derivation differently. An appeal to the Federal Circuit must be taken

---

[76] The Federal Circuit also has jurisdiction over the derivation proceedings that have replaced interferences. Further, the AIA amended § 1295(4)(A) to grant express federal jurisdiction in matters dealing with post-grant review, ex parte reexaminations, and inter partes review.

within two months of the Patent Trial and Appeal Board decision unless the Director of the PTO grants an extension. 37 C.F.R. § 1.304.

2. REISSUE

A patent holder may surrender a patent that, because of error, is inoperative or invalid because of defective specifications, drawings, or the scope of its claims in exchange for a reissued patent for the invention disclosed in the original patent. 35 U.S.C. § 251. A reissued patent may also be available to the legal representatives or assigns of the patent holder.

The reissue may even result in several reissued patents for distinct parts of the invention though none may exceed the balance of time remaining on the original patent. A reissued patent, to the extent that its claims are identical with the original patent, constitutes a continuation of the original patent and has effect from the date of the original patent. 35 U.S.C. § 251. For reissue to be appropriate, a patent must be inoperative due to correctable error. Likewise, non-joinder or misjoinder of inventors may be cured by reissue.

The reissue provision is based on principles of equity and, although construed liberally, reissue is not available to cure all errors. One significant limitation is found in 35 U.S.C. § 251: a reissued patent may not enlarge the scope of the original patent unless it is applied for within two years of the grant of the original patent. For example, in *Dart Industries, Inc. v. Banner*, 636 F.2d 684 (D.C. Cir. 1980), the patent holder filed an initial patent application claiming its engine carburetor design and two subsequent applications for amendments. In the initial application, the patentee disclosed—but did not claim—a particular feature of his invention: a "venturi" or flared tube that creates a pressure differential and assists in mixing fuel with air before it is sent to the pistons. The patent holder neither disclosed nor claimed this feature in the second application, but both disclosed and claimed the feature in the third application, arguing that it had been disclosed in the grandparent application and therefore was not new matter under § 251. The court rejected this argument, concluding that the patent holder's failure to maintain continuity of disclosure was uncorrectable.

Moreover, reissue cannot cure a defect caused by a breach of the duty of candor. As stated in *In re Clark*, 522 F.2d 623 (C.C.P.A. 1975), "[w]here inequitable conduct has occurred during prosecution, it cannot be purged or cured after the patent has issued."[77]

---

[77]   The plain language of the 35 U.S.C. § 251 as amended by the AIA removes the innocence requirement from correctable error. How this will be treated in the courts remains to be seen. It seems somewhat difficult to imagine that Congress intended to create a safe harbor for intentional misrepresentation.

3. REEXAMINATION

Reexamination allows "any person at any time" to question the validity of a patent in light of prior art. 35 U.S.C. §§ 302–07. An inventor of a third party can have a U.S. patent reexamined by a patent examiner to verify that the subject matter it claims is patentable. To have a patent reexamined, an interested party must submit prior art, in the form of patents or printed publications, that raises a "substantial new question of patentability." There are three primary reasons reexaminations are initiated:

1. Prior to filing a lawsuit for infringement, an inventor may file for a reexamination of their own patent to ensure it is valid in light of prior art they may have discovered since the issuance of a patent.

2. Third parties involved in an infringement lawsuit may seek reexamination to invalidate the patent while keeping legal fees low. With judicial endorsement, trial proceeds can be stayed pending the outcome of reexamination.

3. The PTO may initiate a reexamination order by the Director if there is a substantial new question of patentability affecting any claim of a patent is raised.

Ex parte reexamination involves minimal participation of a third party challenger of a patent's validity. A challenger may anonymously request the reexamination of a patent by producing relevant prior art and may only reply to proofs adduced by the patentee in response, but may not otherwise participate or appeal. To initiate an ex parte reexamination, under 35 U.S.C. § 303(a), the challenger must request the reexamination in writing and point to specific prior art that tends to raise a substantial new question of patentability of the challenged claim. The PTO must immediately notify the patent owner of a reexamination request and must decide within three months whether a substantial question of patentability exists. The PTO can also initiate a reexamination, regardless of whether the prior art cited was considered when the patent was originally granted. If the PTO determines that there is no substantial question of patentability, that decision is final and non-appealable. Under 35 U.S.C. § 304, if the PTO determines that a reexamination is warranted, both the challenger and patentee must be notified. The patentee has a reasonable time of at least two months to file a statement on the question, including any amendment to the patent and new claims. The patent holder must also serve a copy of its statement on the challenger, who may respond within two months. The patentee then proceeds under 35 U.S.C. § 305 and attempts to distinguish its patent from prior art, proceeding as if the patentee was protesting an initial rejection of the patent.

In an ex parte reexamination, participation of the requester and the patentee is limited to the submission of statements allowed under 35 U.S.C. § 304. The patentee is the only party that can file an appeal the PTO's ex parte reexamination of a patent under 35 U.S.C. § 306. The appeal will initially go before the Patent Trial and Appeal Board (PTAB).[78] The PTAB consists of three

4. POST-GRANT REVIEW

Post-grant review (PGR) is authorized by 35 U.S.C. § 321 and is a trial proceeding conducted before the PTAB to review the patentability of one or more claims in a patent on any ground that could be raised under § 282(b)(2) or (3). Unlike pre AIA reexamination procedures which were limited to prior art in the form of patents and publications, the PGR substantially broadens the scope for challenge by allowing evidence of on-sale activities, public uses, prior filed but not yet issued patents, other types of disclosures, and issues concerning enablement.

Post grant review process begins with a third party filing a petition on or prior to the date that is 9 months after the grant of the patent or issuance of a reissue patent. The patent owner has two months to file a preliminary response to the petition setting forth reasons why the PGR should not be granted, but cannot present new evidence of patentability. After the filing the PTO has three months to determine if the PGR should be granted. 35 U.S.C. § 324(c). The Director may not authorize a post grant review unless it is determined that it is more likely than not that at least one claim challenged unpatentable. 35 U.S.C. § 324. A PGR can also be authorized if the Director determines that the petition raises a novel or unsettled legal question that is important to other patents or patent applications. 35 U.S.C. § 3324(b).

Once the PGR is authorized the PTO can require the patent owner to file additional evidence and expert opinions to support the owner's response. The patent owner can respond in a variety of ways including filing substituted or amended claims as long as it finds support in the original patent specification and does not broaden the scope of the original claims. Discovery is limited to evidence directly related to the assertions put forth by either party. Sanctions are available for misuse of discovery to harass or cause unnecessary delay. If the proceeding is instituted and not dismissed, a final determination by the PTAB will be issued within 1 year (extendable for good cause by 6 months). Although the decision not to commence a PGR decision is not appealable, final PGR decisions are appealable to the Federal Circuit.

---

[78] The AIA contains a provision giving Fed. Cir. Appeals Ct. exclusive jurisdiction over any appeals of PTO reexamination decisions. District court can no longer hear re-exam cases.

A party is barred from filing a PGR petition if they have already filed a civil action. However, if a civil action is filed after the PGR petition, the action will be stayed until the patent owner files a counterclaim or requests that stay be lifted.

5. INTER PARTES REVIEW

The AIA has done away with the Inter Partes Reexamination process and has replaced it with the Inter Partes Review (IPR) procedure 35 U.S.C. § 311. Inter partes review is a trial proceeding conducted at the PTAB to review the patentability of one or more claims in a patent only on a ground that could be raised under §§ 102 or 103, and only on the basis of prior art consisting of patents or printed publications.

For first-inventor-to-file patents, inter partes review process begins with a third party (a person who is not the owner of the patent) filing a petition after the later of either:

1.   9 months after the grant of the patent or issuance of a reissue patent;

2.   or if a post grant review is instituted, the termination of the post grant review.

These deadlines do not apply to first-to-invent patents. The patent owner may file a preliminary response to the petition. An inter partes review may be instituted upon a showing that there is a reasonable likelihood that the petitioner would prevail with respect to at least one claim challenged 35 U.S.C. § 312. Because the ex partes reexamination process is subject to the lower standard of "substantial new question of patentability" under 35 U.S.C. § 303(a), it may be easier to initiate a reexamination than an IPR.

The AIA attempts to coordinate with other proceedings and avoid duplication. To accomplish this 35 U.S.C. § 315(e)(1) estops an IPR petitioner from challenging in district court or International Trade Commission (ITC) enforcement action[79], any claim that was raised or reasonably could be raised in an IPR. An IPR must be filed before a declaratory action is filed by the patent challenger in district court 35 U.S.C. § 315(a)(1). District court actions filed after an IPR are automatically stayed during the IPR proceedings 35 U.S.C. § 315(a)(2). The stay can only be lifted if:

1.   The patent owner requests the stay to be lifted;

2.   An infringement action is filed by the patent owner in district court;

---

[79]   Domestic and foreign companies seeking to block the importation of products that infringe United States intellectual property rights or otherwise compete unfairly are subject to Section 337 of the Tariff Act of 1930. Under the Statute, the International Trade Commission has the power to exclude infringing products from entry into the United States.

3. The declaratory judgment patent challenger dismisses the district court action.

In the event that the patent owner files an infringement action, and the infringer counterclaims based upon patent invalidity, the automatic stay provision is not triggered 35 U.S.C. § 315(a)(3). An accused infringer must request an IPR proceeding within a year from the date the patentee files an infringement action 35 U.S.C. § 315(b). If the proceeding is instituted and not dismissed, a final determination by the Board will be issued within 1 year (extendable for good cause by 6 months).

6. COVERED BUSINESS METHOD REVIEW

The transitional program for covered business method patents (TPCBM) is a trial proceeding conducted by the PTAB to review the patentability of one or more claims in a covered business method patent. A covered business method (CBM) patent is defined in 35 U.S.C. § 18 as a patent that "claims a method or corresponding apparatus for performing data processing or other operations used in the practice, administration, or management of a financial product or service, but is not for a "technological" invention.

TPCBM proceedings employ the standards and procedures of a post grant review, with certain exceptions. For example, for first to invent patents only a subset of prior art is available to support the petition. Further, a person may not file a petition for a TPCBM proceeding unless the person or the person's real party in interest or privy has been sued for infringement of the patent or charged with infringement under the patent.

The USPTO has published a Trial Practice Guide explaining CBM procedures and amplifying its regulations on what is not a technological invention:

1. Mere recitation of known technologies, such as computer hardware, communication or computer networks, software, memory, computer-readable storage medium, scanners, display devices or databases, or specialized machines, such as an ATM or point of sale device.

2. Reciting the use of known prior art technology to accomplish a process or method, even if that process or method is novel and non-obvious.

3. Combining prior art structures to achieve the normal, expected, or predictable result of that combination.

The standard for whether the PTAB will institute a CBM proceeding is whether a petition by an interested party (ordinarily, a party that the patentee sued for patent infringement) requesting institution of the proceeding establishes that it is more likely than not that at least one claim of the challenged patent is unpatentable. Any statutory ground of invalidity may be considered, including patent ineligibility under 35 U.S.C. § 101. The procedure for conducting TPCBM review took effect on September 16, 2012, but only applies to covered business method patents. The program will sunset for new TPCBM petitions on September 16, 2020.

7. DERIVATION PROCEEDING

With the transition from first-to-invent to first-inventor-to-file rule under the AIA, the patent interference proceedings were eliminated after March 15, 2013. In its place, Congress established the derivation proceeding under 35 U.S.C. § 135 to determine if patent applicant derived or misappropriated the invention of another. The derivation proceeding is a trial proceeding conducted by the PTAB to determine whether

- a. an inventor named in an earlier application derived the claimed invention from an inventor named in the petitioner's application, and
- b. the earlier application claiming such invention was filed without authorization.

An applicant subject to the first-inventor-to-file provisions may file a petition to institute a derivation proceeding only within 1 year of the first publication of a claim to an invention that is the same or substantially the same as the earlier application's claim to the invention.[80] The petition must be supported by substantial evidence that the claimed invention was derived from an inventor named in the petitioner's application.

8. ENFORCING PATENTS

United States District courts have original and exclusive jurisdiction over any civil action arising under the patent laws. On appeal, jurisdiction lies in the United States Court of Appeals for the Federal Circuit. The Federal Circuit applies its own law to patent matters and the law of the circuit in which the originating district court sits for non patent matters in the case.

Under 28 U.S.C.A. § 1400(b), the proper venue for patent cases is in judicial districts where (1) the defendant resides or (2) where the acts of infringement were committed and the defendant has a regular and established place of business. Following *TC Heartland LLC*,[81] "residence," as it applies to domestic corporations, only means the state in which the organization is incorporated for the purposes of patent infringement.

---

[80] Or one year after patent issuance if the application was never published under 35 U.S.C. § 122.

[81] *TC Heartland LLC v. Kraft Foods Group Brands LLC*, 137 S.Ct. 1514 (2017).

Further, *In re Cray Inc.*[82] has postulated that a regular and established place of business is restricted to places where a company regularly carries on business, not just where its employee have offices. Finally, the ruling in *In re BigCommerce, Inc.*[83] clarified that there is only one correct venue, where a company has its principal place of business and its registered office, to bring an infringement suit, you cannot sue in every district of a state in which the company resides. These changes suggest that the existing standards for venue in patent infringement cases are currently in flux and should continue to be watched by litigators.

Infringement includes any unauthorized manufacture, use, sale, offer to sell, or importation into the United States of any patented article. Infringement is a strict liability cause of action; the intent of the infringer is only relevant in the determination of damages.

In conducting an infringement analysis, the court construes the claims for the patent and then determines if the allegedly infringing device "reads on" every limitation of the claims, either identically or under the doctrine of equivalents.

The construction of the claims to determine infringement is similar to the construction used in patent prosecution; claims are construed according to their express language in light of the specification, drawings, and the file wrapper. Extrinsic evidence may be used, but not if it contradicts the express language of a claim.

The doctrine of equivalents broadens the scope of patent protection to cover insubstantial or trivial nonfunctional changes that do not literally infringe. An element is equivalent to a limitation of a patent claim if it performs substantially the same function in substantially the same way to obtain substantially the same result as the claim limitation.

Direct infringement is the manufacture, use, sale, or importation of the infringing device and requires that the accused device meet every limitation of the claim, either literally or under doctrine of equivalents. Indirect infringement includes both contributory infringement and inducement to infringement and requires direct infringement as a prerequisite to liability.

Contributory infringement occurs when one sells a material component of another's patented invention that is not itself a staple article or commodity of commerce suitable for substantial non-fringing use. Inducement to infringement occurs when one actively induces another to engage in direct infringement. Common defenses to infringement include

---

[82]   *In re Cray Inc.*, 871 F.3d 1355, 1364 (Fed. Cir. 2017) (*finding*, that "the mere fact that a defendant has advertised that it has a place of business or has even set up an office is not sufficient; the defendant must actually engage in business from that location. In the final analysis, the court must identify a physical place, of business, of the defendant.").

[83]   *In re BigCommerce Inc.*, 890 F.3d 978 (Fed. Cir. 2018).

invalidity of the patent, misuse, shop rights, prior use, safe harbors, and non-patent defenses including that the accused device did not infringe or lapse of the statute of limitations. Defendants asserting patent invalidity carry the burden of proof but may use any of the grounds required for patentability to make the challenge such as by negating novelty, non-obviousness, utility, etc.

Misuse is generally asserted as a defense when the patent holder has allegedly abused the patent monopoly with any arrangement by requiring the purchase of unpatented goods with the patent or conditioning the grant of a license upon acceptance of another different license or some similar tying arrangement or unlawful restraint of competitive trade.

Shop rights grant an employer the right to use an invention patented by an employee under equitable circumstances, such as when the employer provided the material and the employee developed the invention in the course of their employment.

A defendant that continuously used the patented method for at least a year prior to the date the patent issued may continue using the method if it was developed independently of the patentee.

Injunctions are the most common remedy for patent infringement and are issued on equitable principles identical to those for non-patent injunctions. There are two types of injunctions commonly used in patent infringement proceedings, preliminary and permanent injunctions. Preliminary injunctions require a clear showing of patent validity and patent infringement. Once these two conditions are met there is a rebuttable presumption of irreparable harm to the patentee. Prior to eBay v. MercExchange, the courts would, as a general rule, issue permanent injunctions in patent infringement cases, absent exceptional circumstances. Now, to receive a permanent injunction, the claimant must pass the four-factor test set forth in eBay v. MercExchange (patent holders are required to show that they have suffered irreparable injury, that money damages are inadequate, balance of the hardships, and that the public interest would not be disserved). The difference between the standards for each type of injunction is that the analysis for a preliminary injunction combines the inadequacy of legal remedies and irreparable harm into a singular prong of the analysis. Additionally, the preliminary injunction requires an evaluation of the likelihood of success on the merits, while a permanent injunction is not considered until after adjudication

Patent holders may also receive money damages for their lost profits if they can prove them with requisite certainty but more often the measure of damages is a reasonable royalty. A reasonable royalty is calculated by what a willing licensor and licensee would bargain for in a hypothetical negotiation. The court may treble the damages in a case of willful infringement or bad faith, but cannot increase damages as a compensatory measure.   In exceptional cases, such as those involving willful infringement, inequitable conduct, or vexatious litigation, the prevailing party in a patent infringement action may receive an award of its reasonable attorneys' fees.

S. COPYRIGHT LAW

Copyrights, like patents, are designed to foster a public policy of incentivizing creativity and innovation.   By protecting works from unauthorized copying, society motivates authors and artists to produce useful works that benefit society.   The federal government's power to protect copyrights is derived from the same source as patent law: Article 1, Clause 8 of the United States Constitution. The vast majority of federal copyright law is found in Title 17 of the United States Code.

The first Congress enacted the first federal statutes on patent and copyright law in 1790. Since then, there have been a number of revisions to copyright law—primarily to increase the types of works that are eligible for copyright protection. The Copyright Act of 1976 overhauled United States Copyright law and replaced the Copyright Act of 1909. Among other things, the 1976 Act granted copyright protection from the moment a work is fixed in tangible form and extended the duration of copyright protection. In 1989, as part of the United States' decision to join the Berne Convention, Congress made substantial revisions to the notice provision and other formalities required by the 1976 Act.   Congress continues to update copyright protection to adapt to changing technologies and an expansion in the public's perception of artists rights. For example, in 1990, Congress expanded architects' rights to their plans and buildings constructed based on their plans, and in 1992, the Act was amended to afford record companies and performers additional protection in response to the development of digital recording machines.

T. STATE AND COMMON LAW COPYRIGHTS

Two types of copyrights existed prior to 1978: statutory and common law. Statutory copyright protection extended only to works that were published and common law copyrights protected unpublished works. Statutory copyright protection was limited to a term of years, and common law copyright protection was perpetual. However, common law copyright was largely abolished with the passage of the Copyright Act of 1976. Under § 302(a), works are copyrightable once they are fixed in tangible form. The preemption provisions of 17 U.S.C. § 301, preempt, as of January 1, 1978, all legal and equitable rights within the general scope of copyright as specified in § 106 with regard to all copyrightable subject matter, regardless of the date of publication. Likewise, § 106A pertaining to moral rights, § 113(d), and related sections preempt all state law governing rights within the scope of § 106A with regard to "undertakings commenced" after § 106A became effective.

The preemption provisions of do not preempt state law regarding subject matter beyond the scope of §§ 102 or 103, state law governing the violation of rights beyond the general scope of § 106, and state or local landmark, historic preservation, zoning, or building codes. Moreover, state law rights and remedies regarding sound recordings made before February 15, 1972 are not preempted until February 15, 2067, and § 301 neither "annuls [nor] limits any rights or remedies" otherwise available under federal law.

State law is not preempted to the extent that it either grants rights that are not equivalent to those conferred by §§ 106 and 106A or governs activities violating legal or equitable rights that extend beyond the life of the author. Common law copyrights received before January 1, 1978 are entitled to protection only where the common law cause of action arose from undertakings commenced prior to 1978. § 301(b)(2).

U. COPYRIGHTABLE SUBJECT MATTER

The Copyright Act protects "original works of authorship fixed in any tangible medium of expression, now known or later developed, from which they can be perceived, reproduced, or otherwise communicated, either directly or with the aid of a machine or device." 17 U.S.C. § 102(a). Under § 102(a), works of authorship include:

- literary works;

- musical works, including any accompanying music;

- pantomimes and choreographic works;

- pictorial, graphic, and sculptural works;

- motion pictures and other audiovisual works;

- sound recordings; and

- architectural works.

The types of copyrightable works expand as technology advances. For example, in *Williams Electronics, Inc. v. Artic International, Inc.*, 685 F.2d 870 (3d Cir. 1982), the defendants argued that a videogame was not a fixed expression because new images were displayed every time the game was played. However, the court held that videogames were suitably fixed and consequently were protectable by copyright. Similarly, the copyrightability of computer programs was uncertain in the last quarter of the twentieth century. Because computer programs cannot be expressed without the aid of a computer, there were doubts as to whether the programs were copyrightable. Congress concluded that computer programs should be eligible for protection and amended the Copyright Act to specifically include computer programs in 1980.

The Constitution uses two terms that are particularly important to determine the scope of copyright law: authors and writings. From the earliest stages of copyright law, these terms have been given broad meaning. For example, in *Burrow-Giles Lithographic Co. v. Sarony*, 111 U.S. 53 (1884), responding to a challenge on the status of photographs as copyrightable works, the Supreme Court addressed the meaning of the term writings. The Court concluded that writings encompasses all forms of writing, printing, engraving, etching, and the like whereby the ideas of the author are "given visible expression," including the somewhat mechanical process of photography.

In § 102(b), the Copyright Act describes works to which copyright protection cannot be extended, including any "idea, procedure, process, system, method of operation, concept, principle, or discovery." This restriction reflects the constitutional grant of power to protect writings, which have been construed to include only tangible expressions. Additionally, copyright protection is not available for works that are not original or that lack minimal creativity.

1. FIXED AND TANGIBLE

To qualify for copyright protection, a work must be "fixed in any tangible medium of expression, now known or later developed, from which [it] can be perceived, reproduced, or otherwise communicated, either directly or with the aid of a machine or device." 17 U.S.C. § 102(a). "Tangible medium of expression" is a broad category that separates copyrightable expressions from patentable processes and methods. For example, in *Baker v. Selden*, 101 U.S. 99 (1879), the inventor of a bookkeeping system argued that the system was protected by his copyright in a book that described the system. The Supreme Court concluded it was not, because copyrights protect the author's expression of an idea, while patents protect the use of the idea itself. The idea of the bookkeeping system had been placed in the public domain, precluding patent protection, but the book explaining it was protected under copyright.

Copyright attaches at the moment an idea is fixed as a tangible expression. Generally this requirement is easily met. For example, the idea for a book is fixed when it is written. In a more complex example, § 101 provides that a live broadcast "consisting of sounds, images, or both, . . . is 'fixed' for purposes of this title if a fixation of the work is being made simultaneously with its transmission."

2. ORIGINALITY

To be copyrightable, a work must be original, meaning it is (1) the independent creation of its author, and (2) at least minimally creative. The requirement of creativity is minimal and most works satisfy the requirement. For a work to be creative, it needs only to possess some creative spark.

Historically, the sweat of the brow doctrine justified a finding of originality for any compilation of factual information. The sweat of the brow doctrine required only that the author invest original work into the final product. As a result, maps, charts, and telephone directories were copyrightable works. The Supreme Court rejected the sweat of the brow doctrine in *Feist Publications, Inc. v. Rural Telephone Service Co.*, 499 U.S. 340 (1991), in which the Court denied copyright protection for a telephone directory. The Court held that the information was factual and not eligible for a copyright. The *Feist* Court was clear that originality—not sweat of the brow—is required for copyright protection in directories and other fact-based works. Originality can exist in the selection, coordination, and arrangement of public information, but the Court concluded that the "entirely typical" alphabetical organization of the telephone directory in *Feist* indicated that the "creative spark [was] entirely lacking or so trivial as to be virtually nonexistent."

However, even a copy of an original work (like an art student's painting of another artist's work) may satisfy the creativity requirement if it possesses sufficient variation. Basically, anything more than a direct copy is generally considered creative.

3. EXPRESSION NOT IDEAS

It is the expression of an idea that is copyrightable, not the underlying idea itself (but a patent can be used to secure an idea described in a copyrighted work). The difference between the idea embodied in a work of authorship and the particular expression of that idea is critical to this inquiry. For tangible articles, the difference between the useful and aesthetic elements of the article determine the boundary between aspects of the article that are copyrightable and aspects that are patentable.

4. EXPRESSIVE NOT UTILITARIAN

A work is not protected by copyright to the extent that it is purely functional. If the work is utilitarian, but also has aesthetic or expressive qualities, it might be eligible for a copyright if these qualities are sufficiently separable.

Courts have used different approaches to distinguish between expressive and utilitarian elements. For example, in *Brandir*

International, Inc. v. Cascade Pacific Lumber Co., 834 F.2d 1142 (2d Cir. 1987), the court considered whether a bicycle rack inspired by abstract-expressionist sculpture qualified for copyright protection. The court found that the utilitarian aspects of the bicycle rack were not separable from the creator's expressive choices and the rack was thus ineligible for copyright protection.

Contrast the outcome in *Brandir* with that in *Pivot Point International, Inc. v. Charlene Products, Inc.*, 372 F.3d 913 (7th Cir. 2004), where the plaintiff alleged that its copyright to a successful hair-stylist's mannequin had been infringed by the defendant's sculpturally similar model. The court concluded that the plaintiff's copyright protected the facial modeling of their mannequin, holding that conceptual separability exists when the artistic aspects of an article can be conceptualized as existing independently of their utilitarian function.

On the other hand, in *Galiano v. Harrah's Operating Co.*, 416 F.3d 411 (5th Cir. 2005), the plaintiff clothing designer alleged that the defendant casino had infringed upon her design for casino uniforms by continuing, after the expiration of their contract, to purchase uniforms manufactured according to her design. The court considered whether there was substantial likelihood that, even if the uniform had no utilitarian use, it would still be marketable simply because of its aesthetic qualities. The court found that the uniforms would not have been marketable but for their utility and held that the uniform design was therefore not copyrightable. The court stated that is utility test was somewhat subjective, but justified the test on the grounds that it was easy to administer.

5. MERGER DOCTRINE

The merger doctrine is related to the utility analysis. It holds that when an idea necessarily involves certain forms of expression, those forms of expression are not copyrightable. The idea behind the merger doctrine is that such a copyright would effectively copyright and thus monopolize underlying idea.

6. TYPEFACE

Mechanical typeface has been categorically denied copyright protection under the merger doctrine. Eltra Corp. v. Ringer, 579 F.2d 294 (4th Cir. 1978). However, as noted by the court in *Adobe System Inc. v. S. Software Inc.*, 45 U.S.P.Q.2d 1827 (N.D. Cal. 1998), "scalable" computer generated fonts are copyrightable because they cannot be copied without an infringement upon the underlying (and independently copyrightable) source code.

7. COMPUTER PROGRAMS

Computer programs have also implicated the merger doctrine. A computer program is protected as a "set of statements or instructions to be used directly or indirectly in a computer in order to bring about a certain result." 17 U.S.C. § 117. The literal elements of the computer software (the source code) are copyrightable as a tangible medium of expression. In this way, computer programs are protected as literary works.

The non-literal elements of the computer program, "the structure, sequence and organization of the program, the user interface, and the function, or purpose, of the program," are also copyrightable as long as they are not the only possible expression of an underlying idea. Johnson Controls, Inc. v. Phoenix Control Systems, Inc., 886 F.2d 1173 (9th Cir. 1989).

V. THE COPYRIGHT PROPERTY INTEREST

A copyright arises automatically once a protective work has been fixed in a tangible medium of expression. Under § 201(a), ownership of a copyright initially vests in the author. Ownership of a material object that embodies the copyrighted work does not give the owner any copyrights in the work. For example, the owner of a reproduction of a painting does not thereby own the copyright to the painting, and the owner of this book does not own the copyright to it.

Authors possess the exclusive rights of § 106 and may exploit the copyrighted work themselves or may transfer all or some of those rights to others. The character of the author is important, and it is determinative of the duration of copyright protection. If the copyrighted work is the product of joint authors, each author may exploit it. A work for hire vests the copyright in the employer rather than the natural person who created the work.

1. JOINT AUTHORSHIP

All authors of a joint work have rights in the copyrighted work. A joint work is "a work prepared by two or more authors with the intention that their contributions be merged into inseparable or interdependent parts of a unitary whole." 17 U.S.C. § 101. Authors can manifest the requisite intent to create a joint work either by working together to produce the work or by acknowledging that their works will be merged together. The authors' independent contributions to the joint work do not have to be equal in any sense, whether measured by quality, quantity, or economic value. However, the contribution of each must be independently copyrightable. For example, in *Childress v. Taylor*, 945 F.2d 500 (2d Cir. 1991), the court held that an actress was not the joint author of a play, even though she had conducted research for and met regularly with the playwright, because she had not actually written any portion of the play.

To mitigate the possibility of abuse from subordinate authors, there must be evidence of a mutual intention to share authorship, such as shared credit or shared approval of revisions, if the authors did not collaborate directly.

Co-owners of joint works are treated as tenants in common. Each co-owner has an undivided, independent right to the entire work, subject only to a duty of accounting for profits to other co-owners.

Each co-owner has the exclusive rights of § 106 and may license or authorize other persons to use those rights. However, absent an agreement otherwise, any profits gained by licensing or assigning the exclusive rights are subject to the duty of accounting and must be shared between co-owners.

2. WORKS FOR HIRE

When a work is made as part of employment or hire, "the employer or other person for whom the work was prepared is considered the author. . . and unless the parties have expressly agreed otherwise in a written instrument signed by them, owns all of the rights comprised in the copyright." 17 U.S.C. § 101. A work for hire is:

(1) a work prepared by an employee within the scope of employment; or

(2) a work specially ordered or commissioned for use as a contribution to a collective work as part, a motion picture or other audio-visual work, as a translation, a supplementary work, as a compilation, an instructional test, as a test, as answer material for a test, or as an atlas, if the parties expressly agree in a written instrument signed by them that the work shall be considered a work made for hire.

17 U.S.C. § 101. A work cannot be made into a work for hire by contract after it has been completed; rather, a prior or simultaneous contract is required.

Section 101(1) does not define employee or scope of employment and courts apply the federal common law of agency to make this determination. Many factors are considered, including:

(1) The hiring party's right to control the manner and means by which the product is accomplished;

(2) The skill required;

(3) The source of the instrumentalities and tools involved;

(4)   The location of the work;

(5)   The duration of the relation between the parties;

(6)   Whether the hiring party has the right to assign additional projects to the hired party;

(7)   The extent of the hired party's discretion over when and how to work;

(8)   The method of payment;

(9)   The hired party's role in hiring and paying assistants;

(10) Whether the work is part of the regular business of the hiring party;

(11) Whether the hiring party is in business;

(12) The provision (or lack of) of employee benefits; and

(13) The tax treatment of the hired party.

A work cannot be converted into a work for hire after its production. For example, in *Billy-Bob Teeth, Inc. v. Novelty, Inc.*, 329 F.3d 586 (7th Cir. 2003), a company that manufactured the prosthetic teeth featured in the *Austin Powers* movies claimed the teeth as works for hire, although the company's founders had actually designed the teeth prior to the manufacturer's incorporation. The court held that the teeth could not be works for hire because the corporation claiming them as such could not have employed or commissioned the designers prior to its legal existence.

3. DURATION

The duration of copyright protection depends on when the work was created and the identity of the work's author. Currently, a copyright expires 70 years after the author's death or, in the case of a jointly authored work, 70 years after the death of the last surviving author. 17 U.S.C. § 302(a). However, works created before January 1, 1978, expire 28 years from the date they were first copyrighted and may be renewed for an additional 67 years. 17 U.S.C. § 304. For works created before January 1, 1978, but not published by that date, copyright subsists from January 1, 1978, and endures for the life of the author plus 70 years—the term provided for in § 302(a). In no case, however, shall the term of copyright in those works expire before December 31, 2002; and, if the work was published on or before December 31, 2002, the term of the copyright does not expire before December 31, 2047. 17 U.S.C. § 303. Anonymous works, pseudonymous works, and works for hire are protected for the shorter of 95 years after their first publication or 120 years after they were created. 17 U.S.C. § 302(c). At the end of a work's copyright term, the work enters the public domain.

Since passage of the first copyright laws, Congress has repeatedly lengthened copyright duration. As amended, § 302(a) of the Copyright Act stated that the "[c]opyright in a work created on or after January 1, 1978, subsists from its creation and endures for a term consisting of the life of the author and fifty years after the author's death." In 1998, when the European Union added 20 years to its member nations' copyright terms, the United States amended the standard duration under § 302(a) to life plus 70 years.

When congress modifies copyright duration, problems arise in deciding what works will fall under the new provision. For example, in 1998, the Sonny Bono Copyright Term Extension Act extended the terms of works published in the 1920s and 1930s by an additional 30 years. These works had been caught in between the 1909 Copyright Act and the 1976 Copyright Act and would have expired in 1998 (less than 75 years after their publication) without the extension.

Other duration problems arise regarding works written under pseudonyms, jointly-authored works, works for hire, and works by authors whose dates of death are uncertain. Section 302(c) provides that copyrights in anonymous works, pseudonymous works, and works made for hire expire 95 years from the first publication or 120 years from the year of its creation, whichever expires first. In the case of joint works, the copyright term is the life of the last surviving author plus seventy years. 17 U.S.C. § 302(b). Sections 302(d) and 302(e) govern what is considered to be a death record and specify how to determine a copyright's expiration date in the absence of documentation of death.

4. TRANSFERABILITY

If the work for hire doctrine does not apply, ownership of a copyright initially vests in the authors, and the authors may transfer their rights to another person or entity. 17 U.S.C. § 201(d)(1). Any of the rights included in a copyright may be individually transferred or conveyed to another person or entity, and the new owner is entitled to all the protections and remedies afforded to that exclusive right. 17 U.S.C. § 201(d)(2).

The Copyright Act distinguishes between exclusive and nonexclusive copyright transfers. Section 204(a) requires a writing (similar to the statute of frauds) for exclusive transfers of copyrights or portions of copyrights. Section 101 defines "transfer of copyright ownership" to include both assignments and exclusive licenses. Therefore an assignment or exclusive transfer of any portion of the copyright must be evidenced by a properly executed writing. Without such writing, signed by the assigning or transferring party, a transfer of copyright ownership (other than by operation of law) is not valid. 17 U.S.C. § 204(a). In contrast, a nonexclusive license need not be in writing.

The Copyright Act also addresses priority between competing transferees. Under 17 U.S.C. § 205(d), a first assignee can secure priority over later assignees by recording the assignment with the Copyright Office within one month of the execution of the assignment (extended to two months if the assignment was executed outside of the United States). A subsequent assignee can gain priority only if they satisfy three conditions:

(1)   The earlier assignee must not have recorded their assignment within the one month allowed by 205(d);

(2)   The subsequent assignee must be the first to record their assignment with the Copyright Office; and

(3)   The subsequent assignee must take their assignment in good faith, for value, and without notice of the earlier assignment.

During a period of 5 years that begins 35 years after a transfer by an author of an interest in any particular work, the author or the author's successors-in-interest may terminate the transfer and recapture their rights in the work.   17 U.S.C. § 203(a)(3).   The termination is effected by serving advance notice on the copyright owners that, on a date within that 5-year period, the copyright will revert to the author or his successors in interest, notwithstanding any agreement to the contrary. 17 U.S.C. § 203(a)(4)–(5). 17 U.S.C. § 304.

At an author's death, the author's termination rights pass to his heirs in accordance with § 304(c). The rights are first divided equally between the author's surviving spouse (if any) and other heirs, and are apportioned thereafter among the author's lineal descendants on a per-stirpes basis.

W. SECURITY INTERESTS IN COPYRIGHTS

Copyrights, along with other intellectual properties such as patents and trademarks, often represent a significant portion of an entity's value and can be a useful source of collateral for secured transactions. To maintain priority, lenders must properly create and perfect their security interests in intellectual property.

Article 9, which has been adopted by all fifty states, governs the creation and perfection of security interests in intellectual property, which is categorized as a general intangible. U.C.C. § 9–102. A security interest is defined as "an interest in personal property or fixtures which secures payment or performance of an obligation." A security interest is not enforceable against either a debtor or third parties and does not attach to the collateral unless

(1)   the secured party has given value in exchange for the collateral,

(2)   the debtor has rights in the collateral, and

(3) the debtor has signed a security agreement that provides a description of the collateral.

U.C.C. § 9–203(b). Lenders must ensure that the debtor has rights in the intellectual property collateral prior to obtaining the security interest.

Perfection is the method by which a secured party achieves and maintains the highest available priority for its security interest in collateral. An unperfected security interest may be effective against the debtor, but it is of little value against third parties. In bankruptcy, the difference between a perfected security interest and an unperfected security interest often means the difference between a full recovery as a secured creditor and either little or no recovery as an unsecured creditor.

A security interest is perfected when it attaches if the applicable requirements are satisfied before attachment. The process of perfecting a security interest in most types of personal property is accomplished when a properly completed UCC–1 financing statement is filed with the appropriate state office, most often the office of the secretary of state. The financing statement must name both the debtor and the secured party and must describe the collateral covered by the financing statement. The U.C.C. no longer requires the debtor to sign an electronically filed financial statement, although the debtor must authorize the filing. The relative priorities of creditors who hold conflicting security interests are straightforward. Under the U.C.C.,

(1) if the conflicting security interests are perfected, they rank according to priority in time of filing or perfection;

(2) a perfected security interest has priority over a conflicting unperfected security interest; and

(3) if the conflicting security interests are unperfected, the first security interest to attach has priority. However, under § 9–109(c)(1), Article 9 does not apply to the extent that it is preempted by federal law.

Filing a financing statement is neither necessary nor effective to perfect a security interest in collateral that is subject to a separate federal filing requirement. In such cases, compliance with such a federal requirement is equivalent to filing a properly completed UCC–1 financing statement, and compliance with federal law is the only means of perfection. U.C.C. § 9–311(b). However, even in cases where federal law governs the perfection of security interests, Article 9 governs the relative priorities of conflicting security interests unless federal law also establishes separate priority rules. Sections 9–109 and 9–311 raise distinct issues. Under § 9–109, federal law preempts Article 9 where the former governs ownerships rights in the property secured as collateral. Under § 9–311, the U.C.C. defers to federal law regarding perfection if federal law has defined a filing requirement. The distinction between these property rights governed by federal law must be perfected in accordance with federal law or the U.C.C. Because of uncertainty regarding what law controls, financing statements in patents, trademarks, or copyrights should be filed with both state and federal offices.

The method of perfecting security interests in copyrights is substantially different from perfecting interests in patents and trademarks. The United States Copyright Act of 1976 provides for the recordation with the Copyright Office of "[a]ny transfer of copyright ownership or other document pertaining to a [registered] copyright. . ." 17 U.S.C. § 205(a). A "transfer of copyright ownership" is defined in section 101 of the Copyright Act as "an assignment, mortgage, exclusive license, or any other conveyance, alienation, or hypothecation of a copyright or any of the exclusive rights comprised in a copyright, whether or not it is limited in time or place of effect, but not including a nonexclusive license." The mortgage and hypothecation categories include pledges of property as security or collateral for a debt, which must be recorded to provide constructive notice of the facts stated in the recorded document. 17 U.S.C. § 205(c).

Some courts have held that, because the Copyright Act duplicates the state filing provisions of Article 9, a U.C.C. filing is neither necessary nor adequate to perfect a security interest in a registered copyright. *See In re* Peregrine Entertainment, Ltd., 116 B.R. 194 (Bankr. C.D. Cal. 1990); *In re* AEG Acquisition Corp., 127 B.R. 34 (Bankr. C.D. Cal. 1991); *In re* Avalon Software, Inc., 209 B.R. 517 (Bankr. D. Ariz. 1997); *In re* World Auxiliary Power Co., 303 F.3d 1120 (9th Cir. 2002). Perfection of a security interest in a copyright therefore requires only (1) proper registration of the copyright with the United States Copyright Office and (2) the filing of a security agreement or copyright mortgage with the United States Copyright Office.

At present, security interests in registered copyrights are properly perfected under Title 17 by recordation with the Copyright Office. Although unregistered copyrights are most likely perfected by filing a UCC–1 financing statement with the appropriate state office, a secured party should require the debtor to register all copyrights prior to obtaining a security interest in them. Ultimately, Congress may need to resolve the question of how unregistered copyrights are perfected.

A security agreement should reference copyrights as "general intangibles" and identify each copyright by title and registration number. To guard against unregistered copyrights, the agreement should oblige the debtor both to notify the secured party of all registered copyrights and to complete the registration of copyrights that are pending. Copyright Office filings under Title 17 relate only to existing copyrights, and blanket liens against subsequent registrations are not permitted. 17 U.S.C. § 205(c)(1). Therefore, the security agreement should also obligate the debtor to notify the secured party of all subsequent copyrights, to promptly register those copyrights with the Copyright Office, and to execute supplemental security agreements.

A security agreement should reference copyrights as "general intangibles" and identify each copyright by title and registration number. To guard against unregistered copyrights, the agreement should oblige the debtor both to notify the secured party of all registered copyrights and to complete the registration of copyrights that are pending. Copyright Office filings under Title 17 relate only to existing copyrights, and blanket liens against subsequent registrations are not permitted. 17 U.S.C. § 205(c)(1). Therefore, the security agreement should also obligate the debtor to notify the secured party of all subsequent copyrights, to promptly register those copyrights with the Copyright Office, and to execute supplemental security agreements.

In the event of default, both the U.C.C. and the security agreement itself govern the rights of the parties. Under U.C.C. § 9–601(a), a secured party may reduce the claim to judgment, foreclose on the collateral, or enforce the claim or security interest by any other available judicial means. These rights are cumulative and may be exercised simultaneously according to U.C.C. § 9–601(c). If possible without a breach of the peace, a secured party may also take direct possession of the collateral without resort to the judicial process according to U.C.C. § 9–609(a)–(b).

Foreclosure can occur through either a public or private sale, or the secured party may enforce his rights through a strict foreclosure—the seizure of the collateral in satisfaction of the debt—and so acquire the debtor's interest in the collateral without a sale. U.C.C. § 9–620, cmt. 2. A strict foreclosure requires the secured party to send its proposal to the debtor, any other secured creditors with perfected security interests in the collateral, and any guarantors of the security interest. U.C.C. § 9–621(a)–(b). Prior to the Article 9 revisions in 2001, a secured party could accept the collateral only in full satisfaction of the obligation; however, under Revised Article 9, the secured party may accept the collateral as either full or partial satisfaction of the obligation it secures.

Acceptance of collateral by the secured party in either full or partial satisfaction of the debtor's obligation

(1) discharges the obligation to the extent consented to by the debtor;

(2) transfers to the secured party all of the debtor's rights in the collateral;

(3)   discharges the security interest and any subordinate security interest; and

(4)   terminates any other subordinate interest.

U.C.C. § 9–622(a). Subordinate interests are discharged even if the secured party does not comply with the requirements of Article 9. U.C.C. § 9–622(b). However, the debtor, guarantors, and any other secured parties retain the right to redeem the collateral by satisfying the obligations secured by the collateral and paying any reasonable expenses (including attorney's fees) incurred by the secured party. U.C.C. § 9–623(a)–(b).

A debtor may either consent to strict foreclosure or object to force a sale. U.C.C. § 9–620(a). Additionally, all parties entitled to receive a proposal under U.C.C. § 9–621 have the opportunity to object. If the secured party receives any objection, he must dispose of the collateral— either by sale, lease, license, or otherwise—though public or private proceedings. U.C.C. § 9–610(a). If the secured party foreclosing on the collateral is also the transferee receiving the collateral, he may lack the incentive to maximize the sales price. In such cases, if the sales price is significantly below what would have been realized if the interested party had not been involved in the transaction, U.C.C. § 9–615(f) provides for calculating the deficiency.

The purchaser at sale is entitled to a transfer statement, authenticated by the secured party, stating

(1)   that the debtor has defaulted in connection with an obligation secured by the collateral purchased;

(2)   that the secured party has exercised his post-default remedies;

(3)   that, by reason of the exercise, the transferee has acquired rights of the debtor in the collateral; and

(4)   the name and mailing address of the secured party, the debtor, and the transferee.

U.C.C. § 9–619(a). A transfer statement entitles the transferee to records of all the debtor's rights in the collateral, and any official filing, recording, registration, or certificate of title system covering the collateral. U.C.C. § 9–619(b). The transfer statement may be filed with the Copyright Office to document the transfer. 17 U.S.C. § 204.

In sum, it is better practice to require the debtor to register all copyrights prior to obtaining a security interest in them and to perfect under Title 7 by recordation with the Copyright Office and also perfect under the U.C.C. by filing a proper security agreement with the appropriate state office.

X. ENFORCING COPYRIGHTS

The Copyright Act of 1976 provides that copyright attaches to the work upon creation; consequently the formal registration process is no longer the vital step that it once was under prior law. However, the formalities of publication, registration, and notice remain important because they allow the copyright holder the full gamut of rights, remedies, and means of enforcement.[84]

1. REGISTRATION

Because the work is copyrighted from the moment of creation, registration is not required in order for a copyright to be valid. However, there are many incentives to register a work and registration remains a fairly important step in the copyright enforcement process. The registration process has several steps:

(1) application and payment of the required fee;

(2) deposit of a copy of the work in the Copyright Office;

(3) examination by the Register of Copyrights;

(4) registration, or denial of registration by the Register; and

(5) issuance of certificate of registration.

17 U.S.C. §§ 408, 410. Additionally, the copyright owner must deposit with the Copyright Office two copies of any published work or one compete edition of the work if it is unpublished, collective, or foreign work.

> The benefits of registration are substantial. Authors must have registered their copyright in order to commence an action for copyright infringement. There is an explicit exception to the registration requirement for works that were first published in other nations that adhere to the Berne Convention.

Furthermore, if a work is infringed upon before it is registered, the holder of the copyright will not be able to seek statutory damages or attorneys' fees from the infringing party unless registration is secured within three months of the works first publication. Registration made within five years after the work's first publication constitutes *prima facie* evidence of the validity of the copyright.

---

[84] Note that in the recently decided *Naruto v. Slater*, 888 F.3d 418 (9th Cir. 2018), the enforcement of copyrighted material has narrowed with respect to establishing standing to sue. In *Naruto* People for the Ethical Treatment of Animals (PETA) filed a lawsuit as "next friends" on behalf of a primate named Naruto, who had taken a selfie that was later used for commercial purposes. Under *Naruto* to "establish next friend status for a petitioner, the putative next friend must establish: (1) that the petitioner is "unable to litigate his own cause" due to mental incapacity, lack of access to the courts, or other similar disability; and (2) that the next friend has some "significant relationship" with and is truly dedicated to the best interests of the petitioner." *Id.* at 421.

2. NOTICE

In 1989, as part of the United States' decision to join the Berne Convention, Congress revised the notice provision so that failure to include a copyright notice will not result in any loss of copyright. However, the absence of notice may allow a defendant to raise an innocent infringer defense, while the presence of notice forecloses that defense.

Under the 1909 Copyright Act, failure to place proper copyright notice on copies distributed to the public would generally be fatal to the copyright and the work would become part of the public domain. The Copyright Act of 1976 significantly softened the consequences of a failure to provide proper notice in 17 U.S.C. § 405.

With respect to copies and phonorecords publicly distributed by authority of the copyright owner before the effective date of the Berne Convention Implementation Act of 1988, the omission of the copyright notice described in 17 U.S.C. §§ 401 through 403 from copies or phonorecords publicly distributed by authority of the copyright owner does not invalidate the copyright in a work if—

(1) the notice has been omitted from no more than a relatively small number of copies or phonorecords distributed to the public; or

(2) registration for the work has been made before or is made within five years after the publication without notice, and a reasonable effort is made to add notice to all copies or phonorecords that are distributed to the public in the United States after the omission has been discovered; or

(3) the notice has been omitted in violation of an express requirement in writing that, as a condition of the copyright owner's authorization of the public distribution of copies or phonorecords, they bear the prescribed notice.

For example in *O'Neill Developments, Inc. v. Galen Kilburn, Inc.*, 524 F. Supp. 710 (N.D. Ga. 1981), the plaintiff sought to cure its failure to include proper notice on brochures it distributed through registration of the work within five years after the publication without notice, and made a reasonable effort to add notice to all copies that were distributed after the omission had been discovered. The Court interpreted discovery in to include " 'discovery' of the fact that the existence of a copyright has become an issue."

The notice requirements of §§ 401 and 402 apply only to published works—narrowly defined as the transfer of ownership or lease of copies or phonorecords, for purposes of distribution, public performance, or public display. 17 U.S.C. § 101. But, mere public performance or public display alone does not constitute publication.

If a copyright notice appears, it must consist of:

(1)   the symbol ©, or the word "Copyright", or the abbreviation "Copr.";

(2)   the year of first publication of the work; and

(3)   some clear identification of the copyright owner.

17 U.S.C. § 401(b). The requirements are essentially the same for a phonorecord, except that instead of bearing the symbol © or equivalent mark, it must bear a ℗ (the letter P in a circle) symbol. 17 U.S.C. § 402(b)(1). The copyright notice must be situated on the item in such a way as to give "reasonable notice of the claim of copyright" and otherwise as prescribed by the Register of Copyrights. 17 U.S.C. §§ 401(c), 402(c).

Fixing adequate notice to copyrighted computer software presents unique issues. Under Copyright Office regulations, notice is fixed and positioned so as to provide reasonable notice of the claim of copyright when it appears:

(1)   either near the title or at the end of material printed from the software;

(2)   displayed at the user's terminal when the user signs on;

(3)   continuously on display on the computer terminal while the software is in use; or

(4)   durably fixed to either the device on which the software is stored or on the container used as a permanent receptacle for the software storage device.

37 C.F.R. § 201.20(g).

The chief benefit of a properly affixed notice is that it negates any claim by an infringer that they did not know the work was copyrighted, foreclosing a defense of innocent infringement. 17 U.S.C. §§ 401(d), 402(d). Aside from its evidentiary value, the copyright notice serves to encourage copyright owners to either enforce their rights or allow material to slip into the public domain, to identify the copyright owners, and to allow users to calculate the term of the copyright by the date affixed to the item.

Y. TRADEMARK LAW

1. INTRODUCTION

Trademark law allows providers of goods and services to distinguish their products from those of their competitors. Trademarks play an important role in all commercial transactions by providing a way for consumers to distinguish products and identify their sources. The goodwill corresponding to a trademark can be among a business's most important assets. Assuring the integrity of trademarks is the chief aim of trademark law. In the United States, both state and federal law apply to trademarks.

A trademark is a distinctive mark, symbol, or emblem used by a business to identify and distinguish its goods from those of others. A trademark enables a consumer to identify a product and its source. In the Lanham Act, the principal federal trademark law, Congress has further defined a trademark as

> [a]ny word, name, symbol, or device, or any combination thereof, (1) used by a person, or (2) which a person has a bona fide intention to use in commerce and applies to register on the principal register established by this Act, to identify and distinguish his or her goods, including a unique product, from those manufactured or sold by others and to indicate the source of the goods, even if that source is unknown.

15 U.S.C. § 1127. In essence, trademark law is based on the traditional property law notion that a right in property is a legally enforceable power to exclude others from using a resource.

The character of trademark has changed over time. Originally, trademarks indicated ownership of a particular item. As commercial trade grew more sophisticated and extensive, the marks shifted to a purpose of identifying the source of goods offered for sale in a marketplace. Historically, the Romans and medieval English guilds used trademarks to identify their products. Guilds used trademarks to fix responsibility for defective goods and protect their manufacturing monopolies, a system that eventually developed into the modern trademark system. As distribution networks extended into expanding markets, manufacturers began to adopt marks solely to allow consumers to identify their goods and purchase them with confidence based on the reputation of the manufacturer. The United States adopted the English trademark law to prevent unfair competition through the misappropriation of marks.

Trademark law protects manufacturers against free riding and ensures that consumers can confidently identify the origin of, and anticipate the quality and uniformity of, the goods they purchase. As stated in 15 U.S.C. § 1127, the express purpose of the Lanham Act is to protect the owner's rights and those of the public.

For example, Nike relies heavily on trademarks in its business practices. Both the name "Nike" and the ubiquitous Nike "swoosh" are trademarks that allow consumers to easily recognize the Nike brand and rely on the associated product quality. Because those trademarks consistently correspond to a predictable quality, they reduce consumers' cost of searching. Without Nike's trademarks and adequate protection of those trademarks, it would be difficult for consumers to distinguish Nike shoes from those made by other companies.

The trademark system also protects service marks, collective marks, and certification marks. A service mark is a mark used by a company to identify and accumulate goodwill toward specific intangibles such as services. 15 U.S.C. § 1127. "Merry Maids" is a service mark used by a cleaning services company. A collective mark is a mark that distinguishes membership in an association, union, or other group. "Girl Scouts of America" and "Realtor" are collective marks. A certification mark is used by third parties to guarantee that certified goods or services meet certain criteria. The "Good Housekeeping Seal of Approval" and Underwriters Laboratory's "UL" are certification marks. The Lanham Act extends these three other types of marks the same protections as a traditional trademark if the owner has a bona fide intent to use the mark in commerce.

2. SOURCES OF U.S. TRADEMARK JURISPRUDENCE

In the United States, trademarks are protected by federal law, state statutory law, and common law. Federal rights and registration requirements are governed by the Lanham Trademark Act of 1946, codified in Title 15, of the United States Code. The Lanham Act is rooted in the Commerce clause of the U.S. Constitution. 15 U.S.C. § 1127 states that ". . . it is the intent of this chapter to regulate commerce within the controls of Congress by making actionable the deceptive and misleading use of such marks in such commerce." In the *Trade-Mark Cases*, 100 U.S. 82 (1879), the Supreme Court held that, because the common law property interest in a trademark arose from use rather than originality, trademarks are not among those property interests protected by the Copyright clause. Therefore, state trademark law is not preempted by the Lanham Act, so a dual system of state and federal trademark law exists. The federal system has developed primarily to register and establish the priority of trademarks.

- Anyone has the right to place a mark not used by another on products she manufactures or distributes to distinguish them from other products in the market.

- This allows her to inform the public of the origin of the product and thus develop a reputation in the market.

- A trademark is both a sign of the quality of the article and an assurance to the public that it is the genuine product of the manufacturer.

- A trademark owner may petition the court to protect her right to the mark's exclusive use and to prevent others from using the mark.

- This protection benefits the trademark holder, the market, and the public.

Every state has enacted legislation to protect trademarks, usually derived from the Model State Trademark Bill, which is very similar to the Lanham Act.

Alabama	ALA. CODE § 8–12–6 et seq.
Alaska	ALASKA STAT. § 45.50.010 et seq.
Arizona	ARIZ. REV. STAT. § 44–1441 et seq.
Arkansas	ARK. CODE ANN. § 4–71–201 et seq.
California	CAL. BUS. & PROF. CODE § 14200 et seq.
Colorado	COLO. REV. STAT. § 7–70–102 et seq.
Delaware	DEL. CODE ANN. tit. 6, § 3301 et seq.
Florida	FLA. STAT. ANN. § 495.011 et seq.
Georgia	GA. CODE ANN. § 10–1–440 et seq.
Hawaii	HAW. REV. STAT. § 482–1 et seq.
Idaho	IDAHO CODE ANN. § 48–501 et seq.
Illinois	ILL. COMP. STAT. § 1036/5 et seq.
Indiana	IND. CODE § 24–2–1–0.5 et seq.
Iowa	IOWA CODE ANN. § 548.101 et seq.
Kansas	KAN. STAT. ANN. § 81–202 et seq.
Kentucky	KY. REV. STAT. ANN. § 365.561 et seq.
Louisiana	LA. REV. STAT. ANN. § 51:211 et seq.
Maine	ME. REV. STAT. tit. 10, § 1521 et seq.
Maryland	MD. CODE ANN., BUS. REG. § 1–401 et seq.
Massachusetts	MASS. GEN. LAWS. ANN. ch. 110H, § 1 et seq.
Michigan	MICH. COMP. LAWS ANN. § 429.31 et seq.
Minnesota	MINN. STAT. ANN. § 333.001 et seq.
Mississippi	MISS. CODE ANN. § 75–25–1 et seq.
Missouri	MO. REV. STAT. § 417.005 et seq.
Montana	MONT. CODE ANN. § 30–13–301 et seq.
Nebraska	NEB. REV. STAT. § 87–127 et seq.
Nevada	NEV. REV. STAT. ANN. § 600.240 et seq.
New Hampshire	N.H. REV. STAT. ANN. § 350–A:1 et seq.
New Jersey	N.J. STAT. ANN. §§ 17:16Y–1 et seq., 56:3–13a et seq.
New Mexico	N.M. STAT. ANN. § 57–3B–2 et seq.
New York	N.Y. GEN. BUS. LAW § 360 et seq.

North Carolina	N.C. GEN. STAT. ANN. § 80–1 et seq.
North Dakota	N.D. CENT. CODE ANN. § 47–22–01 et seq.
Ohio	OHIO REV. CODE ANN. § 1329.54 et seq.
Oklahoma	OKLA. STAT. tit. 78, § 21 et seq.
Oregon	OR. REV. STAT. § 647.005 et seq.
Pennsylvania	PA. CONS. STAT. ANN. § 1101 et seq.
Rhode Island	RI. GEN. LAWS ANN. § 6–2–1 et seq.
South Carolina	S.C. CODE ANN. § 39–15–1105 et seq.
South Dakota	S.D. CODIFIED LAWS § 37–6–4 et seq.
Tennessee	TENN. CODE ANN. § 47–25–501 et seq.
Texas	TEX. BUS. & C. § 16.01 et seq.
Utah	UTAH ADMIN. CODE § 70–3a–102 et seq.
Vermont	VT. STAT. ANN. tit. 9, § 2521 et seq.
Virginia	VA. CODE ANN. § 59.1–92.2 et seq.
Washington	WASH. REV. CODE ANN. § 19.77.010 et seq.
West Virginia	W. VA. CODE ANN. § 47–2–1 et seq.
Wisconsin	WIS. STAT. ANN. § 132.01 et seq.
Wyoming	WYO. STAT. ANN. § 40–1–101 et seq.

3. TYPES OF TRADEMARKS

Courts and commentators have traditionally divided potential trademarks into four different categories:

(1) generic,

(2) descriptive (including deceptively misdescriptive),

(3) suggestive, and

(4) arbitrary or fanciful.

The categories tend to bleed together at the edges, but courts use them as guidelines when determining whether a mark deserves trademark protection. The ultimate question, however, is whether the mark is distinctive. It is important to remember the following rules, as the level of protection varies with each category of mark:

- Generic marks are never distinctive and are not eligible for protection.

- Descriptive and deceptively misdescriptive marks are eligible for protection only if they acquire secondary meaning.

- Deceptive marks and geographically deceptively misdescriptive marks adopted after 1993 are ineligible for trademark protection.

- Suggestive, arbitrary, and fanciful marks are considered inherently distinctive and, if otherwise valid, are eligible for protection when used.

Trademark Types and Protections

Type of Mark	Whether Protected
Generic	Never
Descriptive	With Secondary Meaning
Misdescriptive	With Secondary Meaning
Deceptive	Never
Primarily Geographically Misdescriptive	Never (if adopted after 12/93)
Suggestive	When Used
Arbitrary	When Used

a. Generic Marks

A generic mark is the common name of an article or service. A generic term merely describes the character of a product as opposed to identifying its source. For example, apple is a generic mark when used in connection with the actual piece of fruit (rather than a computer). "A generic term answers the question 'What are you?' while a mark answers the question 'Where do you come from?' " Colt Defense LLC v. Bushmaster Firearms, Inc., 486 F. 3d 701 (1st Cir. 2007).

Because generic marks do not distinguish between different equivalent products, generic marks are ineligible for trademark protection. Many companies that enjoy trademark protection for their products would lose it if the trademarked term became generic. 15 U.S.C. § 1064(3).

At one time marks such as cellophane and aspirin had secondary meaning and were protected, but they have become generic terms—describing the good rather than its source—and consequently lost their former status as protected trademarks.

b. Descriptive and Deceptively Misdescriptive Marks

Merely descriptive and deceptively misdescriptive marks are ordinarily not protected by trademark law. 15 U.S.C. § 1052(e)(1). Descriptive marks identify a product based on a characteristic or quality, such as color, smell, function, or ingredient. Deceptively misdescriptive marks do the same thing—only the description is inaccurate. However, if the marks have acquired a secondary meaning in the minds of the consuming public, they can receive trademark protection. The secondary meaning shows that the descriptive term is not merely a description of the good, but is also an indication of the producer of the good. In other words, if consumers recognize it as signifying the good's origin, it has acquired secondary meaning.

c. Descriptive Marks and Secondary Meaning

In *In re Bayer Aktiengesellschaft*, 488 F.3d 960 (Fed. Cir. 2007), the applicant sought to register "Aspirina" for use on analgesic pain relievers chemically similar to generic aspirin. On appeal, the Federal Circuit concluded that, given the character of the substance to be sold under the mark, the mark was merely descriptive and therefore ineligible for trademark protection. Similarly, an aloe vera derivative product called "Alo" and an optometry center called the "Vision Center" both use descriptive terms to identify goods or services and, absent secondary meaning, are not eligible for trademark protection. *See* Aloe Crème Laboratories, Inc. v. Milsan, Inc., 423 F.2d 845 (5th Cir. 1970); The Vision Center v. Opticks, Inc., 596 F.2d 111 (5th Cir. 1979).

However, a merely descriptive term may become distinctive and therefore protectable if it develops a secondary meaning that indicates the origin of goods rather than simply describing their character. For example, in *Schmidt v. Honeysweet Hams, Inc.*, 656 F. Supp. 92 (N.D. Ga. 1986), the court held that although "Honey Baked Ham" is plainly a descriptive mark, it had gained a secondary meaning sufficient to justify federal registration and trademark protection. Particularly persuasive were surveys showing that 53% of participants volunteered "Honey Baked" as a distinct brand, "nearly double the percentage of brand name recall for any other major brand name of pre-cooked sliced hams," 96% recognized the brand, and when shown a picture of defendant's store, 29% believed the defendant sold "Honey Baked" brand hams.

A merely descriptive mark that has become incontestable is a valid trademark, regardless of whether it should have been registered in the first place, because 15 U.S.C. §§ 1064 and 1065 do not include descriptiveness as a reason to cancel a mark. For example, in *Park 'N Fly, Inc. v. Dollar Park and Fly, Inc.*, 469 U.S. 189 (1985), the plaintiff used the mark "Park 'N Fly" in its airport pay-to-park business. The Court held that although the mark was purely descriptive for that purpose, its incontestable status was conclusive as to the mark's validity and plaintiff's exclusive right to the mark.

Under 15 U.S.C. § 1052(e)(2), unless the applicant shows that its mark has a secondary meaning, a mark that is primarily geographically descriptive of the goods is unregisterable, except as an indication of regional origin specifically registerable as a certification mark under § 1054.

Even if a registrant can prove secondary meaning, if a particular product or service is associated with a particular place, the strength of a mark incorporating that place-name is likely diminished. The consumer is likely to associate the place-name with products or services other than those sold under the registrant's particular mark. For example, in *Vail Associates, Inc. v. Vend-Tel-Co., Ltd.*, 516 F.3d 853 (10th Cir. 2008), the plaintiff, which operated a Vail, Colorado ski resort, claimed that its incontestable service mark "Vail Ski Resort" was infringed by the defendant ski-resource hotline's "1-800-SKI-VAIL" mark. Although the plaintiff's mark was incontestable—which is conclusive proof of its secondary meaning—the court held that the mark was exceptionally weak given that it contained no inherently distinctive elements, and that "[t]he presence of secondary meaning. . . does not provide the mark holder with an exclusive right to use the mark in its original descriptive sense." In view of the mark's weakness and with no evidence of actual confusion, the court held that confusion was unlikely, concluding that "[i]f some confusion exists, such is the risk [the plaintiff] accepted when it decided to identify its services with a *single word* that is primarily descriptive of a geographic location." Both users in *Vail Associates, Inc. v. Vend-Tel-Co., Ltd.*, 516 F.3d 853 (10th Cir. 2008), used their marks in relation to the provision of services actually provided in Vail, Colorado. Thus any bar to registration arose under § 1052(e)(2).

d. Deceptively Misdescriptive Marks

A mark is deceptively misdescriptive if it misdescribes a product in a way that is plausible but inaccurate. Deceptively misdescriptive marks are a subset of descriptive marks for which § 1052(e)(1) raises an impediment to registration. Deceptively misdescriptive marks are only eligible for trademark protection if they have obtained secondary meaning. A deceptively misdescriptive mark is distinct from a deceptive mark only in that any misdescription is not likely to be a material factor in the consumer's purchasing decision.

For example, in *Glendale International Corp. v. U.S. Patent & Trademark Office*, 374 F. Supp. 2d 479 (E.D. Va. 2005), the court affirmed the PTO's determination that the plaintiff's use of the mark "Titanium" for recreational vehicles was deceptively misdescriptive given that titanium is a lightweight metal commonly used in the automotive industry. Thus, the mark plausibly but inaccurately described the vehicles, but, because consumers were not likely to purchase the RV because of their confusion as to its titanium content, the mark was not deceptive.

Likewise, in *In re Woodward & Lothrop Inc.*, 4 U.S.P.Q.2d 1412 (T.T.A.B. 1987), the Trademark Trial and Appeal Board found the mark

"Cameo" to be deceptively misdescriptive of jewelry because none of the jewelry to be sold under the mark included or incorporated any actual cameos—a type of jewelry in which the stone around a design is cut away leaving the design in relief, typically against a contrasting background— although a mistaken belief that it did was unlikely to induce consumers to make a purchase.

Hence, a misdescriptive mark is not necessarily invalid provided that it will not cause confusion among consumers as to the character of the goods.

As with descriptive marks, even clearly misdescriptive marks that have become incontestable cannot be challenged on the grounds of being misdescriptive.

e.   Deceptive Marks

Unlike deceptively misdescriptive marks, which merely inaccurately state a fact, deceptive marks that induce the purchase because of that inaccurate fact are not eligible for trademark protection.   15 U.S.C. § 1052(a). A mark is deceptive if the inaccurate information conveyed by a misdescriptive designation is likely to influence the purchasing decisions of a significant amount of prospective consumers. These marks are not eligible for protection because of policy concerns about inducing reliance on an intentionally inaccurate fact. *See, e.g., In re* Budge Manufacturing Co., 857 F.2d 773 (Fed. Cir. 1988) ("Lovee Lamb" on synthetic seat covers held deceptive); Neuman & Co. v. Overseas Shipments, Inc., 326 F. 2d 786 (C.C.P.A. 1969) (Dura-Hyde for plastic material with the appearance of leather held deceptive).

15 U.S.C. § 1052(e)(3) raises an independent bar to the registrability of primarily geographically deceptively misdescriptive marks. Unlike the bar imposed by § 1052(e)(2), the prohibition on registration of primarily geographically deceptively misdescriptive marks is absolute, regardless of any secondary meaning the mark may have acquired. These marks are not protected under the Lanham Act.   Section 1052(f) provides a limited exception to that prohibition with regard to primarily geographically deceptively misdescriptive marks that became distinctive by acquiring secondary meaning prior to December 8, 1993, the date that the North American Free Trade Agreement (the "NAFTA") was passed into law.

After the passage of NAFTA and revision of to bar primarily ge-ographically deceptively misdescriptive marks, the Federal Circuit applied a two-part test to determine whether a mark was barred.

> [t]he examiner has the initial burden of proving that: (1) the mark's primary significance is a generally known geographic location;   and   (2)   consumers   would   reasonably   believe   the

applicant's goods are connected with the geographic location in the mark, when in fact they are not.

In re Save Venice New York, Inc., 259 F.3d 1346 (Fed. Cir. 2001).

In 2003, the Federal Circuit added a third prong to the analysis. In *In re California Innovations, Inc.*, 329 F.3d 1334 (Fed. Cir. 2003), the PTO refused to register the applicant's California Innovations mark for use on a range of sewn goods including backpacks and thermal insulated bags and wraps—koozies—for cans to keep the containers cold or hot. The basis of the PTO's decision was that the word California is primarily geographically descriptive, and consumers might mistakenly believe that the goods sold under the mark were manufactured in California. The court found the PTO's analysis entirely lacking, holding that "the relatively easy burden of showing a naked goods-place association without proof that the association is material to the consumer's decision is no longer justified." Under the court's reformulated test, the PTO may not refuse registration of a mark under § 1052(e)(3) unless the examiner can show that:

(1) the primary significance of the mark is a generally known geographic location,

(2) the consuming public is likely to believe the place identified by the mark indicates the origin of the goods bearing the mark, when in fact the goods do not come from that place, and

(3) the misrepresentation was a material factor in the consumer's decision.

f.   Suggestive Marks

Suggestive marks are inherently distinctive and are protectable without any proof of a secondary meaning. A suggestive mark simply suggests a particular characteristic of the goods or services and the consumer must exercise imagination in order to draw a conclusion as to the nature of the goods and services. For example, Golden Bake pancakes, Mouse Seed mouse poison, and Coppertone suntan lotion are suggestive trademarks as each requires that consumers exercise some degree of imagination to discern the nature of the item being sold.

Where a question exists as to whether a mark is merely descriptive or suggestive, the PTO's prior determination serves as prima facie evidence of the strength of the mark and raises a rebuttable presumption as to the mark's strength.

g.   Arbitrary or Fanciful Marks

Arbitrary or fanciful marks are those that bear no relationship to the products or services to which they are applied. A fanciful trademark is essentially a made up word created solely for use as a trademark. For example, Kodak is a fanciful term developed to mark photographic supplies. An arbitrary mark, although a real word, has no real relation to the product it is identifying and is used in an unfamiliar way to mark a product. Ivory is an arbitrary term to mark soap. Like suggestive terms, arbitrary or fanciful terms do not need a secondary meaning to receive trademark protection. Arbitrary and fanciful marks are generally considered the strongest types of trademarks and, as such, receive the highest trademark protection.

Z. TRADE DRESS

1. TRADE DRESS GENERALLY

Trademark protection may be extended to trade dress, which encompasses the overall appearance of a product's design as presented in the marketplace. Trade dress typically includes decor, packaging, wrappers, labels, and all other materials used in presenting the product to the consumer. When the design or packaging of a product is distinctive enough to identify the manufacturer of a product, and meets the other requirements of a trademark, it may be protected as trade dress. However, the distinctive qualities of the design must be nonfunctional for trademark protection to apply.

2. FUNCTIONALITY

Under 15 U.S.C. §§ 1052(e)(5) and 1064, a mark is ineligible for registration and can be cancelled at any time if it "comprises any matter that, as a whole, is functional." As a general rule, trademark rights cannot be claimed in a product's functional shapes or features. This rule serves two purposes:

(1) it prevents trademark law from becoming unduly anti-competitive by ensuring that competitors remain free to copy useful product features; and

(2) the functionality doctrine addresses the conflict with patent law by preventing a trademark monopoly of possibly unlimited duration on utilitarian features.

This limitation is particularly relevant with regard to trade dress. A product feature is functional when it is essential to the device's use or purpose or when it affects the device's cost or quality. Functionality is fact dependent, and what is functional in one instance might not be functional in another context.

In deciding whether to apply trademark protections to a product's trade dress, courts distinguish between functional and non-functional trade dress. The common law distinguishes between de jure and de facto trade dress functionality.

3.   DE FACTO FUNCTIONALITY

A design is functional in the de facto sense when, despite the fact that the product is capable of performing its intended function, elements of the design are arbitrary or superfluous. Both nonfunctional ornamentation and arbitrary combinations of entirely functional elements can qualify for protection as trade dress, though in either case they must also carry a secondary meaning to indicate a product's origin.

4.   DE JURE FUNCTIONALITY

De jure functionality is the legal conclusion that a particular trade dress is unfit for trademark protection, either because the product's overall appearance is the consequence of entirely and necessarily utilitarian considerations or because the design does not serve to indicate the product's source. A design is de jure functional if it is one of a limited number of equally efficient options available to competitors, and free competition would be unduly hindered by according the design trademark protection.

5.   TRADE DRESS AND PATENTS

Trademark protection of trade dress may overlap with patent law since design patents may be granted to protect a "new, original, and ornamental design" for a manufactured article. This distinction is important because patent protection is only granted for a limited amount of time, while trademark protection typically extends as long as a valid trademark continues to be used in commerce. Because a design patent cannot be issued for a design that is essential to the utility of an article, a design patent is presumptive evidence of nonfunctionality, which may support a similar trademark claim for the design.

The party asserting trade dress protection bears the burden of proving that the allegedly protected design is nonfunctional, and the existence of any other protections based on functionality weigh heavily against them.

AA.   TRADEMARK REQUIREMENTS

A trademark can be virtually anything used to identify the source or origin of goods or services provided it is distinctive and is in use or there is a bona fide intent to use the mark at the time of registration.

1. SUBJECT MATTER

Almost any objective signifier that helps consumers identify a product can be protected as a trademark. Words or symbols are most typical. Trademarks are any word, name, symbol, or device or any combination thereof used to identify and distinguish particular goods and to indicate the source of the goods. 15 U.S.C. § 1127.

Words can be protected as trademarks against their phonetic equivalents.

Symbols, such as the Nike swoosh, are also commonly entitled to trademark protection. Even a unique color may be afforded trademark protection. For example, in *In re Owens-Corning Fiberglas Corp.*, 774 F.2d 1116 (Fed. Cir. 1985), the court held that the bubblegum pink color of Corning's fiberglass insulation served no function but as an indication of origin and should be afforded trademark protection.

2. DISTINCTIVENESS

To be eligible for trademark protection, the mark must be distinctive—it must serve the purpose of identifying the origin of the goods or services. As detailed earlier, the categories of distinctiveness are generic, descriptive, suggestive, arbitrary, or fanciful. The further along this spectrum a term or mark fall, the more likely it is to be distinctive.

The distinctive quality of a trademark can be either inherent or acquired. For example, in *Playtex Prods. v. Georgia-Pacific Corp.*, 390 F.3d 158 (2d Cir. 2004), the court considered plaintiff Playtex's trademark Wet Ones for its pre-moistened towelettes and whether the defendant's mark Quilted Northern Moist-Ones was confusingly similar. The court held that the marks were not confusingly similar because the Wet Ones mark was a well established mark that had acquired distinctiveness in the marketplace.

Suggestive, arbitrary, and fanciful marks are inherently distinctive. In contrast, a descriptive mark is distinctive only to the extent that the mark has acquired a secondary meaning and is recognized in the market. A mark acquires distinctiveness as consumers begin to recognize the mark as denoting the source of particular goods and disassociate the mark from any prior connotations. The question is whether the mark's distinctiveness outweighs its descriptiveness.

3. USE OF A TRADEMARK

Historically, United States trademark protection was not available to marks not actually in use. That changed in 1988, when the Lanham Act was amended to allow registration of a trade, service, certification, or collective mark where the registrant has a bona fide intention to use the mark in commerce. 15 U.S.C. §§ 1127, 1051–54.

The Lanham Act defines a trademark as "used in commerce" when:

(1) It is placed in any manner on the goods or their containers or the displays associated therewith or on the tags or labels affixed thereto, or if the nature of the goods makes such placement impracticable, then on documents associated with the goods or their sale, and the goods are sold or transported in commerce, or

(2) When it is used or displayed in the sale or advertising of services and the services are rendered in commerce, or the services are rendered in more than one State or in the United States and a foreign country and the person rendering the services is engaged in commerce in connection with the services.

15 U.S.C. § 1127. The commerce to which § 1127 refers is interstate commerce subject to Congressional regulation, rather than simply for-profit activity.

The standard of use necessary to establish priority is minimal. All that is required is that the mark be adopted and thereafter used in a way sufficiently public to identify the marked goods or services to the appropriate segment of the public, regardless of any actual sales.

A person or organization that applies for a mark with a bona fide intention to use the mark in commerce will be issued a notice of allowance, assuming the mark otherwise qualified for protection. 15 U.S.C. § 1063(b)(2). Within six months of the date of issuance of the notice of allowance, the trademark holder must file a verified statement with the PTO that the trademark has been used in commerce. 15 U.S.C. § 1051(d)(1). Subject to examination and acceptance of the statement, the PTO will issue a certificate of registration of the mark. The six-month period will be extended another six months upon written request of the applicant, and up to a total of twenty-four months upon a showing of good cause. 15 U.S.C. § 1051(d)(1), (2). In essence, the Act allows temporary or provisional protection to an applicant with a bona fide intention to use the mark in commerce.

4. PRIORITY

Use of a mark in commerce is essential to establishing priority because the right to a given trademark typically belongs to the first party that uses the mark in connection with the sale of goods or services. That person is the senior user and persons who later use the same or allegedly similar marks are junior users.

However, what constitutes use is somewhat ambiguous, where, for instance, a mark is contested as between the manufacturer of goods sold under that mark and the goods' exclusive distributor, because both parties played an integral role in bringing the marked goods to market. All else being equal, in a dispute between manufacture and exclusive distributor, the manufacturer is presumed to own the trademark. However, that presumption is rebuttable, and in order to discern whether it has been rebutted a court considers:

(1) which party invented and first affixed the mark onto the product;

(2) which party's name appeared with the trademark;

(3) which party maintained the quality and uniformity of the product; and

(4) with which party the public identified the product and to whom purchasers made complaints.

A registered mark confers a nationwide right of priority against any other person except for a person who used the mark prior to the filing. 15 U.S.C. § 1057(c)(1). Thus a nonregistrant may rebut the presumption of validity and ownership if it can show that it used the mark in commerce first. To satisfy this burden a registrant user must prove:

(1) that it actually adopted and used the mark in commerce prior to the other party's registration in such a manner that sufficiently associated the mark with the prior user, and

(2) that its use of the marks has been continuous and not interrupted.

Department of Parks and Recreation for the State of Calif. v. Bazaar Del Mundo, 448 F.3d 1118, 1125–26 (9th Cir. 2006).

If a trademark has not been registered, an entity asserting priority in ownership can prevail only if it shows prior use of the mark in a way sufficiently public to identify or distinguish the marked goods in an appropriate segment of the public mind as those of the adopter of the mark. Although the standard of use is minimal, the use must be continuous from its first instance until ownership is asserted in order to preserve the user's priority.

BB. TRADEMARK REGISTRATION

1. INTRODUCTION

The federal government, as well as every state, maintains trademark registration services. On the federal level, the PTO is in charge of receiving, reviewing, and registering all federal trademarks in the United

States. Each state employs a trademark registration system that is separate from the federal system. The state systems aim to determine whether an identical trademark already exists and issue a state registration if it does not. The federal PTO, however, reviews each trademark application and analyzes the proposed mark for registerability.

2. WHAT REGISTRATION GIVES THE HOLDER

Rights in a trademark are acquired by use, not registration. However, registration of a mark on the Principal Register is prima facie evidence of its validity and the owner's exclusive right to use the registered mark in commerce on the goods or services described in the registration. 15 U.S.C. § 1115(a). Registration provides constructive notice of the registrant's ownership in the mark and forecloses a later user of the same or confusingly similar mark from claiming innocence, good faith, or lack of knowledge. 15 U.S.C. § 1072. Thus, once a mark is registered with the PTO, it is afforded national protection regardless of where it is used. 15 U.S.C. § 1072 provides for constructive notice of registration and modifies the common-law rule that allowed acquisition of concurrent rights by users in distinct geographic areas if the subsequent user adopted the mark without knowledge of the prior use.

In general, the duration of a registered mark is 10 years. However, a mark will be automatically cancelled six years after its registration date unless the registrant files an affidavit or declaration that the mark is in use in commerce or an affidavit showing that the non-use is excusable. Registration may be perpetually renewed for periods of 10 years within one year of the end of each successive 10 year period. Marks registered or renewed prior to November 16, 1989, remain in force for twenty years, provided an affidavit of use or excusable non-use was filed within the sixth year after registration. Registration of these marks may also be renewed every 10 years. 37 C.F.R. § 2.181(a)(1).

3. WHAT CANNOT BE REGISTERED

15 U.S.C. § 1052 sets forth the various grounds for refusal to register a mark. Unregisterable marks include, *inter alia*, those that are merely descriptive and lack secondary meaning; are deceptive or primarily geographically deceptively misdescriptive; or are confusingly similar to a prior mark and marks that are misdescriptive geographic indications of wine or liquor where the marks were first used on or after January 1, 1996 (*e.g.*, a mark that includes the "Bordeaux" for a wine that does not come from that region in France). Although Section 1052 does not specifically bar the registration of generic marks, the Federal Circuit in *BellSouth Corp. v. Data National Corp.* 60 F.3d 1565 (Fed. Cir. 1995) stated that a generic term is "the ultimate in descriptiveness" and thus should be barred.

4. THE SUSPECT PROVISIONS OF SECTION 1052(a)

As enacted by Congress, Section 1052(a) of the Lanham Act deemed unregistrable marks that were immoral, deceptive, or scandalous, or were disparaging in nature. Historically, the guidelines for determining whether a mark should be barred as disparaging under this section were particularly vague, exposing applicants to a highly subjective registration process in the PTO.[85] However, in 2017 the Supreme Court resolved the ambiguities in application of the statute by declaring that a ban on disparaging trademarks under § 1052(a) violates the Free Speech Clause of the First Amendment.[86] The case which prompted the Court to strike the law as invalid arose from the denial of trademark rights to *The Slants*— an Asian-American rock band who sought to register the name of their group, and thereby reclaim the pejorative term.[87]

The Court's unanimous decision to invalidate the disparagement bar to registration was rooted in the fact that the clause operated as a form of viewpoint discrimination. Justice Alito authored the unanimous holding and stated that the disparagement provision "denie[d] registration to any mark that is offensive to a substantial percentage of the members of any group. But in the sense relevant here, that is viewpoint discrimination: Giving offense is a viewpoint."[88] Because the government failed to provide sufficient justifications to satisfy even the more relaxed Constitutional analysis under *Central Hudson* (which requires a restriction of speech to serve "a substantial interest," and be "narrowly drawn" to that interest), under no circumstances could the disparagement provision be sustained.

Although the implications of the *Tam* decision have not yet been fully realized, one significant dispute was immediately resolved in light of the Court's holding. The Washington Redskins professional football team had faced a string of legal disputes concerning its name since the REDSKINS mark was first challenged by a Native American tribe in 1992.[89] Twenty-

---

[85] *See, e.g.*, In re In Over Our Heads, Inc., 16 U.S.P.Q. 2d 1653 (T.T.A.B. 1999), the court considered whether the "Moonies" mark was disparaging to members of the Unification Church, who are sometimes referred to as "moonies." In approving the application for trademark registration, the Board stated that "if a group does find the mark to be scandalous or disparaging, an opposition proceeding can be brought and a more complete record can be established." *See also* In re Hines, 32 U.S.P.Q. 2d 1376 (T.T.A.B. 1994), the Board reconsidered its earlier decision to deny registration to the mark "Budda Beach Wear" on the ground it was disparaging, noting that "it is imperative that the Board be careful to avoid "interposing its own judgment for that of Buddhists'."

[86] Matal v. Tam, 137 S. Ct. 1744 (2017).

[87] THE SLANTS was registered as a trademark on November 9th, 2017.

[88] *Tam*, 137 S. Ct. at 1763.

[89] The procedural history of the cases is quite complex: "In 1992 seven Native American Indians filed a petition before the Trademark Trial and Appeal Board to cancel six trademark registrations owned by Pro-Football that used the terms "Redskin" or "Redskins" as a mark to indicate the Washington Redskins professional football team and related goods. After the Trademark Board in 1999 granted the petition to cancel the registrations, the team appealed to the District Court in the District of Columbia. The District Court in 2003 reversed and ordered summary dismissal of the petition on two alternative grounds: the claim of disparagement was not

five years later, the case was finally dismissed in view of *Tam*, as the petitioners no longer had grounds to challenge the validity of the mark.

While the Supreme Court did not address the other portions of § 1052(a) in *Tam*, the arguments used to invalidate the disparagement clause were equally applicable to other portions of the statute. Thus, the Court of Appeals for the Federal Circuit has extended *Tam* to invalidate the "immoral" and "scandalous" statutory bars of the Lanham Act on the same Constitutional grounds.[90] Such barriers to registration comprised content-based restriction, as the bar applied to particular speech on the basis of the "topic discussed or the idea or message expressed."[91]

The remaining portions of § 1052(a) may remain intact, as the Constitutional concerns underpinning the *Tam* decision are not implicated by the remainder of the statute. Thus, Section § 1052(a) will likely continue to preclude the registration of marks which "falsely suggest a connection with persons, living or dead, institutions, beliefs, or national symbols, or bring them into contempt, or disrepute. . ." This rule is designed primarily to protect persons and institutions from exploitation of their persona by others. Hence, it embraces the concepts of both the right to privacy and the right to publicity. To bar registration on this ground,

(1) the mark must be unmistakably associated with a person or institution—the same or a close approximation of their name or identity;

(2) it must be clear that the person or institution identified by the mark is not connected to the goods or services associated with the mark; and

(3) the fame or reputation of the person or institution is such that a connection would be presumed.

---

proven by the evidence; and the petition was barred by a laches defense because of the long delay in seeking a cancellation. The petitioners appealed to the D.C. Court of Appeals, which in 2005 reversed and remanded, but only on the issue of the laches defense, not addressing the merits. On remand, the District Court in 2008 upheld the laches defense. On appeal in 2009, the Court of Appeals affirmed and the case appeared to be over. But the challenge continued. A different group of five Native Americans filed a new petition to cancel. The parties stipulated that the evidence in the new case would be the same as in the previous case with the addition of the depositions of the five new petitioners. In the new case, the Trademark Board held in 2014 by a 2–1 majority that laches was not a defense and that the Redskins mark was disparaging of Native Americans. On appeal, in 2015 the District Court in Virginia affirmed cancellation of the registrations, finding that: the disparagement bar was not unconstitutional; that the evidence established that the REDSKINS registered marks are barred by § 2(a) because may disparage Native Americans; and that the laches defense was not proven." 3 McCarthy on Trademarks and Unfair Competition § 19:77.25 (5th ed. 2018). The case was on appeal to the Fourth Circuit when the *Tam* decision was rendered.

90   In re Brunetti, 877 F.3d 1330, 1342, 125 U.S.P.Q. 2d 1072 (Fed. Cir. 2017) (The application for FUCT for wearing apparel was originally rejected by the PTO under § 2(a) as being immoral or scandalous.)

91   *See* 3 McCarthy on Trademarks and Unfair Competition § 19:77 (5th ed. 2018).

In *In re North American Free Trade Association*, 43 U.S.P.Q. 2d 1282 (T.T.A.B. 1996), the Appeals Board affirmed the PTO's refusal to register the mark NAFTA as a service mark for the applicant, concluding it suggested a false connection with the NAFTA treaty. On the other hand, in *Lucien Piccard Watch Corp. v. Since 1868 Crescent Corp.*, 314 F. Supp. 329 (S.D.N.Y. 1970), the court held that the mark Da Vinci on plaintiff's jewelry products did not falsely suggest a connection with Leonardo Da Vinci since no one was likely to believe he was connected with the goods.

5. ALTERNATIVE GROUNDS FOR REFUSAL UNDER SECTION 1052

15 U.S.C. § 1052(c) bars registration of a mark that "[c]onsists of or comprises a name, portrait, a signature identifying a particular living person except by his written consent" or "the name, signature or portrait of a deceased President of the United States during the life of his widow, if any, except by the written consent of the widow." The written consent requirement under § 1052(c) also applies to a nickname if it identifies a particular living individual.

15 U.S.C. § 1052(b) bars registration of any mark that "[c]onsists of or compromises the flag or coat of arms or any other insignia of the United States, or of any State or municipality or of any foreign nation or any simulation thereof." This category is relatively narrow and includes only those emblems and devices that represent authority and are of the same class and character as flags and coats of arms. Such insignia include the Great Seal of the United States, the Presidential Seal, and the seals of government departments.

The term simulation in § 1052(b) refers to something that gives the appearance or effect or has the characteristics of the original item. In *In re Advance Industrial Security, Inc.*, 194 U.S.P.Q. 344 (T.T.A.B. 1977), the Board concluded that a mark containing the words Advanced Security in the upper third portion along with an eagle that was similar to the United States Coat of Arms was not a simulation of the United States Coat of Arms or Great Seal. The Board noted that the mark created an overall commercial impression distinctly different from the Great Seal.

6. INCONTESTABLE MARKS

After a mark is registered and in continuous use without challenge for five years, and the filing of an affidavit to that effect with the PTO, a mark becomes incontestable and is further insulated and protected from attacks by later users or infringers. 15 U.S.C. § 1065; 1115. Section 1115(a) provides that incontestable status is conclusive evidence of registration and validity of the mark, and the registrant's ownership and exclusive right to use the mark. If a mark has become incontestable it cannot be challenged on the ground that it is merely descriptive and has not acquired secondary meaning. Section 1115 sets forth myriad other defenses available in the case of an incontestable mark.

A mark cannot acquire incontestable status if it is or has become generic. 15 U.S.C. § 1065(4). Also, under § 1064(3), registration of a mark may be cancelled at any time—even after becoming incontestable—for a limited number of reasons. The most important reasons for cancellation of registration include that:

> [T]he registered mark becomes the generic name for the goods or services, or a portion thereof, for which it is registered, or is functional, or has been abandoned, or its registration was obtained fraudulently. . .

7. SUPPLEMENTAL REGISTER

A mark that does not meet all the requirements for registration on the PTO's Principal Register, but that is capable of distinguishing the applicant's goods or services, may be registered on the PTO's Supplemental Register. Thus, a mark that is merely descriptive may be registered on the Supplemental Register if it is capable of later becoming distinctive of acquiring secondary meaning. If the mark later acquires distinctiveness through use in commerce it will become eligible for registration on the Principle Register.

Supplemental registration confers significantly fewer advantages than principal registration. Registration on the supplemental register is not evidence of the mark's validity, or the registrant's ownership of or exclusive right to use the mark. However, it enables the registrant to satisfy the home registration requirement of some foreign countries and creates jurisdiction in a federal forum for disputes involving the mark.

CC. LOSS OF TRADEMARK RIGHTS

Trademark owners can lose their rights to the mark if the mark becomes generic or if they abandon the mark. 15 U.S.C. § 1064(3). Marks are considered abandoned if (1) use of the mark is discontinued with the intent not to resume use, or (2) there is a course of conduct by the owner that "allows the mark to become generic." 15 U.S.C. § 1127. Owners may also cancel their trademark registration on their own accord.

1. GENERICIDE

A trademark may also lose protection if it becomes generic. Terms like aspirin, cellophane, nylon, thermos, and escalator, at one point, were all trademarks protected under United States trademark law. Lifelong protection of a trademark is not a certainty. If consumers come to associate a trademark with the class of product instead of a particular brand, the mark will become generic and its owner will lose rights to it.

Generic terms are not registerable and a registered term may be cancelled at any time on the grounds it has become generic. 15 U.S.C. § 1064(3). A registered mark will not be deemed to be the generic name of goods or services solely because the mark is also used as a name of or to identify a unique product or service. 15 U.S.C. § 1064(3). Congress added this language in 1984 to clarify that it is not destructive of the trademark function to identify a product by the name coined by its purveyor.

In determining whether a mark has become generic, the issue is whether the trademarked term has become synonymous with the nature or class of products of which it is a part. In *Bayer Co. v. United Drug Co.*, 272 F. 505, 509 (S.D.N.Y. 1921), the case in which aspirin was found to be generic, Judge Learned Hand stated: "The single question as I view it, in all these cases is merely one of fact: What do buyers understand by the word for whose use the parties are contending?" Similarly, in *King-Seeley Thermos Co. v. Aladdin Industries, Inc.*, 321 F.2d 577 (2d Cir. 1963), the court determined that the trademark thermos had become generic, holding that once the public expropriates a trademark as its own, it is unfair to restrict the rights of competitors to use the word. In other words, thermos bottle and vacuum bottle had become virtually synonymous. Not surprisingly, owners of popular marks often engage in extensive policing efforts to prevent them from becoming generic and falling into the public domain. The actual primary significance of the mark to purchasers is controlling, however. In other words, even the best efforts of the trademark owner to prevent public appropriation of the mark as a generic description can be unsuccessful.

2. ABANDONMENT

A trademark owner forfeits all right in any mark they have abandoned under 15 U.S.C. § 1064(3), and abandonment is a defense to infringement under § 1115(b)(2). Trademarks may be found to have been abandoned because of non-use, assignments in gross or naked licensing.

Under 15 U.S.C. § 1127, a mark is abandoned because of non-use when its owner has ceased using the mark with an intent not to resume its use. At common law, a party alleging abandonment had to prove intent to abandon, but because trademark owners could overcome any circumstantial proof of their intent to abandon simply by testifying that they did not intend to abandon their marks, the Lanham Act reformulated the test. Under § 1127, proof of three consecutive years of non-use establishes a prima facie case of intent not to resume use, which the trademark owner must then rebut with objective proof of its intent to resume use of the mark. Thus, "an affirmative desire not to relinquish a mark" is no longer the determinative factor. This change helps ensure that the Lanham Act does not allow the warehousing of unused trademarks by their owners.

Whether a mark has been abandoned through non-use is a question of fact, and the owner's intent is inferred from the circumstances, aided by the statutory presumption. Because a finding of abandonment results in the forfeiture of a property interest by the trademark owner, the party alleging abandonment bears the burden of proof on their claim and abandonment must be proven by clear and convincing evidence.

3. NON-USE

To trigger the presumption raised by three consecutive years of non-use, the party alleging an abandonment must show that during those three consecutive years the trademark owner did not employ its mark for any purpose that qualifies as use within the meaning of Title 15. Under § 1127:

> The term "use in commerce" means the bona fide use of a mark in the ordinary course of trade, and not a use made merely to reserve a right in a mark. For purposes of this chapter, a mark shall be deemed to be in use in commerce
>
> (1) on goods when—
>
>> (A) it is placed in any manner on the goods or their containers or the displays associated therewith or on the tags or labels affixed thereto, or if the nature of the goods makes such placement impracticable, then on documents associated with the goods or their sale, and
>>
>> (B) the goods are sold or transported in commerce, and
>
> (2) on services when it is used or displayed in the sale or advertising of services and the services are rendered in commerce, or the services are rendered in more than one State or in the United States and a foreign country and the person rendering the services is engaged in commerce in connection with the services.

Thus, to be used within the meaning of § 1127, the mark must be affixed to goods, and the goods must be either sold or transported in commerce, all in the ordinary course of trade. Token use for the purpose of establishing and reserving a right in the mark is insufficient.

In order to qualify as use, any bona fide use in the ordinary course of trade must also be in commerce, defined by as "all commerce which may lawfully be regulated by Congress." Thus, only use within the United States, and therefore subject to Congressional authority, is relevant for trademark purposes.

4. REBUTTAL

Under § 1127, "[n]onuse for 3 consecutive years shall be prima facie evidence of abandonment." Therefore, once the party alleging abandonment has established that the trademark owner either did not use the mark at all, or did not put the mark to bona fide use in the ordinary course of trade for three consecutive years, a presumption arises that the mark has been abandoned. Thereafter, the trademark owner bears the burden of production to show that despite the non-use it intended to resume use of the mark.

The presumption of abandonment is generally rebutted by showing that the registrant made efforts to resume use or by showing that the non-use was excusable, both of which indicate that the non-use was not coupled with an intent not to resume use, or an intent to abandon. Proof of the trademark owner's active efforts by the trademark owner to resume use of the mark during the period of non-use will usually overcome the presumption of abandonment.

A trademark owner may also rebut a prima facie case of abandonment by showing that the non-use was not the result of an intent to abandon or lack of intent to resume use of the mark, but rather that it was provoked by some excusable external pressure—e.g., labor strikes, litigation, war, bankruptcy, or government restrictions. In most cases rebuttal requires proof of an intent to resume use in the reasonably foreseeable future.

Changing the use of a mark from one product to another generally will not result in abandonment if the products are similar. Moreover, non-use must be nationwide to amount to abandonment; any lingering interstate activity will defeat a claim of abandonment, though proof of intrastate activity will not.

If a trademark owner cannot rebut the presumption of abandonment raised by the prima facie case described in § 1127, the resulting cancellation of its federal registration will leave the trademark owner with only those rights arising under state and common law from their actual use of the mark. In most cases, the non-use proved to establish the prima facie case of abandonment was a total non-use, and so the trademark owner will be left without any rights in the mark. Thereafter, the mark will be equally available to all prospective users, including the former owner, and the first to meet the statutory preconditions after the date on which the court has deemed the mark abandoned may register the mark anew.

Assignments in gross and naked licensing may also result in abandonment and strip the owner of trademark rights. This is consistent with the purposes of a trademark: to identify goods or services of a particular quality or point of origin. Stripped of these purposes, the trademark may be deemed abandoned.

DD. PROPERTY INTERESTS IN TRADEMARKS

The property interest in a trademark can be characterized as a right to exclude or the right of exclusive use. However, it bears emphasizing that, unlike other types of intellectual property, property rights in trademarks are shaped by consumer perception. For the right to be created, a mark must be used in commerce and must distinguish the goods or services from those of others in the minds of current or potential consumers. 15 U.S.C. §§ 1052, 1127. Similarly, violation of trademark rights depends on consumer perception—are they confused or deceived by use of a similar mark or has such use made the mark distinctive to consumers. *See* 15 U.S.C. § 1125.

As property rights, trademarks can be sold (assigned) and licensed (allowing a limited right to use). The property interest in a trademark, trade name, service mark, collective mark, or certification mark rests in the goodwill associated with the mark. Property rights in a trademark exist solely as a right appurtenant to an established business or trade in connection with which the mark is employed. In other words, there is no right in a trademark in gross; the right to a trademark is connected with the trademarked product or service and associated goodwill.

1. ASSIGNMENTS

15 U.S.C. § 1060(a)(1) addresses trademark assignments and provides that a mark "shall be assignable with the goodwill of the business in which the mark is used, or with that part of the goodwill of the business connected with the use of and symbolized by the mark." Assignments of a mark without the goodwill of the business associated with the mark are often referred to as assignments in gross or naked assignments and will be invalidated (and may also lead to a finding of abandonment).

The prohibition on assignments in gross is intended to prevent consumer confusion or deception. Where a mark has accumulated consumer goodwill as an indication of the origin of a particular good or service, the mark is at best of no assistance to consumers attempting to discern between the quality or origin of goods or services that are different. At worst, an assignment in gross can result in genuine confusion amongst consumers, or even "in a fraud on the purchasing public who reasonably assume that the mark signifies the same thing, whether used by one person or another." Marshak v. Green, 746 F.2d 927 (2d Cir. 1984).

The possibility of invalid assignment in gross poses a risk of abandonment, as an assignor may cease its use of the ostensibly but ineffectually assigned mark, which after time may result in an abandonment. Once the trademark has been abandoned, it cannot be re-assigned because there is no property right to be transferred from another.

2. LICENSES

Prior to enactment of the Lanham Act, many courts held that a trademark represented to the consumer the physical source or origin of the goods and services. By that reasoning, licensing of a trademark was held to effect an abandonment of the mark. As the use of trademarks shifted to identify a standard of quality to consumers rather than a geographical source, courts held that licensing was permitted, provided the owner of the mark retained sufficient control over the quality of the goods or services provided. Under 15 U.S.C. § 1055, the Lanham Act specifically recognizes that the use of a mark by a licensee inures to the benefit of the trademark owner. This is the basis for modern franchising in the United States.

A trademark licensor must take precautions to ensure that the quality of goods sold under its mark remains consistent over time and between licensees. Thus § 1055 provides that only use by a related company will inure to the benefit of a trademark owner. Section 1127, in turn, defines a related company as "any person whose use of a mark is controlled by the owner of the mark with respect to the nature and quality of the goods or services on or in connection with which the mark is used." If a court determines that a trademark owner has not exercised sufficient control over its licensees, the owner will be held to have abandoned its mark by granting a naked license.

The exercise of actual control over licensees—rather than the mere reservation of a right to control through the license agreement—is the key to avoiding a naked license. This typically requires a showing of more than casual control.

EE. SECURITY INTERESTS IN TRADEMARKS

The amount of control that a licensor must exercise over its licensee varies with the circumstances, and the critical inquiry regards whether the amount of control exercised by a licensor is sufficient to ensure that goods manufactured, or services provided by, a licensee under the licensing agreement will remain of the consistent, predictable quality expected by consumers. Under some circumstances, the licensor need not exercise any actual quality control over its licensee. In most instances, an unsupervised license will be held valid only where there was a familial or close working relationship between the licensor and licensee.

Trademarks, along with other intellectual property such as copyrights and patents, often represent a significant portion of a corporation's value and can be useful source of collateral for secured transactions. Failure to take a security interest in trademarks can actually devalue a secured party's collateral. For example, consider the foreclosure value of a fast-food franchise's business assets without its trademarks.

To maintain the priority of their security interests, lenders must know how to properly create and perfect their security interests in intellectual property. Security interests in intellectual property are governed by both the federal law and Article 9 of the Uniform Commercial Code.

Article 9, which has been adopted by all fifty states, governs the creation and perfection of security interest in intellectual property, which is categorized as a general intangible. A security interest is defined as "an interest in personal property or fixtures which secures payment or performance of an obligation." U.C.C. § 1–201(b)(35). A security interest is not enforceable against either a debtor or third parties, and does not attach to the collateral, unless

(1) the secured party has given value in exchange for the collateral,

(2) the debtor has rights in the collateral, and

(3) the debtor has signed a security agreement that provides a description of the collateral.

U.C.C. § 9–203(b). Lenders must therefore ensure that the debtor has rights in the intellectual property collateral prior to obtaining the security interest.

Perfection is the method by which a secured party achieves and maintains the highest available priority for its security interest in collateral. An unperfected security interest may be effective against the debtor, but it is of little value against third parties. In bankruptcy, the difference between a perfected security interest and an unperfected security interest often means the difference between a full recovery as a secured creditor and little or no recovery as an unsecured creditor. 11 U.S.C. § 544.

A security interest is perfected when it attaches if the applicable requirements are satisfied before attachment. The process of perfecting a security interest in most types of personal property is accomplished when a properly completed UCC–1 financing statement is filed with the appropriate state office, usually the office of the secretary of state. The financing statement must name both the debtor and the secured party, and must describe the collateral covered by the financing statement. The U.C.C. no longer requires the debtor to sign an electronically filed financial statement, although the debtor must authorize the filing.

The relative priorities of creditors who hold conflicting security interests are straightforward. Under the U.C.C.

(1) if the conflicting security interests are perfected, they rank according to priority in time of filing or perfection;

(2)   a perfected security interest has priority over a conflicting unperfected interest; and

(3)   if conflicting security interests are unperfected, the first security interest to attach has priority.

However, under § 9–109(c)(1), Article 9 does not apply to the extent that it is preempted by federal law.

Filing a financing statement is neither necessary nor effective to perfect a security interest in collateral that is subject to a separate federal filing requirement.   In such cases, compliance with such a federal requirement is equivalent to filing a properly completed UCC–1 financing statement, and compliance with federal law is the only means of perfection. U.C.C. § 9–311(b).   However, even in cases where federal law governs the perfection of security interests, Article 9 governs the relative priorities of conflicting security interests unless federal law also establishes separate priority rules.   Sections 9–109 and 9–311 of the U.C.C. raise distinct issues. Under § 9–109, federal law preempts Article 9 where the former governs ownership rights in the property secured as collateral, while under § 9–311, the U.C.C. defers to federal law regarding perfection if federal law has defined a filing requirement.   The distinction between these sections is unclear, and it is equally unclear whether security interests in intellectual property rights governed by federal law must be perfected in accordance with federal law or the U.C.C. Because of this uncertainty, financing statements in patents, trademarks, or copyrights should be filed with both state and federal offices.

Security interests in both common law trademarks and state-registered trademarks are perfected by filing a UCC–1 financing statement with the appropriate state office.   The steps to properly perfect a security interest in a federally registered trademark are less clear.   Under the Lanham Act:

> A registered mark or a mark for which an application to register has been filed shall be assignable with the goodwill of the business in which the mark is used. . . An assignment shall be void against any subsequent purchaser for valuable consideration without notice, unless the prescribed information reporting the assignment is recorded in the United States Patent and Trademark Office within 3 months after the date of the assignment or prior to the subsequent purchase.

15 U.S.C. § 1060(a)(1) and (4).   Thus, the Lanham Act provides for a recordation of "assignments" and contains a limited priority rule.

The Lanham Act does not define assignment, and it is unclear whether security interests must be recorded with the PTO.   Nevertheless, to give third parties notification of legal ownership or other equitable interests, the PTO does accept and file documents that create security interests in trademarks.

The courts have narrowly interpreted the Lanham Act, holding that—despite the PTO's acceptance of filings creating security interests—it was not intended to govern security interests in trademarks and does not preempt Article 9. Furthermore, courts have consistently held that a security interest in a trademark must be perfected according to the U.C.C. requirements.

Although the courts have consistently held that the U.C.C.—not federal law—governs the perfection of security interests in trademarks, the prudent approach to perfecting any security interest in a trademark is to both file a UCC–1 financing statement with the appropriate state office and to record that security interest with the PTO. Dual filing avoids any confusion regarding the term assignment under the Lanham Act and forecloses any risk that a security interest will be lost to a bona fide purchaser. The Lanham Act's limited priority rule addresses only the validity of an assignment "as against any subsequent purchaser for a valuable consideration without notice." 15 U.S.C. § 1060(a)(4). Subsequent lien creditors are not mentioned. However, because registering a trademark with the PTO serves as constructive notice of trademark ownership, 15 U.S.C. § 1072, filing the security interest with the PTO may also provide constructive notice of the secured party's interest to any prospective bona fide purchaser of the trademark.

Regardless of the method of registration, a security interest in a trademark is always at risk of being invalidated as an assignment in gross. Trademarks, unlike patents and copyrights, cannot be freely bought and sold, but may only be assigned along with the associated goodwill. 15 U.S.C. § 1060. Any transfer of a trademark unaccompanied by the underlying goodwill will be invalid as an assignment in gross. Because a security interest in a trademark may ripen into an assignment, unless the foreclosing creditor also holds a security interest in the goodwill associated with the trademark, the trademark assignment will be unenforceable. A secured party should specifically identify the debtor's trademarks and the associated goodwill of the business in both the security agreement and the financing statement. This is generally the case when a secured party also has a blanket lien or security interest in the business assets associated with the use of the mark.

Finally, because the U.C.C. definition of general intangibles includes both rights in a trademark and the associated goodwill, U.C.C. § 9–102, cmt. 5(d), a reference in the security agreement to general intangibles may be sufficient to cover trademarks. However, it is better practice to include a specific list of existing marks, registration numbers, and references to the goods, products, or services with which the trademarks are associated.

FF. EXCLUSIVE RIGHTS PROTECTED UNDER TITLE 17

1. GENERALLY

The Copyright Act gives the author the exclusive right to:

(1) reproduce the copyrighted work;

(2) prepare derivative works based upon the copyrighted work;

(3) distribute copies of the work through sale, rental, lease or lending;

(4) perform copyrighted works publicly;

(5) display the copyrighted work publicly; and

(6) perform the copyrighted work publicly through digital audio transmission (in the case of sound recordings).

17 U.S.C. § 106. The copyright owners may exercise these rights exclusively, or may authorize others to do so.

The first three of the exclusive rights listed in apply to all copyrightable works. The rights to perform and display copyrighted works are limited to works that can be performed or displayed. The right to perform copyrighted material publicly applies to literary, musical, dramatic, choreographic works, pantomimes, motion pictures, and other audiovisual works. The right to display copyrighted work publicly applies to literary, musical, dramatic, choreographic works, pantomimes, and pictorial, graphic, or sculptural works, including the individual images of a motion picture or other audiovisual work. Finally, the right to public performance through digital audio transmission is limited to sound recordings.

2. REPRODUCTION

A copyright owner has the exclusive right to reproduce the work in the form of phonorecords or copies, which are terms of art. 17 U.S.C. § 106(1). Phonorecords capture and convey sound while copies capture images and convey those images visually. The parallel treatment of copies and phonorecords under Title 17 is purposeful. The statutory grant to the copyright owner of an exclusive right "to reproduce the copyrighted work in copies or phonorecords" reflects the distinction under Title 17 between copies—defined in § 101 as "material objects, *other than phonorecords*, in which a work is fixed by any method now known or later developed"—and phonorecords—defined as material objects in which sounds, other than those accompanying a motion picture or other audiovisual work, are fixed by any method now known or later developed.

The exclusive right to reproduce encompasses changing mediums for conveying copyrightable material. Thus, compact discs, digital video discs, and other newer forms of phonorecords and copies are protected in addition to vinyl records, paper photocopies, and other, older forms of recordation. For example, unauthorized fax copies and unauthorized uploading of images produced by a scanner are considered infringements. In *Pasha Publications, Inc. v. Enmark Gas Corp.*, 1992 WL 70786 (N.D. Tex. 1992), the court held that the defendant had violated the author's exclusive right to reproduction by faxing a copyrighted newsletter to its employees. Similarly, in *Playboy Enterprises, Inc. v. Webbworld, Inc.*, 991 F. Supp. 543 (N.D. Tex. 1997), the plaintiff's infringed upon Playboy's exclusive right to publish its copyrighted images by collecting images scanned and posted online by third parties, and re-posting them on its members-only website.

Likewise, the right to duplicate digital music files is protected in addition to vinyl records and other, older forms of recordation. For example, in *Metro-Goldwyn-Mayer Studios Inc. v. Grokster, Ltd.*, 545 U.S. 913 (2005), the Supreme Court reversed a lower court grant of summary judgment in favor of the defendants' peer-to-peer computer networks Grokster and StreamCast. The networks had been sued by a consortium of music publishers and copyright owners alleging inducement to infringement and contributory infringement. The defendants had advertised themselves as alternatives to Napster and had actively encouraged users to infringe on copyrighted material, conduct which the Court held unlawful.

Title 17 outlines several exceptions to the exclusivity of reproduction and performance rights otherwise reserved to copyright owners.

Sections 112 and 117 impose limitations on the exclusivity of a copyright owner's right to reproduce copyrighted works. Section 117 allows computer software licensees to back-up their software, and even to alter it if necessary to render the software functional for their needs. Section 112 provides a similar defense to broadcast-programming licensees who make backup recordings of copyrighted material for later rebroadcast and archival purposes.

Section 117 specifically forbids software purchasers from reselling their backup or archived copies of copyrighted software except as "part of the lease, sale, or other transfer of all rights in the program" and even then only with the copyright owner's permission. The safe harbor of § 117 for backup or archival purposes does not allow the software purchaser to actually *use* the copies they have made. For example, in *Wall Data Inc. v. Los Angeles County Sheriff's Department*, 447 F.3d 769 (9th Cir. 2006), where the defendant held 3,500 licenses to use a computer program, but installed and used the program on more than 6,000 computers, the copying fell outside of the § 117 safe harbor.

Rebroadcasters' freedom to make copies of performances and sound recordings for rebroadcast purposes under § 112 is an important right that gives broadcasters control over their programming schedules, provided that they comply with the restrictions imposed by the statute. To avail itself of the exception, a broadcaster must meet three conditions:

(a)   the broadcaster must make only one copy, and that copy must be used only by its maker;

(b)   the copy must be used only for rebroadcast within the maker's local service area; and

(c)   the copy must be destroyed within six months unless preserved for archival purposes.

The importance of § 112 was evident in *Agee v. Paramount Communications, Inc.*, 59 F.3d 317 (2d Cir. 1995), in which defendant Paramount infringed upon the plaintiff's reproduction rights in copyrighted sound recording synched to the credits of the program, Hard Copy. The program was then transmitted to the codefendant affiliate stations, which complied with the requirements of § 112. The court held that although Paramount had infringed, the affiliate's compliance with § 112 insulated them from liability for unauthorized reproduction of the plaintiff's sound recordings.

Both the Audio Home Recording Act of 1992 (the "AHRA") and the Intellectual Property and Communications Omnibus Reform Act of 1999 address the author's exclusive right of reproduction in the context of evolving technology.   AHRA broadly prohibits the manufacture, importation, or use of devices that are capable of serial copying—defined as "the duplication in a digital format of a copyrighted musical work or sound recording from a digital reproduction of a digital musical recording" 17 U.S.C. § 1001(11)—but not if they conform with recognized systems by which the unauthorized duplication of digital recordings can be restricted. 17 U.S.C. § 1002. AHRA provides for:

(1)   a serial copy prevention system under which consumers are permitted to make an infinite number of copies directly from a lawfully purchased prerecorded tape but, due to digital copy that is inserted into any initial copy of the purchased tape, are prevented from making further copies from any initial copy;

(2)   a two percent royalty levy on the transfer price of digital recorders and a three percent royalty levy on the transfer price of blank recording media;

(3)   the deposit of these royalties into the Copyright Office for distribution by the Copyright Royalty Tribunal under a sound recording fund and a musical works fund; and

(4)   various civil remedies and the arbitration of certain disputes.

H.R. Rep. 102–873(II), at 3 (1992). The first provision described above is embodied in § 1008, which prohibits any claim of infringement "based on the noncommercial use of [a device capable of serial copying] by a consumer [to make] digital musical recordings or analog musical recordings." 17 U.S.C. § 1008. In providing this limited exception, Congress extended to licensees a right to copy recordings which would otherwise constitute infringement.

The Omnibus Reform Act prohibits both the circumvention of a "technological measure that effectively controls access to a work protected under this title," 17 U.S.C. § 1201(a), and any activity that would make available for use technology designed, anticipated or known to be used "for use in circumventing a technological measure that effectively controls access" to a copyrighted work. 17 U.S.C. § 1201(a)(1)(A).

However, several exceptions are specifically permitted. The Librarian of Congress has the authority to exempt from the general prohibition any class of work if the overly zealous protection of it might impede non-infringing use of protected works. 17 U.S.C. § 1201(a)(1)(D). Furthermore, software licensees are permitted, where necessary, to develop, apply, and disseminate the means to decode and decrypt any protections on licensed software for the purpose of enhancing the interoperability of the "independently created computer program with other programs. . ." 17 U.S.C. § 1201(f). There are also other narrower exceptions scattered throughout the text of § 1201.

3. DERIVATIVE WORKS

The exclusive right to make or authorize derivative works of a copyrighted work is especially valuable. Derivative works are those "based upon one or more pre-existing works, such as a translation, musical arrangement, dramatization, fictionalization, motion picture adaptation, sound recording, artistic reproduction, abridgment, condensation, or any other form in which a work may be recast, transformed, or adapted." 17 U.S.C. § 101. In addition, revisionary works, including those that consist of editorial revisions, annotations, elaborations, or other modifications which, as a whole, represent an original work of authorship, are derivative works. For example, authors have the right to convert novels into motion pictures, to translate articles into other languages, or to make orchestral arrangements of popular hits. Authors also have the right to license others to authorize the production of these derivative works.

The standard for proving that a work is derivative and therefore infringes upon the copyright holder's rights is not as strict as the standard for copyrightability of a derivative work. A derivative work is copyrightable only if it satisfies 17 U.S.C. § 102, but infringing on another's exclusive right to create derivative works involves even less than infringing on the right to reproduce the work. A work is derivative if it has been substantially copied from prior copyrighted work. Further, a derivative work does not have to be fixed in a tangible medium to be an infringement upon the copyright owner's rights. In *Herbert v. Shanley Co.*, 242 U.S. 591 (1916), for example, the Supreme Court held that the live performance of a copyrighted arrangement of a comic opera was an infringement, even though no admission was charged to the audience. In addition, words do not necessarily have to be borrowed from the copyrighted work. In a classic derivative rights case, *Kalem Co. v. Harper Bros.*, 222 U.S. 55 (1911), the Court held that a silent motion picture adaptation of the novel *Ben Hur* was a derivative work of the book and constituted infringement.

Editing and abridging a work, along with expansion of a work, can infringe upon the exclusive right to derivative works. In *Gilliam v. American Broadcasting Companies*, 538 F.2d 14 (2d Cir. 1976), a broadcast network heavily edited television programs without the permission of the comedy group that produced them (Monty Python). The court concluded that the network had infringed upon the group's copyright to the program scripts and sua sponte enjoined ABC from continuing to broadcast properly licensed but roughly edited episodes of Monty Python's Flying Circus, which the court described as "a mere caricature of [the group's] talents." Although the court briefly discussed moral rights, and even hinted at an "actionable mutilation" of the plaintiff's work, its opinion rested more securely on a traditional theory of the performer's copyright in the script, since the edits exceeded both reasonable expectations and the editorial rights ABC claimed under the license agreement.

4. DISTRIBUTION

Under 17 U.S.C. § 106(3), the copyright owner has the exclusive right to distribute copies or phonorecords of the copyrighted work to the public through sale, rental, lease, lending, or other transfer of ownership. The classic example of infringement through distribution is that an infringer hands out copies of a copyrighted work, and thereby infringes upon the copyright owner's exclusive right of distribution. For example, in *Tangorre v. Mako's, Inc.*, 2003 WL 470577 (S.D.N.Y. 2003) (unreported decision), the plaintiff had photographed the defendant club's "girls" in anticipation of a promotional calendar. The defendant refused to pay the plaintiff, but published the calendar using the plaintiff's photographs, and distributed copies to patrons. The court held that by allowing its customers to take copies of the calendar containing unlicensed copies of the plaintiff's photographs, the defendant had infringed upon the plaintiff's right of distribution.

The rise of the Internet has provided increased low-cost opportunities for infringement and also somewhat altered the dynamic. For example, in

A&M Records, Inc. v. Napster, Inc., 239 F.3d 1004 (9th Cir. 2001), the court addressed whether the users of an online file-sharing network had infringed upon the plaintiff's exclusive rights in copyrighted music. Finding that the music was indeed copyrighted, the court held that users had infringed on the plaintiff's distribution and reproduction rights, in that "Napster users who upload files to the search index for others to copy violate plaintiffs' distribution rights. Napster users who download files containing copyrighted music violate plaintiffs' reproduction rights."

Taken alone, 17 U.S.C. § 106(3) would make it an infringement for a bookseller to sell books or a person to loan a movie to a friend, but under the first sale doctrine, these activities are not infringement. In *Bobbs-Merrill Co. v. Straus,* 210 U.S. 339, 350 (1908), the Supreme Court concluded that a person who has "sold a copyrighted article, without restriction, has parted with all right to control the sale of it." The first sale doctrine is codified in 17 U.S.C. § 109(a).

The purchaser of a book that was sold with permission of the owner of the copyright may sell it again, but cannot publish a new edition of it. Essentially, the first sale of a copyrighted work extinguishes the right of the copyright owner in that particular edition or embodiment of the copyright. Thus, a book dealer can resell antique books but she cannot remove the illustrations from those books and produce a new compilation of antique illustrations. For sound recordings and computer programs, this rule applies only to for-profit operations and explicitly excludes nonprofit libraries. 17 U.S.C. § 109(a)(2).

Copyright infringement is a strict liability cause of action. It is irrelevant whether an infringer knew or had any reason to suspect that by purchasing or selling particular goods they infringed upon another's copyright. *Pinkham v. Sara Lee Corp.*, 983 F.2d 824 (8th Cir. 1992) states:

> Once a plaintiff has proven that he or she owns the copyright on a particular work, and that the defendant has infringed upon those "exclusive rights," the defendant is liable for the infringement and this liability is absolute. The defendant's intent is simply not relevant. . .

5. PERFORMANCE

The copyright holder has the exclusive right to performance for all works except for pictorial, graphic, sculptural works, and sound recordings. The exclusion of sound recordings from those works covered by the exclusive right to performance seems surprising, but that exclusion does not leave music unprotected. In *Lodge Hall Music, Inc. v. Waco Wrangler Club, Inc.*, 831 F.2d 77 (5th Cir. 1987), the court held that playing copyrighted records in a late-night bar would constitute infringement of the copyright holder's exclusive right to public performance. But an author's right to exclusive performance of underlying musical compositions only applies to performance for a live audience. In 1995, Congress extended the ownership of a copyright in a sound recording to cover the public performance of the work by means of digital audio transmission. 17 U.S.C. § 106(6). This expansion of the performance right to sound recordings is of increasing importance as the popularity of the Internet and other digital music services grows.

To infringe on the copyright owner's exclusive right, the performance must be public. 17 U.S.C. § 106(4). To perform a work publicly means:

> [t]o perform or display it at a place open to the public or at any place where a substantial number of persons outside of a normal circle of a family and its social acquaintances is gathered or to transmit or otherwise communicate a performance or display of the work to [such a gathering] or to the public. . . by means of any device or process. . .

17 U.S.C. § 101. A motion picture or other audio-visual work is performed by showing its images in any sequence or making the sounds accompanying it audible. With regard to movies and other audiovisual works, 17 U.S.C. § 101 defines the copyright owner's exclusive right as the right "to show [the movie's] images in any sequence or to make the sounds accompanying it audible."

The House Report that accompanied the 1976 revisions further explained that even "performances in 'semipublic' places such as clubs, lodges, factories, summer camps, and schools are 'public performances' subject to copyright control," but Congress concluded that "routine meetings of businesses and governmental personnel would be excluded because they do not represent the gathering of a 'substantial number of persons.'" H.R. Rep. No. 94–1476, at 64 (1976).

Prior to the Copyright Act of 1976, copyright owners were only protected against for profit public performances. The Copyright Act of 1976 did away with the for-profit requirement, but created certain exceptions that benefit many non-profit groups. Section 110(3), for example, allows the performance and display of works of a religious nature in the course of worship services.

Section 110(4) provides a similar, although somewhat more limited, defense for the live performance of copyrighted work provided there is no cost of admission to the public or the performance is for charitable purposes. However, the exception allowed by § 110(4) does not protect infringers if they obtain any commercial benefit from the infringement. For example, in *Morganactive Songs, Inc. v. Padgett*, 2006 WL 2882521 (M.D. Ga.), the plaintiff alleged that three of its copyrighted songs had been performed in the defendant's club during a children's charity fundraiser. Despite the overall charitable character of the event, the court concluded that the defendant had obtained a direct commercial benefit from alcohol sales the night of the performance, and was therefore ineligible for the exception allowed under § 110(4).

Sections 111, 119, and 122 limit the exclusivity of a copyright owner's performance rights in favor of those who retransmit, for commercial purposes, programming copyrighted by the original broadcaster.

Section 111(a) allows hotels, educators, governmental bodies, and nonprofit organizations to retransmit broadcast programming. Section 111(c) allows for the simultaneous secondary transmission of broadcast signals by cable television providers. Section 111(e) allows U.S. cable providers operating outside of the contiguous 48 states to make single recordings of broadcast programming for a single non-simultaneous retransmission subject to certain further conditions. Cable providers that retransmit broadcast signals under §§ 111(c) and (e) may not alter the programming or commercial content of the broadcast signals they retransmit, and are subject to statutory licensing requirements described in excruciating detail in § 111(d). Those requirements are too intricate to cover here, but amount to a requirement that cable providers pay royalties, collected and disbursed by the Copyright Office, for the copyrighted broadcast programming they carry. Sections 119 and 111 impose similar statutory licensing requirements on satellite television service providers.

Under § 114(a), the owner of a copyright in a sound recording has no exclusive right of performance with regard to that work, except as provided in § 106(6) with regard to "digital audio transmission." Section 114(d) provides that with the exception of "nonsubscription broadcast transmissions," digital audio transmissions are subject to statutory licensing requirements described traditional "over-the-air" broadcasts. *Public Performance of Sound Recordings: Definition of a Service, Final Rule*, 65 Fed. Reg. 77292 (Dec. 11, 2000). In *Bonneville International Corp. v. Peters*, 347 F.3d 485 (3d Cir. 2003), the National Association of Broadcasters sued the copyright office, challenging its definition of "nonsubscription broadcast transmission" in hopes of escaping statutory licensing requirements for their simultaneous online broadcast of "over-the-air" programming. The court rejected that interpretation, holding that "nonsubscription broadcast transmissions" include only over-the-air broadcasts, extended to include retransmissions and digital rather than more traditional analog signals, but not to include simultaneous streaming webcasts.

6. DISPLAY

The copyright holder's right of public display applies to all copyrighted works except sound recordings. 17 U.S.C. § 106(5). This right of public display compliments the right of public performance reserved to the owners of copyrights in sound recordings or other works with a temporal dimension, such as movies or pantomimes. With regard to audiovisual works, the copyright owner has both a performance right and a display right under § 106. 17 U.S.C. § 101 explains that displaying a work means showing, "a copy of it, either directly or by means of a film, slide, television image, or any other device or process or, in the case of a motion picture or other audiovisual work, to show individual images nonsequentially." Thus, showing individual frames from a motion picture infringes upon the copyright owner's right of display, but not its performance right. The same definition of public that applied to the performance right applies to the public display right. Including a picture of a piece of artwork on a website that can be viewed by the public, even if they view it alone in a private setting, is therefore a public display and will constitute infringement unless the copyright owner has given permission for the display.

Congress created an exception to the general rule of public display to strike a balance between the copyright owner's rights and the interests of a person who owns a physical copy of a work. 17 U.S.C. § 109(c) provides that an owner of a lawful copy of a work or a person authorized by that owner may display that copy to viewers present at the place where the copy is located. Section 110(s) allows public venues, like restaurants and bars, to play the radio or television without violating the copyright owner's right of performance or display, subject to some restrictions regarding the size of the display system.

CHAPTER 6

SOURCES OF CAPITAL AND SECURITIES LAWS

■ ■ ■

A. INTRODUCTION

When starting a small business, it is typical that at least part of the initial funding will come from the founders' own funds. However, most small businesses at one point or another will need to obtain outside sources of financing for the business. From a business strategy standpoint, the entrepreneur must decide whether debt financing or equity financing is most suitable for achieving the goals and objectives of the business. The obvious benefit of debt financing over equity financing is that if the business succeeds, the entrepreneur will reap all the future profits. Therefore, if there is high confidence that the business will succeed and the business has the opportunity to secure financing, a loan is a more attractive source of money than an equity investment from a third party who would then own a share of the business and receive a share of the profits. The downside of debt financing, however, is that if the business fails and the entrepreneur has personally guaranteed the loan, it must be repaid with the entrepreneur's personal funds. By contrast, the entrepreneur would not have to repay the equity investors if the business fails. This section will discuss the process, documentation, and regulatory requirements that surround and impact debt and equity financing of the business.

B. PROMISSORY NOTES

One of the most fundamental forms of debt financing is the loan. The loan can be from such sources as a friend, family member, wealthy investor, or a bank. A lender will almost always want the business's founders to sign a promissory note to evidence the debt. A promissory note is an instrument, under which one party (the maker or issuer) makes an unconditional promise in writing to pay a sum of money to the other (the payee) or at the payee's order. The payment may be scheduled for a fixed time, for determinable future time, or on demand of the payee, under specific terms. Unlike a loan agreement, a promissory note need only be signed by the payor. The terms of a note usually include the principal amount, the interest rate, the parties, the date, the terms of repayment (which usually includes interest), and the maturity date. Sometimes, provisions are included concerning the payee's rights in the event of a default, which may include foreclosure of the maker's assets, although these provisions are most often found in an accompanying loan or security agreement.

While a friend or relative may be willing to lend money on a handshake, it is always a better business practice to put the terms of the loan in writing and to delineate a specific interest rate and repayment plan. Borrowing money without a written agreement often leads to unrealistic expectations and misunderstandings between the parties. Furthermore, a written and signed a promissory note is often instrumental for tax and record keeping purposes.

While the obligation is outstanding, a photocopy of the signed note, marked "COPY" should be kept for the business's records, as the original will be in the possession of the payee or its assignee. The issuer of a promissory note is entitled to get the note back when the note is paid off, and the note should be marked "paid in full" and signed by the payee to evidence satisfaction of the obligation. Avoid having several signed copies floating around that can cast doubt on whether the debt has been paid.

C. COMMERCIAL LOAN AGREEMENTS

When a small business approaches a commercial bank to borrow money, the loan officer will want to know how the borrower intends to use the money loaned. If it is a new business, a business plan and financial statements may be required. The financial statements include the company's balance sheet, income statement, and statement of cash flow. In addition, if the business is a limited liability entity, the financial institution will also request a copy of the business's organizational documents and authorization from the directors, members, or partners to enter into the loan agreement. The bank will often ask the principals of the business for personal guarantees, requiring them to repay the loan in the event that the business is unable to make the periodic payments of principal and interest. Moreover, the guarantors (also known as the co-signers) provide the lender with reassurance that they will repay the money if the borrower defaults.

A bank will require the business to enter into a loan agreement. This agreement sets out the terms and conditions of the loan. The loan agreement is more detailed than a promissory note, which is a mere instrument. The primary difference is that a loan agreement is longer, more explicit, and contains, optimally, all the agreements (covenants), representations, warranties, and other terms of both parties to the transaction. The tenure of the loan, the rate of interest to be paid, covenants, fees, and the guarantees on the loan are also specified in this agreement. If all the vital components are listed, there is little possibility for ambiguity or misunderstanding. In addition, to further assure loan repayment, the lender may require the borrower to take out a life insurance policy on the owners of the business and grant the lender a security interest in the policy and its proceeds.

D. SECURITY AGREEMENTS

The lender will often seek further assurances from the borrower that the loan will be repaid in full. For that, the lender asks the borrower to provide collateral from its assets and the guarantees of some individuals. In the event of default, the lender has the right to sell or acquire the collateral pledged and apply the proceeds to the outstanding balance of the loan. If guaranties are issued, and the principal borrower (aka "debtor") does not make the required payment, the lender can seek repayment from the guarantors.

Although a security agreement may be oral if the secured party (the lender) has actual physical possession of the collateral, the prudent thing to do is to have the agreement reduced to an integrated writing, signed by the borrower. In many cases, the security agreement must be in writing in order to satisfy the statute of frauds, which is the legal requirement that certain types of contracts must be memorialized in a signed writing with reasonable specificity to be enforceable. The security agreement must be authenticated by the debtor, meaning that it must either bear the debtor's signature or be electronically marked. It must contain a reasonable description of the collateral, and it must use words showing intent to create a security interest (the right of the lender to seek repayment of the loan by foreclosing on the collateral).

When the security agreement is executed by the borrower and the borrower acquires the collateral (if they do not already own it), the security interest is said to "attach" to the collateral. In such a case, the agreement is good as between the borrower and the lender; however, it may not give the lender rights in the collateral that are superior to third parties that, for instance, might get a judgment and levy on the collateral. For a security interest in the collateral to be good against the world and to continue to be enforceable (foreclosable) when the collateral has been transferred to subsequent purchasers or assignees, it must be perfected. This means, generally, it must be filed with the appropriate government office or possessed by the lender, both situations that would put a subsequent lender or creditor on constructive notice of the prior creditor's security interest. By perfecting its security interest, a secured party seeks to gain priority over other parties regarding the collateral. If the transaction is a "purchase money security interest" (where the borrower uses the lenders money to make the purchase, the resulting security agreement automatically perfects the security interest in the goods. Otherwise, the lender must record either the agreement itself, or a UCC–1 financing statement, in an appropriate public venue (usually the state secretary of state, a state business commission under that businesses authority) or, in some cases, take possession of the collateral under a control agreement. Perfecting the interest creates constructive notice, which is deemed legally sufficient to inform the rest of the world of the lender's rights in the collateral. It makes the lender's interest in the collateral superior to any later claimant, like a judgment creditor levying on the borrower's property. Where a borrower has used the same property as collateral with respect to multiple security agreements made with different lenders, the first lender to record or otherwise gain first priority has the strongest claim to that property. When foreclosing, the party with priority will be entitled to all the proceeds up to the point at which its debt has been repaid, after which the proceeds will be payable to the secured party that is next in priority or, if there is no other secured party, to the borrower.

Foreclosure can occur through either a public or private sale, or the secured party may enforce his rights through a strict foreclosure—the seizure of the collateral in satisfaction of the debt—and so acquire the debtor's interest in the collateral without a sale. U.C.C. § 9–620, cmt. 2. A strict foreclosure requires the secured party to send its proposal to the debtor, any other secured creditors with perfected security interests in the collateral, and any guarantors of the security interest. U.C.C. § 9–621(a)–(b). Prior to the Article 9 revisions in 2001, a secured party could accept the collateral only in full satisfaction of the obligation; however, under Revised Article 9, the secured party may accept the collateral as either full or partial satisfaction of the obligation it secures.

Acceptance of collateral by the secured party in either full or partial satisfaction of the debtor's obligation:

- discharges the obligation to the extent consented to by the debtor;

- transfers to the secured party all of the debtor's rights in the collateral;

- discharges the security interest and any subordinate security interest; and

- terminates any other subordinate interest.

U.C.C. § 9–622(a).

Subordinate interests are discharged even if the secured party does not comply with the requirements of Article 9. U.C.C. § 9–622(b). However, the debtor, guarantors, and any other secured parties retain the right to redeem the collateral by satisfying the obligations secured by the collateral and paying any reasonable expenses (including attorneys' fees) incurred by the secured party. U.C.C. § 9–623(a)–(b).

A debtor may either consent to strict foreclosure or object to force a sale. U.C.C. § 9–620(a). Additionally, all parties entitled to receive a proposal under U.C.C. § 9–621 have the opportunity to object. If the secured party receives any objection, he must dispose of the collateral— either by sale, lease, license, or otherwise—though public or private proceedings. U.C.C. § 9–610(a). Under Revised Article 9, every aspect of the disposition including the price and method of sale must be commercially reasonable. U.C.C. § 9–615, cmt. 6. If the secured party foreclosing on the collateral is also the transferee receiving the collateral, he may lack the incentive to maximize the sale price. In such cases, if the sale price is significantly below what would have been realized if the interested party had not been involved in the transaction, U.C.C. § 9–615(f) provides for calculating the deficiency, which will then be credited to the debtor.

The purchaser at sale is entitled to a transfer statement, authenticated by the secured party, stating:

- that the debtor has defaulted in connection with an obligation secured by the collateral purchased;

- that the secured party has exercised his post-default remedies;

- that, by reason of the exercise, the transferee has acquired rights of the debtor in the collateral; and

- the name and mailing address of the secured party, the debtor, and the transferee.

U.C.C. § 9–619(a).

A transfer statement entitles the transferee to records of all the debtor's rights in the collateral, as well as any official filing, recording, registration, or certificate of title system covering the collateral. U.C.C. § 9–619(b).

E. PRIVATE EQUITY INVESTMENT

Debt is not generally well suited for very high-risk investments in start-up companies. Since the business must usually repay a portion of the loan's principal and interest each month regardless of whether its operations have begun to generate revenue, the business will have to use a portion of the loan proceeds to pay back the loan until its revenues are sufficient to make payments on the loan from operating cash flows. Furthermore, the interest rate charged must be high enough to compensate the bank for the amount of risk that it is incurring in making the loan. Because raising funds through debt presents the dual problem associated with lack of immediate cash flow from revenues and the lender's limitation on balancing high risk with a reasonable prospect of a suitable return, entrepreneurs are often faced with issuing equity as the only source of capital.

While equity can be issued in the form of stock or membership interests to friends and family to obtain the necessary funds for the new business, it is more likely that the entrepreneur it will have to rely on the private equity market. Private equity is an asset class consisting of debt or equity securities in businesses that are not publicly traded on a stock exchange. A private equity investment will generally be made by an angel investor, venture capital firm, or a private equity firm. Each of these categories of investors have their own set of goals, preferences, and investment strategies; each providing working capital to a business to nurture expansion, new product development, or restructuring of the company's operations, management, or ownership.

1. ANGEL INVESTORS

An angel investor[1] is an affluent individual who provides capital for a business start-up, usually in exchange for debt that is convertible into equity or just ownership equity. Angel investors are often retired entrepreneurs or executives who may be interested in angel investing for reasons that go beyond pure monetary return. These reasons may include wanting to keep abreast of current developments in a particular business arena, mentoring another generation of entrepreneurs, and making use of their experience and networks on a less than full-time basis. Thus, in addition to funds, angel investors can often provide valuable management advice and important contacts. Because there are no public exchanges listing their securities, private companies meet angel investors in several ways, including referrals from the investors' trusted sources and other business contacts; at investor conferences and symposia; and at meetings organized by groups of angels where companies pitch directly to investors in face-to-face meetings. There is no set investment amount for angel investors, and the range can go anywhere from a few thousand to a few million dollars. Because a large percentage of angel investments are lost completely when early stage companies fail, professional angel investors seek investments that have the potential to return at least 10 or more times their original investment within five years, through a defined exit or harvest strategy, such as plans for an initial public offering or an acquisition. Angel capital fills the gap in start-up financing between friends and family, who provide early seed funding, and venture capital.

2. VENTURE CAPITAL

Venture capital (the "VC") is financial capital provided to early-stage, high-potential, high risk, growth startup companies. The venture capital

---

[1]   The term "angel" originally came from Broadway where it was used to describe wealthy individuals who provided money for theatrical productions.

fund makes money by owning equity in the companies it invests in, which usually have a novel technology or business model in high-technology industries. Generally, venture capitalists can be viewed as financial intermediaries, meaning they first must convince wealthy individuals, pension funds, corporations, and foundations to trust the venture capitalists with their money, which the venture capitalists will use to make equity investments in privately held companies. Obtaining investments is a difficult task, requiring venture capitalists to prove that they have the experience and track record of making equity investments in companies, monitoring and assisting in their growth, and exiting those investments in such a way as to make substantial profits for themselves and the investors.

Venture capital firms are typically structured as limited partnerships where the general partners serve as the managers of the firm and will serve as investment advisors for the venture capital funds raised. Investors in venture capital funds are limited partners and are generally either wealthy individuals or institutions with large amounts of available capital. Common examples are state and private pension funds, university financial endowments, foundations, insurance companies, and pooled investment vehicles. Venture capitalists are compensated through a combination of management fees and carried interest (often referred to as a "two and twenty" arrangement). Management fees are annual payments made by the investors in the fund to the fund's manager to pay for the limited partnership's investment operations. In a typical venture capital fund, the general partners receive an annual management fee equal to up to two percent of the committed capital. Carried interest is the share of the profits of the fund (typically 20%), paid to the limited partnership fund's general partners as a performance incentive. The remaining eighty percent of the profits are paid to the fund's limited partners.

Venture capital is attractive for new companies with limited operating history that are too small to raise capital in the public markets and have not reached the point where they are able to secure a bank loan or complete a debt offering. In exchange for the high risk that venture capitalists assume by investing in smaller and less mature companies, venture capitalists usually get significant control over company decisions, in addition to a significant portion of the company's ownership (and consequently value).

Venture capital is invested in exchange for an equity stake in the business. As a shareholder, the venture capitalist's return is dependent on the growth and profitability of the business. This return is generally earned when the venture capitalist exits by selling its shares when the business is sold to another owner. Venture capitalists are typically very selective in deciding what to invest in and are most interested in ventures with exceptionally high growth potential. These opportunities are likely capable of providing the financial returns and successful exit event within the required timeframe (typically three to seven years), which venture capitalists expect.

Because venture capital investments are illiquid (there is no public market for them) and require the extended timeframe to grow and prosper, venture capitalists will carry out detailed due diligence (investigation and analysis of the business) prior to investment. The venture capitalist's due diligence will require the business to provide the following type of information:

- Name, address, phone, and e-mail address for the business's executives, directors, attorneys, and accountants;

- Minute book, including articles of organization/articles of incorporation, bylaws/operating agreement, minutes, resolutions, actions taken upon written consent, and stock/membership transfers;

- Certificates of good standing (corporate and tax) for all jurisdictions where the company has assets, operations, or conducts business;

- Names and addresses of shareholders/members and number of shares/membership interests outstanding, along with annual securities and other state and federal regulatory reports;

- Financial statements (preferably audited), tax returns, and quarterly budgets and management reports for the previous three years;

- Schedule of all insurance policies and pending claims;

- Agreements and documents related to secured and unsecured borrowing;

- Schedule of all inventory and its value based upon the company's accounting method valuation policy;

- List of senior executives and management, including their compensation, perquisites, fringe benefits, deferred compensation, options, and severance pay arrangements;

- Description of all pending or threatened litigation, judgments, settlement agreements, administrative proceedings, and government investigations;

- List of the company's customers, purchase orders, and management projections for future revenue and expenses, including assumptions used;

- Agreements with all suppliers, distributors, and joint ventures;

- List of all competitors and market share;

- Description of all intellectual property owned or used by the company along with related patents, copyrights, trademarks, trade secrets, and licenses;

- List of all real property owned by the company and copies of all agreements for leased real property.

Venture capitalists also are expected to nurture the companies in which they invest by providing advice and contacts, which help increase the likelihood of reaching an Initial Public Offering ("IPO") or sale stage when valuations are favorable. Like meeting angel investors, private companies meet venture capital firms and other private equity investors in several ways, including referrals from the investors' trusted sources and other business contacts; investor conferences and symposia; and summits where companies pitch directly to investor groups in face-to-face meetings. In addition, there are some new private online networks that are emerging to provide additional opportunities to meet investors.

The need for high returns makes venture funding an expensive capital source for companies and most suitable for businesses having large up-front capital requirements that cannot be financed by cheaper alternatives such as debt. This situation is most commonly the case for businesses involving development of intangible assets such as pharmaceuticals, software, and other intellectual property whose value is unproven. In turn, this explains why venture capital is most prevalent in fast-growing technology and life sciences or biotechnology fields. If a company has the qualities venture capitalists seek, including a solid business plan, a good management team, investment, passion from the founders, a good potential to exit the investment before the end of their funding cycle, and target minimum returns in excess of forty percent per year, entrepreneurs will find it easier to raise venture capital.

3. PRIVATE EQUITY FIRMS

Private equity firms typically make minority investments in relatively mature companies that are looking for capital to expand, restructure operations, enter new markets, or finance a major acquisition without a change of control of the business. This form of financing is often referred to as "mezzanine round financing." Such financing is either a subordinated debt or preferred equity instrument that represents a claim on a company's assets, which is senior only to that of the common shares. Mezzanine financings can be structured either as debt (usually an unsecured and subordinated note) or preferred stock. Companies that seek growth capital will often do so in order to finance a transformational event in their life cycle. These companies are likely to be more mature than venture capital funded companies, able to generate revenue and operating profits but unable to generate sufficient cash to fund major expansions, acquisitions, or other investments. Because of this lack of scale, these companies generally can find few alternative sources to secure capital for growth. So, access to growth equity can be critical to pursue necessary facility expansion, sales and marketing initiatives, equipment purchases, and new product development. The primary owner of the company may not be willing to take the financial risk alone. By selling part of the company to private equity, the owner can take out some value and share the risk of growth with partners. Capital can also be used to effect a restructuring of a company's balance sheet, particularly to reduce the amount of debt the company has on its balance sheet.

While private equity investors are willing to incur investment risk when providing capital to promising companies, they try to mitigate such risk as much as possible. For example, it is typical for such investors to take preferred stock that is convertible into common stock at their option in return for their investment, rather than taking straight common stock. Such preferred stock will generally carry a dividend and have priority over common stock in the payment of dividends and upon liquidation. The convertibility feature of the preferred stock allows its owner to convert the preferred stock into common stock so that the investor can participate in the appreciation of the common shares should the business perform well and go public or otherwise engage in a change in control transaction. Another possible alternative is a hybrid debt and equity security, which in essence is a loan whose outstanding balance can be converted into common stock at the investor's discretion. Finally, an additional transactional option for private equity is to structure the investment as debt with a warrant[2] or other attached equity instrument that allows the debt to be repaid while allowing the investor to have a continuing right to receive equity in the company.

4.   CROWD FUNDING

While there are numerous definitions for the word "crowdfunding," crowdfunding allows businesses and other organizations to raise money, through either donations or investments from the public, using the internet as a medium. Crowdfunding emerged as a new form of capital formation following the 2008 financial crisis, which increased the financial difficulties faced by startup businesses. Having since gained widespread popularity (largely due to the creation of crowdfunding mediums, such as Kickstarter and GoFundMe), crowdfunding has emerged as a popular alternative to more traditional capital raising methods like going public or taking out a loan with a financial institution. There are five models of crowdfunding: Donation-based crowdfunding; Rewards-based crowdfunding; Royalty-

---

[2]   A warrant is a right to buy a stated number of shares of stock at a defined price.

based crowdfunding; Debt-based crowdfunding; and Equity-based crowdfunding.

In donation-based crowdfunding, backers donate varying amounts of money to an initiative and typically receive nothing is return for their contribution. Donation-based crowdfunding is most often used for social causes, charities, and political campaigns rather than for startup businesses. Rewards-based crowdfunding, also called "perks-based," allows the backer to receive a token gift of appreciate or a pre-purchase of the company's service or product in exchange for funding. One of the biggest benefits of the rewards-based crowdfunding model is that, by acting as a pre-sale, the startup does not have to repay the money and therefore does not begin operations in the red. Though less common than the other crowdfunding models, royalty-based crowdfunding gives backers a share in a unit trust that will acquire a royalty interest in the intellectual property of the company. Over time a percentage of revenue is paid out to the funder from this interest. Debt-Based crowdfunding, also known as lending-based crowdfunding, gives backers a debt instrument that will pay out with a fixed rate of interest in exchange for funding. Debt-based crowdfunding may be more appealing to backers for two reasons. First, debt-based crowdfunding allows backers to receive a profit on the investment in the form of interest. Second, debt-based crowdfunding places the backer in a senior position to equity lenders, which gives some security to the lenders if the startup goes belly up. Finally, equity-based crowdfunding exchanges equity instruments for capital. Equity-based crowdfunding allows a backer to receive a share in the profitability of the venture, which has unlimited potential for financial gain.

5. DETERMINING VALUATION

Before investing in a start-up, potential investors will want to determine the new venture's valuation. Valuation is the price that a reasonable person would pay to own the future cash flows of a business less any debt owed plus all cash on hand. Valuation of a pre-revenue company is often one of the first points of contention that must be negotiated between an investor and entrepreneur. Entrepreneurs want the value to be as high as possible and potential investors want a value low enough so that they own a reasonable portion of the company for the amount they invest.

Valuing a startup is intrinsically different from valuing established companies. Without profits or assets to use as determining variables, the valuation methods of small startup businesses greatly differ from those used to determine the value of large ongoing businesses. Because of the high level of risk and often little or no revenues, traditional quantitative valuation metrics like comparing Price/Earnings, EBITDA (Earnings Before Interest, Taxes, Depreciation and Amortization) or discounting free cash flows with those of its peers are of little use. Startup valuations are largely determined based on qualitative attributes.

Popular methods for the valuation of small startups include: the Venture Capital Method; the Berkus Method; the Risk Factor Summation Method; and the Scorecard Valuation Method. The venture capital method breaks the valuation of a startup into the following equation: Return on Investment = Terminal (or Harvest) Value / Post-Money Valuation. The terminal or harvest value is the estimated selling value of the company at some point in the future. Selling value may be determined by estimating a reasonable expected revenue for the company in the sale year. The venture capital method calculates post-money valuation by accounting for the time and risk the backer takes. Using the expected rates of return upon exit from the market, the backer may then estimate the current valuation with the following equation: Pre-Money Valuation=Post-Money Valuation-Investment.

The next valuation method for startups is the Berkus method. Created in the mid-1990s, the Berkus method identifies four major elements of risk faced by young companies and assigns a financial valuation to each of these elements in addition to some basic value for the quality of the idea. Though the Berkus method initially restricted maximum value of $500,000 for each element, this maximum value is suggestive. The maximum value for each element should be reflective of the nature of the industry that the startup will enter. Similar to the Berkus method, the risk factor summation method compares twelve characteristics of a startup to what is expected in a fundable startup business. Each risk factor is assessed on a +2 to −2 scale[3] and is given a valuation based on this assessment. Each corresponding valuation is then added to or subtracted from the average pre-money valuation of companies in the region to determine the startup's overall valuation.

The Scorecard Valuation Method is based upon a good understanding of the average (and range) of pre-money valuation of pre-revenue companies in a region. With this data in hand, the Scorecard Method gives investors subjective techniques to adjust the valuation of a target company for seed and startup rounds of investment. Savvy entrepreneurs can use these tools to prepare for negotiations of valuation with investors.

Entrepreneurs should recognize that valuation is a function of a variety of different factors, none of which will apply equally when evaluating any two companies. Some of the factors that influence valuations include:

---

[3]   +2: very positive for growing the company and executing a wonderful exit; +1: positive; 0: neutral; −1: negative for growing the company and executing a wonderful exit; −2: very negative. *See* Bill Payne, *Valuation 101: The Risk Factor Summation Method*, Investing for Beginners (Nov. 15, 2011) http://blog.gust.com/valuations-101-the-risk-factor-summation-method/.

- Determine Amount of Required Capital—Consider the current burn rate (amount of money that the company is currently spending), and the time it will take to achieve revenues. Consider how much money will be required for 18 months operations before there is a need to raise additional capital. Clearly identify, how the money will be used with realistic estimates.

- Market Conditions—Valuations are nothing more than opinions and agreements, they always come down to what the market is willing to pay. Timing is important, start-up valuations tend to be higher when overall economic conditions are good.

- Realistic Projections—Valuations are merely estimates based upon financial projections and growth rates. Growth rate projections should not be unreasonable within the context of the economic conditions of the market that in which you are competing.

- Valuations as Operating Metrics—Startup valuations are not only useful when it comes to fundraising. If calculated in a reliable way, a valuation can turn into a metric to use when tracking the company's progress and growth.

- Present a Valuation Range—A good valuation is not the one that calculates the perfect number, it is one that shapes the discussion in an open and constructive manner. Determine a range of outcomes and present the range instead of a fixed number. This will send a signal to investors that you are knowledgeable about the value of your startup but also open to negotiate.

- Team Strength—Investors commonly value startups based on the strength of their entrepreneurial team and value previous entrepreneurial experience. Investors tend to highly value previous entrepreneurial experience. If the founder, advisors or team members have strong expertise in the field, make sure to capture it in the valuation.

- Consider All the Terms of the Deal—Investors often include liquidation preferences in their investment contracts. Such preferences often give the investors the right to be paid ahead of other parties and may transfer ownership of the company's intellectual property to the investors upon dissolution of the company.

- Calculating the Company's Fair Value—In essence, every funding round in is a partnership with the investors. The investors will be around until the company either succeeds or fails. The start-up valuation and the investment process should result in a win-win deal which will establish a productive working relationship going forward.

6. TERM SHEETS

A term sheet is used to set forth the basic terms and conditions for a business deal. This document is primarily used to serve as a letter of intent, which specifically outlines the intentions and terms agreed upon between the parties to the deal. A main function of a term sheet is to summarize and define the financial and legal terms pertaining to the transaction. A well-executed term sheet can help to eliminate misunderstanding and confusion among the parties. A second important function of a term sheet is to quantify the value of the transaction, both in qualified terms and numbers. When both functions are executed properly, a term sheet can serve as the basis on which to draft additional legal documents for the remainder of the business deal.

Term sheets are used in a number of situations in the business world. Most often, term sheets are used by investors as they consider financing an entrepreneur's business idea. However, term sheets can be used in almost any financing situation or business deal. Term sheets are valuable to the entrepreneur because they narrow the parties' focus to the essence of the business deal. This helps to save costs on legal fees, while also speeding up the process of closing the deal.

Typically, the investor or funding firm considering investing in the deal will produce the first draft of a term sheet. Once the term sheet has been drafted and published, it becomes a written expression of the investor's interest in investing and an outline of the terms by which they wish to abide. While a term sheet is not a legally binding document, both parties to the business deal have an obligation to negotiate in good faith. Therefore, the term sheet is a reflection of an agreement between two parties, in good faith, to proceed with financing according to the terms and conditions set forth.

A term sheet is not a "one size fits all" document. Therefore, entrepreneurs should seek the advice of an attorney to ensure that the proposed term sheet fits the desires and needs of the entrepreneur before moving forward with the deal. Entrepreneurs should also work with several investors to receive multiple options as they consider which avenue to pursue.

It is of the utmost importance for an entrepreneur to consult with an experienced attorney before agreeing to a term sheet. In addition to having the term sheet examined by an attorney, an entrepreneur should also examine the term sheet for themselves to determine whether the terms align with the interests of her business.

When examining a term sheet, an entrepreneur or attorney should pay special attention to the following sections: price per share, corporate governance, options, and valuation. A close inspection of these key sections will help to ensure that there are no unavoidable mistakes or unfavorable terms within the term sheet. Entrepreneurs and attorneys should also be able to recognize whether a term is favorable to the entrepreneur or the investor.

Generally speaking, term sheets are not legally binding. However, depending on the language contained within the document, a term sheet may be enforceable. If the term sheet contains language stating that the document is non-binding, then the determination of enforceability is quite clear. However, if the term sheet fails to explicitly state that the document is non-binding and begins by stating, "The parties agree as follows," one might argue that the parties intended to be bound by the terms based on the introductory language.

On occasion, a term sheet may include certain provisions that allow for a portion of the terms to be binding and other provisions to be non-binding. For example, many term sheets include binding provisions regarding confidentiality, exclusivity, and the like. These binding provisions are explicitly stated, while the other provisions of the term sheet are left as non-binding terms.

If a business deal goes south, parties may consider terminating the term sheet. Termination refers to the process of removing a party from obligations under the provisions of the document. If the term sheet is non-binding, the parties should have no concerns regarding termination. For example, a non-binding term sheet might include a provision stating, "Either party may terminate this agreement by a simple notice including email before the signing of the definitive agreements. No party is required to give the reasons for the same." On the other hand, if the term sheet is binding, the non-breaching party may seek enforceability. Often the following duties explicitly remain effective and in force despite termination: confidentiality, return of proprietary information, non-compete provisions, and exclusivity.

When reviewing and preparing to sign a term sheet, an entrepreneur should consult with an experienced attorney regarding binding and non-binding language before signing the document. An attorney should review this language with a focus towards eliminating any sense of ambiguity in the document regarding its enforceability.

F. WHAT IS A SECURITY?

For businesspersons who are seeking to sell securities, it is important that both the businessperson and their attorneys understand that every sale of securities, no matter how large or how small, is subject to the registration or exemption requirement. It is critical for attorneys to recognize the security implications of any transaction, as failure to do so can subject the client to financial damages and the attorney to a malpractice claim. When such transactions are beyond an attorney's core competencies, that attorney should associate a firm that has the requisite experience in the field. Legislation is routinely passed which effects changes to the securities laws and also results in new rules and regulations. Unless an attorney specializes in this area, it is difficult to stay abreast of these developments. Nonetheless, generalist attorneys should be able to advise entrepreneurs the general process, costs, and complexities of a securities offering or finding an applicable exemption so as to avoid the need to engage in that process.

There are two primary sets of federal laws that come into play when a company wants to offer and sell its securities to the public. They are the:

- Securities Act of 1933 (the "Securities Act"), and

- Securities Exchange Act of 1934 (the "Exchange Act").

The Securities Act, often referred to as the "truth in securities" law, generally requires companies to give investors full disclosure of all material facts—the facts investors would find important in making an investment decision. The Securities Act also requires companies to file a registration statement with the SEC that includes information for investors. This information enables investors to make informed judgments about whether to purchase a company's securities. While the SEC requires that the information provided be accurate, it does not guarantee it, nor does the SEC evaluate the merits of offerings or determine if the securities offered are good investments. The SEC staff reviews registration statements and declares them effective if companies satisfy their disclosure rules. Investors who purchase securities and suffer losses have important recovery rights if they can prove that there was incomplete or inaccurate disclosure of important information.

The Exchange Act requires publicly held companies to disclose information regularly through quarterly and annual statements about their business operations, financial conditions, and managements. These companies, and in many cases their officers, directors, and significant shareholders, must file periodic reports or other disclosure documents with the SEC. In some cases, the company must deliver the information directly to investors. The Exchange Act empowers the SEC with broad authority over all aspects of the securities industry. This power includes the power to register, regulate, and oversee brokerage firms, transfer agents, and clearing agencies as well as the nation's securities self regulatory organizations (an "SRO"). The various stock exchanges, such as the New York Stock Exchange and American Stock Exchange, are SROs. The National Association of Securities Dealers, which operates the NASDAQ system, is also an SRO. The Exchange Act identifies and prohibits certain types of conduct in the markets and provides the SEC with disciplinary powers over regulated entities and persons associated with them. The Act also empowers the SEC to require periodic reporting of information by companies with publicly traded securities.

The official definition of security, from the Securities Act of 1933 and the Securities Exchange Act of 1934, is:

> Any note, stock, treasury stock, bond, debenture, certificate of interest or participation in any profit-sharing agreement or in any oil, gas, or other mineral royalty or lease, any collateral trust certificate, preorganization certificate or subscription, transferable share, investment contract, voting-trust certificate, certificate of deposit, for a security, any put, call, straddle, option, or privilege on any security, certificate of deposit, or group or index of securities (including any interest therein or based on the value thereof), or any put, call, straddle, option, or privilege entered into on a national securities exchange relating to foreign currency, or in general, any instrument commonly known as a 'security'; or any certificate of interest or participation in, temporary or interim certificate for, receipt for, or warrant or right to subscribe to or purchase, any of the foregoing; but shall not include currency or any note, draft, bill of exchange, or banker's acceptance which has a maturity at the time of issuance of not exceeding nine months, exclusive of days of grace, or any renewal thereof the maturity of which is likewise limited.

Securities Act § 2(1); Exchange Act § 3(a)(10).

Despite what appears to be a comprehensive definitional list, courts must often determine what unconventional investments fall within the definitional framework and also what investments that appear to fall within the framework are actually not securities. For example, while publicly traded stocks and bonds would clearly fall within this definitional framework of a security, courts have found that unconventional investments such as a row of citrus trees that are cultivated, harvested, and marketed by an affiliate of a promoter, fall under the definition of security. *See* SEC v. W.J. Howey Co., 328 U.S. 293 (1946).

The determination of whether a given financial transaction is brought under the oversight of the securities laws often turns on whether it is deemed by the courts as an investment contract. The Supreme Court has provided guidance to this issue in *SEC v. W.J. Howey Co.*, where it developed a test to determine whether a particular financial transaction is an "investment contract."[4] An investment contract under the *Howey* Test means a contract, transaction, or scheme whereby a person invests money or other tangible consideration in a common enterprise and the investor is reasonably led to expect profits solely from the efforts of the promoter or third party—essentially a passive investment. If this test is satisfied, it is immaterial whether the shares in the enterprise are evidenced by formal certificates or nominal interests in physical assets employed by the enterprise.

The term "investment contract" is undefined by the Securities Act or by relevant legislative reports. But, the term was common in many state "Blue Sky Laws"[5] in existence prior to the adoption of the federal statute. Although the term was also undefined by the state laws, it had been broadly construed by state courts so as to afford the investing public a full measure of protection. In determining whether the transaction involved is a security, the *Howey* Court held that form should be disregarded for substance and emphasized that the economic realities of the transaction were paramount. An investment contract thus came to mean a contract or scheme for "the placing of capital or laying out of money in a way intended to secure income or profit from its employment." See State v. Gopher Tire & Rubber Co., 177 N.W. 937, 938. (Minn. 1920). This definition was uniformly applied by state courts to a variety of situations where individuals were led to invest money in a common enterprise with the expectation that they would earn a profit solely through the efforts of the promoter or of someone other than themselves.[6]

The most significant modification of the *Howey* test first appeared in *SEC v. Glenn W. Turner Enterprises, Inc.*, 474 F.2d 476 (9th Cir.), *cert denied*, 414 U.S. 821 (1973). In that case, the court analyzed a transaction which, but for the minimal effort required of the investors for them to receive a profit, otherwise would have met the *Howey* test. Recognizing that Congress intended that a flexible approach be employed, the court

---

[4]   Some state courts have used a risk capital test to identify when the states securities laws apply to investment transactions. *See, e.g.,* Silver Hills Country Club v. Sobieski, 361 P.2d 906 (Cal. 1961); State ex rel Healy v. Consumer Business Systems, Inc., 482 P.2d 549 (Or. Ct. App. 1977); State v. George, 362 N.E.2d 1223 (Ohio Ct. App. 1975). This test is viewed as being easier to satisfy in that it does not require commonality nor that profits be derived from the efforts of others. For example, in *Silver Hills Country Club v. Sobieski*, memberships in recreational clubs were found to be securities when the memberships were used to finance the club facilities.

[5]   Blue Sky Laws are so named because they were intended to prevent unscrupulous parties from selling investments that were nothing but interests in the clear blue sky. *See,* Hall v. Geiger-Jones Co., 242 U.S. 539 (1917).

[6]   *See,* State v. Evans, 191 N.W. 425 (Minn. 1922); Klatt v. Guaranteed Bond Co., 250 N.W. 825 (Wis. 1933); State v. Health, 153 S.E. 855 (N.C. 1930); Prohaska v. Hemmer-Miller Development Co., 256 Ill. App. 331 (1930); People v. White, 12 P.2d 1078 (Cal. Ct. App. 1932); Stevens v. Liberty Packing Corp., 161 A.193 (N.J. Ch. 1932). *See also* Moore v. Stella, 127 P.2d 300 (Cal. Ct. App. 1942).

held that an investment contract existed when "the efforts made by those other than the investor are the undeniably significant ones, those essential managerial efforts which affect the failure or success of the enterprises." *Id.* at 482. This modification, which effectively eliminated the word "solely" from the *Howey* test, is generally applied in all jurisdictions today, including by the Supreme Court itself in *United Housing Foundation v. Forman,* 421 U.S. 837 (1975); *but see* King v. Pope, 91 S.W.3d 314 (Tenn. 2002).

Whether a particular ownership interest in a business entity is a security depends to a large extent on the legal form of the organization. However, organizational form under state law is not always an accurate reflection of the economic realities surrounding the parties' relationship. For example, although the term "limited partnership interest" does not appear in the definition of a security under the federal securities statutes, courts have generally held that the sales of limited partnership interests are "investment contract" securities. *See, e.g.,* Reeves v. Teuscher, 881 F.2d 1495 (9th Cir. 1989); *In re* Longhorn Securities Litigation, 573 F. Supp. 255 (W.D. Okla. 1983).

Not all limited partnership interests are securities. Under the Uniform Limited Partnership Act, a limited partner (unlike the interest of the general partner) can have no significant input into the management and control of the limited partnership. So the key element in the analysis of a limited partnership interest is whether the limited partner exhibits any management and control in the entity. That is why courts have held limited partnership interests are not securities when the limited partner has control over the management of the partnership. *See* Steinhardt Group v. Citicorp, 126 F.3d 144 (3rd Cir. 1997) (limited partner's interest are not securities if the limited partner exercises pervasive control over the partnership). This is especially true when the limited partnership interest is owned by a general partner, a director of a general partner, or a parent corporation of a corporate general partner. *See, e.g.,* Bamco v. Reeves, 675 F.Supp. 826 (S.D.N.Y. 1987); Bank of America National Trust & Savings Association v. Hotel Rittenhouse Associates, 595 F.Supp. 800 (E.D. Pa. 1984).

By applying this same analysis to a general partnership interest one would conclude that because a general partner has the right to participate in the management of the partnership, that the partnership interest would not be a security. *See* Odom v. Slavik, 703 F.2d 212 (6th Cir. 1983) (since general partners have the right to participate in the management of the partnership, there is a strong presumption that a general partnership interest is not a security). But some general partnership interests can be securities. The test for determining whether or not a general partnership interest is a security was first set out in *Williamson v. Tucker,* 645 F.2d 404 (5th Cir.), *cert denied,* 454 US 897 (1981). Under this test, a general partnership interest is not a security unless the investor can establish one of the following:

- an agreement among the parties leaves so little power in the hands of the partner or venturer that the arrangement in fact distributes power as would a limited partnership;

- the partner or venturer is so inexperienced and unknowledgeable in business affairs that he is incapable of intelligently exercising his partnership or venture powers; or

- the partner or venturer is so dependent on some unique entrepreneurial or managerial ability of the promoter or manager that he cannot replace the manager of the enterprise or otherwise exercise meaningful partnership or venture powers.

The *Williamson* test has also been applied to limited liability partnerships in order to determine whether the limited liability partnership interest is an investment contract security. Since under state law the limited liability partnership has all of the attributes of the general partnership, with the additional benefit of limited liability of all the partners, it should not be surprising that the application of the test in this context should produce similar results. *See* SEC v. Lowery, 633 F. Supp. 2d 466 (W.D. Mich. 2009); SEC v. Merchant Capital, LLC, 483 F.3d 747 (11th Cir. 2007).

Membership interests in limited liability companies are also not included in the definition of securities under the federal securities laws, although some states have amended their statutory definition of security to include such membership interests.[7] Courts generally apply the *Williamson* test to determine whether a membership interest in a limited liability company is an investment contract security. Much like the case with a general partnership, investors in a limited liability company must demonstrate that, despite the organizational form that the investment took, they were unable to exercise meaningful management and control of the entity. This application has led to the generalization that most

---

[7]   *See e.g.,* Section 421–B:2, XX-a of the New Hampshire statutes. The definition of a security in Kansas states that an investment contract may include an interest in a limited liability company. KAN STAT § 17–12a703(28)(E). In California, Section 25019 of the California securities statute provides: Security means any note; stock; treasury stock; membership in an incorporated or unincorporated association; bond; debenture; evidence of indebtedness; certificate of interest or participation in any profit-sharing agreement; collateral trust certificate; preorganization certificate or subscription; transferable share; investment contract; viatical settlement contract or a fractionalized or pooled interest therein; life settlement contract or a fractionalized or pooled interest therein; voting trust certificate; certificate of deposit for a security; interest in a limited liability company and any class or series of those interests (including any fractional or other interest in that interest), except a membership interest in a limited liability company in which the person claiming this exception can prove that all of the members are actively engaged in the management of the limited liability company; provided that evidence that members vote or have the right to vote, or the right to information concerning the business and affairs of the limited liability company, or the right to participate in management, shall not establish, without more, that all members are actively engaged in the management of the limited liability company; . . . .

manager-managed LLCs are securities, while most member-managed LLCs are not securities. Because members of a manager-managed LLC are not relying on their own management, but rather the management of the manager, they are more likely to be passive investors, and as such, are more likely to need the protection of the federal securities laws. In contrast, members of a member-managed LLC are more likely to actively participate in the management of the entity and are less likely to need such protections. Such generalizations cannot be strictly relied upon, and the LLC is the sort of entity that requires case-by-case analysis into the economic realities of the underlying transaction to determine its securities status.

Some cases do follow the general rule. In *Keith v. Black Diamond Advisors, Inc.,* 48 F. Supp. 2d 326 (S.D.N.Y. 1999), the court held that a membership interest was not a security in a member-managed LLC, because the investor had the authority under the operating agreement to actively participate in the management of the LLC even though in practice he assumed a more passive role. Other courts have noted that the mere fact that the investor has some nominal involvement in the operation of the business is not enough, "the focus is on the dependency of the investor on the entrepreneurial or managerial skills of the promoter or other party." SEC v. Merchant Capital, LLC, 483 F.3d 747, 755 (11th Cir. 2007). The court in this case determined that the entity distributed power as if the LLC were a limited partnership; therefore, the membership interest was a security.

Although it is fairly clear that a typical investment in the stock of a business is a security,[8] it is difficult to give generalized guidance regarding the security status of a particular investment interest in a business entity because it is so fact and circumstances dependent. While it is critical that thoughtful consideration is given to such issues when determining which form of business entity is appropriate for a particular business for purposes of registration of securities, such issues typically arise after the fact. Issues often occur when a disappointed investor is attempting to use the federal securities laws to redress their grievances against the promoter of a business.

The term notes can also be considered within the Act's definition of security.[9] Courts have found that notes in traditional consumer and

---

[8]   There have been circumstances where even stock has been determined not to be a security. The Supreme Court held in *United Housing Foundation v. Forman*, 421 U.S. 837 (1979), that the definition of a security must reflect economic reality and that the stock held in a cooperative housing corporation were not securities because they had none of the attributes of a stock investment. Since the investment was for the purpose of obtaining living quarters for personal use and not the expectation of investment profit from the efforts of others the stock was determined not to be a security.

[9]   The Securities Act § 2(1) and Exchange Act § 3(a)(10) define a security to include "any note." However, the Securities Act exempts from registration a note that "arises out of a current transaction "and that matures within nine months. *See* Securities Act § 3(a)(3). This exemption

commercial transactions are not securities. However, if the seller's purpose is to raise money for the general use of a business enterprise or to finance substantial investments, and the buyer is interested primarily in the profit the note is expected to generate, courts will likely find that the instrument is a security. *See* Reeves v. Ernst & Young, 494 U.S. 56, 66–67 (1990). In *Reeves*, the Supreme Court developed the family resemblance test to determine when a note is a security. *Reeves* establishes a rebuttable presumption that every note is a security unless it falls into a category of instruments that are not securities. The following are the four factors to be considered while applying the family resemblance test:

- The motivation that prompts a reasonable buyer and seller to enter into the transaction in question (if used for general business purposes it is more likely a security, if used to buy consumer goods or commercial purpose it is more likely not a security);

- The plan of distribution of the instrument (if offered and traded widely, it is more likely a security, if offered in direct negotiations with a limited number of sophisticated investors, it is more likely not a security);

- The reasonable expectations of the investing public (if a reasonable buyer views the note as an investment, it is more likely a security); and

- The existence of an alternate regulatory scheme reducing the risk of the instrument (if the note is secured, collateralized, or regulated by a banking authority, it is more likely not a security).

Although none of these factors are dispositive, when viewed as a whole they provide the court guidance as to whether a note is a security or merely a consumer/commercial transaction.

There are other situations where it is difficult to tell whether a particular investment scheme is an investment contract and therefore a security. For example, a sale-leaseback transaction[10] is typically viewed as a type of secured financing; however the Supreme Court in *SEC v.*

---

was intended to exclude the issuance of commercial paper for business transactions from the burdens of securities registration. Similarly, the Exchange Act excludes from the definition of security any note that matures within nine months. *See* Exchange Act § 3(a)(10). Because many notes given in consumer and commercial transactions should not be treated as securities, courts have relied on the introductory phrase of the Securities and Exchange Acts "unless the context otherwise requires," to exempt such instruments from securities registration. *See* Securities Act § 2(1); Exchange Act § 3(a)(10).

[10] A sale-leaseback is a financial transaction where the owner of a fixed asset (*e.g.*, real property, plane, automobile) sells the asset and leases the asset back from the purchaser for a specified period of time. This arrangement allows the initial buyer to make full use of the asset while not having capital tied up in the asset. Such a transaction may also offer tax advantages to the parties.

Edwards, 540 U.S. 389 (2004) found that sale-leaseback transaction for pay telephones can amount to an investment contract under the *Howey* test, even though the seller was only promised a fixed rate of return. The Court focused on the fact that such an interpretation furthered the purpose of the securities laws when dishonest promoters promised guaranteed fixed returns to the elderly and to unsophisticated investors. A real estate transaction can also amount to an investment contract and thus a security. For example, when a developer offers the sale of resort condominiums, with a collateral management agreement that limits the purchaser's right of occupancy and makes the property available for rental, with the owner receiving a pro rata share of the pooled net income from the condominium resort. *See* Hocking v. Dubois, 885 F.2d 1449 (9th Cir. 1989) (en banc).

In sum, although the term security is defined in both federal and state statutes, courts have broadened the definition over the years to include a variety of financial transactions that fall within the framework of an investment contract. The case law that has expanded the definition of security, which arises primarily from actions taken by investors who have entered into financial transactions in unregistered securities. Yet, a good understanding of the analysis the courts undertake in defining an investment contract is instructive when determining when a particular investment in a business venture should seek registration or exemption from federal and state securities laws.

G. FEDERAL REGISTRATION OF OFFERS AND SALES OF SECURITIES

Under the Securities Act of 1933, it is against the law for any company, or issuer, to sell securities without either registering the securities with the SEC pursuant to Section 5 of the Securities Act or relying upon a valid exemption from the registration requirements. Similarly, pursuant to each individual state's Blue Sky Laws, it is generally against the law to sell securities within a state without either registering the securities with the state's securities regulatory agency or relying upon a valid state exemption from registration. If an issuer registers securities with the commission, it then becomes a public company subject to the periodic reporting requirements of the Exchange Act and the conduct rules of the exchange on which its securities are listed. Additionally, registering securities with the commission or with one or more states (even without a concurrent registration with the commission) requires an issuer to expend an enormous amount of time and expense that small businesses generally cannot afford. As a result, most small business issuers seeking to sell securities will seek to rely upon an exemption from registration in lieu of a public offering.

There are benefits and new obligations that come from raising capital through a public offering registered with the SEC. While the benefits are attractive, attorneys and businesspersons should be aware that that the company will also assume new obligations. Some benefits include:

- Access to capital will increase, since the company can contact more potential investors.

- The company can obtain financing more easily in the future if investor interest in it grows enough to sustain a secondary trading market in the securities.

- The controlling shareholders, such as the company's officers or directors, may have a ready market for their shares, which means that they can more easily sell their interests at retirement, for diversification, or for some other reason.

- The company may be able to attract and retain more highly qualified personnel if it can offer stock options, bonuses, or other incentives with a known market value.

- The image of the company may be improved or more widely known.

The company will have new obligations which include:

- The company must continue to keep shareholders informed about the company's business operations, financial condition, and management, incurring additional costs and new legal obligations.

- The company, officers, and directors may incur liabilities if they do not fulfill their new legal obligations.

- The founders may lose some flexibility in managing the company's affairs, particularly when shareholders must approve their actions.

- The public offering will take time and money to accomplish.

If the small business decides to embark on a registered public offering, the Securities Act requires the company to file a registration statement with the SEC before the company can offer its securities for sale. A company cannot actually sell the securities covered by the registration statement until the SEC staff declares it effective, even though registration statements become public immediately upon filing. Registration statements have two principal parts:

- The Prospectus—The prospectus is the legal offering or selling document that must describe the important facts about the company's business operations, financial condition, and management. Everyone who buys the new issue, as well as anyone who is made an offer to purchase the securities, must have access to the prospectus.

- Additional Information—The registration statement must also include detailed information that the company does not otherwise have to deliver to investors. Anyone can see this information by requesting it from one of the SEC's public reference rooms or by looking it up on the SEC website.

Form S-1 is an SEC filing used by companies planning on going public to register their securities with the SEC. S-1 forms are filed with the SEC's Electronic Data Gathering, Analysis, and Retrieval system (EDGAR). The online form is only 8 pagers long, however, one should not be deceived by the simplicity of the form's design. The Office of Management and Budget (OMB) estimates that it takes approximately 972.5 hours to complete. Much of the time and effort in preparation of the form is being used to collect and display information about the corporate filer seeking registration. When the company files this form, it must also describe each of the following in the prospectus:

- a description of the company's business, properties, and competition;

- the plan for distributing the securities;

- the intended use of the proceeds of the offering;

- information about the management of the company;

- the identity of its officers and directors and their compensation;

- material transactions between the company and its officers and directors;

- material legal proceedings involving the company or its officers and directors.

Information about how to describe these items is set out in SEC rules. Registration statements also must include financial statements audited by an independent certified public accountant.

In addition to the information expressly required by Form S-1, the company must also provide any other information that is necessary to make the disclosure complete and not misleading. It also must clearly describe any risks prominently in the prospectus, usually at the beginning. Examples of these risk factors are:

- lack of business operating history;

- adverse economic conditions in a particular industry;

- lack of a market for the securities offered; and

- level of company dependence upon key personnel.

SEC staff examines registration statements for compliance with disclosure requirements. If a filing appears incomplete or inaccurate, the staff usually informs the company by letter. The company may file correcting or clarifying amendments. Once the company has satisfied the disclosure requirements, the staff declares the registration statement effective. The company may then begin to sell its securities. The SEC can refuse or suspend the effectiveness of any registration statement if it concludes that the document is misleading, inaccurate, or incomplete. Registration statements and prospectuses become public shortly after filing with the SEC. When filed by U.S. domestic companies, the statements are available on EDGAR.

H. UNDERWRITING THE SECURITIES OFFERING

The process of going public involves more than registration with the SEC. The issuer will engage an investment banking firm as an underwriter to act as a financial intermediary in making the securities offering available to the public. The issuer and underwriter will enter into an underwriting agreement which will specify the price and amount of the securities to be offered. The underwriter will generally request that the issuer's counsel and accounting firm provide comfort letters assuring the underwriter that the soundness or backing of the company. The issuer's counsel will opine that their client is incorporated, that the securities are authorized, and that there are no outstanding contingencies that have not been disclosed. They will also be required to provide an opinion letter regarding the company's corporate law compliance, which will be filed with the registration statement.

The underwriting agreement can define the underwriter's role in a variety of ways:

- The issuer offers the securities directly to the public and the underwriter agrees, for a fee, to assume the insurance risk of purchasing any of the securities not purchased by the public;

- The issuer directly offers a portion of the securities to the public, and the underwriter agrees to use its best efforts to act as an agent for the issuer in finding investors for the remainder of the offering;

- The issuer sells the securities directly to the underwriter at an agreed price and the underwriter then resells the securities to the public or to brokerage firms. The participants are compensated by the spread between the purchase price and the public offering price.

In large offerings, an underwriting syndicate may be assembled under the management of the lead underwriter. The managing underwriter will negotiate the terms with the issuer and make arrangements with the other underwriters to purchase a percentage of the total offering. Each underwriter bears the responsibility to sell the securities to investors and each underwriter profits from the spread of the purchase price and the public offering price. The underwriters often enter into agreements with brokerage firms who will act as retailers for the offering.

A public offering can be expensive. The issuer can expect professional fees to range from $500,000 to $1,000,000 for each issuers legal counsel and its auditing firm. This cost is in addition to filing fees, listing fees, and printing costs, which can add an additional $200,000 to $500,000, to bring the securities public.

I.   REGULATORY REPORTING REQUIREMENTS

In addition to issuing securities in an offering registered under the Securities Act, a company can become public by registering the company's outstanding securities under the Exchange Act requirements. Both types of registration trigger ongoing reporting obligations for the company. In some cases, the Exchange Act also subjects the company's officers, directors, and significant shareholders to reporting requirements.

Once the SEC staff declares the issuer's registration statement effective under the Securities Act, the Exchange Act requires the company to file reports with the SEC. The obligation to file reports continues at least through the end of the fiscal year in which the registration statement becomes effective. After that, the company is required to continue reporting unless it has fewer than 300 shareholders of the class of securities offered or it has fewer than 500 shareholders of the class of securities offered and less than $10 million in total assets for each of its last three fiscal years.

Companies with more than $10 million in assets whose securities are held by more than 500 owners must file annual and other periodic reports. If a company is subject to the reporting requirements, it must file ongoing information with the SEC about:

- its operations;
- its officers, directors, and certain shareholders, including salary, various fringe benefits, and transactions between the company and management;
- the financial condition of the business, including financial statements audited by an independent certified public accountant; and

- its competitive position and material terms of contracts or lease agreements.

All of this information becomes publicly available when the reports are filed with the SEC. Even if a company has not registered a securities offering, it must file an Exchange Act registration statement if it has more than $10 million total assets and a class of equity securities, like common stock, with 500 or more shareholders or it lists its securities on an exchange or on NASDAQ. If a class of a company's securities is registered under the Exchange Act, the company, as well as its shareholders and management, are subject to various reporting requirements.

In addition to issuing securities in an offering registered under the Securities Act, a company can become public by registering the company's outstanding securities under the Exchange Act requirements. Both types of registration trigger ongoing reporting obligations for the company. In some cases, the Exchange Act also subjects the company's officers, directors, and significant shareholders to reporting requirements.

A company with Exchange Act registered securities must comply with the SEC's proxy rules whenever it seeks a shareholder vote on corporate matters. These rules require the company to provide a proxy statement to its shareholders, together with a proxy card when soliciting proxies. Proxy statements discuss management and executive compensation, along with descriptions of the matters up for a vote. If the company is not soliciting proxies but will take a vote on a matter, the company must provide to its shareholders an information statement that is similar to a proxy statement. The proxy rules also require a company to send an annual report to shareholders if there will be an election of directors. These reports contain much of the same information found in the Exchange Act annual reports that a company must file with the SEC, including audited financial statements. The proxy rules also govern when a company must provide shareholder lists to investors and when it must include a shareholder proposal in the proxy statement.

If a company has registered a class of its equity securities under the Exchange Act, persons who acquire more than five percent of the outstanding shares of that class must file beneficial owner reports until their holdings drop below five percent. These filings contain background information about the beneficial owners as well as their investment intentions, providing investors and the company with information about accumulations of securities that may potentially change or influence company management and policies.

A public company with an Exchange Act registered security that faces a takeover attempt, or third party tender offer, should be aware that the SEC's tender offer rules will apply to the transaction. The same is true if the company makes a tender offer for its own Exchange Act registered securities. The filings required by these rules provide information to the public about the person making the tender offer. The company that is the subject of the takeover must file with the SEC its responses to the tender offer. The rules also set time limits for the tender offer and provide other protections to shareholders.

Section 16 of the Exchange Act applies to a company's directors and officers, as well as shareholders who own more than ten percent of a class of a company's equity securities registered under the Exchange Act. It requires these persons to report their transactions involving the company's equity securities to the SEC. Section 16 also establishes mechanisms for a company to recover profits an insider realizes from a purchase and sale of a company security within a six-month period, known as short swing profits. In addition, Section 16 prohibits short selling by these persons of any class of the company's securities, whether or not that class is registered under the Exchange Act.

J. EXEMPTIONS FROM SECURITIES ACT REGISTRATION

The company's securities offering may qualify for one of several exemptions from the registration requirements. Although a particular offering may be exempt from registration, one should keep in mind that all securities transactions, even exempt transactions, are subject to the antifraud provisions of the federal securities laws. So, corporate directors, officers, and the company will be responsible for false or misleading statements, whether oral or written. The government enforces the federal securities laws through criminal, civil, and administrative proceedings. Some enforcement proceedings are brought through private law suits. Also, if all conditions of the exemptions are not met, purchasers may be able to obtain refunds of their purchase price. The issuer seeking the exemption bears the burden of demonstrating that it has met the exemption's requirements. In addition, offerings that are exempt from provisions of the federal securities laws may still be subject to the notice and filing obligations of various state laws.

1. REGULATION A EXEMPTION

Section 3(b) of the Securities Act authorizes the SEC to exempt small securities offerings from registration. By this authority, the SEC created Regulation A, which was designed to make access to capital possible for small and medium-sized companies that could not otherwise bear the costs of normal SEC registration and allow non-accredited investors to participate in the offerings 17 C.F.R. 230.251–230.263. If a company chooses to rely on this exemption, it must file an offering statement on SEC

Form 1-A consisting of a notification, offering circular, and exhibits for the SEC to review.

Rules governing Form 1-A were revised in 2015 to allow the statement to be used for offerings up to $50 million. The statement can be used for two segments of offerings limited by their value. Tier 1 is capped at $20 million for the aggregate offering price and aggregate sales of securities offered over a 12-month period. Tier 2 is limited to $50 million in securities offerings in a 12-month period. These aggregate limits include a restriction that for Tier 1 offerings no more than $6 million can be offered by all selling security holders that are affiliates of the issuer. The limit for Tier 2 offerings is $15 million for all selling security holders that are affiliates of the issuer.

Submissions of Form 1-A may include additional information as a supplemental part of the filing. This can include a statement regarding whether or not the amount of compensation to be paid to the underwriter was cleared with the Financial Industry Regulatory Authority (FINRA). The supplemental information can also include reports referenced in the offering circular or used externally by the issuer or principal underwriter in relation to the offering. Regulation A offerings share many characteristics with registered offerings. For example, the company must provide purchasers with an offering circular that is similar in content to a prospectus. Like registered offerings, the securities can be offered publicly and are not restricted, meaning they are freely tradable in the secondary market after the offering. The principal advantages of Regulation A offerings, as opposed to full registration, are:

- the financial statements are simpler and do not need to be audited;

- there are no Exchange Act reporting obligations after the offering unless the company has more than $10 million in total assets and more than 500 shareholders;

- companies may choose among three formats to prepare the offering circular, one of which is a simplified question-and-answer document; and

- companies can test the waters to determine if there is adequate interest in the securities before going through the expense of filing with the SEC.

If a company tests the waters, it can use general solicitation and advertising prior to filing an offering statement with the SEC. Doing so gives it the advantage of determining whether there is enough market interest in the securities before it incurs the full range of legal, accounting, and other costs associated with filing an offering statement. The company may not, however, solicit or accept money until the SEC staff completes its review of the filed offering statement and the prescribed offering materials are delivered to investors.

All types of companies that do not report under the Exchange Act may use Regulation A, except blank check companies, those with an unspecified business, and investment companies registered or required to be registered under the Investment Company Act of 1940. A blank check company is one that is in the developmental stage that either does not have an established business plan or has a business plan that revolves around a merger or acquisition with another firm. In most cases, shareholders may use Regulation A to resell up to $1.5 million of securities. In addition, the Regulation A exemption is available only to issuers that are not disqualified under the Securities Act "bad boy" provisions which include:

- issuers under pending SEC administrative review;

- issuers subject to SEC orders in the last five years;

- issuers convicted or enjoined for federal or state securities violations or postal fraud in the past 5 years;

- issuers whose executives or ten percent shareholders have been subject to similar SEC sanctions or court orders; and

- issuers who use an underwriter with a comparable tainted past.

2. REGULATION D EXEMPTIONS

Regulation D exemptions are a series of rules promulgated by the SEC that includes three nonexclusive exemptions from the registration requirements of Section 5 of the Securities Act. Traditionally Regulation D exemptions were the exemptions most commonly used by small businesses to avoid the federal registration requirements.

One of the key concepts under Regulation D is determination of whether a purchaser of securities qualifies as an accredited investor. Under Rule 501 of Regulation D, in order to qualify as an accredited investor, the purchaser must be a bank, insurance company, registered investment company, business development company, or small business investment company;

- an employee benefit plan, within the meaning of the Employee Retirement Income Security Act, if a bank, insurance company, or registered investment adviser makes the investment decisions, or if the plan has total assets in excess of $5 million;

- a charitable organization, corporation, or partnership with assets exceeding $5 million;

- a director, executive officer, or general partner of the company selling the securities;

- a business in which all the equity owners are accredited investors;

- a natural person with a net worth of at least $1 million;

- a natural person with income exceeding $200,000 in each of the two most recent years or joint income with a spouse exceeding $300,000 for those years and a reasonable expectation of the same income level in the current year; or

- a trust with assets of at least $5 million, not formed to acquire the securities offered, and whose purchases are directed by a sophisticated person.

The Restoring American Financial Stability Act, more commonly referred to as the Dodd-Frank Act or the Wall Street Reform Act, now requires that the value of a person's primary residence be excluded from the net worth calculation used to determine the person's accredited investor status. Under the amended net worth calculation, indebtedness secured by the person's primary residence, up to the estimated fair market value of the primary residence, is not treated as a liability, unless the borrowing occurs in the sixty days preceding the purchase of securities in the exempt offering and is not in connection with the acquisition of the primary residence. In such cases, the debt secured by the primary residence must be treated as a liability in the net worth calculation. This is intended to prevent manipulation of the net worth standard, by eliminating the ability of individuals to artificially inflate net worth under the new definition by borrowing against home equity shortly before participating in an exempt securities offering. In addition, any indebtedness secured by a person's primary residence in excess of the property's estimated fair market value is treated as a liability under the new definition. In addition, upon the fourth anniversary of its enactment, and then at least every four years thereafter, the Dodd-Frank Act directs the commission to review the entire definition of accredited investor as applied to natural persons (including the $1 million net worth standard) and permits the commission to make appropriate adjustments to the definition.

Regulation D establishes three exemptions from Securities Act registration: Rule 504, Rule 505, and Rule 506.

Rule 504 provides an exemption for the offer and sale of up to $1,000,000 of securities in a twelve-month period. The issuer may use this exemption so long as it is not a blank check company and is not subject to Exchange Act reporting requirements. Like the other Regulation D exemptions, a company may not use public solicitation or advertising to market the securities, and purchasers receive restricted securities, meaning that they may not sell the securities without registration or an applicable exemption. However, a company can use this exemption for a public offering of its securities and investors will receive freely tradable securities under the following circumstances:

- the offering is registered exclusively in one or more states that require a publicly filed registration statement and delivery of a substantive disclosure document to investors;

- the offering is registered and sold in a state that requires registration and disclosure delivery or sold in a state without those requirements, so long as it delivers the disclosure documents mandated by the state in which it is registered to all purchasers; or

- the securities are sold exclusively according to state law exemptions that permit general solicitation and advertising, so long as they are sold only to accredited investors.

Even if a company conducts a private sale where there are no specific disclosure delivery requirements, it should take care to provide sufficient information to investors to avoid violating the antifraud provisions of the securities laws. This means that any information that is provided to investors must be free from false or misleading statements. Similarly, it should not exclude any information if the omission makes what you do provide investors false or misleading. Finally, the issuer must electronically file a Form D (Notice of Exempt Offering of Securities) with the SEC within 15 calendar days of the first sale of securities pursuant to the offering.

Rule 505 provides an exemption for offers and sales of securities totaling up to $5 million in any twelve-month period. Under this exemption, a company may sell to an unlimited number of accredited investors and up to thirty-five other persons who do not need to satisfy the sophistication or wealth standards associated with other exemptions. Purchasers must buy for investment only and not for resale. The issued securities are restricted, and the company must inform investors that they may not sell for at least a year without registering the transaction. In addition, the company may not use general solicitation or advertising to sell the securities.

The company may decide what information it gives to accredited investors, so long as it does not violate the antifraud prohibitions. However, the company must give non-accredited investors disclosure documents that generally are the same as those used in registered offerings. Any information provided to accredited investors must also be provided to non-accredited investors. The company must also be available to answer questions by prospective purchasers.

This type of offering requires that the company's financial statements are certified by an independent public accountant. If a company other than a limited partnership cannot obtain audited financial statements without unreasonable effort or expense, only the company's balance sheet, to be dated within 120 days of the start of the offering, must be audited. Limited partnerships unable to obtain required financial statements without unreasonable effort or expense may furnish audited financial statements prepared under the federal income tax laws. There are no express information delivery requirements for accredited investors, but for all other investors, the issuer must meet the express information delivery standards set forth in Rule 502. Since Rule 502 requires the issuer to give non-accredited investors disclosure documents that generally are the same as those used in registered offerings, many issuers view the information delivery requirements as so onerous that most will opt to offer securities under Rule 505 (or Rule 506) only to accredited investors.

Rule 506 is the most flexible of the Regulation D exemptions and has several significant advantages over the Rule 504 and Rule 505 exemptions. First, Rule 506 is available to any issuer. Second, there is no limit as to the amount of securities that may be offered and sold pursuant to Rule 506. Lastly, NSMIA amended Section 18 of the Securities Act so that offerings pursuant to Rule 506 are exempt from state Blue Sky securities laws, except that the states can require an issuer to submit a filing fee, file a copy of the Form D, and consent to service of process.

In a Rule 506 offering, the issuer can sell securities to an unlimited number of accredited investors (the same group identified in the Rule 505) and up to thirty-five other purchasers. Unlike Rule 505, all non-accredited investors, either alone or with a purchaser representative, must be sophisticated. They must have sufficient knowledge and experience in financial and business matters to make them capable of evaluating the merits and risks of the prospective investment. There are no express information delivery requirements for accredited investors. But, for nonaccredited investors, the issuer must meet the express information standards set forth in Rule 502. The issuer cannot engage in general solicitation or advertising of the offering and must electronically file a Form D with the SEC within fifteen calendar days of the first sale of securities pursuant to the offering. Any securities issued pursuant to Rule 506 are deemed to be restricted and can only be resold in connection with a registration or a valid exemption from registration.

The Dodd-Frank Act further directed the SEC to issue rules regarding the availability of Rule 506 to certain issuers. The SEC adopted bad actor disqualification on July 10, 2013. The disqualification and related disclosure provisions appear as paragraphs (d) and (e) of Rule 506 of Regulation D. As a result of Rule 506(d) bad actor disqualification, an offering is disqualified from relying on Rule 506(b) and 506(c) of Regulation

D if the issuer or any other person covered by Rule 506(d) has a relevant criminal conviction, regulatory or court order or other disqualifying event that occurred on or after September 23, 2013, the effective date of the rule amendments. Under Rule 506(e), for disqualifying events that occurred before September 23, 2013, issuers may still rely on Rule 506, but will have to comply with the disclosure provisions of Rule 506(e).

Such rules would limit the availability of this exemption to anyone who was subject to final order based on a violation of any law or regulation that prohibits fraudulent, manipulative, or deceptive conduct within the ten-year period ending on the date of the filing of the offer or sale of securities.

Regulation D offerings are governed by integration and aggregation principals. This means that all offers and sales of a Regulation D offering must meet all of the conditions of the relevant exemption. Integration means that different offers and sales of securities are treated together to determine if the conditions of the relevant exemption are satisfied. Aggregation involves calculating the amount financed during a twelve-month period to determine if the dollar amount exceeds the Rule 504 or 505 dollar limit.

3. EQUITY-BASED CROWDFUNDING

Equity-based crowdfunding is the newest form of crowdfunding, only made possible by the Jumpstart Our Business Startups Act (JOBS Act) passed by Congress in 2012.[11] The JOBS Act amended the Securities Act of 1933 to expand the number of investors that companies can solicit and also the amount of money that may be raised privately. Title II (Access to Capital for Job Creators) Title III (Crowdfunding),[12] and Title IV (Small Company Capital Formation) focus on helping start-ups and small businesses obtain the private equity they need to develop and grow.[13] Crowdfunding allows a company to raise up to $1 million dollars in the private equity market in a twelve-month period, which may meet the needs of seed and early stage companies.[14] Both Title II and IV provide an opportunity for growth or later stage enterprises to access the private capital market for even greater levels of equity funding.

It took more than a year for the SEC to promulgate rules and implement Title II of the JOBS Act. Prior to this time, it was illegal to advertise and generally solicit private placement securities offerings. Companies can now undertake wider marketing efforts to obtain unregistered private equity funding; however, they must first take steps to

---

[11]   *See* Jumpstart Our Business Startups Act, Pub. L. No. 112-106, § 101, 126 Stat. 307 (2012).

[12]   CROWDFUND stands for "Capital Raising Online While Deterring Fraud and Unethical Non-Disclosure Act . . . ." *Id.* at §§ 201, 301.

[13]   *See generally id.* at §§ 101–08, 201, 301–12.

[14]   *Id.* at § 302(a)(6)(A).

verify that the purchasers are accredited investors.[15] Now that the general solicitation ban has been lifted, start-ups and small businesses can seek a much greater amount of capital and leverage the internet for marketing their fundraising and access investment platforms to attract potential investors.

Title II requires relatively streamlined reporting requirements, filing a Form D with the SEC before solicitation and disclosing details of the general solicitation to them within fifteen days from such solicitation.[16] Strict verification is required to confirm that investors are accredited. The penalty for not following the general solicitation requirements with the SEC is being banned from fundraising for a full year,[17] a penalty that would prove disastrous to a start-up seeking necessary funding.

Title III amends Section 4(a)(6) of the Securities Act of 1933[18] and allows companies to sell a small amount of stock to a large number of people via web sites called funding portals. Additionally, it exempts securities sold pursuant to Section 4(a)(6) from the registration requirements of Section 12(g) of the Securities Exchange Act of 1934.[19] The SEC adopted final rules for equity crowdfunding that became effective on May 16, 2016.[20] Unlike Title II, the sale of securities to individuals do not have to be accredited investors. It allows a company to raise $1 million in a twelve month period, sets limits on how much an unaccredited investor can invest,[21] and requires the transaction to be conducted through a broker or "funding portal that complies" with 15 U.S.C. § 77d–1.[22] A "funding portal"

---

[15]   § 201. Individuals are accredited investors if their net worth (including spouse net worth) is more than $1 million notwithstanding the value of their primary residence or they meet three income requirements: (1) individual income of $200,000 annually for the two most recent years, (2) annual family income greater than $300,000 for the last two years, and (3) has a "reasonable expectation" of maintaining those income levels in the present year. 17 C.F.R. § 230.501(a)(2017). The Code of Federal Regulations also has qualifying levels for banks, savings and loan associations, broker, dealers, insurance companies, investment companies, business development companies, trusts, and other entities. *Id.* at (a)(1). An investment company is an issuer of securities whose primary business dealings involve investing, reinvesting, or trading securities, engages in "the business of issuing face-amount certificates of the installment type," or has assets comprised of greater than 40% of its total assets. Investment Company Act of 1940, PUB. L. 112-90 § 3(a)(1) (2012). A business development company is defined as a publicly traded business entity who is functionally an investment company that also "makes available significant managerial assistance" to companies if they comprise 70% of its total assets and makes an election under section 55 of the Investment Company Act of 1940. *Id.* at § 2(48)(B). Business development companies came about in 1980 by amendment to the Investment Company Act. Kevin Mahn, *The ABCs of Business D.*

[16]   § 201(a)(1); § 230.503(a)(1).

[17]   *See* 15 U.S.C. § 78c (a)(39)(B)(II).

[18]   *See* § 302(a)(6); § 77(d)(a)(6).

[19]   §§ 77d(a)(6)(c)–(d), 77d–1(a).

[20]   *Crowdfunding*, SECURITIES AND EXCHANGE COMMISSION, https://www.sec.gov/rules/final/2015/33-9974.pdf.

[21]   The language from the JOBS Act lays out several investor income requirements. *See* §§ 302(a)(6)(A), (B).

[22]   *Id.* at § 302(a)(6)(C).

is a financial intermediary that can sell stock online to non-accredited investors.[23]

One of the objectives of the JOBS Act was to encourage small business and startup funding by easing federal regulations and allowing average individuals to become investors. However, in order to protect the unsophisticated investor and prevent fraud, there are still a significant number of regulations and disclosure requirements with which the issuing company and financial intermediary must comply. Any financial intermediary engaging in crowdfunding must register with the SEC and the Financial Industry Regulatory Authority (FINRA). The funding portal may not advertise for securities on its website, pay anyone to solicit investors, manage customer funds or securities, or offer investment advice or recommendations.[24]

The issuing company must register with the SEC and provide comprehensive company information to both the intermediary facilitating the offerings and the potential investors. The Crowdfunding rules require investors have access to business plans, financial statements, the price of the security and how it was determined, and how the proceeds from the sale will be used. The price of professional services to complete the required documents and assist in compliance, can be costly. The SEC estimates that raising $100,000 may cost up to $39,810[25] and as much as $151,660 for a $1 million dollar raise.[26] If, during the course of advertising, an issuer[27] "makes an[y] untrue statement of material fact or omits to state a material fact" that makes any "means or instruments of transportation or communication" misleading, the JOBS Act specifically creates liability for the investor against the issuer.[28]

In June 2015, the SEC issued final rules under Title IV that amended Regulation A of the Securities Act to apply to public offerings of securities that do not exceed $50 million dollars in a one-year period.[29] Commonly referred to as Regulation A+, Title IV allows non-accredited investors to

---

[23] § 78c(a)(80). *See* Joan Macleod Heminway, *The New Intermediary on the Block: Funding Portals Under the* CROWDFUND *Act*, 13 U.C. DAVIS BUS. L. J. 177, 190–91 (2013) (citation omitted).

[24] 15 U.S.C. §§ 78c (80)(a)(A)–(E).

[25] For raises of less than $100,000 cost estimates range from $12,960–$17,960. For raises between $100,000 and $500,000 cost estimates range from $39,810–$69,810. *Id.*

[26] *Id.* For raises between $500,000 and $1 million cost estimates range from $76,660 – $151,660. *Id.*

[27] In this context, issuer includes a director or partner of the issuer, the CEO, CFO, and "principal accounting officer" or controller of the issuer. 15 U.S.C. § 77d–1(c)(3) (2012).

[28] *Id.* at 77d–1(c)(2). The communication must also use means of or travel in interstate commerce. *Id.* Also, it is a defense if the purchaser knew of the "untruth or omission." *Id.*

[29] *See* Press Release, U.S. Securities and Exchange Commission, SEC Adopts Rules to Facilitate Smaller Companies' Access to Capital, (Mar. 25, 2015) (on file at website), https://www.sec.gov/news/pressrelease/2015-49.html.

participate in private offerings, subject to certain provisions.[30] The rule establishes two tiers under Regulation A.[31]

Tier 1, which covers exempt public offerings of up to $20 million within a twelve-month period, retains many of the previous requirements of Regulation A.[32] Tier 2 allows exempt public offerings of up to $50 million within twelve months but requires more robust initial and ongoing reporting.[33] Tier 2 offerings are intended to preempt state securities laws known as Blue Sky laws.[34] Tier 1 offerings will continue to be subject to state securities law registration and qualification requirements.[35] However, Tier 1 issuers may be able to benefit from the multistate review protocol for Regulation A filings that was implemented by the North American Securities Administrators Association, Inc. (NASAA).[36]

The above three titles of the JOBS Act all promise to increase the amount of private equity available to entrepreneurs in need of capital. While it is impossible to predict how much additional capital will be brought to market through these new funding mechanisms, it is estimated that $1 billion was invested online under Title II in 2014 and $2.5 billion in 2015.[37] There is also an estimated 8 million accredited investors in the United States, and only 3% of them have ever invested in a start-up.[38] There is approximately $26 trillion in savings and long-term investments in the United States. If only 1% of that amount was shifted to private

---

[30] *Id.*

[31] *Id.*

[32] *Id. See generally Amendments for Small and Additional Issues Exemptions under the Securities Act*, U.S. SECURITIES AND EXCHANGE COMMISSION 7–9, https://www.sec.gov/rules/final/2015/33-9741.pdf (containing citations to codified sections of Regulation A). Companies utilizing the Regulation A exemption are still required to file offering statements with the SEC; however, the companies utilizing the exemption are given distinct advantages over companies that must fully register. *Id.* The issuer of a Regulation A offering must give buyers documentation with the issue, similar to the prospectus of a registered offering. *Id.*

[33] SEC Adopts Rules to Facilitate Smaller Companies' Access to Capital, *supra* note 29.

[34] *Id.* Companies rarely used the previous Regulation A exemption for public offerings. The JOBS Act required the Comptroller General of the Government Accountability Office (GAO) to study the effect of state securities laws on Regulation A offerings. In its report to Congress, the GAO discussed factors that contributed to the limited use of Regulation A, including the small size of the offerings, the significant time and cost of complying with both federal and state securities laws and the availability of other offering exemptions. *Amendments for Small and Additional Issues Exemptions under the Securities Act, supra* note 32, at 31.

[35] SEC Adopts Rules to Facilitate Smaller Companies' Access to Capital, *supra* note 29.

[36] *See Coordinated Review*, NASAA, http://www.nasaa.org/industry-resources/corporation-finance/coordinated-review/.

[37] Chance Barnett, *Trends Show Crowdfunding To Surpass VC in 2016*, FORBES (June 9, 2015, 5:33 PM) [hereinafter *Trends Show*], http://www.forbes.com/sites/chancebarnett/2015/06/09/trends-show-crowdfunding-to-surpass-vc-in-2016/#56dfe399444b. Since this is "private equity," accurate statistics are difficult to collect.

[38] Chance Barnett, *SEC Democratizes Equity Crowdfunding With JOBS Act Title IV*, FORBES (Mar. 26, 2015, 8:41 PM) [hereinafter *SEC Democratizes*], http://www.forbes.com/sites/chancebarnett/2015/03/26/infographic-sec-democratizes-equity-crowdfunding-with-jobs-act-title-iv/#1585185f5a71.

equity through these exemptions, an additional $260 billion could be used to support small and start-up businesses.[39]

4.   INTRASTATE OFFERING EXEMPTION

Section 3(a)(11) of the Securities Act of exempts an offering involving "any security which is part of an issue offered and sold only to persons resident within a single state. . . where the issuer of such securities is. . . a corporation incorporated by and doing business within such state." The criteria for the intrastate exemption are:

- all offers and sales to investors must be made only to bona fide residents of a single state;

- the state where offers and sales are made must be the state in which the company was organized; and

- the company making the offering must be doing business within that state.

There is no fixed limit on the size of the offering or the number of purchasers. The company must determine the residence of each purchaser. If any of the securities are offered or sold to even one out-of-state person, the exemption may be lost. Without the exemption, the company could be in violation of the Securities Act registration requirements. If a purchaser resells any of the securities to a person who resides outside the state within a short period of time after the company's offering is complete (the usual test is nine months), the entire transaction, including the original sales, might violate the Securities Act. Since secondary markets for these securities rarely develop, companies often must sell securities in these offerings at a discount.

It will be difficult for a company to rely on the intrastate exemption unless you know the purchasers and the sale is directly negotiated with them. If a company holds some of its assets outside the state, or derives a substantial portion of its revenues outside the state where it proposes to offer its securities, it will probably have a difficult time qualifying for the exemption. A company that is unsure of whether it wishes to conduct a private placement across state lines may not test the waters by making offers to non-residents and thereafter switch to the intrastate offering exemption. In addition, if the securities that are offered on an intrastate basis are resold to non-residents, the availability of the exemption may be lost under certain circumstances.

In other words, the federal securities laws require that the intrastate-offered securities come to rest in the hands of residents.

---

[39]   *See* AMY CORTESE, LOCAVESTING: THE REVOLUTION IN LOCAL INVESTING AND HOW TO PROFIT FROM IT 16 (2011) (citation omitted) (noting that more money needs to go into local businesses).

Because of the vague nature of what constitutes coming to rest, the SEC promulgated a safe harbor rule that allows the company to assume that its securities have come to rest if no re-sales occur within nine months of the last sale made in reliance on this exemption. Any subscription documentation related to the intrastate offering should prohibit the resale or transfer of securities to non-residents for a period of nine months after the offering closes. The small businessman conducting an intrastate offering should not forget that the antifraud provisions of the federal securities laws still apply. As a result, extreme caution should be taken to ensure that investors are not misled in any verbal or written communication concerning the affairs of the company or the attributes and risks of the investment.

Due to the absence of direct federal regulation, a state's interest in this type of offering becomes paramount. Thus, the company must independently analyze whether an exemption from registration is available on the state level or whether registration with state authorities will be necessary. The requirements for exemption and registration vary among the states. State antifraud provisions, on the other hand, generally conform to the federal regulatory scheme.

Although there are no limitations on the amount of capital that can be raised or the number of investors who may invest strictly in reliance upon this federal exemption, most state regulations will impose these limitations. Because of the greater the number of investors, there is a greater the risk that securities may come to rest or be transferred out-of-state, thus destroying the exemption. The company has the burden of complying with the exemption's requirements, not the individual investor. If the elements of the exemption are not satisfied, the company may become subject to civil liability or may be required to return invested money. To minimize the significant risk of destroying the availability of the intrastate offering exemption, the offering documentation should be carefully drafted by the company.

An intrastate offering may be attractive to small businesses and entrepreneurs in view of the cost savings associated with avoiding direct federal regulation. Moreover, if the company's products and business have local appeal, investors may be more inclined to invest in the offering. If entrepreneurs do not have the resources or contacts to conduct a successful out-of-state offering, the intrastate offering exemption may be a preferable alternative.

5. THE PRIVATE PLACEMENT EXEMPTION

Section 4(2) of the Securities Act exempts from registration "transactions by an issuer not involving any public offering." To qualify for this exemption, the purchasers of the securities must:

- have enough knowledge and experience in finance and business matters to evaluate the risks and merits of the investment (the sophisticated investor), or be able to bear the investment's economic risk;

- have access to the type of information either through their positions with the issuer as an insider or through adequate disclosure (usually a private placement memorandum); and

- agree not to resell or distribute the securities to the public.

Other key elements of a valid Section 4(2) offering include an absence of any general solicitation or advertising and a relatively discreet number of purchasers. Given that the existence of a valid Section 4(2) exemption is dependent upon so many fact-specific elements, securities practitioners will generally rely upon the Section 4(2) exemption only when the offering is to a very small number of purchasers who are all insiders or there is no other federal exemption available to the issuer.

The precise limits of this private offering exemption are uncertain. As the number of purchasers increases and their relationship to the company and its management becomes more remote, it is more difficult to show that the transaction qualifies for the exemption. If securities are offered to even one person who does not meet the necessary conditions, the entire offering may be in violation of the Securities Act.

6. EMPLOYEE BENEFIT PLANS EXEMPTION

Rule 701 under the Securities Act is an exemption that allows eligible companies to issue stock or grant stock options or other similar securities to their employees as part of the employee compensation packages. The Rule 701 exemption is available to any issuer except those subject to Exchange Act reporting requirements or investment companies registered or required to be registered under the Investment Company Act of 1940. The securities must be offered pursuant to a written compensatory benefit plan or a written compensation contract, a copy of which must be delivered to the purchaser of the securities. Rule 701 exempts offers and sales of company's securities to its employees, directors, general partners, trustees (where the issuer is a business trust), officers, consultants, and advisors. There is no limitation on the amount of securities offered pursuant to 701; however, the aggregate sales price or amount of securities sold in reliance upon Rule 701 during any consecutive twelve-month period cannot exceed the greatest of

- $1 million;

- fifteen percent of the issuer's total assets as of the issuer's most recent annual balance sheet date; or

- fifteen percent of the outstanding amount of the class of securities being offered and sold in reliance upon Rule 701, determined as of the issuer's most recent annual balance sheet date.

Any securities issued pursuant to Rule 701 are deemed to be restricted and can only be resold in connection with a registration or a valid exemption from registration.

7. STATE REGISTRATION OF OFFERS AND SALES OF SECURITIES

While the SEC directly, and through its oversight of the National Association of Security Dealers (the "NASD") and the various stock exchanges, is the main enforcer of the nation's securities laws, each individual state has its own securities laws and rules. As discussed earlier, Blue Sky Laws are state laws that regulate the offering and sale of securities to protect the public from fraud. Although the specific provisions of these laws vary among states, they all require the registration of all securities offerings and sales, as well as of stock brokers and brokerage firms. Most states securities laws are modeled after the Uniform Securities Act of 1956. Approximately forty states have used this Act as the basis for their state Blue Sky Laws. While most Blue Sky Laws are modeled after the Uniform Securities Act of 1956, as a practical matter there is little uniformity among state securities laws. To make matters more complicated, although some states may have virtually identical statutory language or regulations covering particular activities or conduct, their interpretation may differ considerably from state to state. Therefore, it is essential that each state's statutes and regulations be researched before undertaking any securities sales activities in a state to determine what is permitted in any given state. Each state has a regulatory agency that administers the law, typically known as the state Securities Commissioner.

Recently, federal legislation was enacted that limits the ability of the states to review and restrict the sale of most securities. The National Securities Markets Improvement Act of 1996 (the "NSMIA") was designed to eliminate the duplicative nature of the federal and state securities laws. This legislation limits the state's authority to review registration of securities offerings that are offered on a national basis. However, there are notice and filing requirements in each state that must still be complied with. In addition, NSMIA did not affect the ability of the state regulators to conduct investigations and to bring fraud actions.

Among other changes, NSMIA amended Section 18 of the Securities Act of 1933, thereby creating a class of securities referred to as covered securities, the offer and sale of which (through licensed broker-dealers) are no longer subject to state securities law registration requirements. Covered securities include:

- securities listed (or approved for listing) on the NYSE, AMEX and the NASDAQ/National Market, and securities of the same issuer that are equal in rank or senior to such listed securities;

- mutual fund shares;

- securities sold to certain qualified purchasers;

- certain securities exempt under Section 3(a) of the Act (including government or municipal securities, bank securities, and commercial paper);

- and securities exempt from registration under the Act if sold in transactions complying with Rule 506 of Regulation D under the Act.

Although NSMIA preempts state securities registration requirements, NSMIA preserves the right of the states to investigate and prosecute fraud.

As a result of NSMIA, states may no longer require the registration of covered securities. However, states may, as permitted under NSMIA, require filings and the payment of fees for offers and sales in their state of covered securities other than those that are listed (or approved for listing) on the designated exchanges. This also includes securities senior to such securities (i.e., preferred shares or debt securities of an issuer with common stock listed on the designated exchanges). Additionally, since NSMIA only preempts state securities registration requirements, broker-dealer and agent/salesperson registration requirements (applicable to individuals engaged in the offer and sale of covered securities) must still be examined to determine whether action is required to be taken in connection with a particular offering or transaction. Therefore, although covered securities are no longer subject to substantive state review, Blue Sky action with respect to offerings of covered securities is still necessary.

However, despite NSMIA, many smaller and local offerings remain subject to state Blue Sky Laws. As such, registration is required before securities can be offered and sold in a state. There are different kinds of registration depending on the perceived risk of the offering. For a company that makes an SEC registered offering of other than covered securities the issuer need only file a of the federal registration with a states securities administrator. For a seasoned issuer, with a history of healthy net earnings and not in default on a debt, a state registration of an offering exempt from federal registration requires only a short form filing. The procedural requirements for short form filings differ depending on the state of incorporation but generally consist of basic corporate information and a required filing fee.

For other companies making non-preempted offerings such as the intrastate exemption or the small offering exemptions of Rules 504 and 505 of Regulation D, registration by qualification is more complex. The company must file a registration statement, provide disclosure information to investors, and receive administrative approval in each state where the securities are offered or sold.

In an attempt to reduce these burdens on small issuers, most states have adopted the Small Offerings Registration (the "SCOR"), under the auspices of the North American Securities Administrators Association (the "NASAA"). SCOR, available in certain state offices, allows the issuer to use a fill-in-the blank form for offerings that do not exceed $1,000,000, which complements the SEC's 504 exemption.

In the case of larger offerings, some states have adopted the Coordinated Equity Review (the "CER"), allowing an issuer to file one standard application where it wants to offer and sell securities. The state that reviews the application and SEC registration statement, works with the issuer to resolve all regulatory issues. Once approved by the lead state, the offering may be made in all CER participating states.

Because of all of the described complexities in the state securities registration process, when offering any security for sale in any state, experienced Blue Sky counsel should be retained to review the applicable state Blue Sky Laws and take any action necessary to permit the offering to be made in the particular state. This is particularly true for small start-up companies that are making smaller local offerings.

In sum, businesspersons should work with their attorney to make sure that: the most effective and correct form of financing is chosen; all parties are in compliance with and well versed in the securities law; they are aware of regulatory reporting requirements; and exemptions from the Securities Act registration are recognized and used to the business' advantage. If business owners and attorneys work together to understand, comply with, and take advantage of these key concepts, both parties are certain to benefit.

BIBLIOGRAPHY

■ ■ ■

Block, Cheryl D. *Corporate Taxation*, Fredrick, MD: Aspen Publishers 4th edition Copyright 2010.

Branson, Douglas M., Heminway, Joan Macleod, Loewenstein, Mark J., Steinberg, Marc I., Warren, Manning Gilbert III., Business Enterprises: *Legal Structures, Governance and Policy: Cases, Materials, and Problems*, Newark, NJ: LexisNexis Copyright 2009.

Choi, Stephen J. & Prichard, A.C. *Securities Regulation: the Essentials*, Fredrick, MD: Aspen Publishers Copyright 2008.

Drake, Dwight, *Business Planning: Closely Held Corporations*, St. Paul, MN: Thompson Reuters 3rd edition Copyright 2011.

Ehrlich, Scott B. & Michael, Douglas C., *Business Planning*, Newark, NJ: LexisNexis Copyright 2009.

Foonberg, Jay G., *How to Start And Manage A Law Practice*, Chicago, IL: American Bar Association., 5th edition Copyright 2004.

Fox, Charles M., *Working With Contracts* (Practicing Law Institute) 2nd edition Copyright 2008.

Goldsby, Michael G., *The Entrepreneuer's Toolkit*, Chantilly, VA: The Great Courses Copyright 2014.

Gevurtz, Franklin A., *Business Planning*, New York, NY: Thompson Reuters/Foundation Press 4th edition Copyright 2008.

Gruner, Richard S., Ghosh, Shubha, Kessan, Jay P. *Intellectual Property In Business Organizations: Cases and Materials*, Newark, NJ: LexisNexis Copyright 2006.

Menell, Peter S., Lemley, Mark A., Merges, Robert P., *Intellectual Property in the New Technological Age: 2018; Volume I: Perspectives, Trade Secrets and Patents,* Clause 8 Publishing Copyright 2018.

Lloyd, Robert M. & Kuney, George W., *Secured Transactions: UCC Article 9 & Bankruptcy,* Knoxville, TN: Robert M. Lloyd and George W. Kuney Copyright 2008.

Klein, William A. & Coffee, John C. Jr., *Business Organization And Finance Legal And Economic Principals*, New York, NY: Foundation Press 10th edition Copyright 2007.

Kuney, George W. & Looper, Donna C., *Mastering Intellectual Property*, Charlotte, NC: Carolina Academic Press Copyright 2009.

Kuney, George W. & Looper, Donna C., *Mastering Legal Analysis and Drafting,* Charlotte, NC: Carolina Academic Press Copyright 2009.

Kuney, George W., *The Elements of Contract Drafting With Questions And Clauses For Consideration,* St. Paul, MN: Thompson Reuters 3rd edition Copyright 2011.

Maynard, Therese H. & Warren, Dana M., *Business Planning: Financing the Start-Up Business and Venture Capital Financing*, Fredrick, MD: Aspen Publishers Copyright 2010.

Painter, William H., *Problems And Materials In Business Planning*, St. Paul, MN: West Publishing Co. 3rd edition Copyright 1994.

Palmiter, Alan, R., *Corporations*, Fredrick, MD: Aspen Publishers 6th edition Copyright 2009.

Palmiter, Alan, R. *Securities Regulation*, Fredrick, MD: Aspen Publishers 4th edition Copy 2008.

Ragazzo, Robert A. & Fendler, Frances S., *Closely Held Business Organizations Cases, Materials, And Problems*, St. Paul, MN: 2nd edition Thompson Reuters Copyright 2012.

Stark, Tina L., *Drafting Contracts: How and Why Lawyers Do What They Do,* Fredrick, MD: Aspen Publishers Copyright 2007.

Braving The Waters: A Guide For Tennessee's Aspiring Entrepreneurs, 9 TRANSACTIONS: THE TENNESSEE JOURNAL OF BUSINESS LAW 2, Buffalo, NY: William S. Hein & Co., Inc., Copyright 2008.